Helping Jesus Fulfill Prophecy

Helping Jesus Fulfill Prophecy

Robert J. Miller

CASCADE *Books* · Eugene, Oregon

Cascade Books
An Imprint of Wipf and Stock Publishers
199 W. 8th Ave., Suite 3
Eugene, OR 97401

www.wipfandstock.com

ISBN 978-1-4982-2896-1

Cataloguing-in-Publication data:

Miller, Robert J. (Robert Joseph), 1954–

Helping Jesus fulfill prophecy / Robert J. Miller.

xviii + 408 p. ; 23 cm. Includes bibliographical references.

ISBN 13: 978-1-4982-2896-1

1. Bible. Gospels—Criticism, interpretation, etc. 2. Bible—Prophecies. 3. Bible. Gospels—Relation to the Old Testament. I. Title.

BS2555.52 M55 2016

Manufactured in the U.S.A.   12/10/2015

Translations of texts from the Hebrew Bible and New Testament are from the New Revised Standard Version (occasionally modified to highlight comparisons of parallel texts and in rendering the divine name—see Preface). Copyright © 1989, Division of Christian Education of the National Council of Churches of Christ in the U.S.A. Used by permission; all rights reserved. Translations of some gospel texts are from the Scholars Version (SV) as found in *The Complete Gospels*, ed. Robert J. Miller, 4th ed., Polebridge Press, copyright © 2010. Used by permission; all rights reserved.

Appendix 2 is used by permission of Polebridge Press.

to Eric Freed

お悔やみ申し上げます

requiescat in pace

Contents

Part 3: The Argument from Prophecy in Patristic Thought

Part 4: Modern Reckoning with the Argument from Prophecy

Preface

THIS BOOK IS WRITTEN for general readers. Since the book is neither short nor easy, it presupposes a keen interest in the subject matter; yet it does not presuppose any specialized knowledge. This book is also for those who want to understand not only what historical-critical scholars think, but why. I strive to explain as clearly as I can the evidence and reasoning that lead to the conclusions I draw. That form of explication entails two particular types of study that call for readers' patience and perseverance. First, the nature of the subject matter often entails the close comparison of texts (usually two versions of a prophecy, or a prophecy and a narration of its alleged fulfillment). Such comparisons sometimes must proceed word for word, with attention to precise nuances in meaning. Second, there are certain passages that require analysis of the ancient Hebrew or Greek or Latin in order to understand them correctly. However, readers need no prior knowledge of those languages to follow the discussion. My hope is that those willing to read and think carefully will be rewarded for their efforts with an enriched understanding of a complex subject, whether or not they agree with all my conclusions.

Terminology

Jew / Christian

There has been much recent discussion among biblical scholars about the precise meanings of the terms "Jew/Jewish" and "Christian," the concern being that modern connotations of those terms might lead to anachronistic misunderstandings when the terms are applied to people or things in Antiquity. At present, there is no clear consensus regarding to whom or what those terms should refer, nor on what other terms to use in cases when "Jew" or

"Christian" would be imprecise. Until scholars reach some broad agreement on what the appropriate terminology should be, I think it best in this book to use "Jew/Jewish" and "Christian" in their general traditional (and, admittedly, inexact) senses, the former in reference to the religion and culture of Israel, the latter in reference to the religion centered on Jesus. An inescapable ambiguity of such usage is that many of the earliest followers of Jesus can be described as both Jews and Christians. They understood themselves to be Jews; if, for our convenience, we refer to them as Christians, that is not because they practiced Christianity—which did not yet exist as a distinct religion—but because they revered Jesus as the Christ, the Anointed One.

Old Testament / Hebrew Bible

The *Hebrew Bible* is the Jewish scriptures in the Hebrew language (though a few pages are in Aramaic). Early Christians knew the Jewish scriptures mostly in Greek translation, and referred to them simply as *hai graphai* ("the writings") and later as *ta biblia* ("the little scrolls," from which derives our word "Bible"). The terminology of "Old Testament" and "New Testament" emerged after some Christian writings came to be regarded as authoritative scripture. The *Old Testament* is thus the Jewish scriptures as adopted, organized, and supplemented by Christians. Since the primary focus of my book is on the Christian interpretation of the Jewish scriptures, I usually refer to them as the Old Testament (OT).

Lord / Yahweh

Out of deference to the traditional Jewish custom of not pronouncing the name of God, most English translations of the Hebrew Bible, including the New Revised Standard Version, use Lord (in capital letters) where the Hebrew text has *yhwh*, the name of the God of Israel. I have modified the NRSV, rendering *yhwh* as "Yahweh," the most likely pronunciation of that name. I reserve "Lord" for the Hebrew word *adon*, which means "lord, master."

Uppercase and lowercase nouns

God/god. I capitalize "God"—out of deference to Judaism and Christianity—when it denotes the deity whom Israel called "Yahweh" and whom Jesus addressed as "Father."

Christ/christology. I capitalize "Christ" because it is a title, but neither "christological," which means "messianic," nor "christology," which refers to beliefs about the identity and spiritual status of Jesus.

Gospel/gospel. The word "gospel" is a common noun that names a literary genre, and is therefore written with a lower case *g*. The "Gospel of Matthew" is a proper noun, the title of a literary work, and is thus capitalized. I follow the same distinction for *letter/Letter, epistle/Epistle, book/Book,* and *psalm/ Psalm.*

Exile/exile. I take the name of the forced relocation of Judeans to Babylon in the sixth century BCE to be a proper name: "the Babylonian Exile." Otherwise I use the lowercase "exile."

Antiquity/antiquity. I capitalize "Antiquity" because it is the name of a historical period, on a par with names like "Middle Ages" or "Renaissance." The word appears lowercased only when it means "old age."

Law/law. I capitalize "Law" when it refers to the Torah.

I lowercase "scripture" because the word is a common noun meaning "an authoritative religious text."

I lowercase the word "gentile" because it is a common noun that means "non-Jew," which to ancient Jews meant "foreigner."

Acknowledgments

I DRAFTED MAJOR PORTIONS OF this book during a nomadic sabbatical from Juniata College in 2009–2010. I began work on the book while visiting the Stockholm School of Theology in the fall of 2009, where I was supported by a generous grant from the Swedish Foundation for International Cooperation in Research and Higher Education, and by the hospitality and friendship of Thomas Kazen. My work continued in winter 2010 as scholar in residence at Eden Theological Seminary in St. Louis, where I enjoyed the hospitality of Stephen Patterson and his family, and in spring 2010 as visiting professor at Stanford University, where I was graced by the friendship and intellectual stimulation of Thomas Sheehan.

Several colleagues donated their time and expertise to reviewing drafts of chapters and suggesting improvements: Cecilia Wassen of the University of Uppsala read the chapter on the Dead Sea Scrolls; Nina Livesey of the University of Oklahoma read the chapter on Justin Martyr; and Belle Tuten of Juniata College reviewed the chapter on Augustine. I am deeply indebted to Charles Hedrick, who generously read my entire draft and offered numerous astute criticisms and suggestions that have greatly improved this book.

This book is dedicated to the memory of a beloved friend, Eric Freed, whose senseless murder robbed so many of an inspiring teacher and a humane and holy priest.

Abbreviations and Short Titles

Ancient Sources

1QpHab	Qumran Habakkuk Pesher
4QpNah	Qumran Nahum Pesher
Acts	Acts of the Apostles
Answer	*In Answer to the Jews* (Augustine)
Ant.	*Antiquities of the Jews* (Josephus)
CD	Cairo Damascus Document
Chr	Chronicles
Cor	Corinthians
DivDem	*The Divination of Demons* (Augustine)
Deut	Deuteronomy
Dan	Daniel
Dialogue	*Dialogue with Trypho* (Justin Martyr)
DSS	Dead Sea Scrolls
Eccl	Ecclesiastes
Eph	Ephesians
Exod	Exodus
Ezek	Ezekiel
Faith	*On Faith in Things Unseen* (Augustine)
Faustus	*Reply to Faustus* (Augustine)
Gal	Galatians
Gen	Genesis
Hab	Habakkuk
Hag	Haggai

Heb	Hebrews
History	*History of the Church* (Eusebius)
Hos	Hosea
Isa	Isaiah
Jer	Jeremiah
Kgs	Kings
Lam	Lamentations
Lev	Leviticus
LXX	Septuagint
Macc	Maccabees
Mal	Malachi
Matt	Matthew
Mic	Micah
MT	Massoretic text
Nah	Nahum
NT	New Testament
Num	Numbers
Obad	Obadiah
OT	Old Testament
Pet	Peter
Phil	Philippians
Prov	Proverbs
Ps	Psalm
Q	the Q Gospel
Rev	Revelation
Rom	Romans
Sam	Samuel
Song	Song of Songs / Song of Solomon
Tob	Tobit
Tr. on John	*Tractates on the Gospel of John* (Augustine)
Wars	*Wars of the Jews* (Josephus)
Wis	Wisdom / Wisdom of Solomon
Zech	Zechariah
Zeph	Zephaniah

Modern Sources

AB	Anchor Bible
AGJU	Arbeiten zur Geschichte des antiken Judentums und des Urchristentums
FC	Fathers of the Church. Washington DC, 1947–
ICC	International Critical Commentary
NRSV	New Revised Standard Version
OTL	Old Testament Library
SV	Scholars Version
SBLDS	Society of Biblical Literature Dissertation Series
SNTSMS	Society of New Testament Studies Monograph Series 36
VTSup	Supplements to Vetus Testamentum
WBC	Word Biblical Commentary

Introduction

THE BELIEF THAT JESUS fulfilled scripture is part of the DNA, as it were, of Christianity. That belief goes back as far as anything historians can trace in early Christianity. Paul, whose letters are the earliest available writings about Jesus, wrote that Christ died for sins "according to the scriptures," and was raised on the third day "according to the scriptures." In expressing these beliefs Paul insisted that he was merely repeating what he had been told by those who were believers before him (1 Cor 15:3–4). The belief that Jesus fulfilled scripture was crucial to the earliest groups of Jesus followers—either Jews or non-Jews who knew that they had joined a Jewish movement—because it was a means to assure themselves of their religious legitimacy. It enabled them to relate what was new (Jesus) to what was old (the scriptures of Israel). Making that connection was essential in a time and culture that regarded old sacred writings with reverence and anything new in religion with suspicion.

From the beginnings of Christianity, then, the belief that Jesus fulfilled prophecy[1] functioned as an attempt to *prove* something of great importance. It is appropriate, therefore, to describe the way early Christians expressed their belief in the fulfillment of prophecy as an *argument*, which I will call in this book the "argument from prophecy." The argumentative quality of that belief has endured in Christian discourse, and is fully on display in contemporary Christianity.

For a representative contemporary example of the argument from prophecy, I turn not to some scholarly writing on the topic, but to a short and simple selection from an Internet blog aimed at a mass Christian audience. Its author, Rick Warren, wrote the hugely popular *The Purpose Driven Life*,[2]

---

1. I use "fulfill scripture" and "fulfill prophecy" more or less interchangeably. As we will see, Jews and Christians regarded numerous passages from the books of the prophets and from other books of scripture as predictions of the future.

2. Zondervan, 2002. According to the book's website (http://purposedriven.com/

1

and is pastor of Saddleback Community Church, a non-denominational evangelical megachurch in Orange County, California. Warren's immense following and his celebrity status among evangelical Christians make it a safe bet that his public beliefs are widely shared by American evangelicals. Here is the essence of one of Warren's devotional postings from 2013.

Biblical Prophesies [sic]: What Are the Odds?

> One of the reasons I can know that the Bible is true and trustworthy is that it has thousands and thousands of prophecies that have come true and will come true in history. Every one of the Bible's prophecies have [sic] either come true exactly as God predicted or will come true sometime in the future.
>
> The Bible contains more than 300 prophecies about Jesus alone—all written a thousand years before he was born . . . What are the odds that I could make 300 predictions about you and every one of them would come true? It's so astronomical, you couldn't write the number down. It takes more faith to believe that the Bible's prophecies were a coincidence than to believe that God planned them.
>
> During Bible times, nobody wanted to be a prophet. The law in Israel was that a prophet of God had to be correct 100 percent of the time. If you were wrong just once, then you were considered a false prophet and would have been put to death. A prophet better be right!
>
> And the Bible prophecies were right—every one of them. You can trust the Bible because what the Bible predicts comes true.[3]

This short piece is an ideal snapshot of popular Christian notions of biblical prophecy and so is worth our close attention. The piece is structured as an argument, that is, as a series of statements that lead to a conclusion (the Bible is true), which is set out strategically at the top of the excerpt and in the last sentence. As the title of the piece indicates, the argument is based on mathematics: "What are the odds?" But one need not be good at math to follow the argument, for it relies not on calculations, but rather on intuitions about impressive numbers ("more than 300 . . . astronomical . . . correct 100% of the time").

What the argument is designed to prove is interesting in that it is somewhat unexpected. One might expect the claim that Jesus fulfilled hundreds of prophecies to point to the conclusion that Jesus was the messiah

books/pdlbook/#purpose), over 32 million copies have been sold.

3. Warren, "Biblical Prophesies [sic]."

foretold by the prophets. Instead, the conclusion of Warren's argument has to do with the Bible, not Jesus. The argument comes down to this: Jesus fulfilled prophecy; therefore, the Bible is true.

A bit of critical thinking can spot the fundamental error in this argument's reasoning. What is the *evidence* that Jesus fulfilled prophecy? Answer: the Bible says he did. So, the argument actually amounts to something like this: I know the Bible is true because Jesus fulfilled prophecy; and I know that Jesus fulfilled prophecy because the Bible says so, and what the Bible says is true. In other words: I believe the Bible is true because I believe the Bible is true.

My aim in this analysis is not primarily to demonstrate that this argument is logically empty but to explore its effect on its intended audience. Who would be persuaded by this argument? Only those who already have faith in the Bible. This insight, simple though it might be, is the key to a major thesis of my book: arguments based on the fulfillment of prophecy are rationally persuasive only to believers. More specifically, arguments that Jesus fulfilled prophecy work only for those who already believe in him. To assert that Jesus fulfilled prophecy is, in effect, to *profess* one's Christian faith; it is not, as it might seem at first, to offer evidence for one's faith. The claim that Jesus fulfilled prophecy is, therefore, not part of a proper argument; it is a profession of faith formatted *as if* it were an argument. Its function is to reaffirm beliefs that are already in place.

What This Book Is About

This book is about how and why Jews and Christians in Antiquity expressed their convictions that the biblical prophets had predicted realities that had been fulfilled either in their recent past or in the time of the origin of their particular religious movement. More specifically, this book is about the argument from prophecy: its origin and development, history, methods, functions, presuppositions, implications, and problems. To explain that list briefly, this book studies:

- the origin and development of the belief that the biblical prophets predicted events that were to occur in the distant future;

- the various concrete ways in which belief in the fulfillment of prophecy was expressed over the centuries;

- the specific methods and techniques that interpreters of biblical prophecy used in their attempts to demonstrate the fulfillment of prophecy in their own time or in the recent past;

- how the argument from prophecy functioned within the religious thought of the writers who presented it and in the thought of the audiences for whom they wrote, and within the literary contexts of their writings;

- what the argument from prophecy presupposes, and what it implies, about prophets, prophecy, and the interpreters of prophecy;

- the problems that the historical-critical interpretation of the Bible creates for the argument from prophecy in contemporary Christianity.

Outline of the Book

This book unfolds in four parts, in historical order.

Part 1 (chapters 1–6):
Prophecy, Prediction, and Fulfillment in Israel

As its title indicates, this book is interested primarily in early Christian beliefs that Jesus fulfilled prophecy. But our study cannot begin with early Christian beliefs, because those beliefs were rooted in more ancient Jewish ones. Part 1 explores the development of Jewish concepts of the nature of prophecy and how it might be fulfilled, from Old Testament times through the first century CE. The first chapter examines the ancient Israelite understandings of what prophets were and of how their pronouncements concerned the future, and the vexing problem of how to tell the difference between true and false prophets. Chapters 2 and 3 investigate some false predictions made by biblical prophets, some subsequent efforts to cope with problems that such predictions created, and what those complications reveal about the nuances in Israelite notions of prophecy. Chapter 4 turns to ancient Greece and its understanding of prophecy as cryptic predictions with unforeseeable fulfillments. Starting from the third century BCE, Greek concepts exerted powerful influence on how Jews, and later Christians, understood the prophetic scriptures. Chapter 5 studies the fascinating claims in the Dead Sea Scrolls that biblical prophecies had been fulfilled in the recent history of an idiosyncratic sect of dissident Jews. Chapter 6, which covers the second century BCE through the first century CE, samples two ancient translations of the Hebrew Bible, one into Greek (the Septuagint) and one into Aramaic (a targum), and the works of the Jewish historian Josephus in order to track the development of Jewish beliefs and literary practices relating to the fulfillment of prophecy—beliefs and practices that

formed the ground from which grew early Christian approaches to the fulfillment of prophecy.

Part 2 (chapters 7–13):
The Fulfillment of Prophecy in the New Testament

This is the heart of the book. Within the New Testament (NT), the belief
that Jesus fulfilled prophecy is expressed most overtly and extensively in the
gospels, primarily in the Gospels of Matthew and John. Chapters 8 through
11 scrutinize each of the NT gospels, analyzing every generic statement
that Jesus fulfilled prophecy and every individual passage that quotes an
Old Testament (OT) scripture and matches it with some event in the gospel
narrative. These analyses have various historical-critical objectives, three of
which are the most important to our topic: (1) to compare the wording of
the scriptures as quoted in the gospels to their wordings in the OT, (2) to
compare the meanings the quoted scriptures have in their own literary and
historical contexts to the meanings they acquire in their new contexts in
the gospels, (3) to discern how the text of a given prophecy might have
influenced the composition of the gospel passage that shows its fulfillment.

I will argue that these detailed literary analyses enable us to understand
the interpretive methods by which the gospel authors, especially the authors
we call Matthew and John, shape their evidence and hone their arguments
that Jesus fulfilled prophecy. It is in these ways that the gospel writers *help*
Jesus fulfill prophecy.

The chapters on the gospels also investigate how the argument from
prophecy functions within the gospels to legitimate the Jesus movement
and to delegitimate Jews who do not follow Jesus. These chapters trace the
specific contours of the anti-Jewish edge on the argument from prophecy,
especially in Matthew and John, where the anti-Jewish polemic is protracted
and acerbic. The chapters on Matthew and John also assess the plausibility
and fairness of their unsubtle arguments that Jews have no excuse for not
believing in Jesus because he had so clearly fulfilled prophecy.

In addition to examining the four gospels, part 2 treats the literary
expression of the fulfillment of prophecy in the rest of the NT by analyzing
representative and interesting examples from the Acts of the Apostles (in
chapter 9), from the writings of Paul (in chapter 12), and from the Letter to
the Hebrews (in chapter 13).

Part 3 (chapters 14–16):
The Argument from Prophecy in Patristic Thought

Patristic authors, also known as the church fathers, were Christian theologians from roughly the second through the sixth century. Building on the NT proclamation of the fulfillment of prophecy, these authors developed the argument from prophecy into a pillar of early Christian theology that functioned as a foundation for how Christians thought about the OT and the relationship of Christians to Jews. Part 3 deals primarily with two giants in the field of early Christian scriptural interpretation: the second-century Justin Martyr (chapter 14) and the fourth- and fifth-century Augustine (chapter 16). Chapter 15, "Between Justin and Augustine," briefly analyzes the work of Eusebius of Caesarea (fourth century) and Theodore of Mopsuestia (fifth century), and samples a few representative excerpts from other authors.

Justin and Augustine each buttressed the argument from prophecy with hundreds of examples of how Jesus or the church fulfilled specific scriptures. Both Justin and Augustine embedded the fulfillment of prophecy within overtly anti-Jewish apologetics. Justin linked the argument from prophecy directly to the belief that Christians have replaced Jews as God's chosen people. Augustine constructed an elaborate argument to show that because the argument from prophecy was so obviously compelling, Jewish unbelief in Jesus must have been willful, and thus sinful, which is why Jews deserved the divine punishment under which they survived as dispersed exiles.

Part 4 (chapters 17–18):
Modern Reckoning with the Argument from Prophecy

With part 4 the book jumps directly from Augustine to the modern period. The opening paragraph of part 4 explains the rationale for this historical gap in the book's outline. Chapter 17, "Modern Christian Thought on the Fulfillment of Prophecy," analyzes a representative sample of modern Christian engagements with the argument from prophecy, a sample that includes modern apologetic uses of the argument, as well as uneasy assessments of it from the perspective of the historical-critical interpretation of the Bible. The chapter gives special attention to the methodological and theological difficulties the argument from prophecy raises for Christian scholars who embrace historical criticism.

Chapter 18 teases out exegetical, historical, and logical problems that historical criticism exposes in the modern use of the argument from prophecy. I will argue that attempts by modern historical-critical scholars to harmonize the NT presentation of the fulfillment of prophecy with historical criticism have failed. I will make the case that the argument from prophecy fails as a rational argument because it depends on faulty presuppositions, breaks basic rules of logic, and is undermined by a fundamental error in its reasoning. The chapter also raises doubts about the ethical status of the argument from prophecy within contemporary Christianity, given the argument's inherent and disturbing anti-Jewish polemic. The book closes by urging Christians to retire the argument from prophecy.

There are two appended chapters. The first, "Muhammad in the Bible?", examines an unusual facet of modern belief in the fulfillment of prophecy: arguments by contemporary Muslims that the prophet Muhammad fulfilled biblical prophecies. Non-Muslims will find those arguments utterly implausible, and rightly so. However, those arguments employ some of the very same interpretive practices by which NT authors argued that Jesus fulfilled prophecy. A second appended chapter, "Adam and Edom," analyzes a fascinating (mis)use of a prophecy from Amos in the Acts of the Apostles. The version of the prophecy quoted in Acts has the opposite meaning from the prophecy found in the Hebrew text of Amos. Ironically, however, Amos' original prophecy proved false, while its transformed version in Acts has come true.

Past and Present

The basic function of scripture in any religion is to speak to the present. In Judaism and Christianity, believers look to biblical writings for guidance, wisdom, inspiration, and insight for their lives. Believers want to know what the Bible *means* to them, in the real-life context of their own circumstances. The academic historical-critical study of the Bible, insofar as its methods are purely academic, embodies a quite different agenda. It is interested in such topics as how, when, why, and by whom the biblical texts were composed; what they *meant* to their original authors and audiences; and what those texts can teach us about the lives and times of the people about and for whom they were written. The knowledge thus attained is *historical* knowledge, valued—as knowledge in the humanities should be—for its own sake, regardless of how people might (or might not) choose to find meaning in that knowledge for their own lives.

In the study of biblical prophecy, the historical-critical approach to the Bible understands the words of the prophets as acts of communication between prophets and their contemporaries. The prophets interpreted their own times in the light of what they believed were God's acts in their past, God's will for their present, and God's plans for their (almost always) short-term future. When a prophet's message included predictions, they were meant to orient those in the prophet's present to the will of God as it was about to be fulfilled in the near future. Even eschatological prophecies (predictions concerning the End of history) were intended to influence the present hopes and behavior of the prophets' contemporary audiences. However, later audiences, hoping to hear the word of God in the words of the prophets, inevitably understood their pronouncements in relation to their own (i.e., the later audience's) time or the time of the origin of its particular religious community. Thus, for example, the Jewish sect responsible for the Dead Sea Scrolls related biblical prophecy to the recent history of its community, and Christians related OT prophecy to their own time or to the time of Jesus.

The purpose of bringing old prophecies to bear on the present was to validate the audience's self-understanding as a community that embodied God's plan for history as it had unfolded up until then. In that way, later audiences appropriated the divine authority of past prophecy for their own self-validation. The means by which they worked that magic was a framework of interpretation in which the ancient prophets were reimagined as visionaries who predicted "us," even though they did not understand what they had foreseen. The early followers of Jesus cultivated an identity as the new people of God, the heirs of God's promises to Israel. A crucial process by which they rationalized their self-understanding was a set of ingenious interpretations that transformed often cryptic scriptural prophecies into (what they believed were) recognizable predictions about Jesus and their church.

That way of understanding the OT prophets and of appropriating their words came naturally in the NT period. The interpretive presuppositions and techniques used in the NT were not invented by early Christians; they were well established within Jewish hermeneutics.[4] The early Christians learned how to interpret scripture from their Jewish tradition. Of course, the overwhelming majority of Jews, who did not embrace Jesus, rejected the specific Christian interpretations of scripture—or would have rejected them if they had been aware of them—but they almost certainly would have

---

4. *Hermeneutics* refers to the disciplined effort to interpret what texts mean for contemporary audiences.

found the interpretive methods used by followers of Jesus unsurprising, perhaps even familiar. And a century or two later, after Christians began to regard the writings that came to be called the New Testament as authoritative scriptures on a par with those from Judaism, the NT interpretations of OT prophecy were themselves endowed with divine authority. Christians therefore reflexively considered those interpretations to be not only true, but obviously and unquestionably true. From the Christian perspective, the old prophecies meant what the inspired authors of the NT said they meant. Christians believed that the word of God in the NT thus revealed the true meaning of the word of God in the OT.

That theological understanding of the Bible and its interpretation retained a monopoly in Christian thought throughout nearly all of Christian history—until the historical-critical study of the Bible began to develop in the wake of the Enlightenment. To those who study the Bible with the modern historical-critical assumptions that the words of the prophets meant what the prophets intended them to mean, the NT interpretations of some of those prophecies can seem far from obvious and quite questionable. Anyone with a decent study Bible can compare the wordings of prophecies as quoted in the NT with their wordings in the OT, or can compare their meanings in the NT with what they seem to mean in their original OT contexts. In many cases, those simple procedures are sufficient to turn NT interpretations of prophecy from obvious into puzzling.[5]

The insistence on, and even interest in, what the prophets originally meant in communicating with their contemporaries is a distinctly modern concern.[6] That concern is the explicit goal of the historical-critical interpretation of the Bible (or historical criticism for short), which is a set of interpretive methods designed to determine what biblical texts mean on their own terms and in their own historical, literary, linguistic, social, religious, and political contexts. Historical criticism proceeds without reference to beliefs that biblical authors were inspired by God. It neither affirms nor denies that biblical passages convey divine revelation. Rather, its concern is with what the scriptural texts meant to those who composed them and those who received them. It is from the perspective of that concern that the various NT passages that feature fulfillments of prophecy raise interesting and serious questions, precisely because those NT passages give OT texts new meanings that they do not—and in many cases cannot—have in their own contexts.

---

5. It was curiosity about those puzzling interpretations that started me on the path toward writing this book.

6. There are some premodern exceptions, but they are very few. See the discussion about Theodore of Mopsuestia, pp. 274–78.

Here I want to be especially clear, because it is easy to misunderstand what that last point implies. The historical-critical assessment that the NT attributes meanings to prophecies that are foreign to their original meanings in the OT could be taken to imply that historical criticism is right and the NT is wrong when it comes to discerning the meanings of prophecies. But that would be a misunderstanding. It is not that historical criticism interprets the prophets correctly and that interpretations derived from the NT are wrong. Rather, those who practice historical criticism interpret prophecies differently than did the NT authors because historical critics ask fundamentally different questions about those prophecies than NT authors asked. The answers we get are always conditioned by the questions we ask. Historical criticism asks, what did this prophetic pronouncement mean in Hebrew, in the specific literary unit in which we find it in the edited text, and in the context of this or that political crisis or social situation in, say, eighth-century-BCE Israel? The NT writers, by contrast, asked questions like these: What light does this divine pronouncement throw on our story about Jesus? How does it help us understand our place in the unfolding of God's will for us, God's people? Historical criticism does not claim to be the *only* legitimate approach to biblical interpretation. Nor does it assert that the only valid meanings of a text are those intended by its author and/or received by its original audience. However, most modern readers who are serious about understanding what they read want to discern what an author meant by what he or she wrote. That kind of aim comes naturally, and seems unavoidable, to the modern mind, and historical criticism is the best means we have for achieving that goal as best we can.

Some Central Theses of This Book

The primary focus of this book is on the Christian belief that Jesus fulfilled prophecy, as that belief was expressed in Christian writings from the first five centuries, especially in the NT. This book examines in detail how those writings claim that Jesus fulfilled specific scriptures. In the process of that examination, I will argue that, in many cases

- the connection between a prophecy and its alleged fulfillment is less than clear, and often seems far-fetched;

- the quotation of a prophecy by the Christian author does not always match the prophecy as it appears in the OT;

- even when the quotation is accurate, the meaning of a prophecy in its OT context is seldom the same as, and usually very different from, the meaning it acquires in its new Christian context.

Awareness of these complications draws our attention to how Christian writers "helped" Jesus fulfill prophecy, which they did in two ways: (1) by manipulating, sometimes subtly and sometimes blatantly, the OT scriptures so that the scriptures could correspond to their fulfillments presented in the stories about Jesus, and (2) by manipulating, sometimes subtly and sometimes blatantly, the stories about Jesus so that they could fit the predictions from the OT.

Scrutinizing how Christian texts present the fulfillment of prophecy also suggests an explanation of *how* Christians identified the numerous scriptural passages that they claimed were fulfilled by Jesus. I will argue that the process of pairing prophecies to, for example, events in the life of Jesus, was, in most cases, a *retrospective* process. That is, Christians worked backwards from events in the story of Jesus to the prophecies those events were believed to fulfill. I will argue that it is *not* the case that there was a more or less standard list of prophecies that the messiah was supposed to fulfill, that Jesus came along and fulfilled them, and that his followers came to believe that Jesus was the messiah *because* he had fulfilled those prophecies. Rather, the process usually worked the other way around: Jesus' followers, believing that he was the messiah, used the story of his life to guide their search for the prophecies he had, in their view, fulfilled.

That explanation leads to another, similar thesis: that the belief that Jesus fulfilled prophecy was prior to, and the basis for, discovering the specific prophecies that he had fulfilled. But that raises the question of how Jesus' followers came to believe that he had fulfilled prophecies *before* they had identified individual prophecies that they could match to events in his life. I will argue that the belief that Jesus fulfilled prophecy emerged as a virtually intuitive inference from the belief that Jesus was the messiah. The reasoning must have gone like this: Jesus was the messiah; the messiah was foretold by the prophets; therefore, Jesus must have fulfilled prophecy.

The belief that Jesus fulfilled prophecy had its origin in, and grew naturally from, the belief that he was the messiah. That account of the origin of the belief that Jesus was the fulfillment of prophecy coheres perfectly with the results of the analysis of Rick Warren's Internet devotional quoted earlier in this introduction—with the finding that claims that Jesus fulfilled prophecy are expressions of faith in Jesus, not rationally persuasive reasons for why one should believe in him.

That understanding of the function of prophecy fulfillment raises the question of the rational effectiveness of the argument from prophecy. The analysis of Warren's simplified argument from prophecy showed that because the argument employs circular reasoning, its very structure is illogical. The argument is persuasive only for those who already believe in the Bible—that is, for those who don't need to be persuaded. But what about more sophisticated versions of the argument that present evidence in the form of specific prophecies matched to particular events and circumstances in the life of Jesus? We find that kind of presentation of the fulfillment of prophecy in the gospels, especially in Matthew and John, and in the writings of patristic theologians. It is a major task of this book to analyze and assess in detail those presentations of scriptural evidence. The results of those analyses will consistently confirm that those who did not already believe in Jesus and who harbored a modicum of skepticism would be extremely unlikely to embrace faith in Jesus as a result of Christian arguments that Jesus had fulfilled a series of specific prophecies.

The thesis that identifying Jesus as the fulfillment of prophecy was (and is) a profession of Christian faith rather than its basis can sharpen our appreciation for how the argument from prophecy actually functions. If it didn't work well in recruiting outsiders to faith in Jesus, what did the argument from prophecy accomplish for early Christians? I will make the case that the argument from prophecy, as we see it deployed in the NT, especially in Matthew and John where it is developed most extensively, enabled followers of Jesus to achieve two complementary goals: (1) to justify their belief in Jesus by the strongest means available at the time, that is, by appealing to the unimpeachable authority of the scriptures of Israel; and (2) to convince themselves that Jews who did not embrace belief in Jesus were wrong not to do so, since their own scriptures predicted him.

That latter prong in the argument from prophecy reveals an anti-Jewish polemic that is built into the argument from its very beginning. It is another major task of this book to understand and reckon with the ethical implications of that polemic, which should disturb contemporary Christians. That anti-Jewish edge is abundantly evident in patristic writings, especially those by Justin Martyr (second century) and Augustine (fourth/fifth century),[7] who devoted prodigious intellectual energy to the argument from prophecy. For both of them the relationship of Christianity to Judaism was a vexing problem, and the argument from prophecy played a central role in how each of them tried to solve it. Justin's writings give evidence that second-century Jews were resisting the Christian argument on the grounds that Christians

---

7. See the detailed studies in chapters 14 and 16.

were misinterpreting the Jewish scriptures. Justin, in response, goes to great lengths to argue that Jews misunderstand their own scriptures. His project can be described in part as a Christian attempt to lay claim to Israel's past by appropriating its scriptures. In effect, Justin argued that those scriptures belonged to Christians and no longer to Jews. Augustine, more than two centuries later, could be more calmly confident than Justin was about the superiority of Christianity, for by Augustine's time that religion had permeated the Roman Empire. To Augustine the argument from prophecy seemed so self-evidently compelling that it became a serious question for him why there were any non-Christian Jews left. Why hadn't they all seen the light, given the overwhelming evidence from their own scriptures? Augustine's fascinating (and to me, surprising) answer to that question centers on the argument from prophecy: Jewish disbelief is a part of a complex divine strategy for bolstering the credibility of the argument from prophecy in the eyes of pagans.

The primary thesis in part 4 of this book is that the historical-critical study of the Bible has undermined the rational credibility and ethical acceptability of the argument from prophecy. When the argument from prophecy is measured by the standards of historical criticism and the canons of logic, it collapses as a rational argument. The argument is also plagued by its inherent anti-Judaism, which makes it ethically dubious, to say the least. Those considerations lead to my final thesis: the argument from prophecy needs to be retired.

PART 1

Prophecy, Prediction, and Fulfillment in Israel

1

Prophecy and Prediction in Ancient Israel

IN THE MODERN WORLD a prophet is a future teller, someone with super-natural knowledge of future events. But in ancient Israel that was not the essence of prophecy. The most basic description of a prophet in Israel was as an intermediary between God and the people. A prophet therefore had two roles: delivering God's words to the people and interceding with God on the people's behalf. The second role is less emphasized in the Bible, and so I will discuss it only briefly by citing a few examples. Moses, the prophet par excellence, several times pleads with God on behalf of the Israelites, most famously after the incident of the golden calf, when Moses dissuades Yahweh from obliterating his people (Exod 32:1–14). Similarly, the prophet Amos twice intercedes with Yahweh to call off devastating punishments (Amos 7:1–6). The clearest example of this prophetic role has to do with Abraham, who is not usually thought of as a prophet. In Genesis 20, Abraham's wife Sarah, whom he represents as his sister, is taken by a Canaanite king. God appears in a dream to the king and threatens him with death because he has taken a married woman. When the king rightly pleads his innocence, God tells him, "Send back the man's wife now; he is a prophet and he will intercede on your behalf, and you shall live" (Gen 20:7). Notice that Abraham's status as a prophet has nothing whatsoever to do with predicting the future.

Spokesmen for God

The central role of biblical prophets was to be spokesmen for God by delivering his words. That understanding of the prophet's role can perhaps best be seen in two short scenes from the Book of Exodus. In the first scene, God commands Moses to carry his words to Pharaoh. Moses complains that he is unfit for the task because he is a poor speaker (Exod 4:10). God tells Moses that he will empower Aaron, his brother, to speak on his behalf. Note how concretely this is put:

> You [Moses] shall speak to him [Aaron] and put the words in his mouth . . . He indeed shall speak for you to the people; he shall serve as a mouth for you, and you shall serve as God for him. (Exod 4:15–16)

What Yahweh means by Moses serving "as God" to Aaron becomes clear in our second scene when Moses and Aaron are about to confront Pharaoh for the first time.

> Yahweh said to Moses, "See, I have made you like God to Pharaoh, and your brother Aaron shall be your prophet. You shall speak all that I command you, and your brother Aaron shall tell Pharaoh to let the Israelites go out of his land." (Exod 7:1–2)

Aaron's being a prophet has nothing to do with his predicting the future. He is Moses' prophet because he is Moses' spokesman. Aaron will speak to the Pharaoh, but the words he speaks will be Moses', not Aaron's. That is the essence of biblical prophecy: to speak on God's behalf.

This concept of prophecy is also evident in how the prophets delivered their divinely given messages. The prophets frequently preface their declarations with "Thus says Yahweh."[1] This "thus says X" was a common formatting device in the ancient world, which scholars call the messenger formula. It was used when a messenger needed to make it clear that the words he was about to speak were those of the one who had sent the message, not the personal words of the messenger himself. The messenger formula thus functioned as oral quotation marks. Here is an example, from a highly dramatic scene during the Assyrian invasion of Israel. The king of Assyria had sent a royal official to persuade the defenders of Jerusalem to surrender. As that official stood outside the city wall, he shouted up to the soldiers looking down from the walls:

> Thus says the king of Assyria: "Make your peace with me and come out to me; then every one of you will eat from your own vine and your own fig tree and drink water from your own cistern, until I come and take you away to a land like your own, a land of grain and wine, a land of bread and vineyards, a land of olive oil and honey, that you may live and not die." (2 Kgs 18:31–32)

1. To take Amos, the earliest of the classical prophets, as but one example, see 1:3, 6, 9, 11, 13; 2:1, 4, 6; 3:1, 12; 5:4, 16.

Note that "me" and "I" refer to the king, not the official delivering the message. By opening his declaration with the messenger formula, the official signaled to the soldiers that the terms of surrender came straight from the king himself. The prophets' constant use of "thus says Yahweh" underlines their sense of being his messengers.

The prophets were speakers, not writers. When Jeremiah dictated his words to his assistant Baruch to be written down on a scroll, it was an exception that proved the rule. Jeremiah could not enter the temple to deliver his divine message, so he had Baruch write it down, which enabled Baruch literally to carry Jeremiah's words into the temple and read them to the people (Jer 36:5–8). Except in extraordinary situations like Jeremiah's, the prophets' words and speeches were written down later in order to preserve them. Even in written form, it is clear that their speeches were meant to be spoken and heard in public, not read in private. Scholars know that because the prophets' speeches are full of the techniques of effective public speaking, techniques aimed at engaging and challenging listeners.[2] This is important because it reinforces what common sense tells us: that the prophets wanted their words to have an impact on their audiences, to influence them to believe certain things, experience certain feelings, or act in certain ways.

The prophet's mission was to tell listeners how their present situation fit or, more often, did not fit, into God's plans, and to challenge the people to act according to God's will, usually as expressed in the covenant. The characteristic task of the great prophets who preached before the Babylonian Exile was to indict the kings, the wealthy aristocrats, often the priests, and sometimes the entire nation for serious violations of the covenant. The prophets often pleaded with their audiences to repent, and threatened them with terrible consequences (usually invasion and exile) if they refused. Sometimes these prophets urged rulers to avoid alliances with other nations, and they backed up their messages with analyses of the diplomatic and military situation.[3] Occasionally the prophets foretold the blessings that God would send if Israel would repent and live in faithfulness to its covenant.[4] In a few passages the prophets look beyond the disasters they see coming to describe how God will have compassion on the chastened survivors, bless them with prosperity, and restore the nation.[5] These latter themes become the primary message of prophets operating after the Babylonian Exile, when

2. See Lundbom, *Hebrew Prophets*, 165–207.

3. For example, Hos 2:14–22; 7:11–16; Isa 7:1–20; 30:1–7; 31:1–5; Jer 27:1–11.

4. For example, Hos 14:1–7; Isa 1:18–20.

5. For example, Isa 4:2–6; 43:1–7; Jer 23:1–8; 31:1–14; 32:26–44; Ezek 36:22–37; Amos 9:11–15.

the nation and its religious institutions had been destroyed. The mission of those prophets was to challenge a conquered and humiliated people to cast off their cynicism and despair, and to dare to hope for a glorious future with the God of Israel.

The Prophets and the Future

Predicting the future was not central to the prophets' task, but it was part of what they did. Their purpose in foretelling the future was to impact their present. For example, announcing that God would send a punishment (such as a drought or an invasion) was meant to emphasize the seriousness of the nation's sins and to give the people a strong incentive to repent. Prophetic threats were usually conditional; the punishments could be avoided if Israel repented. The same goes for many of the divine promises relayed by the prophets; those blessings would come only if the people returned to faithfulness. The future of which the prophets speak in these cases is the *near* future, the future to be experienced by the prophets' living audiences. One could assume as much even without reading actual prophetic passages, because for promises or threats to be meaningful to the prophets' audiences, those promises or threats had to refer to circumstances that would affect the audiences' lives. A prediction that was meant to be fulfilled centuries later would have little relevance to a prophet's mission.

True and False Prophecy

Several passages in the OT wrestle with the problem of false prophecy, and some of these passages prescribe tests for distinguishing true prophets from false ones. These tests are based on the intuition that prophets can be assessed by the accuracy of their predictions. As we will see, these tests are beset with serious problems. Nevertheless, they show one very important thing: the future that concerned the prophets was the *near* future.

Jeremiah's Difficulties

False prophets could be a big problem. Jeremiah, for example, repeatedly issues warnings such as this:

> Do not listen to the words of the prophets who are telling you
> not to serve the king of Babylon, for they are prophesying a lie

to you. "I have not sent them," says Yahweh, "but they are prophesying falsely in my name." (Jer 27:14–15)

The Book of Jeremiah narrates a dramatic confrontation in the temple between Jeremiah and another prophet, Hananiah, whose message contradicted Jeremiah's (Jeremiah 28). Their heated argument devolved into a physical altercation (28:10–11). Here were two men prophesying in the name of Yahweh, and they violently disagreed with one another. What was the audience to make of such a spectacle? Both men acted and spoke like prophets. Hananiah's message was reasonable and hopeful; Jeremiah's was bleak and counterintuitive. How could the people decide which prophet to believe?

Jeremiah asserted, in the middle of his argument with Hananiah, that true prophets prophesy disaster and false prophets prophesy peace (the Hebrew word here, *shalom*, is broader than our English "peace"; it connotes wholeness, health, and well-being).

> The prophets who preceded you and me from ancient times prophesied war, famine, and pestilence against many countries and great kingdoms. As for the prophet who prophesies *shalom*, when the word of that prophet comes true, then it will be known that Yahweh has truly sent the prophet. (Jer 28:8–9)

Jeremiah's point is that a prophet who tells you what you want to hear should be under suspicion of being a false prophet, unless he can prove otherwise by making predictions that come true. According to Jeremiah, a prophet who predicts disaster has no such obligation, apparently because such a prophet is by definition a true prophet. Obviously, Jeremiah is hardly a neutral party; his criteria put the burden of proof on Hananiah. And while Jeremiah's warning is common sense (beware of those who, in the name of God, tell you what you want to hear), it does not work as an objective test, since nearly all the prophets pronounce both doom and *shalom*, including Jeremiah himself (see Jeremiah 31, for example).

Jeremiah's test for true and false prophecy is further complicated by his accusation that God himself had sent false predictions of *shalom*, presumably to prophets.

> Ah, Lord GOD, how utterly you have deceived this people and Jerusalem, saying, "It shall be well with you," even while the sword is at the throat. (Jer 4:10)

In this strange complaint, Jeremiah blames God for sending a false prophecy. According to Jeremiah, the prophets who passed on this message did so in good faith, but they turned out to be spokesmen for a lying God.[6] The betrayal Jeremiah feels at God's duplicity is reflected in his word "deceived"; the Hebrew word here is *nasha'*, the same word Eve uses in the Eden story to describe how the snake misled her (Gen 3:31). (One wonders whether Jeremiah is here reflecting on his own experience. How else could he know that these deceptive messages had truly come from Yahweh?)

In a heartbreaking lament in Jer 20:7–10, the prophet accuses Yahweh of deceiving him (20:7), this time using a different word (*patah*), the word used in 1 Kgs 22:20–22 to describe Yahweh deceiving the prophets with a false prediction. In Jer 20:10 Jeremiah imagines his enemies conspiring against him and hoping that he will be "deceived"—probably by receiving more false prophecies from Yahweh—so that they can denounce and ruin him. In 15:18 Jeremiah compares Yahweh to a "deceitful brook," a desert riverbed that is dry most of the year.

Jeremiah's depiction of Yahweh as a deceiver of prophets is mirrored in a passage from Ezekiel concerning prophets who cooperate with those who worship other gods alongside Yahweh. If such a person approaches a prophet to seek an answer from Yahweh to some question, Yahweh will punish both the inquirer and the prophet. What is interesting here is that Yahweh will deceive the inquirer by sending the prophet a false message.

> If a prophet is deceived into making a pronouncement, I, Yahweh, am the one who has deceived (*patah*) that prophet. I will stretch out my hand against him and destroy him from the midst of my people Israel. (Ezek 14:9)

Deuteronomy's Tests

Considering Jeremiah's test for true and false prophecy, but putting aside its flaws, it is telling that a prophet of peace can overcome the suspicion against him by making a prediction that comes true: "As for the prophet who prophesies *shalom*, when the word of that prophet comes true, then it will be known that Yahweh has truly sent the prophet" (Jer 28:9). The notion that accurate prediction is the acid test of an authentic prophet is supported by the Bible's most important passage dealing with false prophecy:

> Any prophet who speaks in the name of other gods, or who presumes to speak in my name a word that I have not commanded the prophet to speak—that prophet shall die. You may say to

6. Elsewhere Jeremiah insists that prophets who proclaim that all will be well are frauds who do *not* speak for Yahweh (for example, Jer 6:13–14; 14:13–14; and 23:16).

Jest

yourself, "How can we recognize a word that Yahweh has not spoken?" If a prophet speaks in the name of Yahweh but the thing does not take place or prove true, it is a word that Yahweh has not spoken. (Deut 18:20–22)

This passage lays out three tests for identifying a false prophet: first, if he speaks in the name of a god other than Yahweh; second, if he gives a prophecy that Yahweh has not given him; third, if his prophecy does not come true.

The validity of Deuteronomy's first test is, for Israelites at least, obvious. But it is not very helpful. Anyone could claim to speak in the name of Yahweh. Hananiah did. The second test is useless because it is unverifiable. The only one who could use this criterion to spot a false prophet would be Yahweh himself. The third test, on the other hand, seems both straightforward and objective. However, it is neither. Let's consider three problems:

1. False prophets can deliver true prophecies.

2. Some prophecies do not come true, for very good reasons.

3. Biblical prophets made some false predictions.

(1) *False prophets can make true predictions.* A charlatan, or someone who sincerely, but mistakenly, believed himself to be a prophet, could make a prediction based on prudent analysis that came true because the event he predicted was likely to occur. Or a false prophet might have a prophecy fulfilled out of dumb luck. What is more serious is that—according to the Bible—it is God who sometimes gives true predictions to false prophets.

> If prophets or those who divine by dreams appear among you and promise you omens or portents, and the omens or the portents declared by them take place, and they say, "Let us follow other gods and let us serve them," you must not heed the words of those prophets or those who divine by dreams; for Yahweh your God is testing you, to know whether you indeed love Yahweh your God with all your heart and soul. (Deut 13:1–3)

That warning is unsettling because *true* prophets sometimes give signs just like the ones mentioned in order to validate their credentials (see, for example, 1 Kgs 13:3, 5 and 2 Kgs 20:9, 11). According to Deuteronomy 13, however, the fact that one's predictions come true does not by itself guarantee that one is a true prophet; the content of the prophet's larger message needs to be scrutinized. And note that in this passage it is *Yahweh* who arranges for the predictions of false prophets to come true as a way of testing Israel's faithfulness. When we combine Deut 13:1–3 with Jer 4:10, we get a disconcerting matched set: Yahweh sometimes sends true predictions through false prophets and false predictions through true prophets.

(2) *Some predictions of disaster do not come true*, for good reasons: the people repent, or God changes his mind. Why should prophets who relay those messages be considered false prophets? Here I'm not referring to prophetic *warnings*, which are conditional (if you don't repent, a terrible thing will happen) but to unambiguous declarations that divine punishment is coming.

A good example is the centerpiece of the story of Jonah. After fleeing from Yahweh's command to prophesy to the Assyrian city of Nineveh, being thrown overboard during a storm at sea, surviving seventy-two hours in the digestive tract of a giant fish, and then being barfed up on an Assyrian beach, Jonah makes his way to Nineveh and grudgingly announces over and over again to its inhabitants, "Forty days more and this city will be destroyed" (Jonah 3:4). There's nothing conditional about Jonah's message, and he does not call on the Ninevites to repent. But they do, from the king on down to the cattle (Jonah 3:5–9). Much to Jonah's dismay, God calls off the destruction. According to Deut 18:22, that technically made Jonah a false prophet because, contrary to his prediction, Nineveh was not destroyed after forty days. But, of course, neither Judaism nor Christianity regards Jonah as a false prophet. In fact, the Book of Jonah became part of the Bible. The gospels even portray Jesus citing Jonah as a prototype for himself (Matt 12:38–40 and Luke 11:29–30).[7]

Those who argue that Jonah's message really was meant as a warning and not an announcement of doom have to explain away his actual words. And those who argue that God intended Jonah's message to be a call for the Ninevites to repent have no textual evidence for their assertion.[8] Besides, even if it were the case that the message Yahweh entrusted to Jonah was meant as a warning, Jonah would still be a false prophet according to Deuteronomy's second criterion, because the message he actually delivered would not be the one God had given him.

(3) The final problem with the dictum that a false prediction makes one a false prophet is that *the biblical prophets made some false predictions*

---

7. This can seem ironic in light of the fact that in Matt 12:40 Jesus himself makes a prediction that does not come true (see pp. 39–41).

8. One of my students defended the truth of Jonah's prophecy by interpreting "Forty days more and Nineveh will be destroyed" to mean "Forty days more *of your sinning* and Nineveh will be destroyed." Her reasoning was that Jonah's prophecy must have had that meaning because God does not lie. While I admire the ingenuity of this argument, it is based on theological beliefs, not on textual evidence. If Jonah meant "forty days more of your sinning," that was not, according to the text, what he said.

of their own. A counterintuitive claim like that needs to be demonstrated, not just asserted, but to pursue it here at the length it deserves would derail this chapter's train of thought, so we will take it up in the next chapter. The important point here is that the ancient Israelite scholars who collected the words of the prophets and edited them into books we have today in the Bible knew about these false predictions but did not delete them from the written record. Apparently, those scholars did not judge Jeremiah, for example, to be a false prophet even though events proved him wrong, for example, about the circumstances of a certain king's death.[9] The Jewish tradition accepted those writings of the prophets as sacred scripture even though their scholars were aware that they contained some false predictions.

Conclusion

The test that a true prophet is one who makes accurate predictions is beset with serious problems. No matter how appealing that test might be in theory, it is unreliable in practice.

Leaving all that aside, however, and accepting the test at face value—that is, in the spirit in which it was intended—it presupposes something crucial: prophetic predictions concern the near or immediate future. Fulfillment of prophecy, as a test for a true prophet, is useless unless that fulfillment is intended in the near future. This presupposition should be clear enough if we reflect on the reason for having such a test in the first place. People needed to be able to distinguish true from false prophets in order to know which prophets to take seriously and which to ignore. That is why prophets whose predictions did not come true quickly were met with skepticism (see Isa 5:19 and Jer 17:15). What good would it do to have a test for distinguishing true from false prophets if the outcome of that test could not be evaluated until centuries later? So, no matter what we think about the viability of fulfillment of prophecy as a test for sorting out true from false prophets, the test itself surely demonstrates that the people of the OT understood prophetic predictions to refer to their own near-term future.

9. See the analysis of Jer 22:19 on p. 28.

2

False Prophecies from True Prophets

IN THE PREVIOUS CHAPTER we saw that the seemingly simple distinction between true and false prophets is actually quite complicated. One aspect of that complication is that prophets who are considered true prophets in the Bible occasionally make predictions in the name of Yahweh that turned out to be demonstrably false. This chapter considers some false prophecies by biblical prophets, examining in each case exactly what the prophet predicted and then the historical outcome that disconfirmed the prophecy. This chapter analyzes a sizable sample of false prophecies, probably more than is necessary for some readers, but sufficient, I hope, to overcome the initial doubts of open-minded skeptics.

Biblical Disconfirmations

Our first examples of false predictions by biblical prophets are prophecies for which the Bible itself provides the evidence that they did not come true. We will review three such cases. In each one a legitimate prophet makes a prediction about a king's fate, and the Bible reports an outcome different from the one foreseen by the prophet.

Ahab's Blood (1 Kgs 21:19)

First Kings 21 narrates a murder and theft committed by the king and queen of Israel. King Ahab offered to buy a vineyard in the city of Jezreel from its owner Naboth. When Naboth refused to sell, Queen Jezebel conspired with the elders of Jezreel to frame him for blasphemy at a public trial there. Naboth was taken outside the city and executed forthwith, which enabled the king to seize his property. Yahweh sent Elijah the prophet to convey his outrage at Ahab's sin and to announce his punishment.[1]

> You shall say to Ahab, "Thus says Yahweh: 'In the place where dogs licked up the blood of Naboth, dogs will also lick up your blood.'" (1 Kgs 21:19)

The story does not report that dogs licked up Naboth's blood, but the prophecy presumes that his executioners had allowed his body to be disgraced in this fashion.

In the next chapter of 1 Kings, Ahab is mortally wounded in battle, his blood pooling in his chariot (1 Kgs 22:35).

> The king died, and was brought to Samaria; they buried the king in Samaria. They washed the chariot by the pool of Samaria; the dogs licked up his blood, and the prostitutes washed themselves in it, according to the word of Yahweh. (1 Kgs 22:37–38)

Passing over the bizarre bit about the prostitutes, we see the narrative confirming one part of Elijah's prophecy and disconfirming the other. Elijah had predicted that dogs would enjoy Ahab's blood "in the same place where dogs licked up the blood of Naboth" (outside the walls of Jezreel), but it happened in the city of Samaria, more than twenty miles away.

Josiah's Death (2 Kgs 22:20)

Second Kings 22 relates the story of the discovery of a book of Yahweh's law in the temple in Jerusalem. When King Josiah heard what the book said, he tore his clothes, signifying his repentance. Josiah asked the priest to consult a prophet to authenticate the book, and the priest went to Huldah, a female prophet who is mentioned only in this story. She verified the divine origin of the laws in the book and then delivered a prophecy concerning Josiah: because of his humility and repentance Yahweh would grant him a peaceful death: "I will gather you to your ancestors, and you shall be gathered to your grave in peace" (2 Kgs 22:20).

Thirteen years later Josiah led his army to the strategic city of Megiddo to meet Pharaoh Neco, whose army was marching through Josiah's kingdom. "Meet" probably means "meet in battle," but might mean that Josiah met the pharaoh for face-to-face diplomacy. Second Kings 23:29 reports

---

1. Although it was Jezebel who actually engineered the death of the innocent Naboth (after telling Ahab that she will give him Naboth's vineyard), Elijah charged Ahab with the crime (1 Kgs 21:19). The prophets consistently held those who benefit from injustice morally accountable for it.

that Neco killed Josiah at Megiddo. Whether he was killed in combat or was assassinated, his violent death proved Huldah's prophecy false. The Bible tells us next to nothing about Huldah, but it clearly regards her as a true prophet of Yahweh, for it relies on her authority to authenticate the book of the Law that was found in the temple.

Jehoiakim's Fate (Jer 22:19; 36:30)

Jehoiakim was a ruthless king who tried to murder Jeremiah and had murdered another prophet, named Uriah, whose message was the same as Jeremiah's (Jer 26:20–23). Jeremiah prophesied that there would be no mourning when Jehoiakim died, and that he would be denied the honor of a royal burial. Instead, his body would be disposed of like an animal's carcass, thrown into the city dump to rot in the open air:

> With the burial of a donkey he shall be buried—
>> dragged off and thrown out beyond the gates of Jerusalem.
>> (Jer 22:19)

Jeremiah repeats this dire prophecy once more, and adds a further curse: that Jehoiakim will have no heir to inherit his throne.

> He shall have no one to sit on the throne of David, and his dead
> body shall be cast out to the heat by day and the frost by night.
> (Jer 36:30)

Jehoiakim died while the Babylonians were besieging Jerusalem, but we do not know the circumstances of his death.[2] Second Kings 24:6 simply tells that "he slept with his ancestors." The most natural meaning of that report is that he received a royal burial. If his body had been thrown out in the garbage, it is difficult to explain why the narrator does not mention such an extraordinarily shocking humiliation for a king he regarded as evil (2 Kgs 23:37).

The other element in Jeremiah's prophecy about Jehoiakim, that "he shall have no one to sit on the throne of David" (Jer 36:30), is undeniably a false prediction. The biblical history is explicit that, contrary to Jeremiah's prophecy, Jehoiakim did have an heir to his throne: "his son Jehoiachin succeeded him" (2 Kgs 24:6; 2 Chr 36:8). Jehoiachin became king under extremely unfortunate circumstances: Jerusalem was under siege, and he was very young (eighteen years old according to 2 Kgs 24:8

---

2. 2 Chr 36:6 reports that the Babylonians captured him and "bound him with chains to take him to Babylon," though it does not say whether he was actually taken there.

or—improbably—eight years old according to 2 Chr 36:9). He surrendered to the Babylonians after only three months and was succeeded by his uncle, Jehoiakim's younger brother, Zedekiah (2 Kgs 24:17–18; 2 Chr 3:15),[3] who reigned for eleven years. Jehoiakim was thus succeeded on the throne by his son and then by his brother, two legitimate Davidic kings, until 587 when the Babylonians put an end to the Davidic monarchy once and for all (see 2 Kgs 25:1–7).

Contradictory Predictions

Zephaniah 1:2–3 / Genesis 8:21

When two predictions contradict each other, one of them has to be false. An example of this prophetic phenomenon is found in the opening lines of the prophet Zephaniah's announcement of a coming worldwide devastation by Yahweh.

> "I will utterly destroy everything
>> from the face of the earth," says Yahweh.
> "I will destroy humans and animals.
>> I will destroy the birds of the air
>> and the fish of the sea.
> I will make the wicked stumble.
>> I will cut off humanity
>> from the face of the earth," says Yahweh. (Zeph 1:2–3)

Yahweh's terrifying declaration explicitly reverses his promise to Noah after the flood: "I will never again destroy every living creature as I have done" (Gen 8:21). The prophecy in Zephaniah is linked to the flood story in Genesis by two tight verbal connections. (1) Zephaniah uses the same Hebrew verb for "destroy" (*'asaf*) in verses 2 and 3 that is used in Gen 8:21. (2) The double repetition of "the face of the earth" in Zephaniah echoes the identical phrase used in the beginning, middle, and end of the flood story (Gen 6:7; 7:4; 8:8). These verbal links demonstrate that the prophet (or some later editor) deliberately phrased Zeph 1:2–3 to contradict Gen 8:21.

---

3. 2 Chr 36:10 mistakes Zedekiah for Jehoiachin's brother of the same name (see 2 Chr 3:16).

God's words in Gen 8:21 are a promise, not a prophecy, but that difference is a mere formality. Either the prophecy in Zephaniah is false, or God intends to break his solemn promise in Genesis.[4]

Revenge Fantasies

Isaiah 11:12–14

Assyria deported much of the population of the northern kingdom of Israel when it conquered the nation in 721. Assyria likewise deported many Judeans when it conquered the southern kingdom of Judah in 701. The city of Jerusalem was spared, but Judah became a powerless Assyrian vassal. Isaiah 11:12–14 prophesies that Yahweh will gather the deportees of Israel and Judah and reunite the two kingdoms. Together they will plunder and rule over their neighbors: Philistia, Aram (Syria), Edom, Moab, and Ammon.

> They shall swoop down on the backs of the Philistines in the west,
>> together they shall plunder the people of the east.
> They shall put forth their hand against Edom and Moab,
>> and the Ammonites shall obey them. (Isa 11:14)

None of that happened. The tribes of the northern kingdom were dispersed throughout the Assyrian empire and lost to history (they are known in popular history as "the lost tribes of Israel"); the northern kingdom ceased to exist as an Israelite state and was never reconstituted. Also contrary to Isaiah's prophecy, Judah never again achieved military dominance over all its neighboring states.

---

4. A student of mine earned an *A* for effort when he tried to harmonize this contradiction by arguing that, according to Gen 9:14–15, God did not technically promise never to destroy all life—he only promised not to do so with a flood. But that is not what Gen 8:21 says. There are two versions of just about every narrative element in the flood story (e.g., God tells Noah to take one pair of every living thing into the ark in 6:19, and then in 7:2–3 tells him to take seven pairs of birds and clean animals), because Genesis 6–9 is a repetitive blending of two originally independent stories: the Yahwist and the Priestly. To claim that the two versions mean the same thing is to assume what needs to be demonstrated. Besides, it is difficult to imagine what religious comfort anyone can derive from imagining that God was crossing his fingers while swearing his oath to Noah.

Obadiah 17, 18, 21

The one-chapter Book of Obadiah is an oracle against the nation of Edom, Israel's bitter enemy who, according to the prophet, had joined in the plundering of Judah when it fell to the Babylonians in 587 BCE (see also Ezek 35:12). Obadiah makes extravagant predictions about the revenge Judah ("the house of Jacob") will take on Edom ("Esau"). "The house of Jacob shall take possession of those who dispossessed them" (v. 17b). Mount Zion will rule Mount Esau (v. 21). Most chilling of all, Obadiah prophesies that Judah will exterminate the Edomites.

> The house of Jacob shall be a fire
>
> . . .
>
> and the house of Esau stubble;
> they shall burn them and consume then,
> and there shall be no survivor in the house of Esau,
> for Yahweh has spoken. (Obad 18)

Fortunately, this genocide never occurred. Edom was never depopulated.

A similar though lengthier and more vivid prophecy of Edom's utter destruction is found in Isa 34:5–17. "From generation to generation Edom shall lie waste / no one shall pass through it for ever and ever" (Isa 34:10). This land, now part of the nation of Jordan, is still inhabited.

The Exaggerated Downfall of Superpowers

Our next category of false prophecies by true prophets concerns predictions of the destruction of superpowers that had victimized Israel.

Destruction of Assyria (Isa 10:24–27)

Assyria was the Middle Eastern superpower of the eighth and seventh centuries BCE, and a hated oppressor of Israel. In this passage Isaiah urges the people not to fear the mighty Assyrians under whose yoke they are suffering, because "in a very little while" (Isa 10:25) Yahweh will strike down Assyria and free his people from their domination. Isaiah prophesied in the late eighth century BCE, while Assyria wiped out the northern kingdom of Israel in 722 and laid waste the southern kingdom of Judah in 701. Judah remained a vassal to Assyria until breaking free in 622, but Assyria remained a serious threat until it was finished off by the Babylonians around 605.

Isaiah's "very little while" turned out to be nearly a century. A prophecy meant to encourage those who heard it failed to come true until long after they had died.

No more invasions (Nah 1:12, 15)

The Book of Nahum is entirely devoted to prophecy about Assyria, specifically about the destruction of its capital Nineveh (Nah 1:1), which occurred in 612 BCE. Isaiah had proclaimed that Assyria was Yahweh's instrument for punishing Israel (Isa 7:18–20; 10:5–6). Nahum, prophesying a century after Isaiah, announces that now Yahweh's anger has turned against Assyria and he will cease punishing his people.

> Thus says Yahweh,
> "Though they [the Assyrians] are at full strength and many,
>   they will be cut off and pass away.
> Though I have afflicted you [Israel],
>   I will afflict you no more.
> And now I will break off his yoke from you
>   and snap the bonds that bind you." (Nah 1:12–13)

In 1:15 Nahum makes an extravagant promise to Israel: "never again shall the wicked invade you."

Nahum is so focused on the downfall of the hated Assyrians that he predicts that once they are destroyed Israel will henceforth live in security, that never again will Yahweh permit an invasion—not even for the purpose of punishing his people. Nahum apparently did not foresee the Babylonians, who would destroy Israel over a hundred years later, and who, according to Jeremiah, were instruments through whom Yahweh punished his sinful people (Jer 1:14–15; 27:5–8).

Destruction of Babylon (Isa 13:17–22)

This passage prophesies that the Medes (who were vassals of the Assyrians) will conquer the city of Babylon and destroy it so thoroughly that it will never recover.

> [Babylon] will be like Sodom and Gomorrah
>   when God overthrew them.
> It will never be inhabited or lived in for all generations. (Isa 13:19–20)

The Medes did not conquer Babylon. The city was badly damaged by the Assyrians in 689 BCE, but they rebuilt it in 680. It rose to glory as the capital of the neo-Babylonian empire later in the seventh century. Babylon fell to the Persians in 539 without major fighting. The city later suffered damage as the Persians repressed revolts against their rule in 521 and 482,[5] but it remained largely intact and was rebuilt. The Greek historian Herodotus visited Babylon in the fifth century BCE and was impressed with its grandeur.[6] Over the next few centuries, however, the city languished and eventually fell into ruin as its population dwindled away. But it was never destroyed by military violence.

Excursus:

The Rebuilding of Babylon and the Return of Christ

In 1983 Iraqi dictator Saddam Hussein started to reconstruct Babylon, whose ruins lie in the suburbs of Baghdad, as a memorial to his megalomania. I vividly remember that some "end-times" preachers got excited because they took that project as a sign that the End was approaching. Their reasoning was that since Babylon had never been properly destroyed, it would have to be rebuilt before the prophecy of its destruction could be fulfilled. This confidence that Babylon will be rebuilt features prominently in the enormously popular *Left Behind* end-times saga,[7] which stages lots of exciting action in "New Babylon." Hopes for the rebuilding of Babylon continue unabated among enthusiasts of "end-times prophecy." One of the many websites devoted to this topic opens with this announcement: "Scripture says Babylon will be completely destroyed and no one will ever live there again. This prophecy has never been fulfilled. People have lived there and are still living there today. The complete prophetic fulfillment apparently is still in the future."[8]

5. Blenkinsopp, *History of Prophecy*, 277.

6. Herodotus, *Histories* 1.178–200.

7. Sixteen novels between 1995 and 2007 by Tim LaHaye and Jerry Jenkins (published by Tyndale House).

8. Koenig, "Rebuilding of Babylon."

Egypt conquered by Nebuchadnezzar
(Jer 43:8–13; 46:13–26; Ezek 30:10–12)

Jeremiah 46:13–26 prophesies that King Nebuchadnezzar of Babylon will be Yahweh's instrument for punishing Egypt, that Nebuchadnezzar will attack and conquer that nation. "Daughter Egypt will be put to shame; / she shall be handed over to a people from the north [the Babylonians]" (Jer 46:24). There are also specific predictions that Egypt's capital, Memphis, will be devastated (Jer 46:19), and that Yahweh will hand over Pharaoh and the gods of Egypt to Nebuchadnezzar (Jer 46:25–26).

Jeremiah 43:8–13 contains a similar prophecy, with distinctive predictive details that Nebuchadnezzar will burn the temples of Egypt (Jer 43:12), and that he "shall pick clean the land of Egypt, as a shepherd picks his clothes clean of vermin" (Jer 43:12). Ezekiel 30:10–12 also prophesies Nebuchadnezzar's devastation of Egypt, adding the hyperbolic prediction that Yahweh will dry up the Nile (Ezek 30:12, also prophesied in Isa 19:5–10).

Nebuchadnezzar attacked Egypt in 568 BCE, but there is no historical evidence that he conquered it. While the lack of evidence for an event normally does not allow us to conclude that it did not happen, in this particular case the silence is loud and decisive. Babylonia and Egypt were the superpowers of the day and if one had conquered the other it would have shaken the balance of power all through the ancient Middle East. Such an epic event surely would have left traces in the historical record. Nebuchadnezzar's official annals, which brag about his victories, say nothing about conquering Egypt, which would have been his greatest triumph. Both historians who specialize in ancient Egypt and those who study Babylonia are confident that Nebuchadnezzar died in 562 without having conquered Egypt.[9]

Great Expectations

Second Isaiah (Isaiah 40–55)

In the wake of the devastation and exile of 587 BCE, several prophets spoke of hope for the future, and described their visions of the restoration and exaltation of Israel. Some of these visions are grandiose and include such divine promises as superpower military status for Israel, miraculous fertility in the land, and extravagant riches for the people. Here are three representative examples from an anonymous prophet whose prophecies are found in

---

9. See Greenberg, *Ezekiel*, 617, and the sources cited there.

Isaiah 40–55, and whom scholars call Second Isaiah, who prophesied to his fellow exiles in Babylon.

> I will lift up my hand to the nations,
>> and raise my signal to the peoples;
> they shall bring your sons in their bosom,
>> and your daughters shall be carried on their shoulders.
> Kings shall be your foster fathers,
>> and their queens your nursing mothers.
> With their faces to the ground they shall bow down to you,
>> and lick the dust of your feet. (Isa 49:22–23)

> Yahweh will comfort Zion;
>> he will comfort all the waste places,
> and will make her wilderness like Eden,
>> her desert like the garden of Yahweh. (Isa 51:3)

> I will make your pinnacles of rubies,
>> your gates of jewels,
>> and your whole wall of precious stones. (Isa 54:12)

As it turned out, the Persian emperor Cyrus overthrew the Babylonian Empire in 539 and allowed the Jewish exiles in Babylon to return to the land of Israel and to rebuild the temple of Yahweh in Jerusalem. But few actually returned, and life for the returnees was very hard. The territory around Jerusalem still had not recovered from the destruction of the Babylonian invasion half a century earlier. What was formerly the kingdom of David was now a tiny and impoverished province in the Persian Empire. The prophetic visions of a wonderful future were not fulfilled in detail or on the scale promised.[10]

Those who cannot accept the fact that the Bible contains prophecies that did not come true might argue that those predictions in Isaiah are not false prophecies; they are simply unfulfilled ones that will be fulfilled in the future. But this is surely not what the prophet who uttered them meant, for he was addressing his contemporaries in Babylon. The "you" and "your" in Isa 49:22–23 refer to them, not to some indefinite audience in the remote future. The prophet emphasizes that Yahweh's intervention to restore his people is imminent, about to unfold as they watch: "I am about to do a new thing; now it springs forth; do you not perceive it?" (Isa 43:19). Their

---

10. Hill, *In God's Time*, 42.

glorification is so near, in fact, that the prophet can refer to it as having already taken place:

> See, you shall call nations that you do not know,
>> and nations that do not know you shall run to you,
> because of Yahweh your God, the Holy One of Israel,
>> for he *has glorified* you. (Isa 55:5)

Haggai

Despite Second Isaiah's optimistic predictions, the situation on the ground in Jerusalem after the exiles were permitted to return was anything but rosy, and an initial enthusiasm for rebuilding the temple could not be sustained in the face of so much material hardship. It was in those discouraging circumstances that the prophet Haggai announced that their deprivations were Yahweh's punishment for putting their own interests above the completion of the temple (Hag 1:2–11). Zerubbabel, the Persian-appointed governor, and Joshua the high priest took Haggai's message to heart and rallied the people to complete the temple (Hag 1:12–14).

Haggai then foresaw a new era of unprecedented glory and prosperity for Israel just around the corner, an era that would crystallize around two miraculous events: the enrichment of the temple and the exaltation of Zerubbabel. Despite his Babylonian name, Zerubbabel was the grandson of Jehoiachin, the Davidic king who had been captured in the fall of Jerusalem in 587. We know almost nothing else about Zerubbabel, but the references to him in the prophecies of Haggai and Zechariah imply that some had high hopes that he would somehow restore the Davidic monarchy and make Israel great again.

Enrichment of the Temple (Hag 2:6–9)

Even though the rebuilt temple apparently compared poorly with the former temple of Solomon (Hag 2:3), Haggai prophesies that earthshaking events are coming very soon and will bring riches flowing into the new temple.

> "In a little while . . . I will shake all the nations, so that the treasures of all nations shall come, and I will fill this house [the temple] with splendor," says Yahweh. (Hag 2:6–7)

The second temple will be so rich that its splendor will overshadow that of Solomon's temple (Hag 2:9).

That did not come to pass. Six centuries later Herod the Great poured enormous funds into a lavish expansion and remodeling of the temple, making it into a world class tourist attraction. But that cannot count as the fulfillment of Haggai's prophecy. Six centuries is not "a little while," and Herod's makeover of the temple was not paid for by "the treasures of all nations."

Supremacy of Zerubbabel (Hag 2:21–23)

The book of Haggai ends with a mysterious prophecy.

> Speak to Zerubbabel, governor of Judah, saying, "I am about to shake the heavens and the earth, and to overthrow the throne of kingdoms . . . On that day," says Yahweh of hosts, "I will take Zerubbabel my servant . . . and make you like a signet ring; for I have chosen you." (Hag 2:21–23)

The bearer of a king's signet ring could act with the authority of the king himself. According to Haggai's prophecy, therefore, God will soon overthrow the political systems of the earth in a cosmic upheaval and install Zerubbabel as his personal representative.

A new world order anchored by Zerubbabel's authority did not materialize. In fact, history records nothing more about Zerubbabel. It is as if a trapdoor had opened beneath him and he disappeared from the stage of history.

Conclusion

False prophecies in the Bible are worth our attention because of what they entail about the complexities of biblical prophecy and what they can tell us about the authors and editors of the Bible. The authors of 1 and 2 Kings, for example, recorded the very stories that proved that the predictions about the deaths of Ahab and Josiah were inaccurate. The authors and editors of the Books of Kings could have buried those mistakes, either by rewording the prophecies of Elijah and Huldah so that they accurately foretold later events in the narrative, or simply by omitting the reports that contradicted the prophecies. Jeremiah's editors could likewise have left out his prediction that Jehoiakim would die without an heir. The editors of the prophecies of Isaiah, Ezekiel, Zephaniah, Nahum, and Haggai had similar opportunities

Jesus

to omit or modify the false predictions analyzed in this chapter. The entire Book of Obadiah could have been dropped from the approved list of prophetic books, and who would have noticed? For all we know, there might have been many false prophecies that were conveniently "forgotten" or quietly dropped or even erased from the record. That false prophecies have been preserved in the written record, even though they could have been easily covered up, tells us that Israelites assessed the truth of the prophets' messages on a broader basis than whether all of their predictions came true.

Fundamentalists and other literalists, whose beliefs about the Bible are based on what they think the Bible should contain rather than on what it actually contains, have no room in their system of beliefs to acknowledge the existence of false prophecies by biblical prophets. A common way in which literalists explain away such inconvenient facts is to label those prophecies *unfulfilled*, rather than false (see the above discussion of Second Isaiah, for example). But this evasive maneuver is futile. It cannot explain the failed prophecies about Ahab, Josiah, and Jehoiakim, or Nahum's prediction that Israel would never be invaded after the downfall of Assyria. It is true that a few prophecies have vague temporal indicators and so can be read as open-ended, for example, the prophecy of Obadiah (though in this case it is profoundly disturbing that anyone would actually hope that Obadiah's prophecy will eventually come true—that is, that the people of Israel will murder every person within the boundaries of the land of ancient Edom). Most prophecies, however, come with implied expiration dates. As we saw above, Second Isaiah's predictions were intended to encourage his contemporaries. And phrases like "in a little while" (e.g., see Isa 10:25 above) are meaningless unless they refer to time scales within the lifetimes of those whom the prophet originally addressed. Other prophecies concern specific people and therefore expire when those people are no more. Nebuchadnezzar will never conquer Egypt (e.g., Jer 43:13–26), and Zerubbabel will not become God's signet ring (Hag 2:23). The Medes will never destroy Babylon (Isa 13:17–22) because they no longer exist as a people and because Babylon does not exist as a living city.

Epilogue: False Prophecy by Jesus

The gospels attribute numerous prophetic predictions to Jesus, most of them having to do with the End Times. Whether those prophecies were accurate is impossible to determine until the End Times arrive, though some of them certainly seem to predict that the End would arrive within the lifetimes of Jesus' disciples. For example, Jesus promised his apostles that they will "be seated on thrones and sit in judgment on the twelve tribes of Israel" (Matt 19:28; Luke 22:30). After the apostles died, Christians who puzzled over such matters inferred that the apostles will judge Israel either as souls from heaven or after the resurrection of their bodies. However, one of Jesus' prophecies is quite explicit that some of his followers will be alive to witness the end times: "Let me tell you, some of those standing here won't ever taste death before they see the kingdom of God arriving in force" (Mark 9:1, with parallels in Matt 16:28 and Luke 9:27).

Commentators defending the literal truth of the Bible have gone to great lengths to argue that Jesus really didn't mean what he said, usually by asserting that "the kingdom of God arriving in force" does not refer to the end times, and/or that "won't ever taste death" doesn't mean "won't die." Some scholars (myself included) maintain that this prophecy was not spoken by the historical Jesus, but was attributed to him after his death. Whether or not that historical judgment is correct matters little here, because even if Jesus himself never pronounced this false prediction, the gospels present him doing so, and therefore Mark 9:1 remains a biblical prophecy. Anyone who doesn't cling to the doctrine of biblical inerrancy can easily see this prophecy for what is: a false prediction.[11]

I won't belabor this example because although it is a prophecy attributed to Jesus that did not come true, the gospel writers did not know that at the time, and the focus of this chapter is on how biblical authors and editors regarded disconfirmed (i.e., false) predictions made by true prophets. So, is there an example of a prophecy by Jesus that an evangelist knows did not come true? Yes, there is.

> Some of the scribes and Pharisees said to Jesus, "Teacher, we wish to see a sign from you." But he answered them, "An evil and adulterous generation asks for a sign, but no sign will be given to it except the sign of the prophet Jonah. For just as Jonah was for three days and three nights in the belly of the sea monster, so for three days and three nights the Son of Man will be in the heart of the earth." (Matt 12:38–40)

---

11. Some evangelical scholars admit this obvious truth. Not all evangelical scholars defend complete biblical inerrancy, but in a case like Mark 9:1 where it is Jesus who is in error, the problem is acute, and most such scholars are silent on the issue. A rare evangelical scholar who does face the problem tries to solve it with an implausible distinction between error and ignorance. "Jesus prophesied that God would wrap things up within one generation. However, instead of saying that Jesus was mistaken, that he was either a false prophet or a misguided fanatic, we ought to admit that his knowledge of the future was limited." Apparently, false predictions do not constitute error: "he was not wrong"; "Jesus was not mistaken" (McKnight, *New Vision*, 138).

Buried

It's obvious that Matthew understands Jesus' resurrection to be the fulfill-ment of this prophecy, and that the Son of Man's being "in the heart of the earth" refers to Jesus' corpse in the tomb. It's just as obvious that, according to Matthew's own timeline, Jesus was dead for no more than two nights and one day: Friday night, Saturday, Saturday night. Matthew does not reveal at what point on that timeline Jesus came to life and left the tomb. All he tells us is that Jesus' tomb was already empty when an angel opened it at first light on Sunday morning (Matt 28:1). So, Matthew saw Jesus' prophecy about his being buried for three days and three nights fulfilled when Jesus was buried for—at most—half that long.

It's interesting that this prophecy is also found in Luke's gospel, though in a significantly different form: "You see, just as Jonah became a sign for the Ninevites, so the Son of Man will be a sign for this generation" (Luke 11:30). In this version Jesus makes no mention of three days and three nights. This saying shared by Luke and Matthew comes from the Q Gospel,[12] which rais-es the question whether Matthew's or Luke's version is closer to the wording of the saying in Q. It's impossible to be certain since we don't have a copy of that gospel. Most scholars who study Q think that it's more likely that Luke's version of this saying is a better reflection of the Q original, which means that Matthew is probably responsible for adding the three days and three nights to the saying. Why would he do that, when he knew that the predic-tion was not literally true? Probably because he wanted to make the parallel between Jesus and Jonah more detailed than it was in Q. Yet precisely that added detail makes the prediction less than fully accurate. Matthew could have avoided that problem, and still made his point, by making the predic-tion general rather than specific, by writing something like, "Just as Jonah was in the belly of the sea monster for a short time, so too will the Son of Man be briefly in the heart of the earth."

The "three days and three nights" makes the prophecy generally, but not completely, true, and therefore partly false. Is this splitting hairs? That depends on who does the splitting. Those who take the Bible literally and maintain that God-inspired prophecies must come true literally—that is, precisely and in complete detail—face a dilemma. *Either* Jesus' prophecy is only partially true—and therefore also and equally partially false—which makes Jesus something less than a true prophet, *or* prophecies need not come true fully and precisely in order to count as true. Needless to say,

12. The Q Gospel was composed of material, almost entirely of teachings attributed to Jesus, that Matthew and Luke used a source. Although no copy of Q has been found, scholars have inferred its existence and reconstructed its probable contents by examin-ing material shared by Matthew and Luke but not found in Mark. See Miller, *Complete Gospels*, 257–78.

Matthew did not consider Jesus to be a partially false prophet. The conclusion is unavoidable: either Matthew's gospel contains this stark contradiction or Matthew did not presuppose that a true prophet makes predictions that always come true fully and precisely.

3

Fixing Failed Prophecies

THE PREVIOUS CHAPTER INVESTIGATED examples of predictions by true prophets that did not come true. In those examples the books containing those false prophecies betray no uneasiness with them. However, that is not always the case. As the belief that prophecy was *essentially* about predicting the future became more entrenched, it was probably inevitable that some thinkers would face the problem of how to deal with prophetic predictions that had failed to come true. In a few places in the Old Testament we can see the traces of different attempts to come to grips with this problem. We will examine three such examples—two briefly and one in detail.

The Rescheduled Massacre of Moab (Isa 16:13–14)

Isaiah 15–16 contains several prophetic pronouncements concerning the destruction of Moab, a small nation bordering Israel. Isaiah 16:6–11 is a lament over the total destruction of Moab after its invasion by a conquering enemy. Isaiah 16:9–10 emphasize the silence of the land at harvest time, when there should be lots of noise from all the farmwork.

> The shout over your fruit harvest
>> and your grain harvest has ceased.
> Joy and gladness are taken away
>> from the fruitful field;
> and in the vineyard no songs are sung,
>> no shouts are raised;
> no treader treads out wine in the presses;
>> the vintage-shout is hushed. (Isa 16:9b–10)

The land is silent because its inhabitants have been slaughtered. Verse 11 expresses the deep grief the poet feels at the emptiness of this once flourishing land.

Isaiah 16:13–14 is an epilogue to the poem of lament in 16:6–11.

> [13] This was the word that Yahweh spoke concerning Moab in the past. [14] But now Yahweh says, "In three years, like the years of a hired worker, the glory of Moab will be brought into contempt, in spite of its great multitude; and those who survive will be very few and feeble."

This passage has the marks of a later addition to the original lament, for it is in prose rather than poetry and has its own introduction. Verse 14 refers to the large population of Moab, "its great multitude," which suggests that the desolation depicted in vv. 9b–10 has not occurred. Although scholars have been unable to establish the original historical setting of vv. 6–11, vv. 13–14 apparently was written at a time when Moab was thriving. The author of this short passage recognizes that the word of Yahweh in vv. 6–11 has not been fulfilled.[1] But a new prophecy has come: in three years the disaster promised in vv. 8–10 will strike. In other words, God's previous prophecy has not come true, and so God has sent a new, updated one.

Isaiah 16:13–14, written by someone pondering and editing the words attributed to Isaiah, shows how carefully the old prophecies were studied, and how later writers felt both the need and the freedom to update and justify them in the light of subsequent events.[2] Here we see one biblical author coming to terms with the failure of a prophecy. Since there are many believers today who resist the idea that any biblical prophecy can fail, it is important to look closely at the time frame for Isa 16:6–11. It is not worded as a prediction about the future, for the devastation of Moab is envisioned as having already happened, which is why the poet-prophet describes emotions he is feeling as he pronounces the lament (vv. 9, 11), and why he summons "everyone" to join in mourning for Moab (v. 7). So it cannot be the case that 16:13–14 means to say simply that the prophecy in vv. 6–11 will soon be fulfilled. Isaiah 16:13–14 says something much more significant: Yahweh's past word about Moab's destruction did not come true, but now he has a new word on the matter.[3] We cannot know whether the author actually believed that Yahweh had revealed the new prophecy to him in v. 14, or

---

1. Verse 12 is another prose addition to vv. 6–11, which need not concern us here.
2. Blenkinsopp, *History of Prophecy*, 300.
3. Fishbane, *Biblical Interpretation*, 476.

whether he used the phrase "but now Yahweh says" as a literary device to express the conclusion of his own theological reasoning.

The Unprofitable Siege of Tyre (Ezek 29:17–20)

In the previous example from Isaiah, literary analysis of the passage suggests that a later editor had added Isa 16:13–14 to Isa 16:6–11. Making this literary distinction enables us to see that 16:13–14 deal with the failure of the prophecy in 16:6–11. In the present example from Ezekiel it is much easier to see what is at stake because here Ezekiel reports that God himself admits that a prophecy has failed. Chapters 26–28 in Ezekiel contain prophecies against the city-state of Tyre, prophecies that envision its destruction by the Babylonian army of King Nebuchadnezzar. Ezekiel 26:7–14 is especially graphic in its descriptions of the Babylonians' battering down Tyre's walls, slaughtering its inhabitants, and looting its riches. While it might seem odd that Ezekiel gives so much attention to a conflict that does not involve Israel, Ezekiel's underlying theological principle here is that Yahweh is sovereign over all the nations, and that he will use Nebuchadnezzar as his instrument for punishing the sinful arrogance of the people and king of Tyre (see, for example, 27:3 and 28:2).

Tyre was a wealthy city, a center of maritime commerce with a large fleet. The city was built on a fortified island off the coast of Lebanon, and so was unusually difficult to attack. Nebuchadnezzar laid siege to the city, which held out for thirteen years.[4] It finally surrendered without being destroyed or looted. It seems there was no loot to be had, probably because the riches of the city had been used up in the long siege or squirreled away for safekeeping by Tyre's fleet.[5] This lack of loot created a problem for Nebuchadnezzar because plunder was the way ancient kings paid their armies. According to Ezekiel, Yahweh had specifically promised Nebuchadnezzar the plunder of Tyre (26:7, 12). Ezekiel 29:17–20 addresses that problem.[6]

> [17] In the twenty-seventh year, in the first month, on the first day of the month, the word of Yahweh came to me: [18] "Mortal, King Nebuchadrezzar[7] of Babylon made his army labor hard against Tyre; every head was made bald and every shoulder was rubbed bare; yet neither he nor his army got anything from Tyre to pay

---

4. Josephus, *Ant.* 10.228.

5. Allen, *Ezekiel*, 109.

6. Fishbane, *Biblical Interpretation*, 476.

7. The Hebrew Bible spells the name of this king in two ways, sometimes with *n* and sometimes with *r*.

for the labor that he had expended against it." ¹⁹ Therefore, thus says the Lord Yahweh: "I will give the land of Egypt to King Nebuchadrezzar of Babylon; and he shall carry off its wealth and despoil it and plunder it; and it shall be the wages for his army. ²⁰ I have given him the land of Egypt as his payment for which he labored, because they worked for me," says the Lord Yahweh.

Verse 17 dates the oracle to 571 BCE,[8] a year or two after Tyre's surrender. In verse 18 Yahweh admits that Nebuchadnezzar and his army had received no pay (that is, no plunder) for all their labor during the siege. So God comes up with a new plan for paying the troops: he will give Egypt and all its wealth to Nebuchadnezzar to plunder. The logic of verse 20 is extraordinary: Nebuchadnezzar and his army had worked for Yahweh, and so he was obliged to pay them their wages. Since he hadn't made good on his promise of plunder in Tyre, he would provide back pay with the plunder of Egypt (see also Jer 43:12).

Two things about this passage command our attention. The first is the candid, almost casual, way it acknowledges that a prophecy uttered by a true prophet had failed to come true. There is no indication here that Ezekiel was particularly troubled by this. He doesn't try to explain the problem away or find some new or hidden meaning in the previous prophecy that might get Yahweh off the hook. Either Ezekiel did not agree with the definition of a false prophet in Deut 18:21–22 (see pp. 22–23), or he did not know about it. Ezekiel had no doubt that he was a true prophet, so if some prophecy that Yahweh had given him didn't come true, there had to be a reason other than his being a false prophet.[9] It was Yahweh's problem, and Ezekiel was confident that Yahweh was going to fix it.

The second fascinating feature of Ezek 29:17–20 is that Yahweh's new compensation package for Nebuchadnezzar also failed to work out. Nebuchadnezzar attacked Egypt in 568 BCE but did not succeed in conquering it (see p. 34). It is surprising that Ezekiel did not hide the failed prophecy about the Babylonians' plundering Tyre; and it is just as remarkable that those who preserved and transmitted Ezekiel's words did not hide the failed prophecy about Nebuchadnezzar's plundering Egypt.[10]

---

8. Ezek 29:17 begins, "In the twenty-seventh year," which in Ezekiel means the twenty-seventh year since the exile of King Jehoiachin to Babylon (see Ezek 1:2), which occurred in 598 BCE, when Ezekiel himself was also exiled.

9. Greenberg, *Ezekiel*, 617 (quoting David Noel Freedman).

10. Ibid., 617–18.

Yahweh rule
Jr. David

Yahweh's Broken Covenant (2 Sam 7:8–16)

The previous examples of failed prophecies in Isaiah 16 and Ezekiel 29 concern foreign nations and events that are peripheral to Israel's religion. However, the next example concerns momentous events in Israel's history and takes us into the heart of OT theology. We will go into this example in detail.

Second Samuel 7 tells how God made a covenant with King David, a covenant scholars call the Davidic Covenant, to distinguish it from the other great covenant, mediated by Moses, the Mosaic Covenant. While most covenants involved two parties entering into a relationship in which each had duties toward the other, the Davidic Covenant is entirely one-sided: Yahweh makes promises but requires nothing in return.

> ⁸ Now therefore thus you shall say to my servant David: Thus says the LORD of hosts . . . ¹² When your days are fulfilled and you lie down with your ancestors, I will raise up your offspring after you, who shall come forth from your body, and I will establish his kingdom. ¹³ He shall build a house for my name, and I will establish the throne of his kingdom forever. ¹⁴ I will be a father to him, and he shall be a son to me. When he commits iniquity, I will punish him with a rod such as mortals use, with blows inflicted by human beings. ¹⁵ But I will not take my steadfast love from him, as I took it from Saul, whom I put away from before you. ¹⁶ Your house and your kingdom shall be made secure forever before me; your throne shall be established forever. (2 Sam 7:8, 12–16)

The promises that concern us here are two. First, Yahweh will establish a son of David as king (2 Sam 7:12). Second, his son will start a dynasty that will rule Israel forever (2 Sam 7:13). What is remarkable about the Davidic Covenant is that it is absolutely unconditional: nothing that David's descendants do will ever cause Yahweh to take the throne away from them. Saul, David's predecessor, lost his throne because he had disobeyed one of Yahweh's commands (see 1 Samuel 15), but Yahweh guarantees that there will be no such consequences for the house of David. If a descendant of David sins against God, God will punish him, but not by taking away his throne (2 Sam 7:14–15). The prophecy concludes by reiterating that David's line will rule Israel for all time: "Your house and your throne shall be made secure forever before me; *your throne shall be established forever*" (2 Sam 7:16).

But that's not the way it worked out. David became king around 1000 BCE, and his dynasty held the throne in Jerusalem through thick and thin for several centuries. But in 586 BCE Jerusalem fell to King Nebuchadnezzar after a long and bitter siege. The Davidic king, Zedekiah, was captured and brought to Nebuchadnezzar. Zedekiah was forced to watch as his sons were murdered. Then the Babylonians blinded him and hauled him off in chains to prison in Babylon (2 Kgs 25:1–7). Zedekiah was the last king of the house of David.

The destruction of the holy city Jerusalem and of Yahweh's temple, and the humiliating termination of the royal line of David were a devastating blow to Israelites who believed in the Davidic Covenant. We can hear some of their feelings of grief, shock, and betrayal in the book of Lamentations, written shortly after the events (see Lamentations 2, for example).

Psalm 89: Pleading with an Unfaithful God

How can Yahweh have allowed this disaster? Was not his promise in the Davidic Covenant unconditional? Could it be that Yahweh had violated his own covenant? These anguished questions are explored with great literary skill in Psalm 89, an extraordinary blend of praise, accusation, and pleading. We do not know when this psalm was composed. There are no clear clues in the psalm, and scholars are forced to make educated guesses. Some argue that it was written in the early years of the Babylonian Exile, others that it fits better into historical circumstances before or after the Exile.[11] All that we know for sure is that the psalm responds to some disaster that drives the author to the conclusion that Yahweh has broken his covenant with David. A close analysis of this powerful psalm gives us some sense of the religious trauma that many Israelites experienced as they faced their feeling that their God had betrayed them.

The author begins with a stout affirmation of Yahweh's "steadfast love and faithfulness" (Ps 89:1–2), two terms that will be emphasized to great effect a few verses later. The psalm then reminds Yahweh that he had sworn to David, "I will establish your descendants forever and build your throne for all generations" (vv. 3–4). The psalm then detours into a lengthy celebration of God's power as the creator (vv. 5–18), but along the way it carefully re-emphasizes God's steadfast love and faithfulness (vv. 5, 8, 14), qualities that describe reliability in keeping covenants, not the ability to create. The psalm then returns to its primary theme, the Davidic Covenant. Verses 19–37 elaborately describe this covenant by quoting Yahweh's words back to him. The psalmist uses Yahweh's own words to strong rhetorical effect, reminding Yahweh in no uncertain terms that his promise to David was permanent and unconditional (vv. 28–33) and backed up by a solemn oath:

11. Tate, *Psalms*, 416–17.

> I will not violate my covenant,
>> or alter the word that went forth from my lips.
> Once and for all I have sworn by my holiness;
>> I will not lie to David.
> His line shall continue forever,
>> and his throne shall endure before me like the sun. (Ps 89:34–36)

Then the mood abruptly changes: "But now you have spurned and rejected him; you are full of wrath against your anointed one. You have renounced the covenant with your servant" (vv. 38–39). The accusation is stark: Yahweh has broken his word. After painful descriptions of the humiliating defeat of the king and the nation, the psalm expresses pleading bewilderment as the author asks how long Yahweh will let these deplorable circumstances continue. "How long, O Yahweh? Will you hide yourself forever? How long will your wrath burn like fire?" (v. 46). The psalm trails off with an accusation and a reminder, both bitter and poignant.

> Lord, where is your steadfast love of old,
>> which by your faithfulness you swore to David?
> Remember, O Lord, how your servant is taunted;
>> how I bear in my bosom the insults of the peoples,
> with which your enemies taunt, O Yahweh,
>> with which they taunt the footsteps of your anointed one.
>> (Ps 89:49–51)

In effect, the author tries to make Yahweh feel ashamed of himself, hoping that he will change his mind, get over his anger, and live up to his covenant promise.

Those final verses[12] just quoted show that the psalmist hopes that Yahweh will relent and restore the Davidic line. Even though Yahweh has broken his word, the psalmist does not fully despair. Perhaps Yahweh will act on the steadfast love and faithfulness for which he is famous. But perhaps not. The situation implied by the psalm's pleading is one in which it was still possible to cling to some hope that the Davidic dynasty might yet regain power. Yahweh had certainly broken his unconditional promise, but perhaps he could be shamed into doing the right thing.

What is crucial for us to note is that the psalmist is utterly convinced that the Davidic Covenant was unconditional. The psalm does not claim that the Davidic kings were righteous, but there is no hint that the psalmist

---

12. Verse 52 ("Blessed be Yahweh forever, Amen and amen.") was added later, when the individual psalms were collected into an anthology.

even considers the possibility that the disaster that befell the king was a just punishment for his sins. The author confronts Yahweh by quoting in Yahweh's own words his provision that if the heirs of David sin they will be punished, but they will not lose the throne (Ps 89:30–33). So from the psalmist's perspective, the only explanation for the recent disaster is that Yahweh has broken his unconditional guarantee to the Davidic dynasty.[13] If any other explanation were available, it is difficult to imagine that the psalmist would run the risk of blasphemy by daring to accuse Yahweh of breaking his word.

The Deuteronomists' Solution

As the stark reality of the Israelites' circumstances in exile began to sink in, the theological implications became severe. If Psalm 89 was composed early in the exile, as it might well have been, it shows that some clung to the desperate hope that Yahweh might even now repent of his violation of the Davidic Covenant and somehow, miraculously, restore it. But as time went by this anguished faith was increasingly more difficult to sustain. Eventually it became painfully evident that the unthinkable was in fact true: Yahweh had made a false promise to the house of David. The logical inference from this was as unavoidable as it was unacceptable: Yahweh could not be trusted to keep his covenants.

Some of the Israelites in Babylon seem to have accepted the logic of all this, for some (perhaps most) of them turned to the Babylonian gods and gave up the religion of Yahweh.[14] After all, why should they keep faith with a deity who had proven himself untrustworthy? But other Israelites were unwilling to abandon the God of their ancestors. Among them were some scholars who collected the oral and written traditions of Israel and began the intensely creative task of producing a national epic that would explain why Israel's history had ended up in disaster, and why there was still hope for the future of Yahweh's people. The results of the work of those anonymous scholars are some of the core books of the Hebrew Bible, including a sweeping history from the time of Moses to the Exile composed of the books of Joshua, Judges, 1–2 Samuel, and 1–2 Kings. Modern scholars call this grand narrative the Deuteronomic History because its overall analysis

---

13. That the Davidic Covenant was understood to be everlasting is verified by two other passages: 2 Sam 23:5 and Jer 33:19–22. The latter is a late addition to the book of Jeremiah, probably composed in the Persian period among Israelites who still hoped for a revival of the Davidic line (see Carroll, *Jeremiah*, 639). Some hopes die hard.

14. Ackroyd, *Exile and Restoration*, 41–42.

of the rise and fall of Israel is based on the theological principle at the base of the book of Deuteronomy: that Israel would prosper when it kept Yahweh's laws and face disaster when it did not.[15] That, of course, is the fundamental premise of the Mosaic Covenant: that God promised to bless the people when they were faithful to the covenant and threatened to punish them when they were not.

From the Deuteronomistic perspective, the Babylonian Exile posed no theological problem at all. God had given his people a code of laws, but the people, and especially the kings, had more or less continually disobeyed them. God had sent a series of prophets to warn them of the consequences of their infidelity to the covenant, and to urge them to repent. But the kings and the people had refused. For the Deuteronomistic historians the invasion by the Babylonians, the destruction of Jerusalem and its temple, and the exile in Babylon were the just punishments of Yahweh, upholding the Mosaic Covenant.

But how were the Deuteronomistic editors to fit the Davidic Covenant into their theological analysis of Israel's history? To them it probably seemed out of character for Yahweh even to make an unconditional covenant in the first place. Worse yet, the obvious implications of an unconditional Davidic Covenant collided headlong with their understanding of the cause of the destruction of Jerusalem and its ruling dynasty, because that disaster was the result of Israel's, not Yahweh's, unfaithfulness. The Davidic Covenant was therefore a square peg that would not fit into the round holes in the Deuteronomistic pegboard. But there it was, spelled out in the story in which the prophet Nathan reports Yahweh's promises to David (2 Sam 7:12–16).

The Deuteronomists' solution was both audacious and elegant: alter the terms of the Davidic Covenant to mesh with Deuteronomistic theology. They did not tamper with the story in 2 Sam 7:1–17, perhaps because it was so well known. However, later in the narrative when David and then Solomon recount the covenant, it is remembered as a strictly *conditional* one, just the way the Deuteronomists needed it to be for their grand theological theory to work out. The first such scene is at David's deathbed, as he speaks his last words to Solomon. After urging Solomon to assiduously keep Yahweh's laws, David tells him,

> Then Yahweh will establish his word that he spoke concerning
> me: "*If* your heirs take heed to their way, to walk before me in

15. See, for example, the stark life-or-death summary in Deut 30:15–20, the inducements and warnings in Deut 8:11–20, and the numerous formal covenantal blessings and curses in Deut 28:1–45.

> faithfulness with their heart and with all their soul, there shall
> not fail you a successor on the throne of Israel." (1 Kgs 2:4)

The second scene is Solomon's very public prayer during the dedication of the grand temple in Jerusalem. In the relevant verse, Solomon quotes Yahweh as he prays to him.

> Therefore, O Yahweh, God of Israel, keep for your servant my
> father David that which you promised him, saying, "There shall
> never fail you a successor before me to sit on the throne of Israel,
> *if only* your children look to their way, to walk before me as you
> have walked before me." (1 Kgs 8:25)

The Davidic Covenant is also featured in 1–2 Chronicles, a postexilic rewriting of Israel's history based on the books of Samuel and Kings. When it comes to the Davidic Covenant, Chronicles exhibits the same contradiction as its sources. When the prophet Nathan relays Yahweh's words to David about the covenant, it is stated unconditionally (1 Chr 17:13–14). However, when David recounts the covenant, it has the Deuteronomistic condition added to it: "I will establish his [Solomon's] kingdom forever *if* he continues resolute in keeping my commandments and my ordinances" (1 Chr 28:7). The same is true for Chronicles' version of Solomon's prayer at the dedication of the temple (2 Chr 6:16).

The Deuteronomistic rewriting of the terms of the covenant turns up also in one of the psalms.

> Yahweh swore to David a sure oath
>   from which he will not turn back:
> "One of the sons of your body
>   I will set on your throne.
> *If* your sons keep my covenant
>   and my decrees that I shall teach them,
> their sons, also, forevermore,
>   shall sit on your throne." (Ps 132:11–12)

This declaration that the covenant was conditional not only contradicts the original story about the covenant in 2 Samuel 7, but it contrasts starkly with the poignant pleading in Psalm 89 (see above), in which the psalmist emphatically reminds Yahweh that his promises to David's heirs were absolutely unconditional (see especially Ps 89:28–33).

Conclusion

In this chapter we have seen three different ways in which OT authors and editors came to grips with the problem of failed prophecies. Isaiah 16:13–14 looks back on a prophecy and says, in effect, that it didn't come true as promised, but now Yahweh has sent a new prophecy that promises that the earlier one will soon come true. In Ezek 29:17–20 Yahweh himself concedes that a prediction of his has failed. This causes a problem, which Yahweh solves with a new prediction. The problem here is a practical one (how to compensate Nebuchadnezzar and his army for services rendered), but apparently not a theological one. Ezekiel seems to shrug off—or perhaps not even notice—the problem of how a genuine prophecy can fail.

The two prophecies that failed in Isaiah 16 and Ezekiel 29 are obscure ones. The third one analyzed in this chapter, the prophecy of an everlasting Davidic dynasty, is famous. Its spectacular failure occasioned profound theological bewilderment, as Psalm 89, for example, shows. The Deuteronomistic editors' solution is, paradoxically, both more subtle and more blatant than the solutions we see in Isaiah 16 and Ezekiel 29. It is more subtle because it does not openly admit that the prophecy about the Davidic Covenant failed. Nor do the editors do anything as obvious as tamper with the scene in 2 Samuel 7 in which the covenant is first revealed by the prophet Nathan. The Deuteronomists' solution is to have David and Solomon "remember" the terms of the covenant differently than in 2 Samuel 7. Yet this tactic is also daringly blatant because the change it introduces into the wording of the covenant (1) alters its character completely, and (2) is in no way implicit in the earlier version in 2 Samuel 7.

Our first two examples operate on the principle that a failed/false prophecy can be superseded by a new prophecy—implying, in effect, that we should forget what Yahweh had said in the past because he is now saying something new. The last example operates on the principle that a prophecy can be altered to conform to a certain theological outlook—implying, in effect, that if a prophecy doesn't fit your beliefs about the way things should be, you can rewrite it so that it does.

4

Prophecy as Mysterious Revelation

The Influence of Greece

THE PROPHETS OF ISRAEL considered the meaning of their messages to be abundantly clear. Most of their speeches condemned the sins of the people and their leaders, called on them to repent, and warned of the dire consequences if they refused. The prophets' preaching was meant to influence the behavior of those to whom they spoke. To do that their messages, which they presented as the very words of God, had to be intelligible. To take but one example, consider Jeremiah's famous temple speech in Jer 7:1–15. Note the emphatic tone of verse 13: "when I [Yahweh] spoke to you persistently, you did not listen," which alludes to the prophets God had sent time and again with the same message. Those prophets are mentioned explicitly in a summary of the temple speech in Jer 26:1–6. Yahweh threatens to destroy his temple unless the people "heed the words of my servants the prophets whom I send to you urgently, even though you have not heeded them" (Jer 26:5). The problem is not that the people have not understood the prophets, but that they have not heeded them.

The notion that the prophets' messages were not difficult to understand seems to be contradicted by the story of Isaiah's call to be a prophet (Isaiah 6). This scene contains one of the most disturbing instructions in the whole Bible, as Yahweh commands his prophet:

> 9 Go and say to this people:
> "Keep listening, but do not comprehend;
>> keep looking, but do not understand."
> 10 Make the mind of this people dull,
>> and stop their ears,
>> and shut their eyes,

so that they may not look with their eyes,

and listen with their ears,

and comprehend with their minds,

and turn and be healed. (Isa 6:9–10)

Yahweh tells Isaiah that his mission is to make sure that the people do *not* understand his message, for if they did, they would surely repent, and God would forgive them (Isa 6:9–10). This passage has befuddled interpreters with its strangeness, and I will not analyze it here except to draw attention to two things. First, the basic message in the preaching that Isaiah actually does is not at all mysterious and is clearly meant to be understood and acted on. Second, Isa 6:9–10 assumes that the prophetic message is usually *easy* to understand. Look carefully at the flow of thought in verse 10: God tells Isaiah to make the people stupid, deaf, and blind, for otherwise they will understand and respond. The point of this strange commission is that it takes extraordinary intervention to *prevent* the people from understanding the meaning of prophecy.

Isaiah prophesied in the eighth century and Jeremiah in the seventh and sixth centuries BCE. Most of the biblical prophets preached in those centuries as well, prior to and during the Babylonian Exile. A handful of prophets—Haggai, Zechariah, Malachi, Joel, and Third Isaiah (an anonymous prophet, or perhaps prophets, whose words are preserved in Isaiah 56–66)—were active shortly after the return from exile in the late sixth century. After that the living voices of the prophets who have books named after them pass into history, while their words were later preserved in writing.

Our next window into the prophetic tradition in Israel is the book of Daniel, the latest prophetic book[1] in the OT. Though the story the book tells is set in Babylonia in the sixth century, critical scholarship has determined that the book was written around the time of the Maccabean crisis in the mid-second century BCE. The understanding of prophecy and divine revelation in Daniel is markedly different than it is in the time of the classical prophets: divine revelation and the messages of the prophets are seen at this later time as mysterious, unintelligible until an inspired sage can interpret them. In the stories in Daniel 2 and 4 the Babylonian king receives strange symbolic dreams that only Daniel can interpret. Daniel himself has elaborate symbolic visions but cannot understand them until angels interpret them for him (Daniel 7, 8, 10). The strange and wonderful story of the writing on the wall in Daniel 5 illustrates perfectly this understanding of divine revelation. During a royal banquet human fingers appear in the air and

---

1. In the Christian Bible, Daniel is considered a prophet, whereas the Hebrew Bible groups this book with the Writings, not the Prophets.

write something on the palace wall, but none of the king's sages can read the writing, much less discern its meaning (Dan 5:5–8). Daniel, however, is able to decipher the writing—the cryptic *mene mene tekel upharsin*—and explain its hidden meaning (Dan 5:25–28).

Even when the words of God seem to have an ordinary and obvious meaning, they require interpretation to disclose their true hidden significance. Daniel ponders "the words of Yahweh to the prophet Jeremiah" that seventy years "must be fulfilled for the devastation of Jerusalem" (Dan 9:2). In Jeremiah's own context there was nothing mysterious in his words: after the Babylonians had deported most of the Jewish leaders to Babylon, Jeremiah sent a letter to tell them, in the name of Yahweh, that it would be seventy years before Yahweh would bring them back to Jerusalem (Jer 29:1, 10). Jeremiah sent that message to counteract Jewish prophets in Babylon who were claiming that God would end their exile within a few years. Jeremiah tells the exiles to plan for a long stay in Babylon (Jer 29:5–7). All of that is transparently clear in Jeremiah 29. Yet Dan 9:24 finds a hidden meaning in Jeremiah's prediction: seventy years actually means seventy "weeks" of years (70 × 7 years). It's no coincidence that a figure of 490 years makes Jeremiah's prediction point to the century when the Book of Daniel was written.

Clearly something had happened to the understanding of the nature of prophecy between the time of Jeremiah in the sixth century, when the prophets addressed their contemporaries in language that was easy to understand, and the time of the writing of the Book of Daniel in the second century, when prophecy was perceived to be mysterious and intended for a time in the prophet's future. What had happened was the influence of Greek culture on the Jewish world. Following in the wake of Alexander the Great's conquest of the Middle East in the late fourth century, Greek language, art, literature, education, philosophy, architecture, social customs, political structures, even Greek sports, began to exert a broad and lasting influence on the native cultures of the region. The resulting blend of Greek and indigenous traditions is called by historians *Hellenistic* (that is, "Greek like"), as distinct from *Hellenic* (Greek).

Hellenistic Judaism refers to the many-faceted forms of Jewish religion that developed out of the creative engagement of the ancient Israelite traditions (especially the Hebrew scriptures) with the influence of Greek thought, language, and culture. For our purposes, we will focus on how the Jewish understanding of prophets as God's messengers was influenced and transformed by the Greek understanding of prophets as *oracles*.

The Greek understanding of prophecy is important to our topic because of the influence it had on how Jews came to understand their own prophets. Although Judaism came to absorb some basic Greek beliefs about prophecy, the function and practice of prophecy in Israel and Greece differed in important ways. Like the Israelites, the Greeks believed that certain rare individuals relayed messages from the gods; but Greece did not have people like the great prophets of Israel—public figures who offered unsolicited divine criticism of the nation's religious and moral behavior. Prophetic messages in Greece were nearly always addressed to individuals, usually in response to specific inquiries.

Oracles

The most famous manifestation of prophecy in Greece was the oracle, a sacred person who conveyed messages from a god at a shrine dedicated to that deity. (The term *oracle* can also refer to the divine message delivered by the sacred person.) The individuals who served as oracles were anonymous, and we know little about how they were selected for their roles. There were several oracle shrines in Greece, the most prominent being Apollo's at Delphi. People consulted oracles in order to obtain a god's guidance concerning specific decisions or answers to specific questions. Apollo was consulted especially on matters of religious practice; for example, about which deity to approach, which rituals to use to obtain a certain result from the gods, what titles to use in addressing this or that deity, and whether to start up a new festival or revive an old one.[2] The oracle also took questions on mundane matters. Here are some actual questions put to oracles: Will my wife have a baby? Is the baby my wife is carrying mine? Should I buy that house in the city? [From a slave:] Should I run away?[3] The oracle's responses were believed to come straight from the god. Answers could come in plain or symbolic language and range in clarity from unintelligible mutterings to well-crafted verse. The meaning of the answer was usually clear, especially on religious matters.[4] Answers to questions in the form "Should I do x?" included indications of the consequences of doing so. Sometimes the consequences were stated clearly, sometimes ambiguously. The most famous case of an ambiguous reply is the one to King Croesus, who asked the oracle at Delphi whether he should go to war against Persia. The oracle responded that if he did, "he would destroy a great kingdom." Encouraged by this reply, Croesus attacked the Persians and was utterly defeated. The result confirmed the oracle: the kingdom Croesus destroyed was his own.[5]

2. Ferguson, *Backgrounds*, 166.

3. Quoted from Klauck, *Religious Context*, 191–92.

4. Ferguson, *Backgrounds*, 168.

5. Herodotus, *Histories*, 1.46–53.

The New Testament contains an indirect reference to the Delphic oracle and to the widespread belief in its prophetic power. In an episode in the Acts of the Apostles, Paul and his companion Silas encounter "a slave girl who had a prophetic spirit and who made a great deal of money for her masters by pronouncing oracles." She trails Paul for several days, calling out, "These men are slaves of the Most High God, who proclaim to you a way of salvation." Paul becomes annoyed at her shouting and exorcises the spirit within her in the name of Jesus Christ. That exorcism antagonizes her masters, and Paul and Silas wind up being arrested, flogged, and jailed (Acts 16:16–24). The connection of this episode to the oracle at Delphi is found in the description of the spirit possessing the girl: her "prophetic spirit" is literally "a *pythian* spirit" (Acts 16:16). Pytho was the ancient name of the site of the Delphic oracle, and a *Pythia* was a female who relayed oracles from Apollo.[6]

The story in the Acts of the Apostles aims to demonstrate the superiority of Jesus over Apollo, inasmuch as Paul treats Apollo's prophetic spirit as a demon by exorcising it in the name of Jesus. That Apollo is represented by someone of the lowest possible social class, a slave girl, might be intended as a further insult to Apollo. Nevertheless, it is noteworthy that the narrator of Acts does not question the girl's prophetic ability. In fact, her identification of two strangers as agents of the Most High God[7] confirms the prophetic authenticity of the oracular spirit possessing her.

The Old Testament contains several stories in which Israelites consult prophets who act as oracles of Yahweh. In 1 Sam 9:3–10, Saul searches for lost donkeys but cannot find them; so he attempts to find a "seer" who can "inquire of Yahweh" to discover their location. That this kind of oracle seeking was common in early Israel is revealed by the narrator's explanation: "Formerly in Israel, anyone who wanted to inquire of God would say, 'Come, let us go to the seer,' for the one who is now called a prophet was formerly called a seer" (1 Sam 9:9). In some stories no seer/prophet is mentioned, but his presence is implied by the term "inquire of Yahweh/God." For example, "David inquired of Yahweh, 'Shall I go and attack the Philistines?' Yahweh said to David, 'Go and attack the Philistines'" (1 Sam 23:2). As with oracles in Greece, here too the information sought from God is an answer to a very specific question. Another oracle story (1 Kgs 22:1–28) has a fascinating twist. King Ahab consults the prophet Micaiah, who relays a deliberately false reply to the king's question. When the king suspects that the reply is

6. Pervo, *Acts*, 405n49.

7. This term was used both by Jews as a title for Yahweh and by gentiles to refer to Zeus (Pervo, *Acts*, 405n50). Perhaps the author of Acts is deliberately ambiguous as to which deity is meant in this passage.

untrue, Micaiah gives the true reply and then, curiously, explains why Yahweh had tried to deceive Ahab.

Prophetic *Mania*

In addition to oracles stationed at established shrines, Greeks could also obtain prophetic messages from freelance prophets (*theomanteis*) and soothsayers (*chrēsmodoi*)—the difference between them is not clear. Like oracles, these specialists were also believed to be channels through whom the gods spoke. Greeks assumed that when a god spoke through a human instrument, the divine intervention in that person's mind temporarily overrode his or her conscious awareness and induced an altered state of consciousness. Here is how Plato explains it:

> God takes away the minds of these men and uses them as his ministers, just as he does soothsayers and godly seers, in order that we who hear them may know that it is not they who utter these words of great price, when they are out of their wits, but that it is God himself who speaks and addresses us through them.[8]

The Greeks called this altered state of consciousness *mania*. Though some instances of mania were known to be caused by disease, it was usually considered a divine endowment. Plato tells us that "the greatest blessings come by way of *mania*, indeed of *mania* that is heaven-sent."[9] Plato distinguishes four types of divine mania: prophetic (from Apollo), ritual (from Dionysus), poetic (from the Muses), and erotic (from Aphrodite and Eros).[10] Here is Plato's description of the prophetic type of mania.

> It was when they were mad [i.e., manic] that the prophetess at Delphi and the priestesses at Dodona achieved so much for which both states and individuals in Greece are thankful; when sane they did little or nothing. As for the Sibyl and others who by the power of inspired prophecy have so often foretold the future to so many, and guided them aright, I need not dwell on what is obvious to everyone.[11]

8. Plato, *Ion* 534d, quoted from Aune, *Prophecy*, 39.

9. Plato, *Phaedrus* 244a.

10. Plato, *Phaedrus* 265b.

11. Plato, *Phaedrus* 244b.

What Plato describes is the sensation that one is acting under the influence of mysterious forces beyond one's control. Even our culture can occasionally recognize mania, for we know that falling "madly" in love, for example, is a mild form of temporary insanity.

Ancient peoples, and many traditional societies throughout history up until today, have generally considered mental disturbances of every kind to have supernatural causes. Indeed, those experiencing such mental states often feel as if they are in contact with spirits, for good or bad. Our own culture regards all such experiences as pathological; "hearing voices" in our culture is never good, no matter what the voices might say. However, our modern culture is highly unusual in this regard. Most other cultures have believed that "normal" everyday states of consciousness impede human openness to and awareness of the supernatural world. Greek thinkers distinguished divine mania from mania that was caused by disease, but even so the distinction was not hard and fast. Plato recognized that disease can sometimes be a favorable precondition for the manifestation of supernatural abilities.[12] Epilepsy, for example, was widely considered a sign of favor from the gods.

Mania in the Bible

Etymology can be revealing. A Greek word commonly translated "prophet" is *mantis*, which comes from the verb *manteuomai* ("to prophesy" or "to have a presentiment"). But *mantis* is also indirectly related to another verb, *mainōmai* ("to rage"), the root for the noun *mania*. The Bible preserves a few traces of manic behavior among the earliest prophets. Num 11:25–29 reports that seventy elders prophesied when a "spirit" came on them. The text does not describe what this prophesying consisted of, but the terse narration—"when the spirit rested on them, they prophesied" (Num 11:25)—gives the impression that the elders were not in control of themselves. Whatever they were doing, it must have been chaotic if seventy men were doing it all at once.

In 1 Sam 10:5–13, Samuel warns Saul that he will meet a band of prophets and will then fall into some sort of agitated ecstatic state ("prophetic frenzy" in the NRSV): "The spirit of Yahweh will possess you, and you will be in a prophetic frenzy along with them and be turned into a different person" (1 Sam 10:6). Samuel's prediction comes true in 10:10. Later in the narrative (1 Sam 19:19–24) Saul encounters other prophets, supervised by Samuel himself, and again falls into manic behavior, this time described more luridly than before: "Saul stripped off all his clothes, and he too fell

12. Plato, *Timaeus* 71e.

into a frenzy before Samuel. He lay naked all that day and all that night" (1 Sam 19:24).

Biblical scholars refer to this kind of phenomenon as "ecstatic prophecy"—"ecstasy," from the Greek word *ekstasis*, meaning "standing outside (of oneself)," is a near synonym for mania. The prophet Elisha was derogatively called a "madman," *meshugga* in Hebrew[13] (2 Kgs 9:11), an indication that prophecy was popularly associated with occasional ecstatic raving (see also Jer 29:26 and Hos 9:7).

It is noteworthy that in Mark's gospel Jesus is described as having the reputation of being an ecstatic. In Mark 3:21 Jesus' family comes to take him away because people were saying, "He is out of his mind" (the Greek verb here is the counterpart to the noun *ekstasis*). In Mark's context, this judgment about Jesus is not based on anything he says—Mark does not narrate any of Jesus' teaching, apart from a few one-liners, until after this scene—but rather seems to be sparked by his mass healings and the chaotic complications the crowds created in their wake. Mark 3:20–21 exhibits three similarities with OT reports about ecstatic prophets: (1) that altered states of consciousness were associated with the ability to channel divine power, (2) that some regarded such altered states with wary reverence, and (3) that others felt embarrassment (or contempt) for the one acting out in these strange ways.

Enigmatic Messages

The Greeks believed that prophetic messages came straight from the gods. In some cases, this belief was understood quite concretely: it was thought, for example, that at Delphi Apollo took control of the oracle's voice and used it as his own (Apollo's oracular messages were in the first person rather than the third). Because the words of the oracle were believed to originate outside the oracle's mind, and because prophetic personnel relayed the words of the gods while in an altered state of consciousness, the Greeks inferred that their prophets did not know the meaning of the divine words as they uttered them. According to Plato, "prophets and tellers of oracles utter many truths under divine inspiration (*mania*), but have no knowledge of what they are saying."[14] Elsewhere, Plato describes Socrates analyzing how it is that poets can produce such powerful and moving words without being able to explain rationally how they choose them.

13. The Septuagint translates this insult with *epilēptos*, a Greek word that comes into English as "epileptic."

14. *Meno* 99c.

I decided that it was not wisdom that enabled them to write their poetry, but a kind of instinct or inspiration (*mania*), such as you find in seers and prophets who deliver all their sublime messages without knowing in the least what they mean.[15]

One more quotation is germane to our topic. After explaining that a prophet cannot interpret what he says until he comes to his senses, Plato tells us,

For this reason it is customary to appoint interpreters to be judges of true inspiration. Some persons call them prophets, being blind to the fact that they are only the expositors of dark sayings and visions, and are not to be called prophets at all, but only interpreters of prophecy.[16]

Oracles and the Future

Foretelling the future was not the direct purpose of oracles. Those messages from the gods were supposed to instruct the petitioner about the will of the gods, or to answer a direct question, or to give advice about a possible course of action. However, in responding to specific inquiries, some oracles referred to the future, particularly those that forecast favorable outcomes or warned of dire consequences. Because oracles were of divine origin, it was believed that any predictions they made would always be fulfilled. In cases of cryptic or ambiguous oracles, there was plenty of room for speculation about *how* they might be fulfilled. Even when an oracular prediction had seemed to come true, it was still possible to wonder if it had been fulfilled *completely*.

The Greek world was fascinated with puzzling oracles (the modern interest in the inscrutable predictions of Nostradamus or cryptic Mayan prophecies is similar), and Greek culture produced two means of feeding that fascination. One was the practice of collecting oracles in writing.[17] Once oracles were in writing, they could circulate outside their original context, without the questions to which they were the answers. Ambiguous oracles could then be reinterpreted and applied to new situations. There were specialists in Greece who collected and interpreted oracles for a fee.

15. *Apology* 22c.

16. *Timaeus* 72ab.

17. Classics scholar Walter Burkert maintains that "the preservation of oracular utterances was doubtless one of the earliest applications of the art of writing in Greece" (Burkert, *Greek Religion*, 117).

These oracle-mongers were often regarded as con men and suspected of creating some of their oracles from scratch. The fifth-century playwright Aristophanes lampooned oracle-mongers as making up their interpretations as they went along.[18] Aristotle cynically points out that oracle-mongers deliberately make predictions that are indefinite as to when they will be fulfilled. Such vague predictions

> are less likely to be falsified . . . The oracle-monger is more likely to be right if he simply says that a thing will happen than if he says *when* it will happen, and therefore he refuses to add a definite date.[19]

Another way Greeks indulged their interest in enigmatic oracles was through a common type of story in which oracular riddles drive the plot. The oracles in these stories always came true, usually in unexpected ways. Characters would do their best to outwit or preempt the fulfillment of negative oracles, but to no avail. The most famous such story is that of Oedipus, immortalized by the playwright Sophocles in his tragedy *Oedipus the King*.

Oedipus is the son of Laius and Jocasta, king and queen of Thebes. An oracle tells Laius that "he is doomed to perish by the hand of his own son." Seeking to prevent this prediction from coming true, Laius gives the infant Oedipus to a slave and tells him to kill the little boy. The slave cannot bring himself to do that and instead leaves the baby in a field. Oedipus is rescued by a shepherd, who gives him to another shepherd, who takes him to Corinth, where the boy ends up being raised by the king of Corinth as his son. When Oedipus grows up he hears a rumor that he is not the true son of the king. He consults the oracle at Delphi in the hope of finding out who his real parents are. The oracle does not answer his question but instead predicts that Oedipus will "mate with his mother and shed with his own hand the blood of his father." To avoid that terrible fate Oedipus leaves Corinth, believing that its king and queen are his true parents after all.

On the road to Thebes Oedipus encounters Laius. Neither man knows the other's identity. The two fall into a violent argument over whose wagon has the right-of-way and Oedipus ends up killing Laius. Soon after, Oedipus solves the famous riddle of the Sphinx, who has Thebes under a curse. The curse is lifted when Oedipus solves the riddle.[20] His reward is the throne of Thebes and marriage to its queen, Jocasta, his biological mother. Thus the

---

18. Aristophanes, *Birds* 959–91.

19. Aristotle, *Rhetoric* 1407b.

20. The riddle was, "What creature walks on four legs in the morning, two legs at noon, and three in the evening?" Oedipus's solution was, "the human being."

grim oracles are fulfilled without anyone knowing it, and despite everyone's efforts to dodge them.

The story of Oedipus illustrates perfectly the Greek notion not only that prophecies can come true in unexpected ways, but that they can come true in ways that are impossible to anticipate. It was believed that in some cases no one could know what a prophecy was predicting until after it had been fulfilled. So what did people believe was the purpose of mysterious prophecies? It was certainly not to guide behavior. That alone shows that we are in a quite different world from that of the biblical prophets, for they relentlessly urged Israel to repent, or to hope. In Greek drama the purpose of the oracles is, it seems, to teach the audience that the gods, or Fate, control our destinies, that humans are powerless to alter the ultimate courses of their lives, and that the gods might toy with humans, who can only guess at the gods' will.

Influence on Judaism

The notion of God in the Hebrew Bible was, of course, very different from Greek concepts of Fate and the gods. Jews believed that God had spelled out his will for them, clearly and in detail, in the Law of Moses (see Deut 30:11–14). The prophets of the Bible believed that they were not sent to explain mysterious messages from God, but to urge, threaten, and entice the people to heed the clear demands of God. During the Hellenistic era, however, the Greek idea of prophecy had a powerful influence on how Jews thought about their prophets. The "modern" Greek notions of prophecy in the Hellenistic air enabled Jews to think about their prophets in a way that made them relevant to the contemporary culture, and that helped Jews take pride in their religious heritage. Consider how Jews in the Hellenistic era would regard the prophets of their scriptures, men who had lived centuries before modern (i.e., Hellenistic) times. If the messages of those prophets were intended for people who were long dead, those messages would not be of any immediate or obvious relevance for the present. However, if the prophets had foreknowledge of the future, then they had to be supernaturally inspired. The prophets of Israel could then command the respect of a Hellenistic culture, for they spoke of a time far distant from their own, something impossible to do without divine guidance.[21]

The earliest Jewish statement of the Greek-inspired notion of prophecy-as-fate is found in the Book of Tobit, written in the third or second

21. Barton, *Oracles*, 179–80.

century BCE, at a time when Israelite tradition was creatively absorbing and adapting Greek ideas.

> Everything that was spoken by the prophets of Israel, whom God sent, will occur. None of all their words will fail, but all will come at their appointed times . . . Whatever God has said will be fulfilled and will come true; not a single word of the prophecies will fail. (Tob 14:4)

The explicit and repetitive style of this statement hints that it is introducing a new way of understanding prophecy, one that needs reinforcing by repetition. This concept of the nature of prophecy is also found in the Book of Daniel, which was written in the second century BCE. In Daniel, however, this understanding of prophecy is taken for granted, not drummed into the audience as in the Book of Tobit. The author of Daniel assumes that his Jewish audience is familiar and comfortable with its hellenized concept of prophecy. There is no small irony in this, because Daniel was written to help Jews resist the forced hellenization of their native religion by a Hellenistic tyrant. In effect, the author of Daniel adopts an essentially Greek understanding of prophecy, which enables him to portray Daniel as a prophet from long ago sending a divinely inspired message of hope and reassurance to those resisting the influence of Greek religion. In all likelihood the author of Daniel did not think of himself as adopting a Greek understanding of prophecy. For him, that way of thinking about prophets was already traditional and not considered foreign, much less Greek. In the Hellenistic age, some Greek patterns of thought were so pervasive that they seemed obvious and natural, in much the same way that people today who attribute adult emotional problems to early childhood experiences do not consciously think of themselves as using Freudian thought.

We next turn to four sources that help us further understand how Jews in the Hellenistic age regarded prophets and prophecy: the Dead Sea Scrolls (from the first century BCE), the Septuagint (a Greek translation of the Hebrew Bible from the second century BCE), a targum (an Aramaic translation of the Hebrew Bible from the first century CE), and the writings of Josephus (from the first century CE). All of these sources can help us frame the proper context for understanding the New Testament use of Old Testament prophecy.

5

The Fulfillment of Prophecy in the Dead Sea Scrolls

T HE SCROLLS DISCOVERED IN caves at Qumran near the Dead Sea in the mid-twentieth century have greatly expanded our knowledge of ancient Judaism. These writings reflect the beliefs and practices of a Jewish sect that separated itself, both religiously and physically, from the other Jews in the land of Israel. Though the origins of the sect are obscure, scholars generally believe that it began in the first half of the second century BCE and that some of its members moved to Qumran around the middle of that same century.[1]

The Qumran sectarians believed themselves to be the only true and faithful Israelites. They, and they alone, possessed the true interpretation of the Jewish Law and the true understanding of the Hebrew scriptures. Other Jews, they were convinced, were led astray by their corrupt and evil religious leaders. The Qumran movement believed that it was living in the End Times, the last phase of human history, and that God would soon bring history to its climax in a cosmic victory of good over evil. Members of the Qumran community believed that their religious calling was to keep themselves untainted by the larger society and to devote themselves to the study and observance of God's laws while they awaited the End.

Among their many writings are some that interpret biblical prophecies, explaining how some of those prophecies had been fulfilled in the recent history of their sect, how some were being fulfilled in their own day, and how still others were soon to be fulfilled in the near future as the End Times unfolded. Since this way of understanding prophecy closely matches the perspectives of some NT writings, a study of how the Dead Sea Scrolls (DSS) interpret prophecy can provide appropriate historical and religious

1. For the early history of the Qumran community, see Vermes, *Introduction*, 132–38; and VanderKam, *Dead Sea Scrolls*, 127–36.

background for the fulfillment-of-prophecy theme in the NT. By examining first the concepts in the DSS of who the prophets were; second, the concepts in the DSS of the kind of revelation their words convey; and, third, the interpretive methods by which prophetic messages could be applied to the time of the interpreters in the DSS, we can get a sense for the range of beliefs about prophecy in early Judaism.

Out of the many texts discovered at the Dead Sea, it is sufficient for our purposes to look at three: the Damascus Document and the commentaries on the prophets Nahum and Habakkuk.

The Damascus Document

This text is one of the DSS, but it was known to scholars before the discoveries at Qumran. The first copy of it to come to light in modern times was produced in the tenth or eleventh century CE; it was discovered in 1896 in a sealed storeroom in a synagogue in Cairo, which is why the text is known in abbreviation as CD, for Cairo Damascus Document (though some scholars use the simple abbreviation D for this text). Judging from the fact that pieces from ten different copies of CD were found at Qumran, it must have been a popular text there and considered well worth studying. The fragments of CD found at Qumran allow scholars to trace its origin to around 100 BCE.[2]

The Document shows that the sect believed itself to be the true spiritual descendant of the biblical Israel that possessed the true interpretation of the Law of Moses. The mission of the community described in CD was to observe Moses' laws exactly as God intended until the "end of days." The Document frequently quotes or refers to biblical passages and interprets many of them as referring to its own time and circumstances. Some of these interpretations are very strained and seem fanciful to us today. In addition, and important to our investigation, the quotations from the biblical texts can be very free. Not only are the interpretations of the prophecies stretched to fit the community's own situation, but in some cases the words of the prophecies themselves have been rewritten in order to make the prophecies fit the interpretation. We will see that both of these interpretive practices are also found in the Qumran biblical commentaries, as well as in the NT.

The Damascus Document is long and difficult to understand, but for our purposes it will suffice to look briefly at four examples of how CD interprets the scriptures. (In the excerpts in this chapter, quotations from the Bible are in italics, as are the biblical words in the interpretations. The

---

2. Davies et al., *Complete World*, 18.

references in parentheses following the quotations are not, of course, in the original, but have been added by modern editors for convenience.)

(1) In one passage CD refers to the generation of Israelites just prior to its own time as "the congregation of traitors." The document then refers to specific events that led Israel away from the truth.

> These are the ones who stray from the path. This was the time about which it had been written, "*Like a stray heifer so has Israel strayed*" (Hos 4:16), when the Scoffer arose, who scattered the waters of lies over Israel and made them veer off into a pathless wilderness. (CD I 13–15)

CD assumes that its readers know who "the Scoffer" was and what he did when he "scattered the water of lies over Israel." We do not need to know those particulars in order to grasp CD's point, which is that the words of the prophet have come true in recent events.

(2) CD refers again in another passage to those Israelites who are not faithful to the covenant. It then applies to them some words of Moses.

> They have willfully rebelled, walking on the path of the wicked, about whom God says, "*Their wine is serpent's venom and the head of asps is cruel*" (Deut 32:33). The *serpents* are the kings of the people and *their wine* is their paths, and *the head of asps* is the head of the kings of Greece, who came to wreak vengeance on them. (CD VIII 8–12)

The words of Moses in this passage are utterly obscure when quoted out of context, as they are here. But CD understands them as coded references to traumatic events in Israel's recent history. For now we should note that no one reading Deut 32:33 in its own context would ever guess that Moses, addressing the Israelites in the Sinai desert, was actually talking about Greek kings who would appear eleven centuries later.

(3) The next selection from CD illustrates another strategy of biblical interpretation in the DSS: interpreting a verse from scripture by using another, seemingly unrelated verse to bring out its "true" meaning. Here a verse from the prophet Isaiah is used to discover hidden meanings in a verse from the Book of Numbers.

> "*The well was dug by the princes and excavated by the nobles of the people, with a ruler*" (Num 21:18). The *well* is the Torah and those who *dug* it are the penitents of Israel who left the land of Judah to dwell in the land of Damascus. God called them all *princes*, for they sought Him and their honor was not rejected by anyone's mouth. And the *ruler* is the interpreter of the Torah, of

whom Isaiah said, *"He takes out a tool for his work"* (Isa 54:16). *The nobles of the people* are those who come to *dig* the well with the statutes which were ordained by the ruler. (CD VI 3–9)

How the quotation from Isaiah is relevant to the verse from Numbers is not apparent in English translation because there is no clear connection between the ruler mentioned in Numbers and the tool mentioned in Isaiah. In Hebrew, however, the word for "ruler" (*mehoqeq*) is related to the verb *haqaq*, which means "to dig," in the sense of scratching out a hole. *Haqaq* can also mean a "decree," in the sense of something scratched on a tablet. So the Hebrew word for "ruler" (one who issues decrees) sounds the same as the word for one who scratches or digs. Hence, in this passage of CD, the ruler is God's tool for "digging" (that is, interpreting) the "well" of the Torah. (In English, by coincidence, the word "ruler" can denote both a person of authority and a tool.)

(4) The most important example for our study of CD's biblical interpretation is its treatment of a particular prediction of the prophet Amos. But before we get to CD's interpretation, we need to understand this prophecy in its own context in the book of Amos.

> "You shall carry about Sakkuth your king, and Kaiwan your star god, your images which you made for yourselves. Therefore I will take you into exile beyond Damascus," says Yahweh. (Amos 5:26–27)

Sakkuth and Kaiwan are Mesopotamian deities. "Beyond Damascus" means the land to the far north of Israel, i.e., Assyria. According to Amos, Yahweh is indicting the Israelites for violating the covenant by worshiping foreign gods, and he will punish them by sending the Assyrians to devastate Israel and exile its survivors to Assyria.

CD quotes this passage from Amos with a very different wording, which turns the names of the foreign gods into harmless nouns.

> *"I will expel your king's booth and the bases of your images from my tent to Damascus."* The books of the Torah are *the booth of the king;* as God said, *"I will raise up the fallen booth of David"* (Amos 9:11). The *king* is the assembly, and *the bases of the images* are the books of the Prophets whose words Israel despised. (CD VII 14–18)

CD transforms the names Sakkuth and Kaiwan into the words for "booth" and "bases." By rewording the prophecy and interpreting it in this creative way, the foreign gods in Amos' original text become the sacred books of the Law and the Prophets (the scriptures of Israel). While attending to foreign gods (as in Amos) is a sin, attending to the scriptures (as in CD) is not a sin—quite the opposite. Therefore, being deported "to Damascus" (not, as in the original, "*beyond* Damascus" to Assyria) must be a promise of deliverance, not an announcement of punishment.[3] This understanding of the prophecy is quite clear in what CD says immediately preceding the quotation from Amos: "Those who held firmly (to the covenant) escaped to the land of the north" (CD VII 13–14).

CD thus transforms Amos' condemnation into a blessing. CD amplifies this interpretation by adding another divine declaration from Amos 9:11. Since "the booth of the king" is really the Torah, God's promise that "I will raise up the fallen booth of David" now means that God will rescue and exalt the Torah, and also, by implication those who obey it; that is, the Qumran sectarians—in contrast to the rest of Israel, who "despises" the scriptures.

We should look carefully at one transformation in CD's interpretation of Amos 5:26–27—the process by which the god "Sakkuth, your king" in Amos became "your king's booth" in CD. Two things are noteworthy here. First, the name Sakkuth is close to the Hebrew word *sukkoth* ("booth"). Second, the slide from *Sakkuth* to *sukkoth* is assisted by the quotation of Amos 9:11.

Pesharim

Among the DSS are several commentaries on biblical books of prophecy. These commentaries are a distinct kind of religious writing that scholars call "peshers" (or *pesharim*, the Aramaic plural of *pesher*). The word *pesher* means "interpretation" and comes from the root meaning "unbind or release." The word occurs thirty times in the book of Daniel (about half of which is written in Aramaic), where it denotes the interpretation of mysterious dreams or of predictive writing, most dramatically in the famous scene in which Daniel interprets the writing on the wall (Daniel 5).

Modern biblical commentaries attempt to explain the biblical texts within their own historical, religious, and literary contexts, in order to determine what these writings meant to those who wrote them and to their original audiences. An indispensable presupposition for modern commentaries is that meanings are determined by context, which is why the meaning that a word or passage or story had for its ancient author and audience might be very different from the meaning it might have for us. The goal of the modern commentator is to take us back in history and back to a

---

3. Lindars, *New Testament Apologetic*, 279.

Pesher

Interpretation

religious world different from our own so that we can overhear, as it were, what the prophet was saying to the people of his own time.

The peshers from Qumran work in the opposite direction. Rather than take their readers back in history, the peshers bring the prophets' words forward into the time of the Qumran community. The peshers are not interested in what the prophets meant, but only in what their words had come to mean. Qumran peshers presuppose that the words of the prophets were meant for the readers of the peshers, not for the original audiences of the prophets. That way of understanding the prophets makes sense only on the back of two assumptions. First, it assumes that the prophets themselves did not understand the "true" meaning of their own words. Second, it assumes that the pesher authors have had the truth of prophecy revealed to them. Think about it: someone who claims that the prophets were really referring to events of that person's own time has to be assuming that he understands the prophets better than they understood themselves. And someone who assumes *that*—unless he is completely cynical—must also assume that his interpretation of the prophets' words is divinely inspired. Those are huge assumptions and, from our perspective, highly implausible, if not downright arrogant. (We will explore those problematic assumptions in the last chapter of this book.)

Regardless of what we might think of those two assumptions, they were made by the authors of the peshers, and not merely implicitly; they are directly expressed in a revealing passage.

> Yahweh [said to me, *"Write down the vision and make it plain]*[4] *on the tablets, that [he who reads] may read it speedily"* (Hab 2:1–2).

> God told Habakkuk to write down what would happen to the final generation, but He did not make known to him when time would come to an end. And as for what He said, *That he who reads may read it speedily*: interpreted, this concerns the Teacher of Righteousness, to whom God made known all the mysteries of the words of His servants the Prophets. (1QpHab VI 14—VII 5)

Clearly, this Qumran pesher was not trying to discover Habakkuk's intention in delivering his prophetic message. From the pesher's perspective, the words of the prophets come straight from God and contain secret or hidden meanings—see the term "mysteries" in the last line of the passage. These mysteries (note: *all* of them) were revealed to the founder of the Qumran

---

4. Most of the DSS are damaged or fragmentary. Brackets indicate that the enclosed text is missing in the manuscript but has been restored with some degree of confidence by scholarly labor.

community, an obscure and anonymous figure referred to as the "Teacher of Righteousness." Under divine inspiration the Teacher of Righteousness realized that the biblical prophecies actually referred to events and people that concerned his own community from either their recent past or their present or their imminent future. Those events thus provide the key for unlocking the meaning of the biblical prophecies. The Qumran community's belief that the prophecies were really about their own circumstances sets up a mutual, back-and-forth interpretive dynamic between the time the pesher was written and the past prophecies. On the one hand, the prophecies illuminate the situation of the community's present (or recent past), while on the other hand, the events of the community's own time illuminate the putative hidden meanings of the prophecies. Therefore, while the prophecies were thought to disclose the theological significance of the community's history (showing what their history means from the perspective of God's will and plans for history), the community's history can in turn clarify obscurities in the prophecies, according to the peshers' authors. The latter belief enabled the pesher authors to take certain freedoms with the words of the prophets, as we will see below.

Peshers on six books of the prophets were found among the DSS, along with peshers on some of the psalms, which were considered prophetic writings because their purported author, King David, was considered a prophet. All but two of the Qumran peshers survive only in small fragments. A reasonably large section of the pesher on Nahum is intact, and the pesher on Habakkuk is the longest and best preserved. We now turn to those two writings.

The Nahum Pesher (4QpNah)

The Book of Nahum is seldom read in contemporary liturgy[5] and, apparently, was of little interest to early Christians. It is one of the few OT books that is never quoted, nor even alluded to, in the NT. The book was written in the seventh century BCE and its three chapters are devoted entirely to anticipating, and gloating over, the destruction of Nineveh, the capital of the hated Assyrian empire. Nahum's prophecies of doom came true when the Babylonians captured and plundered Nineveh in 609 BCE. Five centuries or so later, the author of the Nahum pesher recycled Nahum's words and

---

5. No reading from Nahum is included in the Revised Common Lectionary (used by many Protestants), the Roman Catholic Sunday Lectionary, or the Jewish Lectionary (Leclerc, *Introduction*, 226).

asserted that they really referred to historical events in the author's day. We will briefly review four such examples.

(1) *He roars against the sea and dries it up* (Nah 1:4).

Its interpretation: the *sea* is all the Kittim. (4QpNah fragments 1+2, line 3)

Kittim is a Hebrew term for people who came to Israel's corner of the world from the Mediterranean Sea (see Gen 10:4). Originally the term denoted the people of Cyprus. The Kittim are also mentioned in Dan 11:30, which contains a thinly-veiled reference to the Roman navy. In the DSS, Kittim is the code name for the Romans, who began to dominate the geopolitics of Israel and its neighbors in the first century BCE.[6] Identifying the Romans with "the sea" in Nah 1:4 makes sense militarily in light of Rome's indomitable navy. It also makes sense theologically because the OT depicts God doing battle with the sea, his mythological enemy (for example, Ps 89:9–10; Isa 27:1; Hab 3:15). The pesher thus classifies Rome as the enemy of God.

(2) *Wherever the lion goes, there is the lion's cub, [with none to disturb it]* (Nah 2:11b).

[Interpreted, this concerns Deme]trius king of Greece who sought, on the counsel of those who seek smooth things, to enter Jerusalem. [But God did not permit the city to be delivered] into the hands of the kings of Greece, from the time of Antiochus until the coming of the rulers of the Kittim. (4QpNah I 1–3)

The lion was the symbol of Assyria (as the eagle was for Rome and is for America), which is the clue that Nahum is referring to the Assyrian empire of his own day. However, the pesher decides that the lion is Demetrius, a Greek king who reigned 95–88 BCE, and who attacked Jerusalem.[7] The pesher also mentions a king Antiochus, who is either Antiochus III (reigned 233–187) or Antiochus IV (reigned 175–164).[8] Demetrius and Antiochus are the only two people mentioned by name in the peshers, which otherwise use nicknames.[9]

"Those who seek smooth things" is probably an insulting nickname for the Pharisees, theological enemies of the DSS community. "Smooth things" in Hebrew is *ḥaloqot*, probably a pun on *halakot* ("laws").[10] The Pharisees

6. Vermes, *Introduction,* 137.

7. VanderKam, *Dead Sea Scrolls,* 68.

8. Berrin, "Pesher Nahum," 653.

9. Ibid.; Davies et al., *Complete World,* 98.

10. Kugel and Greer, *Early Biblical Interpretation,* 79.

seek to follow the laws of Moses, but their enemies at Qumran deride them as those who look for "smooth" (or easy, nondemanding) interpretations of those laws. The writer, from Qumran, sees his community as observing the laws according to strict and rigorous interpretations, in contrast to the Pharisees.

> (3) *The lion catches enough for his cubs and chokes prey for its li-onesses; [and it fills] its caves [with prey] and its den with victims.* (Nah 2:13)

> Interpreted, this concerns the Lion of Wrath [who carries out revenge] on those who seek smooth things, who hangs men alive [from the tree, committing an atrocity which has not been committed] in Israel since ancient times. (4QpNah I 6–8)

The "Lion of Wrath" is a Jewish king, Alexander Jannaeus (103–76 BCE),[11] who took gruesome revenge on Jews who had rebelled against him, cruci-fying eight hundred of them on one horrific day, according to Josephus.[12] "Hanging alive" was a term for crucifixion, which differed from the Israelite custom of hanging the corpse of an executed criminal on a tree for public viewing (see Deut 23:23).[13]

> (4) *They shall say, Nineveh, is laid waste. Who will grieve for her? Where shall I find comforters for you?* (Nah 3:7).

> Interpreted, this concerns those who seek smooth things, whose counsel will perish and whose congregation will be disbanded. They shall lead the assembly astray no more, and the simple folk shall no longer support their cause. (4QpNah III 5–7)

Nineveh, the capital of Israel's cruel conqueror, is equated with "those who seek smooth things," almost certainly the Pharisees. The city's destruction is equated with the Pharisees' loss of religious power. And Nahum's taunt that no one will mourn for Nineveh is taken to mean that "the simple folk" will stop supporting the Pharisees.

The Habakkuk Pesher (1QpHab)

The Book of Habakkuk was written in the last part of the seventh or first part of the sixth century BCE, as the Babylonians swept away the hated

---

11. Berrin, "Pesher Nahum," 653; VanderKam, *Dead Sea Scrolls*, 69.

12. *Ant.* 13.380

13. Berrin, "Pesher Nahum," 654.

Assyrians to become the dominant superpower in the region and then turned their military might against the vulnerable land and people of Israel. The prophet Habakkuk reflects on the role of God's righteousness amid all that violence and suffering. The Book of Habakkuk, like the Book of Nahum, is little known today. Only two of its verses are quoted in the NT.[14] However, Habakkuk was of great interest to the people of Qumran, who found in it (we would say, read *into* it) numerous references to the impact of the Romans on the recent history of the region and to the religious conflicts between the Jewish establishment and the founder of the Qumran movement, the Teacher of Righteousness.

The Habakkuk pesher is relatively well preserved and so gives us the opportunity to observe in some detail the interpretive methods of the Qumran peshers. We will look briefly at eight examples.

> (1) *For behold, I rouse the Chaldeans, that cru[el and determined] nation* (Hab 1:6a).

> Interpreted, this is about the Kittim, who are swift and powerful in war, slaying many. [All the world shall fall] under the dominion of the Kittim and they will not believe in the laws of God. (1QpHab II 10–15)

Here the Chaldeans (a Hebrew synonym for the Babylonians) become the Kittim (Romans). Recall that in the Nahum Pesher it was the *Assyrians* who became the Romans. The Babylonians and the Assyrians were mortal enemies of each another, yet both were interpreted by the Qumran sectarians to be the Romans. The peshers do not try for interpretations that are consistent from one pesher to another, nor even from one passage to another in the same pesher. Each passage bears its own interpretation, as if it were a text unto itself, without context. Scholars call this style of interpretation "atomistic exegesis."[15]

This atomistic approach to the words of the prophets is already implicit to some extent in the term *pesher*. This Aramaic word is found thirty-one times in the OT; as I already mentioned, thirty of these occurrences are in Daniel and have to do with the understanding of dreams and visions (the ancient world did not draw a sharp distinction between the two). When dreams or visions in the OT are interpreted, they are not generally interpreted as a whole. Rather, each detail in the dream or vision is probed for its own meaning.[16] When Daniel interprets King Nebuchadnezzar's dream

---

14. Hab 1:5 in Acts 13:41, and Hab 2:4 in Rom 1:17, Gal 3:11, and Heb 10:38–39.

15. Berrin, "Pesharim," 645.

16. Patte, *Early Jewish Hermeneutics*, 301.

about a statue made of different metals, for example, each separate part of the statue is interpreted individually (see Dan 2:31–45). So when the Qumran commentaries quote a statement from a prophet and then continue with "Its pesher (interpretation) is . . . ," the same style of interpretation applied to dreams and visions is being applied to the words of the prophets.

How did the Qumran commentators justify interpreting the prophets in this manner? We don't know—none of the DSS explains why—but there is a good chance it has to do with an intriguing statement in the Book of Numbers about the special status of Moses:

> When there are prophets among you,
>
>> I, Yahweh, make myself known to them in visions;
>
>> I speak to them in dreams.
>
> Not so with my servant Moses;
>
>> he is entrusted with all my house.
>
> With him I speak face to face—clearly, not in riddles.
>
> (Num 12:6–8)

Here Moses is singled out as the exception. God normally communicates with his prophets in dreams and visions, which carry their meanings the way riddles do. Moses had the unique honor of speaking to God directly ("face to face," which is literally "mouth to mouth" in Hebrew) and in plain in language ("clearly"). A later rabbinic comment on this passage summarizes its message thusly: "God spoke to all the prophets except Moses in dreams and visions."[17] The authors of the Dead Sea peshers also believed that the writings of the prophets carried their meanings concealed in coded language ("in riddles").

(2) Habakkuk Pesher's interpretation of Hab 1:10 and 1:11 describes Rome's military tactics and political system. For the prophet Habakkuk, "they" in 1:10 referred to the Babylonians, but for the Qumran pesher it refers to the Romans (Kittim).

> *They laugh at every fortress; they pile up earth and take it.* (Hab 1:10b)

> Interpreted, this concerns the commanders of the Kittim who despise the *fortresses* of the peoples and laugh at them in derision. To capture them, they encircle them with a mighty army, and out of fear and terror they deliver themselves into their hands. They destroy them because of the sins of their inhabitants. (1QpHab IV 4–8)

---

17. *Sifre on Numbers* 12:6, quoted in Patte, *Early Jewish Hermeneutics*, 301.

The wind then sweeps on and passes (Hab 1:11).

> Interpreted, [this concerns] the commanders of the Kittim who, on the counsel of the House of Guilt, pass one in front of the other; one after another [their] commanders come to lay waste the earth. (1QpHab IV 9–13)

The "House of Guilt" refers to the Roman Senate. The description of the Kittim commanders passing "one in front of the other" and arriving "one after another" refers to the Roman practice of giving command of the army to consuls who hold authority for only one year and are replaced annually by the Senate.[18]

(3) The pesher on Hab 1:13 refers to a power struggle involving the Teacher of Righteousness.

> *O traitors, why do you stare and keep silence when an evil person swallows someone more righteous than himself?* (Hab 1:13b).

> Interpreted, this concerns the House of Absalom and the members of its council who were silent at the time of the chastisement of the Teacher of Righteousness and gave him no help against the Liar who flouted the Law in the midst of their whole [congregation]. (1QpHab V 8–12)

Absalom was a beloved son of David who rose in rebellion against him, which is why the traitors are nicknamed "House of Absalom." They are criticized for not aiding the Teacher of Righteousness when he was harassed by "the Liar." We do not know who this bad guy was, but he was evidently someone with power and influence who made trouble for the Teacher.

An interesting and important feature of this passage is how the pesher misquotes Habakkuk. In the original, this verse is addressed to God: "Why do you look on the treacherous, and stay silent when the wicked swallow those more righteous than themselves?" The pesher alters the verse's wording so that it rebukes traitors instead of questioning God. The pesher also transforms Habakkuk's plural "wicked" and "righteous" into singular nouns referring to specific individuals (the Liar and the Teacher of Righteousness). This kind of textual manipulation is a standard pesher technique. (More on this below.)

(4) The pesher on Hab 2:4 is noteworthy for its reinterpretation of the virtue of faith.

> [*The righteous shall live by faith*][19] (Hab 2:4b).

18. VanderKam, *Dead Sea Scrolls*, 64.

19. As the brackets indicate, this entire sentence is missing in the manuscript but

> Interpreted, this concerns all those who observe the Law in the
> House of Judah, whom God will deliver from the House of Judg-
> ment because of their suffering and because of their *faith* in the
> Teacher of Righteousness. (1QpHab VIII 1–3)

Note that "faith" here is not faith in God, but faith in the Teacher of
Righteousness.

(5) The pesher on Hab 2:8a describes the Romans quite differently
than does the pesher on Hab 1:10.

> *Because you have plundered many nations, all the remnant of the
> peoples shall plunder you* (Hab 2:8a).

> Interpreted, this concerns the last priests of Jerusalem, who
> shall amass money and wealth by plundering the peoples. But
> in the last days, their riches and booty shall be delivered into the
> hands of the army of the Kittim, for it is they who shall be *the
> remnant of the peoples*. (1QpHab IX 3–7)

Here Habakkuk's reference to the Babylonians ("you" in the original) is
made to refer to corrupt priests of Jerusalem, while the "remnant of the
peoples"—a term referring to the survivors of an invasion—becomes the
Romans. While Habakkuk envisioned Babylon's conquered victims rising
up against it, the pesher sees the Romans dispossessing the priests. Note
how the Romans, described as conquerors in the comment on Hab 1:10b,
are here given the role of the surviving victims of invasion, an excellent
example of atomistic interpretation.

(6) Observe how the pesher takes Hab 2:8b in a completely different
direction than it takes Hab 2:8a.

> *Because of the blood of men and the violence done to the land, to
> the city, and to all its inhabitants* (Hab 2:8b).

> Interpreted, this concerns the Wicked Priest whom God deliv-
> ered into the hands of his enemies because of the iniquity com-
> mitted against the Teacher of Righteousness and the men of his
> Council, that he might be humbled by means of a destroying
> scourge, in bitterness of soul, because he had done wickedly to
> His chosen. (1QpHab IX 8–12)

The quotation from Habakkuk consists of a single clause—not even a complete sentence—yet the pesher discovers in it a prediction that God will
punish the Wicked Priest for doing wrong to the Teacher of Righteousness.

---

can be supplied with confidence because the interpretation immediately above it quotes
Hab 2:4a, and the one immediately after it quotes 2:5–6.

(7) The pesher sees the hostility between the Priest and the Teacher foretold also in Hab 2:15.

> *Woe to him who makes his neighbors drunk, who pours out his venom to make them drunk so that he may gaze on their festivals!* (Hab 2:15).

> Interpreted, this concerns the Wicked Priest who pursued the Teacher of Righteousness to the house of his exile that he might confuse him with his venomous fury. And at the time appointed for rest, for the Day of Atonement, he appeared before them to confuse them, and to cause them to stumble on the Day of Fasting, their Sabbath of repose. (1QpHab XI 2–6)

This refers to some event when the Wicked Priest pursued the Teacher of Righteousness to his place of "exile" and committed some offense against him on the Day of Atonement (Yom Kippur, the holiest day of the Jewish year and a day of rest and fasting). The interpretation presupposes what scholars know from other DSS, that the Qumran community followed a religious calendar that differed from that of other Jews. So while it was the Day of Atonement for the Qumran sect, it would not have been for the Wicked Priest; if it had been, he would have been far too busy conducting temple services to have time to track down and "confuse" the Teacher of Righteousness "with his venomous fury." While it is impossible for us to know what exactly the Wicked Priest did, this event apparently was vividly remembered by the Qumran community as an act of severe aggression. Note how little connection the quoted prophecy has to its "fulfillment": only the words "venom" and "festivals" and the strained analogy between getting someone drunk and causing confusion and stumbling. (The word "festivals" does not actually appear in the biblical text of Hab 2:15; more on this below.)

(8) Our final excerpt from the Habakkuk Pesher contains a classic example of how a pesher can assert that "*x* means *y*":

> [For the violence done to Lebanon shall overwhelm you, and the destruction of the animals] will terrify you because of the human blood and the violence against the country, the city, and all its inhabitants (Hab 2:17).

> The interpretation of the word concerns the Wicked Priest, to pay him the reward for what he did to the poor. For *Lebanon* is the Council of the Community and the *animals* are the simple folk of Judah who observe the Law. God will sentence

him to destruction, exactly as he intended to destroy the poor.
(1QpHab XII 1–6)

Note the equation of Lebanon with the council of the Qumran community and the wild animals with the simple people of Judah. To point out the obvious once again: no one hearing or reading Habakkuk's prophecy without the aid of the pesher could possibly guess that those are the real meanings of his words.

Textual Manipulation

The peshers often change the words of the prophets in quoting them. The changes that interest us are not the changes that happen because of copying mistakes but rather the deliberate alterations, often based on subtle differences in the sound or spelling of the Hebrew words, that result in quite different meanings. Here are a few examples.[20]

- *'amal* ("trouble") in Hab 1:3 becomes *ma'al* ("deceit")
- *hayyayin* ("wine") in 2:5 becomes *hayon* ("wealth")[21]
- *melisah* ("mock") in 2:6 becomes *melisi* ("interpreter")

In some cases changes like these were made so that the prophecy would lead more easily to the interpretation.

Here are two examples from the Habakkuk Pesher.

(1) Hab 1:9 describes Babylonian soldiers on the attack:

> They all come for violence,
> with faces pressing forward (*qadimah*, literally "toward the
> east").

The pesher quotes that verse as follows:

> They all come for violence;
> the look on their faces is like the east wind (*qadim*).

Then it gives this interpretation:

> They address [all the people] with anger
> and [wrath and fury] and indignation.

The word for "wrath" has the connotation "burning anger," which picks up the associations with the scorching east wind. (In Judea, wind from the east

---

20. The first three are from Stendahl, *School of St. Matthew*, 185–90.
21. NRSV accepts "wealth" as the more original wording.

is wind from the desert.) Similarly, "fury" is associated with storms, another connection with the east wind.[22]

(2) Hab 2:15 reads:

> Woe to you who make your neighbors drink,
>> pouring out your poison until they are drunk,
>> in order to gaze on their nakedness.

The last line flows logically from the rest of the verse. It makes sense that someone who was drunk might be seen in a shameful condition they would never sink to when sober. In the Habakkuk Pesher, however, the last line reads: "in order to gaze on their festivals." While "their nakedness" is vastly different in meaning from "their festivals," the words are nearly puns of each other in Hebrew: *me'oreyhem* and *mo'edeyhem*.[23] For the pesher author, who encountered these words in writing, they are even closer (מעוריהם and מועדיהם): you have to look very carefully to see the difference; the Hebrew R (ר) and D (ד) can easily be mistaken for each other. The motivation for morphing "nakedness" into "festivals" becomes clear when we look at the interpretation of this verse in the pesher (see example 7, above; p. 78).

The pesher authors manipulated the prophetic texts in the ways described above only because the authors first decided on the interpretations and *then* reworded the prophecies so that they could better support the interpretations.

In a few places the words of the prophet are quoted correctly but are interpreted as if they were different, although similar-sounding, words. As in the preceding example, the difference between the words can be quite small. Sometimes, it is simply a change in the order of the letters in the word. For example, "temple" (*heykal*) in Hab 2:20 is interpreted as if it was the word "he will destroy" (*yiklah*).[24] The two words have the same four Hebrew letters (Hebrew is written without vowels): היכל and יכלה. More often, letters are substituted, as in the comment on Hab 1:12, in which "O Rock" (וצור) is interpreted as if it were "will be distressed" (יצור).[25] In effect, the pesher is interpreting, not the actual text of a prophecy, but a slightly reworded version of it. For example, the Micah Pesher (which is preserved only in small fragments) quotes from Mic 1:6 "a place for planting" (*mata'ey*,

---

22. Patte, *Early Jewish Hermeneutic*, 304.

23. In Hebrew, possessive adjectives are attached to the ends of nouns, which is why "their festivals," for example, is one word. The suffix *-hem* means "their."

24. Patte, *Early Jewish Hermeneutic*, 306.

25. Ibid.

from the verb *nata'*, "to plant"), and then interprets it as if it were from the verb *ta'ah*, "to stray."[26]

It is clear that the authors of the Qumran peshers do more than apply the words of the prophets to the events of their own day; they also alter the words of the prophets to fit their own interpretations. Although such a practice would be dishonest and deceptive in today's world, it seems that the authors of the peshers were sincere in their practice and were confident about what they thought they knew. For them the events affecting their community provided the key to understanding the hidden meanings of prophecies. If a gentle rewording of a few prophecies can help that meaning become more transparent, so much the better. We will see something similar in the way the gospels use prophecy. For the NT authors, not only do the prophecies show the significance of events in the life of Jesus; the life of Jesus sheds light on the true meaning of prophecies, even if a few of them require some rewriting to let that meaning shine through.

Excursus:

Pesher in the New Testament

The pesher technique occurs a few times in the NT. While there are many NT passages in which an OT text is quoted and then applied to Jesus or to some other person or event or Christian teaching, the specific pesher technique—quoting a text and then explaining "this means that"—is relatively rare. Here are three examples.

The first example comes from a speech attributed to Peter in the Acts of the Apostles and is the briefest possible example of biblical interpretation in the pesher format. Peter mentions "Jesus Christ of Nazareth whom you crucified and whom God raised from the dead" and then asserts that "This is *'the stone that was rejected by you, the builders; it has become the cornerstone'*" (Acts 4:11, quoting Ps 118:22). This is an example of the pesher technique stripped of any elaboration or explanation, simply a quotation accompanied by "this is," which identifies the stone with Jesus. The author leaves it to his audience to correlate the crucifixion and resurrection of Jesus with the rejection and "vindication" of the stone.

Our second example is also from the Book of Acts, from the story of Pentecost. Visitors in Jerusalem were amazed as they listened to the disciples who had been filled with the Holy Spirit: people from different countries could hear these Galileans speaking in their own native languages

---

26. Lindars, *New Testament Apologetic*, 15.

(Acts 2:4–12). Peter addresses the crowd (in Greek) and explains that this event "is what was spoken through the prophet Joel."

> *"In the last days it will be,"* God declares,
> *"that I will pour out my spirit on all flesh,*
>> *and your sons and your daughters shall prophesy,*
> *and your young men shall see visions,*
>> *and your old men shall dream dreams."* (Acts 2:16–17,
>> quoting Joel 2:28)

As with the Qumran peshers, so too here: the connection between the quoted text and its application is not obvious, since Joel says nothing about the miraculous linguistic phenomenon (the same speakers being heard in different languages) to which Peter applies it. Nor are there any visions or dreams reported in the story of Pentecost. Nor are the Christian speakers delivering prophecy; the story describes them "speaking about God's deeds of power" (Acts 2:11). The only element connecting Joel's prophecy to the story in Acts is the bestowal of God's spirit.

Our final example of NT pesher is a more sophisticated one that comes from Paul.

> [6] The righteousness that comes from faith says, *"Do not say in your heart, 'Who will ascend into heaven?'"* (that is, to bring Christ down) [7] *"or 'Who will descend into the abyss?'"* (that is, to bring Christ up from the dead). [8] But what does it say? *"The word is near you, on your lips and in your heart"* (that is, the word of faith that we proclaim). (Rom 10:6–8, paraphrasing Deut 30:12–14)

In classic pesher style, Paul here pulls three short phrases out of their context and assigns them brand new meanings quite foreign to the original passage. Here is the passage from which Paul has paraphrased.

> [11] Surely, this commandment that I am commanding you today is not too hard for you, nor is it too far away. [12] It is not in heaven, that you should say, "Who will go up to heaven for us, and get it for us so that we may hear it and observe it?" [13] Neither is it beyond the sea, that you should say, "Who will cross to the other side of the sea for us, and get it for us so that we may hear it and observe it?" [14] No, the word is very near to you; it is in your mouth and in your heart for you to observe. (Deut 30:11–14)

Paul's reinterpretations here are as daring, and as arbitrary, as the ones in the Qumran scrolls. Deuteronomy's statements about the commandment (i.e., the laws of the covenant) are made by Paul to refer first to Christ (Rom 10:6–7) and then to "the word of faith" (Rom 10:8). In its own context the purpose of the Deuteronomy passage is to preempt the excuse that Israelites have not followed the law of God because they did not know about it. Deuteronomy emphasizes that the commandment is accessible to all: it is not far away, neither in heaven nor across the sea. In Paul's interpretations the Deuteronomy phrases are made to emphasize the opposite: Christ is unattainably distant, in heaven and in the "abyss" (the underworld of the dead). Paul's second quotation ("Who will descend into the abyss?") is an especially bold departure from Deuteronomy, which speaks of crossing the sea, not of descending into the underworld. Without his radical resignification of the verse, Paul would have no use for the Deuteronomy passage, because the original "across the sea" cannot be matched to anything about Christ.

Conclusion

The DSS show no interest in what the prophets originally intended to communicate. The Qumran interpreters valued scripture for its contemporary meaning, which they apparently believed had been revealed to them but was unknown to the original authors.[27] This shows that the DSS, although quintessentially Jewish in their beliefs and interests, operate with a thoroughly Greek understanding of the nature of prophecy as oracular pronouncement. The dynamic interpretive interplay between past prophecy and its meaning for the interpreter's present was expressed in the DSS in two complementary modes, which we can call "biblicizing" and "actualizing." "Biblicizing" is the practice of describing present realities and current events in biblical language, as in using biblical names for current groups. For example, the peshers seem to use the name "Judah" to refer exclusively to the Qumran community; Sadducees are called "Manasseh," and Pharisees "Ephraim"; and the Romans are called by the antique name "Kittim."[28] On the other hand, "actualizing" scripture names the effort to make it speak to the time of the interpreter.[29] Biblicizing and actualizing are opposite sides of the same coin: biblicizing refers to the present in terms of the past, while actualizing makes the past refer to the present. Both processes presuppose that for scripture to be meaningful it must relate directly to the present. The past as such was apparently not considered meaningful in itself.

---

27. Berrin, "Pesharim," 645.

28. Kugel and Greer, *Early Biblical Interpretation*, 80.

29. Ibid.

In this chapter's analyses of selected passages from the Damascus Document and the peshers on Nahum and Habakkuk, we can see a set of interesting literary techniques by which the authors actualized scripture. Here I recap four of them and lay out their presuppositions: atomistic interpretation, wordplay, using one prophecy to interpret another, and rewording of prophecies:

1. Atomistic interpretation finds the meaning of scriptural passages not in coherent units in their own literary contexts, but in separate bits isolated from their contexts. Successive clauses in the same passage of scripture can be given entirely different meanings that correlate only inasmuch as they support the desired interpretation, not because they contribute to a complete thought in a coherent sentence in the original passage. Atomistic interpretation treats the biblical text as "a sequence of individual ciphers."[30] Interpreting prophecies in this manner presupposes that the prophets themselves did not know what their speeches really meant. Thus were Hebrew prophets understood in the same way as were Greek oracles.

2. Individual words in scripture can be associated with, or even replaced by, other words that sound or look like them, but that have quite different meanings. This practice assumes that the prophets spoke in code that requires deciphering.

3. The authors of the scrolls sometimes lift words or phrases from one prophecy and juxtapose them to another, seemingly unrelated prophecy, in order to elucidate its meaning. Since the connection between the different passages exists only in the mind of the interpreter, this technique presupposes that the meanings of prophecies are hidden or secret and can be discovered only in light of the community's experience, and only through the interpreter's ingenuity.

4. The scrolls sometimes quote prophecies in wordings that do not match the texts themselves, in a kind of creative misquotation. It comes as no surprise that such rewritten prophecies lend themselves easily to actualizing interpretations, since the prophecies were rewritten precisely for that purpose.

Rewriting scripture in this fashion surely seems audacious to us moderns. We can tolerate a preacher's interpretation of a biblical passage that strikes us as fanciful because we can dismiss that interpretation as mere opinion. But few today would be so tolerant if a preacher deliberately altered

---

30. Davies et al., *Complete World*, 96.

the actual text of the Bible so that it would say what he wanted it to say. Modern sensibilities, however, are often unhelpful when seeking to understand the ancients. When assessing ancient interpreters, we need to try to see things from their perspective, and two insights into the mentality of the Dead Sea interpreters can assist us in that task. First, they apparently believed that God had given them unusual wisdom, or even the same kind of divine inspiration that he had given the authors of scripture,[31] and that this wisdom or inspiration gave them the authority to revise the scriptural text. We cannot know if the interpreters were sincere in that belief, but the principle of charity[32] instructs us to assume that they were. Second, analysis of the peshers shows that significant events in the history of the Qumran community were used as keys that unlocked the hidden meanings of prophecy. It's easy to imagine how this belief could authorize the interpreter to modify the biblical text, provided that those modifications helped to illuminate the hidden meanings of the prophecies.

As we will see in part 2 of this book, there are passages in the New Testament where authors have altered prophecies and proclaimed their fulfillments in Jesus or the church. Are the above two insights into the self-understanding and motivations of the authors of the DSS relevant to the New Testament authors? We do not know whether Paul or the author of the Gospel of Matthew, for example, believed themselves to be divinely inspired. However, their rationale for rewriting prophecies was probably similar to that of the Qumran authors: to help the ancient prophecies disclose their true meanings for God's people in the present.

The underlying theological motivation of the Qumran community's interpretation of scripture was "to present the sect as the true heir of the biblical Israel and to demonstrate that its fortunes are anticipated in biblical texts."[33] As we will see, that was the same motivation for the New Testament authors' presentation of the fulfillment of prophecy.

The Qumran community was a sect,[34] and its members understood themselves to be very different from other Jews. Therefore, we should not assume that the sect's beliefs and practices were representative of other

---

31. Kugel and Greer, *Early Biblical Interpretation*, 60–62.

32. The principle of charity is an element of intellectual etiquette that urges us to construe arguments, especially those that seem dubious to us, in the strongest plausible way. In its broadest sense, the principle of charity is an application of the Golden Rule to the sphere of intellectual discourse.

33. Davies et al., *Complete World*, 18.

34. In the academic study of religion, "sect" refers to a religious group that has separated from the mainstream or majority institutions and traditions of a religion, which it regards with hostility.

versions of Jewish religion. However, there is good reason to think that other Jews shared the general approach to scriptural interpretation that we find in the DSS. "It is only a short hop from Qumran to the sort of typological exegesis known from the New Testament and other early Christian writings, whereby parts of the Hebrew Bible are read as foreshadowing and prediction of the events of the Gospels."[35] Those similarities do not mean that the New Testament authors read the Qumran writings and were directly influenced by them. Rather, the evidence points to a diffuse set of shared Jewish assumptions about the nature of scripture in general and prophecy in particular, and to the desire to hear them speak directly to each generation. The next chapter analyzes diverse manifestations of those assumptions and that desire in important Jewish texts from the Hellenistic period.

---

35. Kugel and Greer, *Early Biblical Interpretation*, 80.

6

The Fulfillment of Prophecy in the Septuagint, the Targums, and Josephus

T HE QUMRAN PESHERS ARE showcase examples of how biblical prophecies could be applied to the circumstances of a later time. By our
modern standards, the interpretations in the peshers are arbitrary in the
extreme, for they ignore the messages the prophecies have in their original
contexts and force the prophecies to address the concerns of the authors of
the peshers. However, the authors at the Dead Sea were by no means unique
in this regard. Similar attitudes towards scripture are evident in interpretations by other Jews from the third century BCE to the early centuries CE.
What unites those diverse interpreters is the desire to make prophecies from
earlier centuries relevant to their recent or current circumstances, thereby
enabling the ancient prophets to speak to the present generation.

This chapter studies selected examples of how that process played out
in three important bodies of literature: the Septuagint (a translation of the
Hebrew scriptures into Greek), the targums (paraphrasing translations of
the Hebrew scriptures into Aramaic), and the writing of the Jewish historian
Josephus.

The Septuagint

This ancient translation of the Hebrew Bible was produced in Egypt in the
late third or early second century BCE in order to make the scriptures available to Greek-speaking Jews who could not read Hebrew. Our ability to
understand the precise relationship between the Septuagint and the Hebrew
text on which it is based is complicated in two ways. First, the Septuagint
seems to have undergone various revisions that continued until the second

century CE,[1] which means we do not always know what its exact wording in every passage was at any given time before then. Second, the Hebrew text of the scriptures was not standardized until the second century CE.[2] Those two inconvenient facts urge caution about drawing definitive conclusions that depend on the precise wording of some passages. Nevertheless, by comparing versions of the Septuagint with the Hebrew Bible, scholars have learned a lot about how ancient Jews interpreted their scriptures.

The Septuagint is important to our study because, while for the most part it stays close to the meaning of the Hebrew text, occasionally it creatively revises prophetic passages so that they refer to events around the time the translation was made. We can see how this works by focusing on a single, highly instructive example in the Book of Isaiah (Isa 8:11–16).[3] Here is the passage translated from the Hebrew.[4]

> [11] For Yahweh spoke thus to me while his hand was strong upon me, and warned me not to walk in the way of this people, saying: [12] "Do not call conspiracy all that this people calls conspiracy, and do not fear what it fears, nor be in dread. [13] But Yahweh of hosts, him you shall regard as holy; let him be your fear, and let him be your dread. [14] He will become a sanctuary, but he shall be a stone of offense, and a rock of stumbling—a trap and a snare for the inhabitants of Jerusalem. [15] And many shall stumble on it; they shall fall and be broken; they shall be snared and taken." [16] Bind up the testimony, seal the teaching among my disciples.

This is a difficult passage, but, fortunately, for our purposes we need understand only its basic structure and message. Then we can see how the Septuagint version of this passage differs from the Hebrew original, what those differences point to, and what they reveal about ancient Jewish beliefs about prophecy.

Structure. In verse 11 Isaiah reports that Yahweh spoke to him. Verses 12–15 are the words Yahweh spoke, referring to himself in the third person in verses 13–14. In verse 16 Isaiah speaks in response to the words of Yahweh in verses 12–15.

Message. Yahweh warns Isaiah not to go along with popular opinion ("the way of this people," v. 11), not to believe conspiracy theories or fear

1. Law, *When God Spoke Greek*, 77–78.

2. Ibid., 79.

3. My analysis of this passage is based on van der Kooij, "Isaiah in the Septuagint," 520–27.

4. The translations from both Hebrew and Greek of Isa 8:11–16 are in van der Kooij, "Isaiah in the Septuagint," slightly modified.

what the people fear (v. 12). He should fear only God (v. 13), who will be for him a source of security (v. 14a) rather than the destructive influence (stumbling block, trap, snare) that he is for the Israelites and the people of Jerusalem (v. 14b). Jerusalem is headed for disaster (v. 15). Because disaster is coming, Isaiah decides to confine his teaching to his disciples (v. 16).

Here is the same passage, but now paired with a translation from the Septuagint for easy comparison.

Hebrew	*Greek (Septuagint)*
11 For Yahweh spoke thus to me while his hand was strong upon me, and warned me not to walk in the way of this people, saying: 12 "Do not call conspiracy all that this people calls conspiracy, and do not fear what it fears, nor be in dread. 13 But Yahweh of hosts, him you shall regard as holy; let him be your fear, and let him be your dread. 14 He will become a sanctuary, but he shall be a stone of offense, and a rock of stumbling for both houses of Israel—	11 Thus says the Lord, "With a strong hand they disobey the course of the way of this people, saying: 12 'Do not say, "it is hard," for whatsoever this people says is hard. Fear not their fear and do not be dismayed. 13 Sanctify the Lord himself, and he himself shall be your fear. And if you put your trust in him, 14 he shall be for you a sanctuary, and you shall not come against him as against a stumbling block, neither as against the falling of a rock. But the house of Jacob is
a trap and a snare for the inhabitants of Jerusalem. 15 And many shall stumble on it; they shall fall and be broken; they shall be snared and taken."	in a snare, and the inhabitants of Jerusalem are in a hollow.' 15 Therefore, many among them shall be powerless and fall and be crushed; and men who are in security shall approach and be taken. 16 Then
16 Bind up the testimony, seal the teaching among my disciples.	shall be manifest those who seal up the Law that they should not learn it."

Structure. The structure of the Septuagint version is quite different from the structure of the Hebrew version and gives the passage a significantly different meaning. Whereas in the Hebrew text God speaks only in verses 12–15, in the Greek version the entire passage is framed as a single message from God, introduced by "Thus says the Lord" in verse 11. God speaks throughout verses 11–16, although in verses 12–14 God is quoting the leaders of the people. In verses 15–16, God again speaks in his own voice. It is important to note that the Hebrew verse 16 reports Isaiah's own words, while the Greek verse 16 is attributed to God. This difference alters the meaning of the whole of 8:11–16, as we will see.

Message. The leaders (those "with a strong hand") are not following "the way of this people" (v. 11). In the Hebrew text, the way of the people is a bad thing—but in the Septuagint it is a good way of life, which the leaders "disobey." This "way" is the way of the covenant and following the commandments of the Torah. Verse 12 is very difficult to understand but reflects a debate about whether "the way of the people" (obeying the laws of Torah) is "hard," that is, severe or difficult. Verses 13–14a describes an alternative to this hard way: a way that honors God with temple worship, in the hope that he will bless the land with security. In verse 14b "the house of Jacob" and the "inhabitants of Jerusalem" refer to "this people" in verse 11; they are now "in a hollow" (they have met with disaster). The leaders' speech in verses 12–14 is their analysis for why they should not follow the "hard" way of the people: the disaster that has befallen them is evidence against the validity of their way. So the leaders resolve to seek Yahweh through (some unspecified) temple worship, rather than through Torah observance.

In verses 15–16 God pronounces judgment on those whose speech he quotes in verses 12–14. Many of those leaders will be destroyed (v. 15a). Describing them as "in security" is therefore ironic: they will "approach" (that is, seek God in the temple), thinking they are safe, but they will "be taken" (v. 15b). Such will be the fate of those leaders "who seal up the Law" to prevent people from learning it (v. 16).

Verse 16 is crucial to the meaning of the whole passage, and a comparison of the two versions of this verse shows how far the Septuagint diverges from the Hebrew original. In the Hebrew, verse 16 mentions "my disciples," which means that it is Isaiah's declaration of his own intentions; in the Greek, verse 16 is God's judgment on the leaders in Jerusalem. In the Hebrew, it is Isaiah's preaching that will be sealed; in the Greek, it is the Law (which is not mentioned in the Hebrew) that is sealed. In the Hebrew, the purpose of sealing the teaching is to preserve it among Isaiah's disciples; in the Greek, the Law is sealed in order to prevent the people from learning it.

The Septuagint passage is clearly more than a translation of the Hebrew—a "rewriting" is a more appropriate term. In Greek, Isa 8:11–16 is by all rights a new text compared to its original. But why have the "translators" taken such liberties? We can see why when we consider the religious controversy that was tearing Judaism apart in the second century BCE when the Septuagint was produced. The Jewish elite in Jerusalem were attempting to "modernize" Jewish life by deemphasizing the ethnically exclusive practices prescribed by the Torah and by embracing a more inclusive

Hellenistic worldview.[5] Jews who held onto traditional ways regarded such changes with horror; see 1 Macc 1:11–15 and 2 Macc 4:7–17 for hostile descriptions of those leaders (who are called "renegades from Israel" in 1 Macc 1:11) from the traditionalist perspective. The Jewish scholars behind the Septuagint, devoted as they were to ensuring the survival and relevance of the scriptures, have turned this passage in Isaiah into a condemnation of the hellenizers in Jerusalem, who were accused of trying to remove the Torah as the basis for Judaism. The alterations in the text introduced by the translators made it possible to read it as a condemnatory prediction of the anti-Torah policies of the leadership in Jerusalem. This prophecy from Isaiah in the eighth century was made to relate directly to a crisis in the second century, when the Septuagint was written. Thus, God, speaking through his prophet, in Greek, predicted and condemned the hellenizing authorities in Jerusalem.

In this passage from the Septuagint, as in the Dead Sea Scrolls, we can see two features of ancient Jewish interpretation of prophecy that we will also see in the NT. First, prophetic passages are interpreted as predictions that come true in the time of the interpreters. Second, the interpreters alter the words of the prophecies in order to make their fulfillment more evident.

The Targums

During the three centuries when most of the Jewish people lived in the Persian Empire (the sixth through the fourth centuries), the Hebrew language gradually fell into disuse as Jews adopted Aramaic, the common language of the Middle East in that period. By the first century BCE Hebrew was no longer the spoken language of ordinary Jews, but it was still used in worship because it was the language of the Bible. Translations of the Hebrew Bible into Aramaic, called *targums* (the Aramaic word for "translation") emerged to meet the needs of Jews who could no longer understand the language of their scriptures. The targums are more than straightforward translations, however, for they paraphrase as often as they translate and frequently add explanatory details, in order to make the scriptures easier to understand.

There is not a single targum for the whole of the Hebrew scriptures but rather separate targums for individual books or groups of books. The targums for the prophetic books originated in the first and second centuries CE, and some were revised for several centuries thereafter.[6] In many places the targums "modernize" as they translate, injecting vocabulary and references

5. See Schäfer, "Hellenistic and Maccabean Periods," 580–85.
6. See Evans, *Noncanonical Writings*, 102–5, and the extensive literature cited there.

from the world of their audiences into the texts. For example, some targumic passages that mention armies and wars refer to Roman military terms or practices, even though the biblical authors wrote centuries before Rome became a world power. So "I will send the sword against them" in Jer 24:10 appears in the targum as "I will hire against them those who kill with the sword."[7] This rendering refers to the hiring of mercenaries, a common practice of the Roman army. In another example, Ezek 30:9 mentions troops sent "in ships."[8] The targum here has "in legions," borrowing the Latin word for this impressive and distinctively Roman military unit.[9] Other examples of the targums' modernizing tendency include the following:

- The original names for money and weights are sometimes changed into names familiar to the targums' own times (like an American translation of the Bible converting money and weights into dollars and pounds).[10]

- The ancient Hebrew names for cities and other geographical locations are often replaced with the names familiar to a targum's audience.[11]

- References to someone's "tent" in Hebrew often appear as "city" in the targums. The audience could thus picture their ancestors as modern city dwellers rather than as primitive nomads.[12]

- Passages about the temple in Jerusalem often describe architectural features introduced during Herod's remodeling of the temple in the first century CE.[13]

Study of the targums is a specialized field in biblical studies, in which much scholarly interest is focused on understanding the numerous differences between the targums and the Hebrew Bible. My purpose here is limited: to examine a few brief passages that a targum has rewritten in order to make the words of the prophets relevant to its time. In the following examples, the targum's version is obviously more than a translation, for the targum has significantly altered both the wording and the meaning of

7. Translations from the Targum in this chapter are by Smolar and Aberbach, *Studies in Targum Jonathan*.

8. The Hebrew text literally reads "messengers," who are sent to wreak military destruction on Ethiopia. The messengers here are clearly soldiers who are instruments of divine punishment.

9. Smolar and Aberbach, *Studies in Targum Jonathan*, 96–97.

10. Ibid., 96.

11. See ibid., 114–28, for specific examples.

12. Ibid., 99.

13. Ibid., 104–5.

the original. In each case we can see how the new wording relates ancient prophecies to the time and circumstances of the targum's audience.

Habakkuk 3:17b

Hebrew text	*Targum*
The flock shall be cut off from the fold, and there shall be no herd in the stalls.	The Romans shall be destroyed, and they shall not collect the tribute from Jerusalem.

The prophet Habakkuk lived in the seventh century BCE, a time when Rome had no power beyond its own region in Italy. The targum here reflects the historical situation in 66 CE, the opening year of the Jewish-Roman war.[14] Jewish forces had driven the Romans out of Judea and thus relieved Jerusalem of its onerous burden of paying annual tribute to Rome. This happy situation did not last, and the war ended in catastrophe for the Jews. Still, the audience of the targum could see that Habakkuk's prophecy had been fulfilled, if only briefly. What we can see, however, and what most of the targum's audience could not, is that the prophecy that was fulfilled in 66 was a prediction made *after* the event, a prediction invented by the targumist, not a genuine prophecy from Habakkuk.

Isaiah 51:20a

Hebrew text	*Targum*
Your children have fainted.	Your children shall be torn to pieces.

This targumic revision also reflects events of the Jewish-Roman war.[15] The verse is addressed to Jerusalem; "your children" therefore refers to the inhabitants of the city. The historian Josephus reports a horrifying atrocity from the siege of Jerusalem in 70 CE. The besieging troops, hearing rumors that refugees fleeing the city were swallowing gold coins to hide them from

14. Ibid., 67.
15. Ibid., 79.

robbers, disemboweled about two thousand Jews in one night.[16] The targum rewrites this line from Isaiah, turning a metaphorical description of a past event (note the "*have* fainted" in the Hebrew text) into a literal prediction of a future one. Of course, what was future from Isaiah's perspective was history for the targumist. This gruesome prophecy could be fulfilled because it had been rewritten to "predict" an event that had already occurred.

Isaiah 22:3b

Hebrew text	*Targum*
All who were found within you [Jerusalem] were captured.	All who were found within you were slain.

The minor revision in this verse probably reflects the course of another war, the one led by Bar Kochba against Rome that ended in defeat in 135 CE.[17] When the Romans destroyed Jerusalem at the end of the Jewish-Roman War in 70 CE, they took thousands of its inhabitants as prisoners, to be sold as slaves. In 135, however, the Romans had more murderous intentions and slaughtered the population wholesale. That catastrophic atrocity, burned into the collective Jewish memory, would doubtlessly be recognized as the fulfillment of the targum's version of Isaiah's prophecy. The targum's audience, however, would not know that the prophecy had been adjusted to match past history.

Isaiah 26:16b

Hebrew text	*Targum*
They poured out a prayer when your chastening was on them.	In their trouble they used to teach the instruction of your Torah in secret.

Here the targum has but the slimmest connection with the original; it preserves only the basic idea that the people responded religiously in a time of difficulty. The mention of teaching the Torah in secret relates the verse to

---

16. Josephus, *Wars* 5.550–52.
17. Smolar and Aberbach, *Studies in Targum Jonathan*, 81.

the time when the Roman emperor Hadrian (in the early second century CE) outlawed Judaism and thus forced its practice underground.[18] Here is another prophecy which the targum's audience could see fulfilled in their relatively recent past.

Isaiah 22:22–25

Our final example involves a longer text than the previous brief quotations. In Isaiah 22:15–25, the prophet addresses a corrupt official named Shebna, the king's chief of staff. Isaiah tells him that he will be replaced by someone named Eliakim (vv. 20–21). Isaiah gives a job description of Eliakim's position (v. 22) and predicts that he will perform his duties honorably (v. 23). However, Eliakim will eventually be overwhelmed by his ever increasing responsibilities (v. 24) and will fail at them (v. 25).

Here are the relevant excerpts where the Hebrew and the Aramaic differ.

Hebrew text	*Targum*
22 I will place on his [Eliakim's] shoulder the key of the house of David.	I will give the key of the temple and the rule of the house of David into his hand.
23 I will fasten him like a peg in a secure place.	I will appoint him a faithful trustee, ministering in the permanent place [the temple].
25 On that day . . . the peg that was fastened in a sure place will give way; and it will be cut down and fall, and the burden that was on it will be cut off.	At that time . . . the faithful trustee who ministers in the permanent place will be removed, and he will be plucked off and fall, and the burden of prophecy concerning him will be annulled.

The targum revises this passage in two important ways. First, it completely rewrites Eliakim's job description, in three particulars: (a) He will have religious authority ("the key to the temple") in addition to a political position; (b) the "key of the house of David" becomes the "rule of the house of David"; thus the position of the king's executive officer turns into the kingship itself; (c) he will be appointed to the office of "trustee." The targum thus makes Eliakim both chief priest and ruler. Such an all-powerful position did not

18. Ibid., 86.

exist in Isaiah's time, but the description fits the Hasmonean rulers of the second and first centuries BCE, rulers who functioned both as chief priests and kings. Likewise, the title "trustee" names a position held by members of those high priestly families.[19]

The targum's second major revision in this Isaiah passage comes at the end: "the burden that was on it will be cut off" in Hebrew becomes in the targum "the burden of prophecy concerning him will be annulled." In the Hebrew original the "burden" refers to Eliakim's office, whereas the "burden of prophecy" in the targum refers to, and effectively cancels, the prophecy in verse 23 that Eliakim "will become a throne of honor to his ancestral house." This startling revision, which has no basis whatsoever in Isaiah's Hebrew text, makes sense from the historical perspective of targumic times. The Hasmonean priest-kings were widely viewed as corrupt and tyrannical. Their power came to an end when Herod the Great defeated the last Hasmonean ruler in 37 BCE. Looking back on that time, the targum sees that those rulers failed to fulfill the prophecy in verse 23 that they will carry out their duties honorably. And thus the passage was rewritten so that Isaiah can predict that they will fail to fulfill his own prophecy. In this way the targumist's creative rewriting ensures that even the failure to fulfill prophecy becomes a fulfillment of prophecy.

Conclusion

Chapter 5 showed that the Dead Sea Scrolls made the scriptures address contemporary events by explicitly interpreting them to do so, by means of the "this is that" format of the peshers. Targums accomplish the same end through a different means: by free translation or paraphrase, which sometimes changes the meaning in the original text so much that the targum's Aramaic text is best described as a *rewriting* of the Hebrew. The examples analyzed above exhibit strategic rewritings that enable the prophets, in the new words attributed to them by the targumist, to speak directly to memorable events that were relatively recent to the time of the targum's writing. Both peshers and targums thus relate scriptures to the times and circumstances of their respective audiences. In both styles of interpretation, the fulfillment of prophecy assures a Jewish audience that the God of Israel who spoke through the prophets in the distant past was still speaking to the present. The audience's ability to verify, via those interpretive methods, the fulfillment of prophecy in their recent past served to confirm their belief in the veracity of the biblical prophets, encouraged them to take pride in their

19. Ibid., 65–66.

ancestral religion, and increased their confidence that the writings of the prophets of old contained ongoing divine guidance for whatever difficulties might lie ahead.

Josephus

The writings of Josephus are a prime source for our knowledge of first-century Judaism and Jewish history. Josephus was a Jewish general in the devastating war with Rome in 66–70 CE. Although his nation was utterly defeated, Josephus survived by surrendering to the Romans, who treated him honorably (more on this below). He retired to Rome and wrote two immense volumes on Jewish history, *Wars of the Jews* and *Antiquities of the Jews*.[20] He is important for our topic because his comments about prophecy let us see how first-century Jews understood it.

Josephus regarded the biblical prophets as predictors of the future, and he believed that the prophets had predicted events of his own time. For example, he saw prophecy fulfilled in the most cataclysmic event of his century: the destruction of the temple in Jerusalem by the Romans in 70 CE.

> Jeremiah denounced beforehand the sad calamities that were coming upon Jerusalem. He also left behind him in writing a description of that destruction of our nation which has lately happened in our days, and the taking of Babylon; nor was he the only prophet who delivered such predictions beforehand to the multitude. So did Ezekiel, who was the first person that wrote, and left behind him in writing two books, concerning these events.[21]

Similarly, Josephus finds predictions in the Book of Daniel that were fulfilled during the time of the Maccabean revolt.[22] Modern scholars agree with Josephus here, but for reasons quite different from his. Josephus assumes that the author of the Book of Daniel was Daniel himself, and that he had lived at the time of the Babylonian exile (in the sixth century BCE), just as Dan 1:1–7 depicts. Modern critical scholars, however, have concluded that the author actually lived in the Maccabean age (in the second century BCE) and that he posed as Daniel, the hero of the narrative, as a literary fiction. From the modern scholarly perspective, therefore, Daniel's prophecies were written *after* the events they "predict," events in the pseudonymous

---

20. For the career of Josephus, see Mason, *Josephus*, 35–51.

21. *Ant.* 10.79.

22. Gray, *Prophetic Figures*, 32.

author's recent past. Josephus, on the other hand, believes that Daniel foretold the sufferings that King Antiochus inflicted on Israel during the time
of the Maccabees, four centuries after Daniel prophesied. But that is not all.
Josephus also believes that Daniel predicted the war between the Jews and
the Romans, in which Josephus himself participated.

> Our nation suffered these things under Antiochus Epiphanes,
> according to Daniel's vision, and what he wrote many years be-
> fore they came true. In the same way, Daniel also wrote about
> the Roman empire and that they would capture Jerusalem and
> destroy the temple.[23]

Josephus's writings provide clear evidence that the belief that the biblical prophets foresaw events far into their future was widespread among
Jews. For example, he tells about a certain high priest, Onias IV, who was
living as a refugee in Egypt during a time of war in Israel. Onias petitioned
the king and queen of Egypt to authorize the building of a temple to Yahweh. This was a religiously suspicious plan because the Law of Moses forbids
temple worship anywhere other than in Jerusalem (Deut 21:1–14). Josephus
informs us that Onias was encouraged in his dubious project "chiefly by the
words of the prophet Isaiah, who had lived more than six hundred years
before and had foretold that a temple to the Most High God was surely to be
built in Egypt by a Jew."[24] In his letter to the king and queen, Onias quotes
Isaiah: "There will be an altar in Egypt to the Lord God."[25]

In the ancient world, dreams, along with prophecy, were believed to
be means by which the gods communicated with humans. Dreams, like
prophecy, were often ambiguous and obscure and so required interpretation. Josephus claims that he was "an interpreter of dreams and skilled in
interpreting the meaning of ambiguous utterances of God,"[26] an ability he
elsewhere describes as a gift from God.[27] Josephus's self-reported insights
into the true meanings of veiled divine messages features prominently in
a fascinating event from his life, as he recounts his own participation in a
tumultuous episode in Jewish history.

In his long account of the Jewish-Roman War, Josephus reports that
one of the major factors motivating the Jews to revolt against Roman rule
was a disastrous misinterpretation of an especially ambiguous prophecy.

---

23. *Ant.* 10.276.

24. *Ant.* 13.64.

25. *Ant.* 13.68, quoting Isa 19:19.

26. *Wars* 3.352.

27. *Ant.* 10.195–96.

> What more than anything else incited the Jews to start this War was an ambiguous oracle that was found in their sacred scriptures, to the effect that at that time someone from their country would become ruler of the habitable earth. The Jews took this prediction to mean someone from their own people and many of the wise men were thereby deceived in their interpretation. This oracle, however, in reality pointed to the reign of Vespasian, who was proclaimed emperor on Jewish soil.[28]

Josephus explains that this prophecy actually referred, not to a Jew, but to Vespasian, the Roman general who prosecuted the war against the Jews. According to Josephus, the reference in the prophecy to "one from their country" fits Vespasian, because he was appointed emperor while he was in Judea with his troops. Josephus tells us that he was able to interpret the prophecy this way because he himself was a prophet; he claims that "God had foretold to him the impending fate of the Jews and the destinies of the Roman emperors."[29]

Josephus was the general in command of the Jewish forces defending Galilee. When the defense collapsed, Josephus surrendered to the Romans and was led to Vespasian. He told Vespasian not to think that he had taken him captive. Rather, Josephus declared that he had been sent by God to Vespasian as a messenger of good news. Josephus told him, "You, Vespasian, are Caesar and emperor, you, and this man your son [referring to Titus who was with Vespasian] . . . You, O Caesar, are lord not only over me, but over the land and the sea, and all humanity."[30]

Vespasian dismissed this prophecy, reckoning that Josephus had said it only to save his own skin. One of Vespasian's associates sarcastically retorted to Josephus that since he was a prophet, it was a shame that he had not foretold the fall of the city of Jotapata (within which Josephus and his men had been besieged) or his own captivity by the Romans. Josephus replied, "I did foretell to the people of Jotapata that they would be taken on the forty-seventh day, and that I should be caught alive by the Romans."[31] He then reports, "Now when Vespasian had inquired of the captives privately about these predictions, he found them to be true, and then he began to believe those that concerned himself."[32]

---

28. *Wars* 6.312–13.
29. *Wars* 3.351.
30. *Wars* 3.401–2.
31. *Wars* 3.406.
32. *Wars* 3.407.

Josephus's prediction about Vespasian came true. In 68 CE the emperor Nero was assassinated while Vespasian was with the army in Palestine. An intense power struggle followed Nero's death. In one year there were four different emperors in Rome. In 69 the Roman army acclaimed Vespasian emperor. He left Palestine for Rome, leaving the war against the Jews in the hands of his son Titus. The rest of Josephus's prophecy came true ten years later, in 79, when Titus succeeded Vespasian.

Mysterious Fulfillments

Josephus believed that the words of the prophets were infallibly true because they came directly from God. However, some prophecies are obscure or ambiguous, and so Josephus reasoned that it was a mystery exactly how they will be fulfilled. Sometimes they are fulfilled in completely unexpected ways. One highly paradoxical result is that two conflicting prophecies can both be true. Josephus analyzes two biblical examples of this paradox in which two prophets predict seemingly contradictory outcomes concerning the fate of the same person. In both cases, the contradicting prophecies both came true.

The first case concerns the prophets Elijah and Micaiah and their prophecies about the death of King Ahab. Ahab's wife, Jezebel, had orchestrated the murder of an innocent man named Naboth so that Ahab could seize his field (see 1 Kgs 21:1–16). While Elijah was in the city of Jezreel, he stood in the field that had belonged to Naboth and prophesied that in punishment for Ahab's murderous land grab, "dogs will lick up Ahab's blood just as they had licked up the blood of Naboth" (1 Kgs 21:19). This prophecy has the grim irony we often see in prophetic predictions of doom in which the punishment fits the crime. Some time later, as Ahab was deciding whether to go into battle at Ramoth, the prophet Micaiah predicted that Ahab would be killed if he launched the attack (1 Kgs 22:15–18). Because Ramoth is a long way from Jezreel, Josephus states that Micaiah was "contradicting a greater prophet than [Micaiah] himself" in saying that Ahab would be killed such a long distance—Josephus describes it as a three-day march—from Jezreel, the city where Elijah had foretold that Ahab would meet his demise.[33] Paraphrasing the biblical story, Josephus reports that Ahab disregarded Micaiah's warning, but took the precaution of dressing as a common soldier so that the enemy troops could not identify him as the king. Nevertheless, during the battle a "random" arrow found a gap in Ahab's armor and mortally wounded him (1 Kgs 22:34). Josephus then tells

33. *Ant.* 8.408.

us that after the battle Ahab's body was taken by chariot (thus covering a three-day march in a much shorter time) to the city of Samaria and buried there;[34] "and when they had washed his chariot in the fountain of Jezreel, which was bloody from the dead body of the king . . . the dogs licked up his blood."[35] This strange turn of events at the end of the story allows Josephus to conclude that "they acknowledged that the prophecy of Elijah was true . . . even though Ahab died at Ramoth, as Micaiah had foretold."[36]

Josephus's argument is clever, but he is wrong about the facts. In his version of the story, Ahab's chariot was washed in the fountain in Jezreel, but the Bible reports that "they washed the chariot by the pool of Samaria" (1 Kgs 22:38), which is over twenty miles from Jezreel. (Josephus seems unaware of the non sequitur in his narrative: the chariot transports the corpse to Samaria, but in the very next clause the chariot is washed more than twenty miles north in Jezreel.) The Bible thus leaves the tension between the predictions of Elijah and Micaiah unresolved.

It is puzzling why Josephus's narrative contradicts the Bible precisely on the one detail on which he rests his case. All our extant copies of the Hebrew Bible and the Septuagint read "Samaria" at 1 Kgs 22:38, so it is extremely unlikely that Josephus saw the word "Jezreel" there. The scholarly sources I consulted do not mention this problem, either because scholars haven't noticed this one small discrepancy among the many hundreds of pages of Josephus's works, or because they have passed over it in silence.

That Josephus got the story wrong, however, does not diminish what we can learn from his argument, for it illustrates how this hellenized Jew had fully assimilated the originally Greek understanding of prophets as oracles. For Josephus, the biblical prophets were conduits of mysterious divine messages whose meanings might not be apparent until they had come true, and whose predictions were the inescapable decrees of fate. Josephus himself emphasizes that last point: "From what happened to this king, we have reasons to consider the power of fate, that there is no way of avoiding it, even when we know it."[37]

Josephus's second example of two apparently contradictory prophecies both coming true involves the prophets Jeremiah and Ezekiel and their predictions concerning the fate of King Zedekiah, the last king of the line of David. Zedekiah was warned by both Jeremiah (in person) and Ezekiel (who sent word from Babylon) that if Zedekiah did not surrender Jerusalem

34. *Ant.* 8.416.
35. *Ant.* 8.417.
36. *Ant.* 8.417.
37. *Ant.* 8.419.

to the Babylonians, who were besieging it, the city and Zedekiah himself would be captured. However, the two prophets seemed to disagree on the details. Jeremiah prophesied that the king would be hauled off in chains to Babylon (Jer 32:4–5), while Ezekiel predicted that Zedekiah would not see Babylon (Ezek 12:13). Because of this discrepancy in the warnings of the two prophets, Josephus reports, Zedekiah disbelieved both of them. "However, all the things foretold about him did come to pass according to their prophecies."[38] The Babylonians invaded Jerusalem, captured Zedekiah, and brought him before Nebuchadnezzar, the king of Babylon. In punishment for Zedekiah's rebellion, Zedekiah's sons were brought before him and he was forced to watch as they were murdered. Nebuchadnezzar then had Zedekiah blinded. He was then "brought to Babylon, but did not see it, according to the prediction of Ezekiel."[39] Josephus's ingenious analysis of what might seem to us to be a loophole reflects his confidence in the predictive power of prophecy.

However, there is a flaw in the logic of Josephus's story about Zedekiah. The point of the story makes sense only if Zedekiah understood Ezekiel's warning that he would not "see" Babylon to mean that he would not be taken there. The problem is that Josephus's obvious implication that Zedekiah understood Ezekiel in this way is plausible only because Josephus does not quote Ezekiel's actual words. The full prophecy that Ezekiel relayed to Zedekiah was, "*I [God] will bring him [Zedekiah] to Babylon*, the land of the Chaldeans, but he shall not see it; and he will die there" (Ezek 12:13). If Zedekiah had heard Ezekiel's full prediction, he could not have misunderstood it to be inconsistent with Jeremiah's—which would have ruined Josephus's clever explanation. We do not know if Josephus was aware of the actual wording of Ezekiel's prophecy. Perhaps Josephus was relying on memory here. Or, as seems equally likely, Josephus intentionally referred only to part of Ezekiel's prophecy, ignoring its obvious meaning and selecting just the words he needed to make his story work.

The belief that prophecies can come true in ways no one expects generates another paradox: even the prophet himself might not know exactly what future realities his words describe. Josephus relates a perfect example of this paradox in a story about an Essene prophet named Judas, whose predictions had all come true.[40] (Josephus did not assume that the prophets in the Bible were the only prophets. As we have seen, he even considered himself a prophet.) This Judas prophesied that one Antigonus, the brother

38. *Ant.* 10.107.

39. *Ant.* 10.141.

40. *Wars* 1.78; *Ant.* 13.311.

of King Aristobolus, would be murdered on a specific day in a place called Strato's Tower (the name of a coastal town, later renamed Caesarea). On the predicted day, Judas was in Jerusalem and was surprised when he happened to see Antigonus in the city. Judas figured that his prophecy would not come true because inland Jerusalem was so far away from Strato's Tower on the coast that Antigonus could not possibly travel there to meet his prophesied death on the same day. It turned out, however, that Antigonus was murdered later that very day, in an underground passageway in Jerusalem that by "coincidence" was also called Strato's Tower. Josephus explains that Judas was not aware before that day that there was a place named Strato's Tower in Jerusalem. Judas's prophecy was thus fulfilled, but not in the way he thought it would be.[41] This story is important for our study because it nicely illustrates an aspect of the ancient understanding of prophecy: the prophet himself can be mistaken about the true meaning of his prophecy. From an ancient perspective, the fact that a prophet does not understand how his prophecy will be fulfilled verifies the divine origin of the oracle.[42] Only after the prophecy has been fulfilled can its true meaning be understood, even by the prophet himself.

We can see that same understanding of prophecy in the New Testament. There is a dramatic scene in the Gospel of John in which Jewish leaders meet to decide what to do about Jesus, whose miracles are attracting large crowds. Soon, they fear, "everyone will believe in him and the Romans will come and destroy both our temple and our nation" (John 11:48). The chief priest lectures them, "You know nothing at all! Don't you realize that you're better off having one man die for the people than having the whole nation wiped out?" (John 11:49–50). What the narrator tells us next is most interesting.

> He didn't say this on his own authority, but since he was that year's chief priest he could prophesy that Jesus would die for the nation. In fact, he would die not only for the nation, but to gather together all God's dispersed children and make them one people. (John 11:51–52)

Because the chief priest had the power of prophecy, what he predicted was guaranteed to come true, but in a way that he could not know. In John's view, Jesus did indeed die to save the people, but as John explains, this salvation meant something very different from anything the chief priest could imagine.

---

41. *Wars* 1.80; *Ant.* 13.313.

42. Aune, *Prophecy*, 145. Aune notes that the story about Judas is a typical example of Greco-Roman stories about ambiguous oracles that are unexpectedly fulfilled. "The story is typically Hellenistic, and its authenticity is therefore dubious" (145).

There is strong irony here, for the chief priest had prefaced his prophecy with, "You know nothing at all." According to John, the chief priest spoke (unknowingly) also about himself. Only those who grasp the true meaning of Jesus' life and death can understand. And that is the cornerstone of the New Testament understanding of the nature of OT prophecy: only in the light of faith in Jesus can the true meaning of prophecy be understood.

Conclusion

Josephus's belief that the prophets from long ago predicted events of his day was widely, if not universally, shared by his fellow Jews, judging from the evidence in the Dead Sea Scrolls, the Septuagint, and the targums. Josephus's various stories and explanations of how prophecies were fulfilled presuppose more specific beliefs that underlie the basic notion that ancient prophecies were fulfilled in a contemporary audience's present or recent past:

- prophecies are deliberately obscure and therefore require interpretation;
- the ability to interpret obscure prophecies is a divine gift;
- prophets did not always know what they were actually predicting;
- prophecies can be fulfilled in unexpected ways, such that their true meaning can be discovered only after their fulfillments.

Those beliefs originated in Greece and were adopted by Jews under the influence of Hellenism (see chapter 4). Yet we should not consider those beliefs foreign to Judaism. Modern historians can identify which beliefs were absorbed into Jewish religion from outside of it, but to Jews in the Hellenistic era, especially by the time of Josephus in the first century CE, such beliefs were simply part of how Jews understood their own religion.

Those beliefs are evident also in the New Testament's presentation of the fulfillment of prophecy in the life of Jesus and the experiences of the early Jesus communities. Occasionally, those beliefs are expressed directly (as in the above example from the Gospel of John), but usually they function as assumptions in the various gospel scenes that explain how Jesus fulfilled specific prophecies. Josephus was writing in roughly the same time period as the authors of the gospels. That the same basic set of beliefs about prophecy are reflected in both the writings of a first-century Jewish historian and the writings of early followers of Jesus is evidence for how broadly they were shared by those who sought to relate the scriptures of Israel to their own circumstances. The creative rewriting of prophetic passages that we have seen in the Septuagint and the targums—by which the scriptural text itself was modified to make it relevant to the recent history of the audience—is an interpretive practice also found in the New Testament, as we will see.

That the New Testament authors shared with their Jewish contemporaries, not only the same beliefs about prophecy, but also some of the same ways of interpreting prophecies, indicates that first-century Christians understood the fulfillment of prophecy within a thoroughly Jewish paradigm. The important point here is that there is little or nothing that is distinctively Christian about how the New Testament uses scriptural prophecy—except that is sees prophecy fulfilled specifically in Jesus.

PART 2

The Fulfillment of Prophecy in the New Testament

Paul

─── 7 ───

The Fulfillment of Prophecy in the New Testament: Introduction

I N THE EARLIER CHAPTERS on the Dead Sea Scrolls and Josephus we saw that Jews in the Hellenistic period (during which the NT was written) regarded prophecy as a form of direct divine revelation in which a prophet receives a message about the future, sometimes a future far distant from his own time. Because prophecy came directly from God, the prophets did not always know the real meaning of the oracles they delivered. Josephus and the authors of the Dead Sea Scrolls believed that the prophets of the Bible had spoken about the times in which the authors themselves were living. In the Dead Sea Scrolls that belief is so intense that their authors could use the recent history of their own community at Qumran as the key to interpreting the prophets. The Qumran community believed itself to be living in the time of the fulfillment of prophecy; all of Israel's history was culminating in their own, and all of the scriptures were pointing to them and their experience. They alone were able to see the true meaning that was veiled in the words of the prophets.

We can see that same perspective in the NT, in Paul's explanation for why he had so little success persuading his Jewish contemporaries that Jesus was the one who fulfilled prophecy. In 2 Cor 3:13, Paul refers to the strange scene in Exodus when Moses puts a veil over his face because it was shining and frightening the people (Exod 34:29–33). Paul then elaborates on the image of that veil.

> To this very day when they [the Jews] hear the reading of the old covenant, that same veil is still there since only in Christ is it set aside. Indeed, to this very day whenever Moses is read, a veil lies over their hearts; but when one turns to the Lord, the veil is removed. (2 Cor 3:14–16)

Paul's point is clear enough: only from the perspective of Christian faith can the meaning of the Jewish scriptures be properly understood.

Another facet of Paul's belief about the scriptures is evident in Rom 15:4: "Whatever was written in former days was written for our instruction." Paul here claims that the OT writings were not intended primarily for their original audiences. Rather, they were written for the sake of future Christians (see also Rom 4:23–24; 1 Cor 9:9–10; 10:11). In this respect Paul agreed with the Qumran authors that the OT prophets, and indeed all the scriptures, were addressing a generation far in their future, though Paul and the Qumran sectarians disagreed about which generation that was. A passage at the end of the Letter to the Romans announces

> the revelation of the mystery that was kept secret for long ages,
> but is now disclosed, and through the prophetic writings is
> made known to all the nations. (Rom 16:25–26)

The role of the prophets here is interesting. A "mystery that was kept secret for long ages" is now revealed. According to Paul, the prophets did not understand that mystery, for only "now" (in Paul's lifetime) has it been revealed. However, now that the mystery has been revealed it can be made known through the writings of the prophets. Again, the true meaning of the scriptures can be understood only from the standpoint of Christian faith. The implication is that not even the prophets themselves grasped the real meaning of their words.

We can see that implication made explicit if we revisit a passage we considered a few pages back (John 11:47–52), which analyzes a prophecy uttered, not by a prophet from the past, but by the chief priest Caiaphas. Speaking to the Jewish Council about its fear that Jesus' growing popularity would incite the Romans to destroy their nation, Caiaphas retorted, "Don't you realize that you're better off having one man die for the people than having the whole nation wiped out?" (John 11:50). John's literary and theological skill is on display in his phrase "for the people": the preposition "for" (*hyper* in Greek) can mean either "in place of" or "for the benefit of." The first meaning makes Caiaphas' rhetorical question a purely political calculation; the second makes the phrase "one man die for the people" into a Christian interpretation of Jesus' death. Caiaphas clearly intended the first meaning, but John explains how it is that Caiaphas's utterance was ultimately true in a way he did not realize.

> He didn't say this on his own authority, but since he was that
> year's chief priest he could prophesy that Jesus would die for
> the nation. In fact, he would die not only for the nation, but to

gather together all God's dispersed children and make them one
people. (John 11:51–52)

John thus tells us that an enemy of Jesus pronounced a prophecy that was
truer than he could know, and thus became a divinely inspired but unwitting witness to Jesus the savior. John's depiction of Caiaphas's prediction
shows how thoroughly the Hellenistic understanding of prophecy was absorbed by early Christianity.

The Gospel of John also mentions three central figures of the OT who
foresaw Jesus. Jesus said, "If you really believed Moses, you would believe
me; after all, I'm the one he wrote about" (John 5:46). Jesus also declared
that "Abraham rejoiced that he would see my day; he saw it and was glad"
(John 8:56). And John explains that "Isaiah saw Jesus' glory and spoke about
him" (John 12:41). It is not clear in these three brief statements whether Moses, Abraham, or Isaiah knew that what they saw, wrote, or spoke about was
Jesus. For John it matters little whether Isaiah, for example, was aware that
the glory he saw was Jesus' glory. What is important for John is that the followers of Jesus understand that he is the reality proclaimed by the prophets.

Paul seems to imply that the prophets were not aware that they were
prophesying about Jesus. The statements in John's gospel about Moses,
Abraham, and Isaiah can be taken as assuming either that these figures knew
about Jesus or that they did not. Neither Paul nor John explains himself
clearly on this matter; their above passages are not concerned specifically
with what the prophets themselves actually knew. But there is one passage
in the NT that is directly interested in this question and that has a clear and
detailed explanation of the matter.

> [10]Concerning this salvation, prophets, who prophesied of the
> grace intended for you, searched and investigated, [11]investi-
> gating to what sort of person or propitious time the spirit of
> Christ within them was referring, bearing prior witness to the
> sufferings destined for Christ and the glories after these suf-
> ferings. [12]To them it was revealed that they were serving not
> themselves but rather you in these things, things that now have
> been announced to you by those who proclaimed good news to
> you through the Holy Spirit sent from heaven, things into which
> angels yearn to gain a glimpse. (1 Pet 1:10–12)[1]

This fascinating declaration makes a number of important assertions.

- The prophets did not know what their own oracles meant.

---

1. Translation by Elliott, *1 Peter*.

- Because the prophets did not know what their oracles meant, they meditated on them ("searched and investigated").

- The prophets were curious about the person and the time to which their oracles referred.

- They predicted the suffering and glorification of the messiah.

- God revealed to the prophets that their oracles were intended for "you" (the readers of 1 Peter), not for the prophets' own times.

- Angels also wanted to find out what the prophets were talking about, but apparently they did not succeed.

- "You" learned what the prophets predicted, not from their writings, but from Christian preachers ("those who proclaimed good news to you").

The author of 1 Peter implies that the prophets were not told the identity of the messiah about whom they prophesied, nor when their prophecies would come true, but only that their oracles were for the benefit of a future generation. Not even the angels could understand the true meaning of the prophetic oracles. The most interesting assertion is in the first part of verse 12, for it shows how the early Christians came to faith in Christ and where the prophecies fit into that process. Referring to what the prophets predicted ("these things"), verse 12 does not tell the readers that they came to believe in Christ because they could see that he had fulfilled prophecy. Rather, it explains that they understood what the prophets had predicted only *after* they were told the good news about Jesus. This is a most important point and the key insight into understanding the early Christian belief that Jesus fulfilled prophecy: that belief was a *result* of their belief that Jesus is the messiah—not the other way around.

At this point we should go back and look closely at how Paul uses the OT when he refers to Moses and the veil. According to the story in Exodus (Exod 34:29–33), when Moses came down from Mount Sinai with the commandments, he was not aware that his face was shining. Although the people were afraid to come near him—presumably because he looked like a god—he gave them the commandments and spoke with them. Only after he had delivered the commandments of the covenant did Moses veil his face.

When Paul refers to that scene, he retells it somewhat differently.

> Moses put a veil over his face to keep the people of Israel from gazing at the end of the glory that was being set aside. But their minds were hardened . . . Indeed, to this day, whenever Moses is read, a veil lies over their hearts. (2 Cor 3:13–15)

Paul's summary of the scene differs from the original in two ways. First, Paul supplies a reason why Moses donned the veil: to prevent the Israelites from seeing "the end of the glory that was being set aside," the "glory" being Paul's roundabout description of Israel's covenant (see 2 Cor 3:7–8).[2] In the Exodus story, however, Moses veils his face *after* passing on the covenant to the people (Exod 34:33). Second, and more problematically, Paul adds that "their minds were hardened" (that is, their minds were closed).[3] The Book of Exodus mentions nothing of the sort.

Paul here has made up his own version of the scriptural story. In itself that is not too troubling. What is disturbing is Paul's motive for riffing on the Jewish Bible: to support his specious claim that Jews do not (and apparently cannot) understand their own scriptures. Paul confidently asserts that only Christians can grasp the true meaning of the OT, yet he distorts the very OT story that he uses to bolster his assertion. This ironic process is one we can see over and over again in the NT: Christian authors altering the OT in order to show what it "really" means.

$\sim$

The chapters in part 2 of this book examine the distinctive ways NT writings present the fulfillment of prophecy in the life of Jesus and the experience of his earliest followers. The four gospels have differing degrees of interest in this theme. Matthew is intensely interested in it, John only slightly less so. Mark and Luke consider it important, but devote much less attention to it than do Matthew or John. The four chapters on the gospels analyze every instance in them when an author claims that prophecy was fulfilled. Such claims are numerous in Matthew and John, and so those chapters are relatively lengthy. Because Matthew's gospel is the one most interested in our topic, the chapter on Matthew includes a critical assessment of how the first evangelist uses prophecy and the polemical implications of that usage. The chapter on John has a similar aim, because that gospel deploys the fulfillment of prophecy to support its anti-Jewish polemic. The chapters on Mark and Luke are somewhat brief, owing to those two gospels' relatively minor

2. Furnish, *II Corinthians*, 203.

3. The passive "were hardened" is ambiguous. It can mean that they misunderstand either because they are unwilling to accept God's message or because God prevents them from understanding it. From an ancient perspective, this kind of ambiguity seemed to point, not to an either/or alternative, but to a mysterious paradox in which both meanings are true. A similar ambiguity pervades the depiction of Pharoah, of whom it is written both that he "hardened his heart" (i.e., closed his mind, the heart being the seat of the will in the ancient world) and that "Yahweh hardened his heart" (see, e.g., the contrast between Exod 9:34 and 10:1).

interest in the fulfillment of prophecy. Luke gives much more attention to prophecy and its fulfillment in the Acts of the Apostles than he does in his gospel; the two writings are analyzed in the same chapter.

Two more chapters, one on Paul and one on the Letter to the Hebrews, round out the NT section of this book. That is because, of the twenty-one NT writings that are classified as letters, only some by Paul and the anonymous Letter to the Hebrews exhibit interest in the fulfillment of prophecy. The other letters (James, 1–2 Peter, 1–3 John, and Jude) contain no overt claims that a specific prophecy has been fulfilled.[4] The Book of Revelation is saturated with the theme of prophecy and its fulfillment, but since Revelation is concerned with prophecies that will be fulfilled in the future, it falls outside the scope of this book.

---

4. 1 Pet 2:6–8 and 22 quote from Isaiah and the Psalms in reference to Jesus, but the quotations are used as exhortations, not as instances of fulfilled prophecy. Jude 14–16 quotes an ominous passage from *1 Enoch* (a noncanonical Jewish apocalyptic text from the first century CE), and claims that it refers to contemporary Christians whom the author excoriates as false teachers. However, the quoted prediction threatens a judgment that the author believes will come in the future.

8

The Fulfillment of Prophecy in the Gospel of Matthew

MATTHEW'S GOSPEL IS BY far the one most interested in the fulfillment of prophecy, and so this gospel demands the lion's share of our attention. After surveying Matthew's examples of prophecy fulfillment, this chapter falls into two main parts. The first part, "How Matthew Helps Jesus Fulfill Prophecy," analyzes Matthew's varied methods of matching prophecies to stories in his gospel. The second part of this chapter, "How Matthew Uses Prophecy," assesses Matthew's repeated assertions that Jesus fulfilled prophecy, and evaluates what those assertions suggest about the Jews who did not accept them.

Overview

There are sixteen scenes in which the narrator (or Matthew's Jesus himself) interrupts the narrative in order to quote a prophecy and point out that it was fulfilled in that scene. There are seventeen fulfillment scenes if we count one more scene that quotes a prophecy and *implies* that it will be fulfilled.[1] Nearly half of those scenes occur early in the story, before Jesus becomes a public figure; five of them are found in the infancy narrative alone. This gospel thus starts with a flurry of fulfillment passages, creating a strong impression that Israel's sacred history has been building up to Jesus.

In ten of Matthew's seventeen scenes it is Jesus who fulfills prophecy. These ten make a curious set. Only one of them has to do with a specific

---

1. In this anomalous scene (21:33–42) Matthew implies that Jesus will fulfill the scripture about the rejected stone becoming the cornerstone when he is resurrected. That implication (in 21:42) is apparent only if the reader interprets the parable about the evil sharecroppers (21:33–41) allegorically. However, the allegory is so unsubtle that there is little danger that the reader will miss the point.

public action of Jesus, and it is an exceedingly strange sight to envision: Jesus riding two animals of different sizes (apparently at the same time) into Jerusalem (21:1–7). Jesus' birth fulfills a prophecy that a virgin[2] will bear a child named Emmanuel, even though that is not his name (1:20–23). Jesus fulfills four prophecies simply by being born in and by moving to or living in certain places: Bethlehem (2:4–6), Egypt (2:14–15), Nazareth (2:23), and Capernaum (4:13–16). He fulfills four more prophecies by teaching in parables (13:34–35), by performing faith healings and exorcisms (8:16–17), by ordering those he had healed not to talk about him (12:15–21), and by being vindicated by God after being rejected by the leaders of his people (21:33–42).

The remaining seven prophecies quoted by Matthew are fulfilled by people other than Jesus:

- Herod, by slaughtering babies in the vicinity of Bethlehem (2:16–18)

- John the Baptizer, by preaching in the desert (3:1–3) and by preparing the way for Jesus (11:10)

- those who hear Jesus' parables, by not understanding them (13:10–15)

- Pharisees, by being hypocrites (15:7–9)

- the disciples, by running away when Jesus is arrested (26:31, 56)

- the priests, by how they spend the money returned by Judas (27:3–10)

Matthew did not invent the notion that Jesus fulfilled prophecy. He found it in his two literary sources: Mark and Q. It must have been a very early notion in the Jesus movement because the belief that Jesus died and rose "according to the scriptures" is among those that Paul, our earliest Christian writer, received from others before him (1 Cor 15:3–4). But Matthew is the writer who develops this belief most extensively and is the only evangelist to make fulfillment of prophecy a major theme in his gospel.

Matthew did not have to start from scratch in documenting how prophecies were fulfilled in the story of Jesus. Four of Matthew's fulfillment scenes are copied from Mark and one from Q.[3] The other twelve are

---

2. I am convinced that Matthew does not believe in the virgin birth (see Miller, "Wonder Baby," 10, 16; and Miller, *Born Divine*, 195–206), but because Matthew's story has always been understood that way, I will not belabor my position here.

3. The Q Gospel was composed of material, almost entirely of teachings attributed to Jesus, that Matthew and Luke used as a source. Although no copy of Q has been found, scholars have inferred its existence and reconstructed its probable contents by examining material shared by Matthew and Luke but not found in Mark. See Miller, *Complete Gospels*, 257–78.

original to him.[4] Of those twelve scenes, there are three in which prophecies are fulfilled by events that only Matthew reports (the journey to Egypt, the massacre of the babies, and the disposition of Judas' money). In these three cases we have to reckon with the probability that Matthew created the scenes precisely to fulfill prophecies (see below). In the remaining nine scenes Matthew discovered prophecies fulfilled in stories that came to him from tradition.[5]

How Matthew Helps Jesus Fulfill Prophecy

This section of the chapter analyzes the different kinds of creativity involved in the ways Matthew matches prophecy to fulfillment: connecting prophecies to events that do not fulfill them in any obvious way, quoting scripture selectively, translating scripture selectively, fabricating prophecies, tailoring stories so that they can fulfill prophecy, and "retrofitting"[6] prophecies so that Jesus can fulfill them.

Awkward Pairings of Prophecy and Fulfillment

Nine of Matthew's fulfillment scenes are based on details in stories that circulated prior to his gospel. For eight out of those nine scenes, however,[7] there is no evidence that anyone other than Matthew noticed that those narrative details fulfilled prophecy. Matthew apparently pondered stories about Jesus in the light of the Jewish scriptures, searching for prophecies that those stories might fulfill. Perhaps he was put on this track by the five fulfillment scenes in Mark and Q, and then his familiarity with the scrip-

4. One of these scenes, Jesus' donkey ride into Jerusalem, occurs independently in the Gospel of John, which quotes the same prophecy as Matthew, though without setting Jesus on two animals. Some scholars argue that Matthew inherited some or all of the other fulfillment scenes from a pre-Matthean source, but the existence of this hypothetical source is very speculative and impossible to confirm. Besides, for our purpose it makes no difference whether Matthew himself came up with these scenes or whether he took them over from earlier Christian thinkers. For our study we can stipulate that "Matthew" designates whoever was responsible for the elements in his gospel that are found nowhere else.

5. In three of those scenes Matthew sees prophecies fulfilled in circumstances to which Luke independently attests (that Jesus was born to a virgin and in Bethlehem) or that are common knowledge (that Jesus was from Nazareth). In the other six fulfillment scenes Matthew attaches a prophecy to a scene he takes from Mark.

6. The term "retrofitting" is explained on p. 139.

7. The scene of Jesus riding a donkey into Jerusalem (noted above) is the only exception.

tures enabled him to see the fulfillment of far more prophecies than others before him had seen.

It is worthwhile asking *why* others had not noticed that prophecies were fulfilled in any of those eight scenes. After all, Matthew's intense interest in the fulfillment of prophecies gives the impression that pointing them out was a primary task of someone telling the story of Jesus' life. Once the New Testament became a fixture in Christianity, Matthew's position as the favored gospel set the tone for what readers expect in all the gospels, all the more so because Matthew loads five fulfillment scenes into his infancy narrative. The first pages of the New Testament are thus dense with prophecy. Christians who learn the life of Jesus starting with Matthew can easily get the impression that Jesus fulfilled so many prophecies that his fulfillments must have been obvious, not only to his disciples, but to anyone who knew the scriptures, especially to the Jewish religious authorities.

Contrary to such an impression, however, Matthew was the only evangelist to notice that prophecies were fulfilled in those eight scenes. Apparently those fulfillments were not as obvious as Matthew makes them seem to be. Why not? If, for example, everyone knew that Jesus was from Nazareth, why didn't they recognize that he thereby fulfilled the prophecy, "He will be called a Nazorean" (2:23)? In this strange case, the answer is simple: no such prophecy exists (see below). But in the other seven cases Matthew quotes authentic scriptures, and two of those are so well matched to what fulfills them that perhaps the only reason Matthew alone made the connection is simply because he knew the prophets better than others in the Jesus movement. Those two cases are Jesus' birth in Bethlehem, which fulfilled a verse from Micah about a ruler of Israel being born in that town (2:6), and Jesus' decision to hide the meaning of his teaching by using parables, which fulfilled God's command to Isaiah to make sure that the people do not understand his message (13:10–15).

In the five remaining scenes in our analysis, the most likely reason why no one other than Matthew identified them as prophecy fulfillments is that the prophecies Matthew quotes are awkwardly paired to the stories that allegedly fulfill them.

(1) *Matt 1:23 (Isa 7:14)*. We should not be puzzled that no one besides Matthew would think that Jesus fulfilled a prophecy that a virgin would give birth to a boy named Emmanuel. Not only was Emmanuel not Jesus' name, but we have no hard evidence prior to Luke's gospel that Christians believed in the virgin birth.[8]

---

8. See Miller, *Born Divine*, 207–8.

(2) *Matt 4:13–16 (Isa 9:1)*. Who could have recognized that Jesus' move to Capernaum fulfilled a prophecy that people who lived all over northern Palestine had seen a great light?

(3) *Matt 8:17 (Isa 53:4)*. It was surely not obvious that Jesus' healing the sick and casting out demons meant that he was the one who "took our infirmities and bore our diseases."

(4) *Matt 12:15–21 (Isa 42:1–4)*. It is counterintuitive, to say the least, that when Jesus ordered those whom he had healed not to tell others about him that he thereby fulfilled the prophecy that God's servant "will not wrangle or cry aloud, nor will anyone hear his voice in the streets," especially since Jesus often taught and argued with opponents in public, presumably in a loud voice.

(5) *Matt 13:35 (Ps 78:2)*. When, in order to reveal hidden truths, Jesus speaks to the crowds only in parables,[9] it is puzzling how he fulfills a verse from a psalm about someone who tells parables in order to explain traditional wisdom (see Ps 78:2–4), especially since Jesus had earlier decided to tell parables as a means of *hiding* the truth (Matt 13:10–15).

We should also note two additional cases of an awkward fit between prophecy and event in Matthew's infancy narrative. First, it is confusing when Matthew tells us that Jesus fulfilled the prophecy "I called my son out of Egypt" (Hos 11:1) by fleeing *toward* Egypt (Matt 2:15). The prophecy refers to the exodus, in which Egypt is the place of slavery and death, whereas in Matthew's story Egypt is the place of safety. Second, it is less than obvious that a massacre of babies in and around Bethlehem fulfilled the prophecy about Rachel weeping for her children in Ramah (Matt 2:18, quoting Jer 31:5), a town twelve miles from Bethlehem. What would really have helped Matthew would be a prophecy about weeping in *Bethlehem*, but since there is no such prophecy, one about Ramah had to do. Readers without a precise knowledge of Judean geography will mistakenly assume that "Bethlehem and all its surrounding region" (Matt 2:16) includes Ramah. However, if a town twelve miles away counts as the surrounding region, so too does a major chunk of Judea, including Jerusalem, which is five miles from Bethlehem.

In each of these above cases the prophecy fits its "fulfillment" only in a vague or tangential way, sometimes in contradiction to what Matthew elsewhere reports about Jesus and sometimes in contradiction to what the prophecy means in its own context (see below). Many of the connections

---

9. Matthew contradicts himself on this point, for it is not true that Jesus teaches the crowds *only* in parables. Matthew tells of Jesus teaching them many things without using parables. For example, the entire speech in chapter 23 is addressed to "the crowds and the disciples," and none of it is in parables.

Matthew draws between prophecy and fulfillment require a generous imagination. Matthew was well aware that he was pressing some of his prophecies into uses that contradicted their natural meanings, as we can see from the skillful ways in which he lifted them out of their original contexts.

Quoting Scripture Selectively

Seven of the prophecies Matthew identifies as fulfilled are quoted out of context in ways that distort their original meanings. By context here I do not mean *historical* context, which Matthew always ignores, as do all ancient authors interested in the oracular meanings of prophecy. Here I am interested in the immediate *literary* contexts of the lines Matthew quotes. What happens to the meanings Matthew sees in these prophecies when we take into account the lines just before or after the ones Matthew selects for quotation?

(1) In *1:23* Matthew applies to Mary and Jesus the prediction that "the virgin will conceive and give birth to a son" from Isa 7:14.[10] Matthew includes the line about naming the boy Emmanuel, for although Jesus was not called by that name, Matthew nonetheless believes that Jesus fulfills its symbolism. However, the next line of the prophecy (Isa 7:15) has no possible application to Jesus. The same is true for the verse preceding the one Matthew quotes (Isa 7:13). Matthew can read Jesus into Isa 7:14 only if he isolates it from the verses immediately before and after it.

(2) In *2:13–15* Matthew correlates "I called my son out of Egypt" to the family's escape to and return from that country. Matthew quotes only one line of Hosea's pronouncement, and it's easy to see why.

> [1] When Israel was a child I loved him,
>
> I called my son out of Egypt.
>
> [2] The more I called them,
>
> the more they went from me;
>
> they kept sacrificing to the Baals
>
> and offering incense to idols. (Hos 11:1–2)

Hosea 11:1a makes it clear that "my son" in 11:1b is a collective reference to Israel. Quoting the whole verse would wreck the correlation to Jesus. This is doubly true for the next verse, which not only refers to the Israelites in the plural, but also speaks of their idolatry. Both features of Hos 11:2 make it impossible for Matthew to read Jesus into it.

---

10. For a detailed philological and literary analysis of Isa 7:14 in its original context in Isaiah and its reuse by Matthew, see Miller, "Wonder Baby."

(3) In **2:16–18** Matthew asserts that Jeremiah's poetry about "Rachel weeping for her children" because "they are no more" (Jer 31:15) was fulfilled in Herod's massacre of the babies in Bethlehem. The verse that Matthew quotes is the beginning of a short poetic unit that ends at Jer 31:17. Jeremiah 31:16–17 comforts Rachel with the promise that her children will return to her. No wonder Matthew selects only 31:15.

(4) Matthew **3:3** claims that John the Baptizer fulfilled a prophecy about someone in the desert urging people to "prepare the way of the Lord." The quote comes from the Greek version of Isa 40:3. Its immediate context in Isa 40:4 makes it clear that it is the "way," not the voice, that is in the desert. However, Matthew (here borrowing from Mark) needs Isaiah's prophecy to be about a *voice* in the desert in order for John, who preached there, to fulfill it. That is why only Isa 40:3 can be quoted. This quotation has also been retrofitted (see below).

(5) In **8:17** Matthew quotes Isa 53:4a ("he bore our infirmities and carried our diseases"), which Matthew sees fulfilled in Jesus' healings and exorcisms. However, Isa 53:4b ("we accounted him stricken, struck down by God, and afflicted"), as well as the immediate context in 53:3–5, indicates that 53:4a means that God's servant is afflicted with diseases that are punishments for the sins of others. The meaning Matthew assigns to verse 4a would not work if he quoted all of verse 4.

(6) In **13:35** Matthew asserts that when Jesus taught in parables he fulfilled "what had been spoken through the prophet, 'I will open my mouth in parables, I will utter secrets that have been hidden since the foundation of the world'" (adapted from Ps 78:2 LXX).[11] Here the purpose of parables is to reveal secrets never before disclosed, a rationale inconsistent with the prophecy about parables fulfilled earlier in Matthew 13, in which parables are intended to *prevent* the people from understanding (Matt 13:10–17). The function of parables in the quotation in 13:35 is also inconsistent with their function in the psalm itself; there the purpose of parables is to explain "difficult sayings from of old, things that we have heard and known, and that our ancestors have told us" (Ps 78:2b–3 LXX). In Psalm 78 parables are meant to shed light on traditional wisdom sayings that every generation knows (see Ps 78:4). Those sayings might be hard to understand but are not secrets, as they are in Matthew's adapted quotation. In order to impute this different meaning to the psalm, Matthew rewrote the second half of Ps 78:2, changing the word that means "difficult things" (*problēmata* in Greek, the source of our word "problem") into one that means "hidden things."

---

11. "LXX" is the symbol for the Septuagint; it is used to tag passages for which the Septuagint's meanings differ in some notable way from meanings in Hebrew.

Matthew's revised version of Ps 78:2 contradicts its plain meaning in its original context: "secrets that have been hidden since the foundation of the world" (as "quoted" by Matthew) cannot be "things that we have heard and known, and that our ancestors have told us" (Ps 78:3).

It's clear why Matthew uses only verse 2 from the psalm; verse 3 would refute his interpretation.

(7) Matthew **26:31** is copied from Mark, who carefully quoted Zech 13:7 out of context so that "I will strike the shepherd and the sheep will be scattered" can be taken as a prophecy about Jesus and his disciples. In Zechariah's own context the sentence Mark extracts expresses God's determination to punish a worthless shepherd and to kill most of his sheep.[12]

These seven cases—two of which come from Mark, and five of which are Matthew's own work—quote the scriptures in such a way as to exclude integral elements in the prophecies that disallow or work against the meanings Matthew reads into them. Matthew's studious process of quoting shows that he is not quoting from memory, for his selective quotations are precise textual maneuvers. It is only because Matthew can consult written texts that he knows exactly which words to include in his quotations and, what is equally important, which words *not* to include. Matthew's deliberate selectivity suggests that he was aware that the prophets he quotes did not think they were prophesying about Jesus. Like the authors of the Qumran peshers, Matthew believes that he has discovered the deeper significance of the prophecies, meanings that God had hidden even from the prophets who uttered them.

Excursus:

Did Matthew quote directly from the scriptures, and does it matter?

We do not, and cannot, know exactly how Matthew obtained the prophecies he quoted. I have described his use of the scriptures as if he had directly consulted actual scriptural texts. That might well have been the case. But it is also possible that the source of Matthew's quotations was what scholars call a "testimony," a pamphlet of sorts containing quotations excerpted from the OT for the purpose of showing that Jesus fulfilled them. Perhaps Matthew copied his quotations verbatim from a testimony source, or perhaps he modified the extracted quotations to suit his own purpose.

12. See pp. 160–61.

Some scholars[13] have theorized that early Christian writers, including some NT authors, relied on such *testimonia* (to use the Latin plural favored by academics). On the one hand, this theory neatly accounts for why the scriptural quotations by Matthew and others are often worded differently than in the OT,[14] and sometimes blend phrases from more than one passage into a novel composite quotation.[15] On the other hand, however, such a theory does not really answer the question of why the quotations are worded as they are; it simply pushes the question one step further back. If a NT author copied his quotations from a testimony, we still have to ask how and why its author, whoever that was, manipulated the texts into the form in which we see them quoted in the NT.

The testimony theory is plausible but suffers from a debilitating weakness: it is unsupported by any direct physical evidence. There are no actual copies of the testimonies that Matthew, or any NT author, supposedly used as sources. However, the more general belief that Christians produced *testimonia* has been at least partly confirmed by Charles Hedrick's recent discovery in Cairo's Coptic Museum of a nearly intact Psalms *Testimonia*. Its Coptic text, presumably translated from Greek, contains about thirty psalm citations correlated to statements about Jesus. "The testimonies are quite similar to those found in the canonical gospels . . . The author of the Psalms Testimony supports traditional motifs from the birth and death of Jesus with citations from the Psalms to show that Jesus' life fulfilled prophecy."[16] The parchment codex was inscribed in the ninth or tenth century, but about the date of the testimony's composition Hedrick cautiously says only that "it appears that it may well have been an early composition."[17] Regardless of its dating, the codex preserves "a virtually complete exemplar of a lost Christian literary genre, the 'handbook' *testimonia*."[18]

Hedrick summarizes the scholarly discussion of the hypothesis that early Christians compiled testimonies into handbooks, and that these were used by NT and patristic authors.[19] He notes the hypothesis's formidable difficulty: "early exemplars of texts written exclusively in 'handbook form' (i.e., a collection of Hebrew Bible texts specifically applied as testimonies to

---

13. See the discussion referenced in note 18 below.

14. For example, the strange quotation in Matt 27:9–10 (see below).

15. For example, the combination of phrases from Isaiah and Zechariah in Matt 21:5 (see below).

16. Hedrick, "Vestiges of an Ancient Coptic Codex," 5.

17. Ibid.

18. Ibid. 6.

19. Ibid., 10–12.

Jesus) have not been found."[20] Hedrick is modest about the significance of his own discovery, arguing that it confirms the testimony hypothesis only "in the broad sense that early Christians collected 'testimonies' to Jesus from the Old Testament and published them as written texts."[21] Hedrick appropriately questions the evidentiary value of *one* document: "Does this testimony handbook represent merely an isolated instance, or does it provide evidence of a lost genre of Christian literature, utilized quite early by Christians, which they later abandoned?"[22]

While nothing indicates that Hedrick's Coptic testimony is a translation of a source used by Matthew, its very existence moves the hypothesis that Matthew used *testimonia* from merely possible to plausible. Still, the existence of such a Matthean source is purely hypothetical, and its contents completely speculative. So such a source has nothing to contribute to the discussion in this chapter. Moreover, it matters not at all to my argument whether Matthew himself, or some earlier author of a hypothetical testimony, was responsible for extracting the scriptural quotations found in the gospel's fulfillment passages. My argument here is that *the Gospel of Matthew* helps Jesus fulfill prophecy by its judiciously selective quotations, regardless of who first produced them.

Therefore, let me stipulate that in all further discussions about how Matthew, or any early Christian writer, manipulated scriptures quoted in his text, names such as "Matthew" designate the author of the text *or* the author of the source from which the author of the text harvested its quotations.

Translating Scripture Selectively

Matthew quoted prophecies selectively because he needed them to carry new meanings. He quoted just the right lines so that the words of the prophets could apply to events in his story once he inserted them into the new contexts he created for them. The careful selectivity with which he extracted his quotations was one way he consciously shaped the prophecies to serve his own purposes.

A similar process by which Matthew selected prophecies has to do with their translation. Some of his quotations of the scriptures accord exactly with the Hebrew text, while others match readings that differ from the Hebrew text.[23] Five of Matthew's fulfillment scenes quote prophecies that

20. Ibid., 12.

21. Ibid.

22. Ibid.

23. It is plausible that Matthew consulted the scriptures in both Hebrew and

Heb vr Greek

differ significantly in the Hebrew and the Greek, and in which the meaning Matthew wants is possible in one version but is ruled out in the other. It makes no difference for our purposes whether Matthew relied on both Hebrew and Greek texts or on different versions of the Septuagint.

(1) *Matt 1:23.* "The virgin will conceive." There is no reference to a virgin in the Hebrew original of Isa 7:14. All versions of the Septuagint use the word *parthenos*, which means "young woman" but can in special circumstances have the meaning of "virgin."[24] Matthew is able to read the meaning he wants into Isaiah only by quoting this prophecy from a Greek translation that allows a meaning not available in the Hebrew text.

(2) *Matt 2:15.* "I called my son out of Egypt." Here Matthew makes the opposite choice. The Hebrew text of Hos 11:1 has "my son" while the Septuagint has "his children." Both versions refer to the people of Israel, but only in the Hebrew wording is it possible for Matthew to see a prophecy about Jesus.

(3) *Matt 8:17.* Matthew asserts that Jesus' many healings and exorcisms fulfilled Isa 53:4, which he quotes in a translation that closely follows the Hebrew: "He took away our illnesses and carried off our diseases." Matthew's translation is accurate, but also creative, for it bends Isaiah's original meaning, which is not that the servant of Yahweh *removes* diseases, but rather that he *suffers* them: "He has borne our infirmities / and carried our diseases." While the translation that Matthew used (or made himself) lets him read this verse as if it were a prophecy about Jesus' healings, the very different Septuagint version cannot be applied to Jesus' healings: "He bears our sins and suffers pain for us" (Isa 53:4 LXX).

(4) *Matt 12:18–21.* Here Matthew quotes Isa 42:1–4. The Hebrew and Greek versions differ only in the final line: "the coastlands wait for his law" (Hebrew) versus "in his name the gentiles will hope" (Greek). The Septuagint here works nicely as a prophecy about Jesus, whereas a rendering that follows the Hebrew text could not.

(5) *Matt 15:8–9.* In this scene, which Matthew copied from Mark, the quoted prophecy is fulfilled by the Pharisees rather than Jesus. In 15:3–6 he criticizes them for devising a law that overrules one of the commandments.

Greek. However, in Matthew's time there were different versions of the Greek translation. Scholars who specialize in the study of the Septuagint have discovered that it underwent a process of revision that lasted several centuries, starting from its origins in the second century BCE—a process "through which some Jewish scribes were working to modify the oldest Greek translation so that they would conform to the tradition behind the Hebrew Bible" (Law, *When God Spoke Greek*, 78). What this means for our study of Matthew is that "even where Matthew follows the Hebrew word for word, he could have been using a Greek revision" (ibid., 100).

24. See Miller, "Wonder Baby," 10; and Miller, *Born Divine*, 189–90.

In this they fulfill Isaiah's prophecy: "This people honors me with their lips, but their heart stays far away from me. Their worship of me is empty, because they insist on teachings that are human regulations" (Isa 29:13 LXX). The last clause of the Hebrew text of Isa 29:13 reads, "their worship of me is a human commandment learned by rote." Only the Septuagint version describes the behavior that Jesus condemns in this scene.

In the five passages just discussed, Matthew is able to connect a prophecy to Jesus only by selecting the version that was right for his purpose. In two cases the prophecies work only because their wording closely follows the Hebrew; in three cases the prophecies are relevant only in a version that departs from the Hebrew original

Fabricating Prophecies

Selective quotation and selectivity in translation are two techniques by which Matthew adopts and adapts the words of the prophets, tailoring them so that they can be fulfilled in his gospel. Both of these techniques show that Matthew knew what he needed his prophecies to say, which guided his careful choices about how and what he quoted from the biblical texts. In two unusual cases, however, Matthew takes a bolder approach by writing prophecies himself and attributing them to the prophets.

Matthew 2:23

"He will be called a Nazorean" is not a quotation from the scriptures, and Matthew knows it. We can tell that he knows it because he presents this prophecy differently than all the quotations in his gospel, in two ways. First, he does not introduce it as a quotation, but instead inserts it into his story in indirect discourse, as a paraphrase: "He [Joseph] settled in a town called Nazareth, in order to fulfill the prediction of the prophets that he will be called a Nazorean." Second, Matthew ascribes the saying generically to "the prophets," rather than to "the prophet" (as in 2:15, for example) or to a named prophet.[25] There is no prophecy about Nazareth in the scriptures; the village is not mentioned anywhere in the OT. Either Matthew created this prophecy out of nothing, or else he got the idea for it from a verse or verses focused on some word that reminded him of the word "Nazorean." Two Hebrew words that could have done the trick for him are *nazir* and

---

25. Paul (e.g., in 1 Cor 15:3–4) refers to the fulfillments of "the scriptures," and Luke to the fulfillments of "the prophets" (Luke 24:25–26 and 44), but in those cases the authors are referring to multiple prophecies, and they do not quote any passages.

netser. A *nazir* (Anglicized as "Nazirite") was a kind of holy man (see Num 6:1–21). Israel's most famous *nazir* was Samson, who identifies himself as such in Judges 16:17: "I am God's Nazirite." (The word is *naziraios* in the Septuagint). *Netser,* Hebrew for "branch," occurs in a prophecy about the Davidic king: "A shoot will grow from the stump of Jesse [David's father], and a branch (*netser*) will spring from its roots" (Isa 11:1).

If either *nazir* or *neṣer* or both are the germ for the mysterious prophecy, it is still an open question whether Matthew came up with "he will be called a Nazorean" from scratch or based it on some verse from scripture. If the latter is the case, scholars can only speculate on where Matthew started and what other passages, if any, he had in mind, for there is no straight line from either Judg 16:17 or Isa 11:1 to Matt 2:23. The only plausible proposal is a Rube Goldberg contraption of bilingual verbal and textual associations, involving three different verses in Isaiah, a Hebrew pun, two variant Septuagint versions of the book of Judges, and a verse from Mark's gospel that Matthew did not include in his own.[26]

Whether Matthew produced this prediction by redoing some verse(s) from the scriptures or directly from his imagination matters little: the fact remains that there is no scripture predicting anything about Nazareth or one of its residents. So why did Matthew go to the trouble of fabricating this prophecy? It was probably because he needed some prophetic legitimation for Jesus' well-known origins in Nazareth, an obscure village with no Davidic or messianic associations. ("Can anything good come from Nazareth?" in John 1:46 has the ring of a derogatory proverb.) Besides, Nazareth is in Galilee, a gentile environment.[27] We can infer from John's gospel that some Jews argued that Jesus could not have been the messiah precisely because he was from Galilee.

> The Anointed One won't come from Galilee, will he? Doesn't scripture teach that the Anointed One is to be descended from David and come from the village of Bethlehem, where David lived? (John 7:41–42; see also 7:52)

A primary purpose of Matthew's infancy narrative was to preempt Jewish objections to Jesus' origins. According to Matthew, Jesus had a legitimate Davidic pedigree through his legal father Joseph.[28] As Matthew tells it, Jesus had been born in Bethlehem and was moved to Galilee as a young child in obedience to a dream sent by God (Matt 2:22). Matthew's final line

---

26. See Miller, *Born Divine,* 117–18, for the details.

27. Matt 4:15 quotes Isaiah, who calls the region "gentile Galilee" (*Galilaia tōn ethnōn,* Isa 8:23 LXX). See also the reference to "gentile Galilee" in 1 Macc 5:15.

28. Miller, *Born Divine,* 89, 91.

in his infancy narrative reports that the family of Jesus settled in Nazareth "in order to fulfill the prediction of the prophets that he will be called a Nazorean." With that, Matthew rests his case that Jesus' origins qualify him to be Israel's true messiah.

Matthew 27:9–10

> [9] And they took the thirty silver coins, the price put on a man's head (this is the price they put on him among the Israelites), [10] and they donated it for the potter's field, as my Lord commanded me.

The prophecy quoted in Matt 27:9–10 is most unusual. It is loosely based on Zech 11:13, from which Matthew quotes a few words and paraphrases some others; finally he adds some of his own. Strangely, Matthew attributes the oracle to *Jeremiah*, to whose prophecy it indirectly alludes, but from which Matthew has taken not a single phrase. There is no convincing explanation for this misattribution, which has perplexed scholars since the earliest centuries of Christianity. A few ancient copyists of Matthew's gospel noticed the mistake, for they corrected the reference, changing Jeremiah to Zechariah, or (strangely) to Isaiah. The fourth-century scholar Eusebius defended Matthew's accuracy, claiming that, either Matthew himself wrote "Zechariah" and a careless scribe was responsible for "Jeremiah," or that the prophecy originally was in the scroll of Jeremiah but was deleted by some evildoer.[29] Eusebius offers no evidence for either theory, and the second one is, frankly, unbelievable. What his lame attempt to exonerate Matthew shows is that Eusebius was unable to identify any text in Jeremiah from which the alleged prophecy might be even loosely paraphrased. No scholar since Eusebius has done any better. Some have speculated that the mistake is due to Matthew's faulty memory,[30] but that is most unlikely; almost certainly Matthew is riffing on a written text, not quoting from memory (see below). Other scholars have theorized that Matthew deliberately wrote "Jeremiah" as a shorthand way to refer to a passage that conflates Zechariah and Jeremiah. That explanation cannot be ruled out but seems implausible because there is no actual material from the text of Jeremiah in Matt 27:9–10. In a few pages I will offer another explanation—an educated guess at best—for the "Jeremiah" in Matt 27:9.

---

29. Eusebius, *Demonstration of the Gospel* 10.4, cited in Davies and Allison, *Matthew 19–28*, 568.

30. As I did in Miller, *Born Divine*, 159.

We can test how the prophecy in Matthew compares to Zechariah's text by analyzing Matt 27:9–10 one phrase at a time. This is unavoidably tedious, but necessary to demonstrate that Matthew himself is the author of the prediction he attributes to a prophet. (Readers who are not intrigued by the nuts and bolts of detailed textual comparison can skip to the conclusion.) For reference, here is Zech 11:13, in both its Hebrew and Greek versions.[31]

Hebrew	*Septuagint*
Yahweh said to me, "Throw it to the potter"—this handsome price at which I was valued by them. So I took the thirty silver coins and threw them to the potter in the house of Yahweh.[164]	The Lord said to me, "Drop them into the furnace, and I will see if it is good metal, as I was proved for their sakes." And I took the thirty silver coins and threw them into the furnace in the house of the Lord.

MATT 27:9A: *"THEY TOOK THE THIRTY SILVER COINS"*

This matches the Septuagint word for word, even though its meaning in Matthew differs on a key particular, the subject of the clause: in Matthew "they" took the money, whereas in Zechariah "I" took it. "I" is the subject in both the Hebrew and the Septuagint, but the Septuagint contains a peculiar ambiguity that Matthew exploits: in this particular tense of the Greek verb (the aorist tense) the first-person singular and the third-person plural forms are spelled alike. The same Greek word (*elabon*) thus means "I took" and "they took"; which of those two meanings is intended in any given sentence must be determined by context, and Zechariah's context clearly requires the verb to mean "I took." There is no ambiguity in the Hebrew text, and so only the Septuagint version of this clause allows Matthew to retrofit[32] it to match his story. This retrofit is crucial to Matthew's point, since his narrative requires the money to be used by priests, not by an individual, and certainly not by the speaker of the prophecy, as in Zechariah. This particular retrofit is an elegant one, for it has altered the meaning of the key word without changing its spelling.

31. This translation is adapted from the NRSV, reading the Hebrew "potter" instead of the Syriac "treasury" (see below).

32. See below (p. 139) for an explanation of "retrofitting."

MATT 27:9B: *"THE PRICE PUT ON A MAN'S HEAD"*

This clause paraphrases the Hebrew, which reads "this handsome price at which I was valued by them." Matthew's rewording again avoids the "I" in the original. The Septuagint has a completely different sense here and matches nothing in Matthew's wording or meaning. So, while Matthew's first clause (v. 9a) is taken from the Septuagint, his second depends on the wording of the Hebrew text. That is why we must infer that Matthew was not quoting from memory but working—carefully and precisely—from texts.

MATT 27:9C: *"THIS IS THE PRICE THEY PUT ON HIM AMONG THE ISRAELITES"*

Neither the Hebrew nor the Septuagint has anything corresponding to this. It seems to be Matthew's own explanatory elaboration on the "by them" in the previous Hebrew clause.

MATT 27:10A: *"AND THEY DONATED IT FOR THE POTTER'S FIELD"*

Most of this appears to be a selective and inventive paraphrase based on two Hebrew phrases in Zechariah ("throw them [the coins] to the potter . . . and I threw them into the house of the Lord into the potter"). Matthew's "field" seems to be an allusion to Jeremiah (see below); Zechariah has no reference to a field.

Most modern English Bibles deviate—with good reason—from the Hebrew text of Zech 11:13 and read "treasury" rather than "potter," relying on the wording in the ancient Syriac and Aramaic translations of this verse. The two words are almost identical in Hebrew: "the potter" is *hayotser* and "the treasury" is *ha'otser*.[33] The Aramaic and the Syriac version were apparently translated from the original wording ("treasury"), which was later miscopied as "potter" (only one letter is different: היוצר versus האוצר) into the standard Hebrew text.[34] Since "potter" makes no sense in the sentence and since "treasury" fits the context, this is one case where the standard Hebrew text is clearly mistaken. Matthew seems to have known this potter/treasury tension in Zechariah's text because Matthew has the priests both

---

33. In transliterating Hebrew, the ' represents the silent letter א.

34. Meyers and Meyers, *Zechariah*, 277.

discuss putting Judas' money into the *treasury* and using it to buy the *potter's* field (Matt 27:6–7).

MATT 27:10B: "AS MY LORD COMMANDED ME"

The "me" is puzzling; since the prophecy concerns what "they" did, how can what "they" did comply with what the Lord commanded "me"? Scholars can only guess at Matthew's inspiration for this phrase, which is not found in Zechariah. The best surmise is that it refers to God's commands to Jeremiah to visit a potter's workshop (Jer 18–19) and to buy a field (Jer 32).[35]

CONCLUSION

The prophecy quoted in Matt 27:9–10 is neither copied nor paraphrased from any biblical text. It is Matthew's own construction, most of it based loosely on Zech 11:13. However, the central action described in the prophecy, and the deed that Matthew narrates as its fulfillment—the purchase of a field from a potter—is not found in Zechariah, and not anywhere else in the Old Testament.

WHY (PERHAPS) MATTHEW ATTRIBUTES
THE PREDICTION TO JEREMIAH

Matthew created the "quotation" in 27:9–10, but he did not make it up from scratch. His erroneous attribution of the prophecy to Jeremiah, whether inadvertent or intentional, tells us where to find the raw material out of which it was created. There are only two parts of the sprawling book of Jeremiah that are relevant to the prophecy Matthew has constructed: Jeremiah 18–19 and 32. In Jeremiah 18–19 Yahweh directs the prophet to visit a potter's workshop, at which Jeremiah receives a revelation (Jer 18:1–11), and to buy an earthenware jug and perform a prophetic sign with it (Jer 19:1–13). In Jer 32:5–15 Yahweh instructs Jeremiah to buy a field for a cousin, for which Jeremiah pays seventeen (not thirty) silver coins (Jer 32:9). Jeremiah 18–19 has a potter but no field; Jeremiah 32 has a field but no potter. Still, there are a few peripheral details that link these two passages with one another and with the story in Matthew 27: Jeremiah 19 mentions a purchase (19:1), "innocent blood" (19:4; see Matt 27:4), and the renaming of a place used for

---

35. Davies and Allison, *Matthew 19–28*, 570.

burials (19:6, 11; see Matt 27:8).[36] In Jeremiah 32 the prophet buys a field with silver coins (32:9) and seals the title deed in an earthenware jar (32:14). So although Matthew did not quote Jeremiah, he seems to have been thinking about him while constructing the prophecy in Matt 27:9–10.

Tailoring Stories to Fulfill Prophecy

The numerous prophecy-fulfillment scenes in Matthew are an obvious indication that the author considers prophecy to be a vital part of his story of Jesus. In a few scenes Matthew goes so far as to treat prophecies as source material for his narrative, using details in the prophecies to shape the scenes in order to spotlight how the actions in the scenes fulfill the prophecies with extraordinary precision. There are three scenes in which it is fairly easy to track how Matthew tailors the stories to fit the prophecies.

Matthew 4:15–16

In recounting the start of Jesus' public career, Matthew follows Mark's outline: Matt 4:12 = Mark 1:14 and Matt 4:17 = Mark 1:15 (see figure 1).

---

36. Ibid., 569.

Figure 1

Jesus moves to Galilee

Mark 1:14–15	Matthew 4:12–17	Isaiah 9:1 (Septuagint)
[14]After John was locked up, Jesus came to Galilee	[12]When Jesus heard that John had been locked up, he headed for Galilee. [13]He took leave of Nazareth to go and settle down in Capernaum-by-the-sea, in the territory of Zebulun and Naphtali, [14]in order to fulfill the prediction spoken through Isaiah the prophet:	
	[15]Land of Zebulun and of Naphtali, the way to the sea,	Region of Zebulun, land of Naphtali, the way of the sea, and those survivors who live on the coast and across the Jordan,
	across the Jordan, Galilee of the gentiles.	Galilee of the gentiles, the remnant of the Judeans.
	[16]The people who languished in darkness have seen a great light, those who have wasted away in the shadow of death, for them a light has dawned.	The people who walked in darkness, look, a great light. Those who live in the region and shadow of death, a light will shine for you.
proclaiming God's good news. [15]His message went: "The time is up: the empire of God is closing in! Change your ways, and put your trust in the good news."	[17]From that time on Jesus began to proclaim: "Change your ways because the empire of Heaven is closing in."	

Between Mark 1:14 and 1:15 Matthew inserts a detailed geographical elaboration of Jesus' movements in Galilee (Matt 4:13), followed by Matthew's fulfillment formula (Matt 4:14) and his quotation of Isa 9:1–2 (Matt 4:15–16). The prophet whom Matthew cites, Isaiah, mentions Galilee along with the old Israelite tribal names Zebulun and Naphtali and locates them on the way to the sea and across the Jordan River (Isa 9:1). In Matt 4:13, Matthew uses the geographical markers from Isa 9:1 to fill out the description of Jesus' movements that he found in Mark. Matthew knows from Mark that Jesus had a house in Capernaum, a town on the coast of the Sea of Galilee. (Mark refers to "his house" in that town in Mark 2:1 and 2:15.) So Matthew reports that Jesus moved from Nazareth to Capernaum, which allows Matthew to work the word "sea" from the Isaiah verse into 4:13. He also describes Capernaum as "in the territory of Zebulun and Naphtali," which is illogical: how can a town be in two territories? (What would Americans think if a town were described as "in the territories of California and Arizona"?) Matthew cannot work Isaiah's "across the Jordan" into 4:13 because Jesus does not cross that river in traveling from Nazareth to Capernaum. All of Galilee is on the west side of the Jordan, and Capernaum is several miles around the lakeshore from the point where that river enters the Sea of Galilee. To be geographically precise, Nazareth is in Zebulun and Capernaum in Naphtali.[37] Strictly speaking, then, Matthew describes Jesus leaving Zebulun to move to Naphtali. But this is a minor detail because Matthew is focused on the phrase "gentile Galilee." For Matthew, that is what brings out the religious point of this prophecy about geography. By portraying Jesus as fulfilling this prophecy, Matthew shows that Jesus was sent for both Jews and gentiles.

Matthew 21:4–5

In this scene Jesus rides into Jerusalem to the cheers of a crowd. Matthew 21:1–9 follows Mark 11:1–10 closely, except for two features (see figure 2).

---

37. Using the maps in the *HarperCollins Study Bible* (2006), compare the locations of the two first-century-CE towns on Map 13 with the eleventh-century-BCE tribal boundaries on Map 3. I know of no map that commits the anachronism of combining first-century town names and eleventh-century tribal areas.

Figure 2

How many animals did Jesus ride?

Mark 11:1–10

[1]When they get close to Jerusalem, near Bethphage and Bethany at the Mount of Olives, he sends off two of his disciples [2]with these instructions: "Go into the village across the way, and after you enter it, right away you'll find *a colt* tied up, one that has never been ridden. Untie *it* and bring *it* here. [3]If anyone says, 'Why are you doing this?' just say, '*Its* master needs *it* and he will send *it* back here right away.'"

[4]They set out and found a colt tied up at the door out on the street, and they untie it. [5]Some of the people standing around started saying to them, "What do you think you're doing, untying that colt?" [6]But they said just what Jesus had told them to say, so they left them alone.
[7]So they bring *the colt* to Jesus, and they throw their cloaks over *it*; then he got on *it*.

[8]And many people spread their cloaks on the road, while others cut leafy branches from the fields. [9]Those leading the way and those following kept shouting,

>Hosanna! Blessed is the one who comes in the name of the Lord!
>[10]Blessed is the coming kingdom of our father David!
>Hosanna in the highest!

Matthew 21:1–9

[1]When they got close to Jerusalem, and came to Bethphage at the Mount of Olives, then Jesus sent two disciples ahead [2]with these instructions: "Go into the village across the way, and right away you will find *a donkey* tied up, *and a colt* alongside her. Untie *them* and bring *them* to me. [3]And if anyone says anything to you, just say, '*Their* Master needs *them* and he will send *them* back right away.'" [4]This happened in order to fulfill the prediction spoken through the prophet:

>[5]Tell the daughter of Zion,
>Look, your king comes to you
>gently, mounted on a donkey
>and on a colt, the foal of a pack animal.

[6]Then the disciples went and did as Jesus instructed them,

[7]and brought *the donkey and colt* and they placed their cloaks on *them*, and he sat on top of *them*. [8]The enormous crowd spread their cloaks on the road, and others cut branches from the trees and spread them on the road. [9]The crowds leading the way and those following kept shouting,

>Hosanna to the son of David!
>"Blessed is the one who comes in the name of the Lord!"

>Hosanna in the highest.

(1) Matthew interrupts the narrative to announce the fulfillment of a prophecy (21:4), which he then quotes (21:5). Matthew 21:5 begins with a phrase from Isa 62:11 and then selectively quotes Zech 9:9.

Matt 21:5	*Isa 62:11*
Tell the daughter of Zion,	Tell the daughter of Zion
	Zech 9:9
Look, your king is coming to you	Look, your king is coming to you,
	righteous and rescuing,
in gentleness,	in gentleness,
mounted on a donkey	mounted on a pack animal
and a colt, the foal of a pack animal.	and a young colt.

Mark's scenario, in which Jesus rides a donkey into Jerusalem while a crowd cheers for the "coming kingdom," apparently reminded Matthew of Zechariah's prophecy. Zech 9:9 seems to mention two animals, a "donkey" and a "colt, the foal of a donkey." In the Hebrew text of Zech 9:9 it is clear that these are two descriptions of the same beast, a juvenile donkey: "mounted on a donkey, / on a colt, the foal of a donkey." Parallel phrasing like this (scholars call it "synonymous parallelism") is quite common in Hebrew poetry. But in the Septuagint version of Zechariah the Greek word for "and" appears: "mounted on a pack animal *and* a young colt." Matthew's "quotation" of Zech 9:9 blends elements from the original Hebrew with the Greek version: the gentle king is "mounted on a donkey / and on a colt, the foal of a pack animal" (Matt 21:5).

(2) Matthew takes the Septuagint wording of this prophecy quite literally, as if it describes a king riding two animals. Accordingly, Matthew rewrites Mark's story so that now the disciples bring a donkey *and* a colt to Jesus and, sure enough, he sits on both of them (Matt 21:7). For consistency, Matthew also goes back earlier in the scene and adds a second animal to the report of the finding of the donkey by the disciples (Mark 11:2//Matt 21:2). He also changes the two pronouns referring to the donkey in the next verse so that Mark's "it" becomes "them" (Mark 11:3//Matt 21:3).

By way of comparison, note that the Gospel of John also quotes Zech 9:9 in connection with its much briefer version of this scene (John 12:12–15). John's version of the prophecy sensibly mentions only one animal.

Matthew 27:9

[handwritten: wrong Prophet]

Figure 3

Thirty Silver Coins

Mark 14:10–11	**Matthew 26:14–15**
[10]And Judas Iscariot, one of the Twelve, went off to the chief priests to turn him over to them. [11]When they heard, they were delighted, and promised to pay him in silver.	[14]Then one of the Twelve, Judas Iscariot by name, went to the chief priests [15]and said, "What are you willing to pay me if I turn him over to you?" They agreed on *thirty silver coins.*

Matthew 27:3–10

[3]Then Judas, who had turned him in, realizing that Jesus had been condemned, was overcome with remorse and returned the *thirty silver coins* to the chief priests and elders. [4]He said, "I've made a serious mistake in turning in this blameless man."

But they said, "What do we care? That's your business."

[5]And hurling the silver into the temple he slunk off, and went out and hanged himself.

[6]The chief priests took the silver and said, "It wouldn't be right to put this into the temple treasury, since it's blood money."

[7]So they devised a plan and bought the potter's field as a burial ground for foreigners. [8]As a result, that field has been called Bloody Field even to this day. [9]Then the prediction spoken through Jeremiah the prophet was fulfilled:

> And they took the *thirty silver coins*, the price put on a man's head (this is the price they put on him among the Israelites), [10]and they donated it for the potter's field, as my Lord commanded me.

Zechariah 11:12–13

[12]They counted out my wages: *thirty silver coins.* [13]Then the Lord said to me, "Throw it into the treasury"—the handsome price at which they valued me. So I took the *thirty silver coins* and threw them into the treasury in the house of the Lord.

Mark 14:10–11 tells of Judas' approach to the high priests and his offer to betray Jesus, for which the priests promise to pay him. When Matthew rewrites this brief scene, he has Judas demand the money up front. Matthew also specifies the amount of money agreed on by Judas and the priests: thirty silver pieces (Matt 26:14–15). Mark does not mention the amount, nor does Luke or John. From what source has Matthew obtained this inside information? Answer: the prophets.

Later in Matthew's story Judas, overwhelmed by guilt, flings the money back at the priests and then commits suicide (Matt 27:3–5). When the priests use the money to buy some land, Matthew informs us that this purchase fulfilled Jeremiah's prophecy about thirty pieces of silver (Matt 27:6–10). The prophecy in question is actually from Zechariah, not Jeremiah. (See above for attempts to explain Matthew's mistake.) A close comparison of

Zech 11:12–13 and Matt 27:3–10 (a scene unique to Matthew's gospel) reveals where Matthew discovered that Judas had returned the money and had done so by throwing it into the temple.

What these three examples reveal about Matthew's use of prophecy

Matt 4:14–16. To position Jesus as fulfiller of prophecy, Matthew chooses descriptive details from Isaiah and crafts them into elaborations on the reports and clues that he found in Mark. The reason why Jesus' movements match the words of prophecy so closely—though not exactly—is that Matthew has derived Jesus' itinerary from those very words.

Matt 21:4–5. Matthew creates a ludicrous scene: Jesus stunt-rides two animals into Jerusalem. The only purpose Matthew could have had in changing Mark's straightforward narrative into such a spectacle is to demonstrate that Jesus fulfilled prophecy to the letter. Obviously, Matthew's Jesus can fulfill this prophecy in this odd manner only because Matthew rigs the story with details cribbed from the "fulfilled" prophecy. This bizarre scene shows to what extremes Matthew was willing to go to portray Jesus as the fulfiller of prophecy.

Matt 26:15 and 27:9. With the thirty silver coins, Matthew again inserts a detail from a prophecy into a story that he borrowed from Mark. A chapter later, Matthew relies on the readers' memory of that detail to confirm that the prophecy was fulfilled to the letter.

Matthew's specification of thirty silver pieces and his report that Judas returned the money are small but lucid examples of how Matthew used the OT as a *source* of information for the story of Jesus. It is not the case that Matthew knew a factually accurate account of the life of Jesus and then realized, from his knowledge of scripture, that the life of Jesus fulfilled prophecy. Rather, the process worked in the opposite direction. *Matthew started with the conviction that Jesus' life must have fulfilled scripture; then he went back to study the scriptures with the intention of finding out more about what had happened in Jesus' life.* That is how he, alone out of the four evangelists, "knows," for example, that Jesus rode two animals into Jerusalem and that Judas was paid thirty silver pieces.

Retrofitting Prophecies

The three scenes analyzed above are passages in which Matthew has crafted his narrative so as to adjust it to prophecy. Those prophecies can be fulfilled only because Matthew adds details from those very prophecies into his narrative. Another process used by NT authors to match prophecy to events works in the opposite direction, altering the prophecies so as to adjust them to the circumstances that fulfill them. We have already seen examples of the results of this process in the way some prophetic passages are reworded in the Septuagint and the Qumran peshers.

I call this process "retrofitting." The term comes from engineering and names a process in which an already built object is added to or changed in some way so that it can perform a function for which it was not originally designed. Applied to the NT, retrofitting is an apt analogy for the manner in which OT passages that by themselves do not work well as predictions about Jesus are rewritten so that they can be more easily correlated with beliefs or stories about Jesus. Sometimes that rewriting involved deleting parts of the OT passage that would ruin the correlation with Jesus. Sometimes it involved changing key words in the passage or adding some new ones. Sometimes it involved stitching together parts of two or more different scriptures to produce a hybrid passage. Some retrofits show a fair amount of textual intervention, whereas others required just a bit of rewriting in just the right place. But the fact that NT writers felt the need to change the OT verses at all shows two things. First, the NT authors were well aware that the OT in its own words often would not be seen as a prediction of Jesus. In other words, they figured that it was most unlikely that someone reading or hearing the OT text in question would think that it was a prophecy about Jesus. The connection the NT author saw between the OT and Jesus was seen *despite* the actual words of the original passage, which is why it needed to be retrofitted. Second, the textual retrofitting also shows that the "flow" of understanding in these cases is *from* Christian beliefs about Jesus *to* the OT, not the other way around. As we will see over and over again, the Christian authors came to understand the OT as they did because they already believed in Jesus. It is, emphatically, not the case that they came to believe in Jesus because of what they read in the OT. If that were the case there would have been no need for the retrofits. Those textual manipulations betray the frustrations of Christian authors hunting for prophecies of Jesus but finding passages that did not really fit with what they wanted to show.

There are five cases of retrofitting in Matthew.

Matthew 1:23

Matthew has made a slight but necessary alteration in the wording of Isa 7:14: he has changed the form of the verb "to name" from second-person singular to third-person plural. In Isaiah (LXX) it is *you* who will name the child, whereas in Matthew "*they* will name him Emmanuel." This grammatical adjustment is necessary because without it the "you" in the prophecy would refer to Joseph and thus contradict the angel's command to him to name the boy Jesus (1:21). So who is the "they" who will call Jesus Emmanuel? According to the way Matthew lays out his sentence, the antecedent of "they" is the people whom Jesus will save from their sins. Matthew's grammatical design here is ingenious because it makes his Christian audience—who are not characters in the story—the ones who will refer to their savior by the name that means "God is with us."

Matthew 2:6

Matthew has altered the text of Micah's prophecy about Bethlehem in two ways. First, he replaces "Ephrathah" with "the land of Judah," probably to make the geographical reference more intelligible to his audience. That is not really retrofitting, but the second alteration is. He adds one Greek word (*oudamōs*) that means "not at all" or "in no way" to the beginning of the second line, emphatically contradicting Micah's assertion that Bethlehem is "the smallest of the clans of Judah."

> *Micah*: You, Bethlehem of Ephrathah,
>> who are the smallest of the clans of Judah.

> *Matthew*: You, Bethlehem, in the land of Judah,
>> *in no way* are you least among the leaders of Judah.

From Matthew's perspective, Jesus had changed the status of Bethlehem. Although it had been a small and unassuming town, it was now famous because it was the birthplace of the Messiah.

Matthew's alteration here is interesting because it was unnecessary. The prophecy would work fine without Matthew's retrofit, but with the new wording it works even better.

Matthew 3:3

This altered quotation came to Matthew already retrofitted by Mark.[38] Isaiah 40:3 LXX calls for the preparation of a "way" (a highway in the desert) for God, which Mark had made into a way for Jesus. This alteration in meaning was effected by changing "the paths of our God" into "his paths," which can then be read as a reference to Jesus' paths rather than God's.

Matthew 11:10

Matthew found this quotation already retrofitted in the Q Gospel: John the Baptizer "is the one about whom it is written, 'See I am sending my messenger before you, / who will prepare your way before you.'" The quotation is based on God's declaration in Mal 3:1 that he is sending his messenger, who "will survey the way before _me_," which Q had tweaked to "will prepare _your_ way before _you_."

Mal 3:1a	Q 7:27 (Mt 11:10)
See, I am sending my messenger	Here is my messenger
	whom I send on ahead of you
to prepare the way before me.	to prepare your way before you

Q's retrofit was necessary because the "way" in Malachi is the way before God ("me"). Only by altering the wording as Q did could the prophecy be made to mean that John prepared the way before Jesus ("you").

Matthew 27:9–10

We saw above how Matthew uses elements in this prophecy to craft the story of the events that fulfill it. Matthew also took great liberties with his prophetic source,[39] wording the prophecy to match his story. In this passage Matthew's extensive textual manipulation goes beyond retrofitting, since he has not only reworded Zechariah, but has freely composed parts of the prophecy himself. In this unusual case it is fair to say that Matthew has created both the prophecy and the event that fulfills it.

38. Mark 1:3; see pp. 157–58.
39. Zech 11:13; see pp. 129–31.

Summary

Looking back over the various textual operations that Matthew performed in presenting prophecies and narrating their fulfillments, it is evident that far more was involved than simply correlating appropriate scriptural predictions with the events that obviously fulfilled them. In five cases the links between prophecies and their fulfillments are quite subtle (or far-fetched, depending on one's perspective). Seven of the prophecies Matthew quotes are in fact pieces of larger prophecies that are lifted from contexts hostile to the meanings Matthew requires. Five prophecies have alternate meanings in their Hebrew or Greek versions that cannot apply to the scenes that fulfill them. Two prophecies do not actually come from the scriptures but are ad hoc fabrications. Three gospel stories borrow key details from the very prophecies they are supposed to fulfill. And five prophecies have been retrofitted to enable them to match the events to which they are correlated.

How Matthew Uses Prophecy

So far we have analyzed the various methods by which Matthew selected, edited, and reworded prophecies in order to show how they were fulfilled by stories in his gospel, some of which he fashioned by integrating into them elements from the prophetic texts. Now we will study how Matthew's fulfillment-of-prophecy theme functions in his gospel, and evaluate the claims inherent in how Matthew uses prophecy in his struggle to legitimize the religious self-understanding of the community for which he wrote.

The first tasks in this section of the chapter are to discuss Matthew's larger agenda in constructing his fulfillment-of-prophecy theme, and to suggest a historical-religious context within which Matthew's message that Jesus fulfilled prophecy had its relevance and force. We have seen the difficulties Matthew confronted in constructing his prophecy-fulfillment scenes. To readers of this gospel, ancient and modern, the whole thing can look fairly obvious, as time and again Matthew highlights some element in his narrative and quotes the scripture it fulfills. However, the appearance of an obvious match between prophetic text and gospel story is the result of the ingenuity and intellectual labor Matthew devoted to finding and/or crafting scriptural passages that had no apparent connection to the story of Jesus and then fitting the text to the story or the story to the text. Think about the challenging tasks this project involved. In some cases Matthew carefully extracted quotations from their literary contexts so that he could give them new meanings incompatible with their original ones. In some cases he compared divergent versions of the same prophecy so that he could select the only one amenable to his new interpretation of it. In some cases he embedded details from the prophecies into the gospel stories as he composed or redacted them. In other cases he altered the wordings of prophecies to ensure a better fit between them and his narrative. And in a couple of cases he created the prophecies themselves. If readers get the impression that Jesus clearly and obviously fulfilled prophecies, that is only because Matthew's meticulous work to create that impression succeeded brilliantly.

Something that demanded so much effort must have been important to the one who worked at it. Why was the fulfillment of prophecy so important to Matthew? What was he trying to achieve with it? The protracted argument that Jesus fulfilled prophecy is a crucial element in Matthew's bitter struggle with the Jewish authorities of his day, a struggle to defend the right of his group of Jesus followers to see themselves as the culmination of God's plan for Israel.[40]

Prophecy and Polemic[41]

It is a deeply rooted Christian belief that Jesus fulfilled prophecy. In its most common version, this belief entails that

- the Old Testament contains a number of prophetic predictions about the coming messiah;

- those prophecies were, in effect, waiting to be fulfilled;

- people would know the messiah when he finally came because he would fulfill those prophecies.

That is how most Christians throughout history have understood the term "Old Testament prophecy," and Matthew's gospel has been instrumental in fostering this notion. His method of quoting numerous specific prophecies and pointing out exactly how they were fulfilled gives the cumulative impression that it should have been fairly clear to people who knew the scriptures that Jesus was the long-awaited messiah. So effective has Matthew's gospel been in this regard that Christianity has long puzzled over why the Jews of Jesus' time "rejected" him. Matthew gives the impression that the Jewish leaders knew (or at least should have known) that Jesus was the messiah but

40. For a superb explication of this widely held scholarly understanding of Matthew's community, see Overman, *Matthew's Gospel*, especially his summary concluding chapter (pp. 150–61).

41. This section recapitulates my earlier argument in Miller, *Born Divine*, 162–64.

fiction

opposed him because of their hypocrisy and hard-heartedness. At the very end of his gospel, Matthew makes his accusation explicit: those authorities knew that Jesus had risen from the dead but conspired to deceive their own people about the truth of his resurrection.

> [11] Some of the guards [at the tomb] returned to the city and re-ported to the chief priests everything that had happened. [12] They met with the elders and hatched a plan. They bribed the sol-diers with an adequate amount of money [13] and ordered them, "Tell everybody, 'His disciples came at night and stole his body while we were asleep.' [14] If the governor should hear about this, don't worry; we'll deal with him." [15] They took the money and did as they had been instructed. And this story has been passed around among the Jews until this very day. (Matt 28:11–15, SV)

We should pause to examine this brief story because Matthew's atti-tude toward the Jewish leaders bears directly on his proof-from-prophecy theme. The first thing to be said about this scene is that there is not a shred of historical evidence for the conspiracy Matthew describes. The conspiracy Matthew imagines is utterly implausible, for it asks us to believe that sol-diers would confess to the most serious offense soldiers on guard duty can commit: sleeping while on watch, which in the Roman army was punishable by death. Besides being stupid, the excuse is also exceedingly lame: if the guards were asleep, how could they know that the disciples had stolen the body? Moreover, if the scenario had happened the way Matthew says it did, he could not have known about it: if the soldiers really "took the money and did as they had been instructed" (28:15), no one could have known about the alleged bribery and the lying. It isn't difficult to conclude that Matthew made this story up. It is fiction. Now the gospels contain many fictions that express truth—stories that, while not historically true, communicate truths that are more important than historical facts. (Jesus' parables and the stories that he multiplied bread and fish are good examples.) But the story about Jewish leaders covering up Jesus' resurrection is not like those benign fic-tions. This story is a lie. That Matthew told it to counteract the accusation that the disciples had stolen Jesus' body helps us understand the motivation for the lie but does not excuse it.

Matthew's argument from prophecy is intertwined with his polemic against official Judaism. He asserts, not only that his people are right to fol-low Jesus as the Jewish messiah, but also that Jews who do not follow Jesus are unfaithful to Judaism. In its simplest form, Matthew's message to his people is:

a. "We" have a right to exist as a Jewish community, despite the fact that "they" say we don't; and

b. "We" are the only real Jews.[42]

The debate between Matthew's people and the Jewish authorities at that time (i.e., the Pharisees) must have been fierce, to judge from the polemical rhetoric in Matthew's gospel. See, for example, the way Matthew's Jesus rips into the Pharisees in chapter 23. We don't expect cool logic in heated debates, which too often end up with each side even more convinced of its own rightness. And that is precisely the sort of framework in which Matthew's use of prophecy must be placed. Matthew's rhetoric was not designed to win over the Jewish opponents of his community. Nor was Matthew's manipulation of scripture meant to persuade the open-minded, if in that situation there were any such people. It was intended to reinforce the belief of Matthew's own people that all of Jewish history had been building up to Jesus, and thus up to them.

Evaluating Matthew's Claims

Matthew labored with diligence and skill to match numerous prophecies to events in the life of Jesus, thereby creating the cumulative impression that it must have been abundantly clear to those who knew the scriptures that Jesus was the messiah. However, our study of the processes by which Matthew created that impression shows that many of the correlations he makes between stories in his gospel and prophecies as they are actually worded in the scriptures are not obvious, to say the least. Inquiring minds should therefore wonder how fair it was for Matthew to heap blame on the Jewish authorities for rejecting Jesus. Matthew's polemic thus invites a critical assessment of the impression he worked so hard to create, which was that the Jewish people (or at least their leaders) should have embraced Jesus as their messiah because he had fulfilled so many prophecies. We can carry out this assessment by probing the gospel from two perspectives, first from within the story world of Matthew's narrative, and then within the real world of Matthew's own historical context. In the first probe we will ask how Jesus' audience in the gospel might reasonably have been expected to recognize that prophecies were being fulfilled in their midst. In the second probe we

---

42. "Matthew and his community claim the same tradition, the same authority—even, at points, the same roles as formative Judaism. Matthew claims quite explicitly to be the heir of God's kingdom and God's true people over against formative Judaism" (Overman, *Matthew's Gospel*, 153).

will ask how Jews of Matthew's day might reasonably have been expected to respond to Matthew's presentation of Jesus as the fulfiller of prophecy.

Who Knew?

We can assess Matthew's implicit but unmistakable assertion that the people of Jesus' day should have embraced him as their messiah because he had fulfilled so many prophecies by asking how many of Matthew's prophecy fulfillment scenes involve public events or common knowledge about Jesus. If the putative purpose of Jesus' fulfilling prophecy was to persuade people that he was the messiah, that purpose would be defeated if the public does not know about the things that fulfill those prophecies. Before we survey the prophecies in Matthew's gospel on this question, a stipulation is in order: "the public" refers to Jesus' audience, not Matthew's. The Christian readers of this gospel know whatever Matthew tells them, including things that happen away from public view. But Matthew's readers don't need to be persuaded that Jesus is the messiah. The people that needed persuading were the ones who saw and heard Jesus firsthand, or who heard about him from others. How many of the things about Jesus that Matthew claims fulfilled prophecy might the public have known? Tracking that will help us evaluate Matthew's insinuation that Jews should have believed in Jesus because he had fulfilled so many prophecies.

What the public could know

Of the fourteen scenes in which Matthew proclaims that prophecy was fulfilled, only five involve things the public could have known about Jesus.

1. Jesus was from Nazareth (2:23).
2. He had a home in Capernaum (4:13–16).
3. He healed people (8:16–17).
4. He taught (only) in parables (13:34–35).
5. He rode donkeys into Jerusalem (21:4–7).

What the public might have known (but probably did not)

Three other circumstances that Matthew believes fulfill prophecy might have been public knowledge but probably were not:

not true

1. Herod's murder of the infants in and around Bethlehem (2:17–18)

2. Jesus' imposition of confidentiality on those he healed (12:15–21)

3. the Pharisees' hypocrisy (15:7–9)

(1) Did Herod slaughter baby boys in the Bethlehem area? No other ancient source besides Matthew mentions this atrocity, so there is no historical evidence that it happened. Matthew invented this story in order to provide the baby Jesus with an escape from a mass murder mandated by a tyrant that parallels the one from which the baby Moses escaped.[43] But even if this had really happened, there is no reason why people three decades later would think it had something to do with Jesus.

(2) Did Jesus order people he had healed not to talk about him? For him to do so would make little sense. If Jesus did not want to be known as a healer, why is he presented as performing healings in synagogues and before crowds—as Matthew reports many times, including both immediately before (12:9–14) and after (12:22–32) the prophecy-fulfillment scene in 12:15–21? Many scholars agree that this motif of Jesus trying to silence those who know of his powers and his true identity, a motif known as "the messianic secret,"[44] is not based on memories about the historical Jesus but is a literary device invented by Mark and subsequently appropriated by Matthew. But even if it were completely historical, it seems unlikely that it was generally known what Jesus had said privately to those whom he had healed.

(3) Were the Pharisees hypocrites? Human nature being what it is, any large group of human beings will almost certainly include some hypocrites; but there is no reason to think that the Pharisees as a group were any more hypocritical than, for example, followers of Jesus. The overwrought polemic against the Pharisees in the NT gospels—and, comparing the polemical rhetoric of the gospels, Matthew has the ugliest of the four—fits the historical context of the evangelists much better than that of Jesus.

What the public did not know

Four out of Matthew's seventeen prophecy-fulfillment scenes relate to alleged events that, if they happened at all, would not have been public knowledge.

43. Miller, *Born Divine*, 108–9, 125–26, 184.

44. The term was coined in 1901 by German scholar Wilhelm Wrede in *Das Messiasgeheimnis in den Evangelien* (*The Messianic Secret in the Gospels*). For a summary and analysis of this landmark study, see Miller, "*The Messianic Secret* by Wilhelm Wrede."

1. Jesus was born to a virgin (1:23).

2. Jesus was born in Bethlehem (2:6).

3. Jesus had lived in Egypt (2:14–15).

4. The chief priests used the thirty silver pieces that Judas returned to them to buy a potter's field (27:3–7).

(1) It was not public knowledge that Jesus was born to a virgin (1:23)—how could it be, since only his mother could possibly have known? Besides, there is no evidence even that any Christians believed in the virgin birth until late in the first century.[45]

(2) The gospels do not indicate that the public thought that Jesus of Nazareth was born in Bethlehem (Matt 2:1). Matthew and Luke independently attest to this belief, but that tells us nothing about what Jesus' contemporaries might have thought. John 7:41–42 most likely indicates that he was thought *not* to be born in Bethlehem, even by the author of the Fourth Gospel.[46]

(3) There is no evidence that the public was aware that Jesus had resided in Egypt as a small boy (Matt 2:14–15). No other gospel mentions this, Luke's narrative rules it out,[47] and it too nicely fits Matthew's christological agenda of having Jesus symbolically recapitulate Israel's exodus. Jesus' time in Egypt is Matthean fiction.[48]

(4) The public had no way of knowing how the chief priests had spent the money that Judas had flung back to them (27:3–7). Only Matthew tells of this, and he describes it as a decision reached in a closed meeting. If what Matthew narrates really happened, only a few insiders would have known about it. If one wonders how Matthew could have known about this, the answer is that Matthew, like all the evangelists, tells his story from the perspective of an omniscient narrator, who by definition knows everything and so can inform readers of things an *actual* narrator would have no way of knowing. It is only because gospel writers are omniscient narrators that Matthew knows, for example, what Pilate's wife told her husband (Matt 27:19), or that Mark knows such things as what Jesus' opponents said among themselves

---

45. Miller, *Born Divine*, 207–8.

46. Ibid., 181–83.

47. In Luke's story, Jesus' family visits the temple in Jerusalem forty days after his birth (Luke 2:22). After that they straightaway return home to Nazareth (Luke 2:39). There are no gaps in this timeline that allow for Matthew's story about the family's taking refuge in Egypt.

48. Miller, *Born Divine*, 167.

(Mark 11:31–32) and the specific words that Jesus prayed while alone in Gethsemane (Mark 14:32–42).

What only Matthew's readers could know

Finally, the remaining two scenarios in Matthew's gospel that fulfill prophecy depend on prior Christian beliefs for their fulfillment: that John the Baptizer prepared the way for Jesus (Matt 11:10), and that God vindicated him (Matt 21:42). First, people might have agreed that John was preparing the way for the messiah, but that he was preparing the way for Jesus is a transparently Christian interpretation of his message. Second, when Matthew unmistakably implies that Jesus is "the stone that the builders rejected that has become the cornerstone" (21:42), he means that Jesus "has become the cornerstone" by being raised from the dead after being "rejected" (killed) by the "builders" (the Jewish authorities). In these two cases, one must believe that Jesus is the risen messiah *before* one can accept that these two prophecies were fulfilled.

Conclusions

The results of this canvass do not bode well for the notion that Jesus' contemporaries should have recognized that he fulfilled prophecy. Of the ten prophecies in Matthew that Jesus allegedly fulfilled, five involve things that, even if they were historically true, would not have been public knowledge. The other five prophecies, those that Matthew relates to things the public could know about Jesus, do not offer much support to Matthew's case against the Jews because it is difficult to see how the public could have been expected to realize that these five things fulfill the scriptures as Matthew says they do. Let's get specific by briefly taking up those five claims one by one.

(1) Jesus was from Nazareth, thereby fulfilling "He will be called a Nazorean." However, this prophecy is not from the scriptures.

(2) Jesus had a home in Capernaum, thereby fulfilling Isa 9:1. How many folks knew that Jesus *of Nazareth* lived in Capernaum? How were those who did know this supposed to understand that this fact fulfilled a prophecy about the people of the region seeing a great light?

(3) Jesus healed the sick and expelled evil spirits, thereby fulfilling half of Isa 53:4. Anyone who knew anything about Jesus would know of his reputation for being a healer who often performed exorcisms. But why should the public connect his healings and exorcisms to a prophecy about

someone who was sick because "he has borne our infirmities and carried our diseases"?

(4) Anyone who knew anything about Jesus would also know that he told parables. (As noted above, it was not true, as Matthew obviously knows, that Jesus taught *only* in parables.) Perhaps a few people steeped in the scriptures might have recalled that a psalm opens with the declaration, "I will open my mouth in parables" (Ps 78:2), but it is asking too much to expect that many would have made this unlikely connection.

(5) The gospels all present Jesus' donkey ride into Jerusalem as a very public event, though only Matthew and John profess that it fulfilled prophecy. If neither Mark nor Luke linked this event to prophecy, after decades of Christian reflection on it, it is unreasonable to think that bystanders would have done so at the time. Besides, the prophecy is about a king, and so only those who believed or hoped that Jesus was a king would have made the connection to Zechariah's oracle.

It is revealing that Matthew does not present any of the above prophecies as comments made by Jesus himself. Matthew does not portray Jesus pointing out to his audience that he is fulfilling this or that prophecy. Instead, Matthew inserts his prophetic quotations into the narrative by using his own quotation formulas, all of which are direct communications between Matthew and his readers. Matthew interrupts his narrative time and again to inform us which prophecy has just been fulfilled. It is as if Matthew knows that his audience won't grasp that what is happening in the story fulfills scripture unless he points it out to them and provides the appropriate quotation. Since Matthew does not expect his own audience to realize that Jesus fulfills prophecy without expert and explicit guidance, it is unreasonable in the extreme for him to insinuate that Jesus' audience should have gotten the point.

Messianic Prophecies?

In addition to thinking critically about how the Jews in the gospel story could have been expected to recognize that Jesus fulfilled prophecies, we also need to analyze the situation from the perspective of the Jews of Matthew's own time, half a century or more after Jesus' death. Let us suppose for the sake of this inquiry that their only information about Jesus would be via Matthew's gospel.

Would Jews who were familiar with the scriptures, and who were not already followers of Jesus, conclude from the presentation in Matthew's gospel that Jesus really had fulfilled what the prophets had predicted about the messiah? For the limited aim of our inquiry, we do not need to ascertain how subjectively persuaded Matthew's coreligionists would be by his gospel, something that is impossible to do in any case. What we can do—and what is sufficient for our purpose—is determine whether the scriptures Matthew quotes in his fulfillment scenes actually are prophecies about the One who is to come. In this exercise we will examine the ten prophecies that Matthew asserts were fulfilled by Jesus and ask two questions of each: is it a prediction, and whom is it about?

The first question aims to determine what type of utterance a quotation is. Not every quotation from the words of the prophets is a "prophecy" in the sense we mean when we speak of the fulfillment of a prophecy. For example, when the prophets speak the word of the Lord about Israel's past history, there is no prediction to be fulfilled. So we can ask of Matthew's quotations whether they are about the prophets' past, present, or future. If a prophecy is about the future, we can ask a second question: is it a prediction about the messiah? Here we should take the term broadly to refer not only to the anointed one, but also to the ideal Davidic king or the son of God, or some such messianic figure.

Matt 1:23 (Isa 7:14)

This passage, at least in the Greek translation in which Matthew quotes it, is a prediction. However, Isaiah's prediction is about his own immediate future: he expects the boy to be born within the next year or so. Jewish interpretation of this prophecy understood it to have been fulfilled in the birth of Hezekiah, son of Ahaz, the king to whom the prophecy was addressed.[49] Contemporary Jewish tradition did not understand Isa 7:14 to be a prophecy about the messiah.[50]

Matt 2:6 (Mic 5:2 + 2 Sam 5:2)

Micah foretells the birth of a Davidic king in Bethlehem. Many Jews of Matthew's time, though by no means all, hoped for a messiah who would be a

---

49. This interpretation is attested by Justin, to his chagrin, in *Dialogue with Trypho* 67:1.

50. Brown, *Birth of the Messiah*, 147n42: "Isa 7:14 was not applied messianically in Jewish usage. A list of 456 such 'messianic passages' is given in Edersheim, *Life*, II 710–41; and Isa 7:14 is not among them. Knowing this, Justin, already in the second century, was accusing . . . Jewish scholars of tampering with OT evidence pertinent to the Messiah (*Dialogue* lxxi–lxxiii)."

powerful king and who would restore Israel to the greatness it had under King David. Since David was from Bethlehem, those who longed for a Davidic military messiah understood Micah 5:2 to be a messianic prophecy.

Matt 2:15 (Hos 11:1)

"I called my son out of Egypt" is not a prediction. Hosea refers to the exodus, an event that had occurred long before his time. Hosea 11:1 is not a prediction waiting to be fulfilled: it does not say "I *will* call my son out of Egypt."

Matt 2:23 (?)

Strictly speaking, "He will be called a Nazorean" is a prediction because it uses the future tense. But it is not an authentic prophecy because it does not exist in any of the books of the biblical prophets, despite Matthew's attribution of it to "the prophets." Since it has no scriptural context, there is no point to asking if it refers to the messiah.

Matt 4:15–16 (Isa 9:1 LXX)

Although this prophecy proclaims the dawning of a new age, it refers to a past event, and Matthew quotes it with verbs that refer to a past event ("the people who *sat* in darkness *have seen* a great light"). It its own context in Isaiah, the proclamation celebrates the recent birth of a prince and heir to the Davidic throne (see Isa 9:6).

Matt 8:17 (Isa 53:4)

This verse comes from one of Isaiah's poems about a mysterious figure called the servant of Yahweh. Although Christian tradition interprets passages that describe the servant's sufferings as prophecies about Jesus, this particular passage from Isaiah is not a prediction. Those in the poem who are pondering the sufferings of Yahweh's servant are reflecting on what has already happened, for the servant has recently been killed (Isa 53:7–9).

Matt 12:18–21 (Isa 42:1–4)

This prophecy is another of Isaiah's poems about the servant of Yahweh, about whom it makes several predictions. But, as the opening line declares, the servant lives in the prophet's present, not his future: "Here is my servant, whom I have chosen." Isaiah here is thus predicting what a figure in the prophet's own time will do.

Matt 13:35 (Ps 78:2)

This quotation features future-tense verbs ("I will open my mouth" and "I will proclaim"), but they are declarations of intent about what the author of the psalm will do in the rest of the psalm: he will explain to future generations (i.e., his readers) the lessons they should learn from the experiences of their Israelite ancestors. The "I" in the quotation is the psalmist himself, not some future messiah.

Matt 21:5 (Isa 62:11 + Zech 9:9)

This prophecy is a prediction about a future king. Since it was widely believed that the messiah would be a king, this quotation qualifies as a messianic prophecy.

Matt 21:42 (Ps 118:22–23)

This quotation from the Psalms describes a past event. We do not know what event the psalmist alludes to in this metaphor, or even whether it is meant to refer to a specific event. Although Matthew makes it obvious that the stone symbolizes Jesus, in the psalm's own context the stone does not refer to the messiah, and need not refer to any person at all. What happened to the stone is a metaphor for any unexpected reversal of fortune.

Results

The results of this uncomplicated analysis are striking. Of the ten prophecies Matthew relates to Jesus, five are predictions, but only three predict events beyond the immediate future of the prophets who pronounced them (2:6; 2:23; 21:5). One of these (2:23) is not actually found in scripture. Thus, *only two out of ten are genuine prophetic predictions*, both of them about a messianic king who will be born in Bethlehem (2:6) and who will ride donkeys into Jerusalem (21:5).

Implications for Understanding Matthew's Use of Prophecy

What are we to make of the above results? That only two of Matthew's prophecies match our common-sense notion of a prophecy about a future messiah exposes a significant gap between what Christians traditionally assume about Matthew's gospel and what this gospel actually delivers. The way Matthew presents his prophecies does not match the traditional Christian assumption that there was a large body of prophecies about a future messiah that were, in effect, waiting to be fulfilled. When that assumption falls, so too does a more important one that presupposes it: that Jews of Jesus' day should have recognized that he was the messiah because he was fulfilling so many prophecies.

Since Matthew presents Jesus fulfilling scriptural statements about events that had occurred *before* the prophets mentioned them, what Matthew means by "fulfilling prophecy" must be more subtle and more expansive than the traditional Christian view of a straightforward correlation between an event in the gospel and a previously "unfulfilled" prediction. What does "fulfill" mean, for example, when Jesus fulfills what the Israelites did during the exodus (Matt 2:15), or when he fulfills a psalmist's announcement of what he intends to write in his psalm (Matt 13:35)? In situations like those, to "fulfill" a prophecy cannot mean to meet expectations about that prophecy, which is what Christians have always taken it to mean. It is not true that Jews were expecting that the messiah would, to use the two previous examples, flee to Egypt or teach in parables. Jewish interpreters of the scriptures did not conclude from Jeremiah's oracle about Rachel weeping for her children that there would be a massacre of baby boys the same age as the messiah. Nor did Jews expect the messiah to be an exorcist on the basis of Isaiah's description of Yahweh's servant as one who was afflicted with diseases. Jews of Jesus' time would have had no clue that Jesus was fulfilling prophecies when he told parables or cast out demons. Nor did Mark, Luke, or John seem to have realized that Jesus' storytelling and exorcisms fulfilled prophecy, despite the benefit of their belief that Jesus was the messiah and the collective hindsight of forty to sixty-five years of Christian reflection on stories about Jesus.

Conclusion

In Matthew's presentation of Jesus fulfilling prophecy, then, it was not the case that the meanings of the prophecies he fulfilled were evident *before* he fulfilled them. It was only later, after Jesus' death, that his followers were able retrospectively to link events in Jesus' life to specific prophecies. (As we will see, Luke and John independently admit this and even explain why the disciples did not realize at the time that Jesus was fulfilling prophecies.) That was not primarily because the prophecies involved were not well known, but rather because *their meanings became clear to Jesus' followers only after they became convinced that he had fulfilled them.* Only after his followers came to believe that Jesus was the promised messiah did they draw the conclusion that he had fulfilled prophecy, for that is what the messiah was supposed to do. Only after they believed that Jesus had fulfilled prophecies were they able to detect the specific prophecies that had reached their fulfillment in his life. And only after his followers had identified which prophecies he had fulfilled did their hidden meanings come to light.

As we have seen time and again, the christological meanings of the prophecies Matthew and others quote are not evident when they are considered in their own contexts in the books of the prophets. But Christians did not look to those contexts to help them discern the meanings of those prophecies; they meditated on them within the new context of belief in Jesus as the messiah. In cases where the scriptural contexts of those prophecies hindered the recognition of their christological meanings, the gospel writers (or some unknown writers before them) could carefully snip the prophecies from their literary contexts and prune "distracting" phrases from their quotations. In cases where the wording of those prophecies, even after this kind of selective quotation, still resisted the new meanings Christians found in them, the prophecies could be retrofitted, rewritten to let their new meanings shine through more clearly.

9

The Fulfillment of Prophecy in the Gospel of Mark

THE VERY FIRST WORDS of the Gospel of Mark announce the fulfillment of prophecy: "The good news of Jesus the Anointed begins with something Isaiah the prophet wrote" (Mark 1:1–2). Mark thus implies that his story about Jesus is good news because it fulfills prophecy. Midway through Mark's narrative, Jesus predicts how it will end: he "is destined"[1] to suffer, be killed, and rise from the dead (8:31). In the scene following that prophecy Jesus explains that his destiny is foretold in the scriptures (9:12). At his Last Supper Jesus announces that "the Human One[2] departs as the scriptures predict" (14:21), and when he is arrested a few hours later he proclaims, "Let the scriptures be fulfilled" (14:49). At major turning points in his narrative, therefore, Mark has planted signposts to assure us that the story of Jesus is unfolding according to prophetic scripture.

When it comes to establishing the fulfillment of specific prophecies, however, Mark has little to say. His gospel has only four scenes in which a quoted prophecy is related to an event or situation that is meant to fulfill it.[3] Mark does not highlight these prophecies with fulfillment formulas, such as we find in Matthew and John, apparently trusting that his audience will infer in these four scenes that a prophecy is fulfilled.

---

1. The Greek *dei* in Mark 8:31 means "it is necessary that"; the force of this meaning can be easily overlooked when translated simply as "must" (as in the NRSV and NAB, for example). In the ancient world, something that *must* happen was believed to be governed by destiny.

2. "The Human One" is the SV translation of *ho huios tou anthrōpou*, traditionally rendered "the Son of Man." See Miller, *Complete Gospels*, 208.

3. In two other scenes (Mark 13:24–25 and 14:62) Jesus makes predictions by quoting prophecies that are about the last days and so cannot be fulfilled within the story line of his gospel.

156

Mark 1:2–3

The first of Mark's fulfillment scenes is the opening scene in the gospel. Mark quotes a prophecy he attributes to Isaiah that is fulfilled when John the Baptizer appears. Here we see a sophisticated adaptation of OT material involving conflation and some subtle retrofitting.

Mark	*(Exod 23:20)*
1:2 Look, I am sending my messenger ahead of you	I will send a messenger/angel in front of you
who will prepare your way,	*(Mal 3:1)* Look, I am sending out my messenger and he will survey the way before me
1:3 a voice crying out in the desert, "Prepare the way of the Lord, make straight his paths."	*(Isa 40:3)* a voice crying out, "In the desert prepare the way of the Lord, make straight the paths of our God."

The quotation conflates Septuagint passages from Exodus, Malachi, and Isaiah. Mark 1:2 combines Exod 23:20 and Mal 3:1, which Mark rewords with one crucial alteration: the messenger in Malachi "will survey the way before *me*" (God), whereas in Mark the messenger "will prepare *your* way." This is a good example of retrofitting, changing the wording of the prophecy so that it can be applied to Jesus. "Your way" in Mark 1:2b is supported by "ahead of you" in v. 2a, another retrofit that borrows a phrase snipped from Exod 23:20.[4]

Mark 1:3 quotes Isa 40:3, but changes its meaning in two ways. First, Mark exploits a syntactical ambiguity in the Greek version of Isa 40:3, which reads literally, "a voice crying out in the desert prepare the way of the Lord." The ambiguity lies in the function of the phrase "in the desert": it can modify either "voice" or "prepare." The context in Isaiah clarifies that the prophet speaks about a road across the desert on which the glory of God will travel with his people as they return to Israel from exile in Babylon (Isa 40:1–5). Mark relates the prophecy to John the Baptizer, who preached in the desert. In Mark's context, therefore, it must be the voice, not the road/

---

4. The "ahead of you" (literally, "in front of your face") in Mark's quotation occurs verbatim in Exod 23:20 LXX (where the "you" refers to the nation of Israel) but is not found in Mal 3:1. English translations of Exod 23:20 use "angel" rather than "messenger," but the two words are the same in Greek (*angelos*).

way (the same word in Greek), that is in the desert. The change in meaning can be seen in English by the shift in quotation marks.

Isaiah: A voice crying out, "In the desert prepare . . ."

Mark: A voice crying out in the desert, "Prepare . . ."

Mark effects a second change in the meaning of Isaiah's prophecy by retrofitting its last line: Isaiah speaks of a way for God, whereas Mark makes this into a way for Jesus. Mark accomplishes this shift in 1:3b by changing Isaiah's "the paths for our God" to "his paths," which allows the term "Lord" (v. 3a) to refer to Jesus instead of God.

Mark 7:6–7

In Mark's second fulfillment scene, Jesus quotes Isaiah and applies his words directly to the Pharisees.

Isaiah prophesied accurately about you hypocrites:

"This people honors me with their lips,
    but their hearts are far from me;

in vain do they worship me,
    teaching human precepts as doctrine." (Isa 29:13 LXX)

Mark 12:10

Mark's third announcement of a fulfilled prophecy comes at the end of the parable about the vineyard (12:1–11). After telling how the owner of the vineyard will destroy its tenants in retaliation for killing his beloved son— the allegorical reference to Jesus is obvious to Christian readers—Jesus says, "Have you not read this scripture: 'The stone that the builders rejected has become the cornerstone?'" (12:10, quoting Ps 118:22). That Jesus fulfills this scripture (which makes no prediction) is implied rather than stated, but it seems clear enough that Mark sees the statement as a coded reference to Jesus' death and resurrection.

Mark 14:27

Mark's fourth fulfillment scene is the most interesting and invites close attention. After Jesus and his disciples finish their last supper, they walk to the Mount of Olives, where Jesus predicts,

> You will all become deserters, for it is written,

> "I will strike the shepherd,
> and the sheep will be scattered." (Mark 14:27)

When Jesus is arrested a couple of scenes later, the disciples fulfill this prophecy: "All of them deserted him and fled" (Mark 14:50). The quotation is from Zech 13:7, and a look at how this verse functions in its own context enables us to see how Mark has put it to a new use.

Zech 13:7 reads somewhat differently in Hebrew than in the Septuagint.

Hebrew: Strike the shepherd so that the sheep may be scattered.

Septuagint: Strike the shepherds and remove the sheep.

Mark: I will strike the shepherd and the sheep will be scattered.

Fortunately, it does not matter which version is the basis for Mark's, since in both the Hebrew text and the Septuagint "strike" is an imperative verb, and in both versions the one who gives the order for the shepherd(s) to be struck also intends the scattering or removal of the sheep. Mark has reworded this prophecy in two ways: Zechariah's "strike" becomes Mark's "I will strike," and "so that the sheep may be scattered" (or "remove the sheep") becomes "and the sheep will be scattered." Both alterations are significant. The first converts a command God gives to others into a declaration of what God himself will do. Rewording the prophecy in that way enables Mark to underline his conviction that God is responsible for what will happen to Jesus, and that God is in control even when Jesus' enemies seem to be. Mark reinforces this way of seeing things at two key moments in the story: first, when Jesus foretells that he will be betrayed, he declares, "The Human One is going as it has been written of him" (Mark 14:21); and second, while Jesus is being arrested, he says, "Let the scriptures be fulfilled" (Mark 14:49). The theological conundrum created by Mark 14:27—why God wants to "strike" Jesus—is left to later theologians to worry about; Mark shows no interest in, nor any awareness of, this problem.

Mark's second revision in the wording of the prophecy transforms the scattering of the sheep from being the *purpose* of God's striking the shepherd into its *result*. According to Zechariah, God clearly wills the scattering of the sheep (see below); according to Mark, God simply predicts it. Mark's Jesus correlates "the sheep will be scattered" to his own prediction that "you will become deserters." The correlation is a bit awkward in that "be scattered" is what happens *to* the sheep, while "become deserters" is what the disciples themselves decide to do. One wonders why Mark didn't straighten out this kink by changing the passive "be scattered" to the active "scatter."

When the prophecy is understood in its original context in the book of Zechariah, we see how its meaning there differs greatly from the meaning it has in Mark. The statement Mark borrowed (and reworded) is one-fourth of one verse in a mysterious oracle.

> [7] Awake, O sword, against my shepherd,
>> against the man who is my associate,
>> says Yahweh of hosts.
> *Strike the shepherd, so that the sheep may be scattered;*
>> I will turn my hand against the little ones.
> [8] In the whole land, says Yahweh,
>> two-thirds shall be cut off and perish,
>> and one-third shall be left alive.
> [9] And I will put this third into the fire,
>> refine them as one refines silver,
>> and test them as gold is tested.
> They will call on my name,
>> and I will answer them.
> I will say, "They are my people";
>> and they will say, "Yahweh is our God." (Zech 13:7–9)

The oracle seems unrelated to its immediate literary context in Zechariah; neither what precedes it (Zech 13:1–6) nor what follows it (Zech 14) helps us grasp its meaning. Perhaps Mark was drawn to this prophecy in part because of its obscurity; he might have seen it as an oracle whose real meaning became clear only after it was fulfilled in the story of Jesus.[5] For our purposes we do not need to understand everything about this difficult oracle. It is sufficient that we discern how it characterizes God's intentions towards the sheep and his attitude towards the shepherd.

Yahweh's intentions toward the sheep are outright hostile: "I will turn my hand against the little ones" (Zech 13:7).[6] Two-thirds of them will be

---

5. Collins, *Mark*, 669.

6. Referring to the scattered sheep as "little ones" seems to emphasize their vulnerability.

killed (Zech 13:8), and the surviving one-third will be made to suffer, as a test through which they can become a faithful people (Zech 13:9). We now can see why Mark has lifted only a single sentence out of this oracle: since the sheep symbolize the disciples, none of the rest of the oracle can be fulfilled in the gospel because it is not God's will that most of the disciples "be cut off and perish."

We do not know who the shepherd in Zech 13:7 is supposed to be, except that Yahweh calls him "my associate." In the ancient Middle East the symbol of the shepherd indicates a king or a prince, but the OT usually uses the symbol to refer to bad political leaders.[7] But why does God want to strike his associate? A passage earlier in Zechariah helps us understand. Zech 11:4–17 is about shepherds and sheep merchants, and it concludes with a prophecy about a "worthless shepherd" who preys on his sheep (Zech 11:15–16):

> Oh my worthless shepherd,
>> who deserts the flock!
> May the sword strike his arm
>> and his right eye.
> Let his arm be completely withered,
>> his right eye utterly blinded. (Zech 11:17)

The next mention of a shepherd in Zechariah is in our oracle in 13:7–9, which opens by picking up the sword imagery: "Awake, O sword, against my shepherd." The shepherd who is being punished in Zech 13:7 can only be the worthless shepherd who is condemned in Zech 11:17. God's calling him "my associate" must therefore be ironic, a reference to his sacred office (king, priest?), not an affirmation that he is faithful. The irony here resembles the irony used in "the one who ate my bread has lifted his heel against me" (Ps 41:9, quoted by Jesus in John 13:18).

Zechariah's prophecy that God will punish a worthless shepherd is obviously unsuitable as a prophecy about Jesus. Not only does it not apply to Jesus, but it goes squarely against everything Christians believed about him. Mark can use only one short sentence in Zech 13:7–9, removing that sentence from the context within which it has its meaning, and even then Mark has to make subtle but significant alterations in its wording in order to fit it to his purpose. Only then can Mark insert it into his own context and thereby give it a new meaning that is nearly opposite its original one.

---

7. See, for example, Jer 23:1–4 and Ezek 34:1–10; King David was an exception (Ps 78:70–72). Mattingly, "Shepherd," 942.

Conclusion

The fulfillment of specific prophecies does not play a major role in Mark's gospel. There are only four fulfillment scenes, and only one of them is about Jesus. One of those four prophecies (1:2–3) is conflated and retrofitted to enable it to function as an appropriate introduction to Mark's narrative. Another one (14:27) has been selectively quoted and then retrofitted to make it cohere with Mark's passion narrative and to reflect his theology. Those two examples demonstrate that Mark was aware that the words of the prophets sometimes need careful reworking before they can serve Christian purposes.

Mark's sole fulfillment scene having to do with Jesus himself (12:1–11) requires one to believe that he was raised from the dead before one can see that he fulfilled prophecy. So although Mark deploys prophecy on a much smaller scale than does Matthew, the same basic principle applies to both gospels: the fulfillment of prophecy serves to confirm faith in Jesus, not to engender it.

10

The Fulfillment of Prophecy in the Gospel of Luke and the Acts of the Apostles

The Gospel of Luke

LUKE'S GOSPEL GIVES US two contrasting impressions about how many prophecies came to fulfillment in Jesus: on the one hand, Luke asserts that Jesus fulfilled numerous prophecies; on the other hand, Luke identifies only two specific prophecies that Jesus fulfilled. We start by examining Luke's assertions about fulfilled prophecy, which are both sweeping and vague. There are four such statements, and each one raises interesting issues.

(1) Early in the narrative, shortly after the birth of John the Baptizer, his father, Zechariah, "prophesies,"

> He has raised up for us a horn of salvation in the house of David his servant.
>
> This is what he promised in the words of his holy prophets of old:
>
> > salvation from our enemies, and from the hands of all who hate us. (Luke 1:69–71)

Given the narrative setting of this prophecy, we might expect that the "horn of salvation in the house of David" is a symbolic reference to Zechariah's newborn son. But that cannot be right, for it is Jesus, not John, who is the Davidic savior in this gospel. Still, Zechariah's declaration that this savior has already come ("He *has* raised up a horn of salvation") is odd, since in Luke's storyline Jesus is not yet born. Zechariah's prophecy, which reiterates what the "holy prophets of old" have promised, is that Jesus (the "horn") will bring "salvation from our enemies." However, it is difficult to see just how Luke intends this prediction to apply to Jesus. While the Christian tradition usually understands Jesus to have brought salvation from sin, this cannot be what Luke means here, since his gospel does not personify sin as an enemy (as Paul does in Romans 5–7, for example). So it is unclear to whom or what "our enemies" and "all who hate us" refer. The only other place in this gospel that combines this vocabulary is the teaching in which Jesus urges his followers to "love your *enemies* and do good to those who *hate* you" (Luke 6:27), which can refer only to human adversaries.

(2) In Jesus' final prediction of his passion he states, "See, we are going up to Jerusalem, and everything that is written about the Human One by the prophets will be fulfilled, for he will be handed over to the gentiles" (Luke 18:31–32). Luke's source here (Mark 10:33) reads, "See we are going up to Jerusalem, and the Human One will be handed over." By adding "and everything that is written about the Human One by the prophets will be fulfilled," Luke emphasizes that Jesus' suffering and death fulfills prophecy. The "everything" implies a large number of prophecies, of which, however, Luke identifies only one (see Luke 22:37).

(3) The third assertion that Jesus fulfills prophecies occurs in the famous scene in which the risen Jesus walks incognito with two of his disciples to the village of Emmaus. The two disciples, who were "prevented from recognizing him" (Luke 24:16), discuss his death and wonder about reports of his resurrection, after which Jesus says to them,

> 25 "You people are so dim, so reluctant to trust everything the prophets have said! 26 Wasn't the Anointed One destined to endure those things and enter into his glory?" 27 Then, starting with Moses and all the prophets, he interpreted for them every passage of scripture that referred to himself. (Luke 24:25–27)

(4) The fourth expression of this theme also occurs after the resurrection and comprises most of the risen Jesus' parting words.

> 44 Then he said to them, "This is the message I gave you while I was still with you: everything written about me in the Law of Moses and the Prophets and the Psalms is destined to be fulfilled." 45 Then he prepared their minds to understand the scriptures. 46 He said to them, "This is what is written: the Anointed One will suffer and rise from the dead on the third day. 47 And all peoples will be called on to repent for the forgiveness of sins, beginning from Jerusalem." (Luke 24:44–47)

Those last two scenes are unique to Luke. No other gospel reports that the risen Jesus explained how he had fulfilled the scriptures. The scope of the two statements is both broad and indefinite; verses 27 and 44 give the impression that many predictions are involved. Verses 26 and 46 state that these many predictions are primarily about Jesus' death and resurrection, though verse 47 adds that some of the predictions are not about Jesus but about what his followers are to do after his death. Neither 24:25–27 nor 24:44–47 hints that Jesus fulfilled prophecy during his lifetime—all the interest is on his death and its aftermath. (We will see this focus confirmed in the ways Acts deals with fulfillment of prophecy.)

Those last two scenes feature the *risen* Jesus, which is important for two interrelated reasons. First, the presence of the risen Jesus in these scenes shows that Luke is aware that Jesus' followers did not realize that he had fulfilled prophecy until after his death (see also John 2:19–22). Luke thus confirms the thesis that the belief that Jesus fulfills prophecy is retrospective, one that arises as those who already believe in Jesus' resurrection look back at the stories about him and ponder them in relation to the OT. As we have seen before, belief in Jesus came first, and belief that he fulfilled prophecy came after—and because of that first belief—not the other way around. Second, because it is about the risen Jesus, Luke 24:45 is quite revealing: "Then he opened their minds to understand the scriptures." According to this verse, the ability to recognize Jesus in the OT is a special gift imparted directly by the risen Jesus. Those not blessed in this way are, by implication, unable "to understand the scriptures." This notion confirms what we have seen before: the claims that Jesus fulfilled prophecy are not convincing except to those who already believe in him.

In summary, the two statements by the risen Jesus in Luke make the following points:

a. Jesus fulfilled many prophecies.

b. The prophecies he fulfilled had to do with his passion, death, and resurrection rather than with details of his life.

c. His followers were unaware that Jesus fulfilled prophecies until they looked back from the perspective of their belief in his resurrection.

d. One must receive spiritual insight from the risen Jesus before one can properly understand the OT.

If we were informed about all that *before* reading the whole gospel—imagine that the Gospel of Luke was a movie and that those two crucial scenes in chapter 24 (Luke 24:25–27 and 44–47, above) were part of the preview—we might well be in doubt about what to expect as the narrative unfolds. On the one hand, since we were told that Jesus fulfilled many prophecies, we might expect Luke to point out some of them along the way, as do Matthew and John. On the other hand, since we were also told that the fulfillment of those numerous prophecies was not apparent to Jesus' followers until after his resurrection, we equally might expect Luke to leave his audience in the same situation as the characters in the story—and so not learn about how Jesus fulfilled prophecies until the risen Jesus drew attention to them.

Luke's narrative follows the second strategy; there are only four scenes in which a specific prophecy is quoted and correlated with an event. Two of these concern John the Baptizer and are taken from Luke's sources: Luke 3:3–6 (based on Mark 1:2–4) and Luke 7:27 (copied from Q). That leaves only two fulfillment scenes for Jesus, both of which are found only in this gospel: in his first recorded public appearance (Luke 4:16–21), and on the night before he died (Luke 22:37).

Luke 4:16–21

Luke reports that after Jesus returned to Galilee following his time with Satan in the desert, "He used to teach in their meeting places and was acclaimed by everyone" (Luke 4:15). The next scene is the first in which Luke lets us hear what Jesus says. As his first recorded public speech in Luke's narrative, this scene lays out major themes of Jesus' teaching in this gospel. The scene is set in the synagogue on the Sabbath. Jesus is invited to read from the scriptures, and so the first words spoken by Jesus in this gospel to the public are also the words of Isaiah. After reading a few lines from that prophet, Jesus announces to the attentive congregation, "Today this scripture has been fulfilled as you listen" (Luke 4:21). It is difficult to determine what Luke intends us to understand here. How can Jesus fulfill a prophecy merely by reading it to his audience? Jesus does nothing in this scene to fulfill this prophecy; he simply announces that it has been fulfilled right then and there. It seems best to take this scene, not as a report of an actual event, but as a kind of overture to the story that follows.

Another reason not to take the scene literally has to do with the prophetic words that Jesus reads. Luke 4:17 tells us that Jesus unrolled the scroll that contained what we call the "book" of Isaiah and that "he found the place where it was written, 'The spirit of the Lord . . .'" Since the quotation from Isaiah in Luke 4:18–19 is made up of selected bits from Isa 61:1–2 and 58:6, deftly edited by Luke, there is no place in the scroll of Isaiah that matches the words that Luke has Jesus read. Here is the quotation, along with the verses from Isaiah.

The spirit of the Lord is upon me,

   because he has anointed me

   to bring good news to the poor.

He has sent me to announce pardon for prisoners

    and recovery of sight to the blind;

     to set free the oppressed,

to proclaim the year of the Lord's amnesty. (Luke 4:18–19)

The spirit of the Lord GOD is upon me,

   because the LORD has anointed me;

he has sent me to bring good news to the oppressed,

   to heal the brokenhearted,

to proclaim liberty to the captives,

   and release to the prisoners;

to proclaim the year of the LORD's favor,

   and the day of vengeance of our God;

   to comfort all who mourn. (Isa 61:1–2)

Is not this the fast that I choose:

   to loose the bonds of injustice,

   to undo the thongs of the yoke,

to set free the oppressed,

   and to break every yoke? (Isa 58:6)

Luke's editorial moves are easy enough to see. First, he has snipped out one phrase from Isa 58:6 ("to set free the oppressed") and inserted it into a quotation based on Isa 61:1–2. Second, he deletes Isaiah's "to heal the brokenhearted." Third, Luke adds a phrase of his own ("recovery of sight to the blind") to Isaiah's prophecy. That modest bit of retrofitting enables Jesus to fulfill prophecy when he later heals the blind (Luke 7:21 and 18:35–43). Last, Luke stops quoting from Isa 61:2 just as it turns ugly. Luke censors the words about "the day of vengeance," obviously because they do not characterize Jesus' teaching. This kind of selective quotation, common in the NT, shows that Luke (and other NT authors) wrestled with the problem of how to present Jesus' fulfilling prophecies when the Christian authors believed that he had fulfilled only certain phrases in those prophecies, not complete passages of the prophets' actual words.

Luke 22:37

The only other prophecy fulfillment concerning Jesus in this gospel, and the only one connected to something Jesus does—or, more precisely, something done to him—is Jesus' announcement immediately prior to his arrest: "I'm telling you, this scripture, 'And he was classed with criminals,' is destined to be fulfilled in me; for what is written about me is reaching fulfillment" (Luke 22:37, quoting Isa 53:12).

Judging from the narrative context, Luke understands this prophecy to be fulfilled in Jesus' arrest, though Luke does not draw attention to its fulfillment. However, long after Luke's gospel was written, a copyist working on the four gospels took this prophecy from Luke and added it to Mark, in a place in Mark's story where it could be fulfilled quite literally: at the crucifixion, immediately after the report that Jesus was crucified between two criminals (Mark 15:27). This scribal addition, traditionally tagged as Mark 15:28, and rightly excluded from most modern NTs—note how the text of Mark in modern Bibles goes from 15:27 directly to 15:29—reads: "And the scripture that says, 'And he was classed with criminals,' was fulfilled."

When we compare Luke's treatment of Jesus' arrest to Mark's, we can see that Luke was aware of a different prophecy associated with Jesus' arrest ("I will strike the shepherd and the sheep will be scattered"—see Mark 14:26–27 above) and chose to ignore it. Luke leaves out this Markan prophecy fulfillment because in Luke's story, unlike in Mark's, the disciples do *not* flee when Jesus is arrested, as we can see when comparing the parallel scenes of Jesus' arrest in Mark and Luke.

Mark 14:48–50	*Luke 22:52–53*
[48] "Have you come to arrest me with swords and clubs as you would an insurgent?	[52] "Have you come with swords and clubs to arrest me as you would an insurgent?
[49] I was with you in the temple area day after	[53] When I was with you day after day in the temple area, you didn't lay a hand on me.
day teaching and you didn't seize me.	But it's your turn now, and the authority of
But let the scriptures be fulfilled!"	darkness is on your side."
[50] And they all deserted him and ran away.	

Luke alters Mark's narrative in two ways: he deletes "all of them deserted him and fled" (Mark 14:50), and rewrites Jesus' command "Let the scriptures be fulfilled" (Mark 14:49) into a declaration to those arresting him, "It's your turn now, and the authority of darkness is on your side" (Luke 22:53). Luke's second alteration is for the sake of consistency: since Luke does not let Jesus predict that the disciples will fulfill prophecy by deserting him (as he does in Mark 14:27), and since Luke does not report that the disciples fled (as they did in Mark 14:50), he consequently has to suppress the Markan Jesus' command that the scriptures are to be fulfilled (Mark 14:49). Later in Luke's narrative, just after Jesus expires, Luke reports that "*all* Jesus' acquaintances, including the women who had followed him from Galilee, were standing off at distance watching these events" (Luke 23:49). This report is based on Mark 15:40–41, which describes some of Jesus' female companions from Galilee, to which Luke adds "all his acquaintances." In Luke's unique version of events the disciples are not scattered when their "shepherd" is struck; on the contrary, they stick together as a group to witness his death. Luke in effect denies that the prophecy quoted by Jesus in Mark ("I will strike the shepherd and the sheep will be scattered") was fulfilled. Luke thereby also contradicts the prophecy Jesus himself makes about his disciples in Mark 14:27 ("You will all become deserters"). Elsewhere in his gospel Luke emphasizes that many (unspecified) prophecies were fulfilled in the events of Jesus' life, but when it comes to the only scene in Mark that depicts Jesus making a prediction based on a specific prophecy, Luke disagrees.

Summary

Luke uses the fulfillment of prophecy in a somewhat paradoxical fashion. On the one hand, he asserts, partly through words he attributes to Jesus, that Jesus fulfilled numerous prophecies. On the other hand, Luke narrates only *two* scenes that claim that Jesus fulfilled a specific prophecy.

The way Luke manipulates texts in those two scenes shows him to be a discriminating user of prophecy. In the first scene (Luke 4:16–21), he carefully edits and retrofits the prophecy he quotes so that Jesus can fulfill it. In the other scene (Luke 22:37), Luke deletes the prophecy quoted in Mark, his source, because Luke rewrites Mark's story in such a way that the prophecy quoted there cannot be fulfilled. In its place Luke substitutes a short quotation more amenable to his distinctive narrative.

In two scenes about the risen Jesus, Luke shows us things seen in no other gospel: Jesus interpreting the scriptures so that his followers can understand their cryptic references to him (Luke 24:27), and Jesus imparting to his followers the ability to "understand the scriptures" (Luke 24:45). Those two scenes are most helpful for our study because they reveal that Luke is aware that the insight that the Jewish scriptures refer to Jesus is available only *after* they are considered from the perspective of belief in the risen Jesus, and only as a result of a spiritual ability imparted by the risen Jesus to his followers.

The Acts of the Apostles

Luke quotes prophecy in the Acts of the Apostles more often than he does in his gospel.[1] The first action the disciples undertake following the ascension of Jesus is prompted by the fulfillment of prophecy (Acts 1:15–26). About half of Peter's first speech (Acts 2:14–36), the first words in Acts spoken in public, consists of quotations of prophetic scripture. Paul's final words at the end of the narrative (Acts 28:25–28) are almost entirely the words of Isaiah.

An examination of the first two prophecies fulfilled in Acts enables us to see how Luke subtly manipulates scripture to make it work in his story. Luke relates his first quotation of scripture to the death of Judas and its effect on a particular plot of land. To explain the relevance of the first prophecy he quotes, Luke gives the reader some background information about how Judas died, drawing on a quite different story than the better known one from Matthew in which Judas hangs himself (Matt 27:3–8).

> This man [Judas] acquired a field with the reward of his wicked-
> ness; and falling headlong, he burst open in the middle and all
> his bowels gushed out. This became known to all the residents
> of Jerusalem, so that the field was called in their language *Hake-*
> *ldama*, that is, Field of Blood. For it is written in the Book of
> Psalms,
>
> "Let his habitation be made desolate,
>   and let there be no inhabitant in it."
> (Acts 1:18–20a, quoting Ps 69:25)

The quotation is adapted from Psalm 69, a lengthy prayer for deliverance and revenge against betrayers and enemies.[2] Luke zeroes in on just the right verse for his story (Ps 69:25); the verse just before (Ps 69:24) is of no use to

---

1. In keeping with the nearly universal consensus of biblical scholars, I presuppose that the Gospel of Luke and the Acts of the Apostles were written by the same author, whom I call Luke.

2. In the Gospel of John, Jesus quotes a different verse from this psalm and applies it to his own enemies: "They hated me for no reason" (John 15:25, quoting Ps 69:4).

Luke, and the one just after (Ps 69:26) would be nonsense if applied to Judas, as we can see when we view verse 25 in its own context:

> 24 Pour out your indignation on them,
>   and let your burning anger overtake them.
> 25 Let their habitation be made desolate;
>   and let there be no inhabitant in their tents.
> 26 For they persecute those whom you have struck down,
>   and those whom you have wounded, they attack still more.
>   (Ps 69:24–26)

Luke quotes verse 25, but since its wording does not quite fit Judas, Luke has adapted it to his story with some careful selective quotation and retrofitting. The quotation is selective because it leaves out "in their tents," a detail obviously inapplicable to Judas. Luke also retrofits the quotation by altering its plural words that refer to many enemies to singular words so that it can refer to Judas as an individual.

The second scripture Luke quotes follows immediately after the first: "Let another take his position of overseer" (Acts 1:20b, quoting Ps 109:8). In its own context in the psalm, this imprecation is one in a long series of curses (Ps 109:6–19) that wicked and deceitful accusers (*satans* in Hebrew, Ps 109:20) utter against an innocent man whom they hope to unjustly convict. In applying the curse to Judas, Luke turns it into a pronouncement of a just punishment, thereby reversing its original meaning. In the Septuagint version of Ps 109:8 the man's position is that of "overseer" (*episkopē*). The Hebrew text lacks this specification. The Septuagint's embellishment is probably what caught Luke's attention because of the unique authority he attributes to the twelve apostles, authority to be inherited by Judas's successor (see Acts 1:21–25).

Just as Luke is more willing to quote scripture in Acts than he is in his gospel, so also is he less reticent about relating specific scriptures directly to Jesus. Acts contains seven scenes in which a character quotes scripture and declares that the quotation refers to Jesus. In addition, there are nine scenes that claim that Jesus fulfilled prophecy but that do not quote specific prophetic passages. In four of those nine scenes the author reports that Paul or Apollos tried to persuade Jews that Jesus fulfilled scripture, with different outcomes on each occasion.[3] In the other five of those nine scenes Peter or Paul asserts that something foretold by the prophets or the scriptures has been fulfilled by Jesus.[4] Two examples suffice to illustrate how Acts invokes

3. Acts 17:2–3; 17:10–12; 18:28; 28:23–24.
4. Acts 3:17–18; 3:24; 10:43; 13:27–29; 26:22–23.

prophecy without quoting actual prophets: "All the prophets testify about him that everyone who believes in him receives forgiveness of sins through his name" (10:43), and "Because the residents of Jerusalem and their leaders did not recognize Jesus or understand the words of the prophets that are read every Sabbath, they fulfilled those words by condemning him" (13:27).

"All the prophets testify about him."

In the nine summary scenes described above, just as in the two summaries in Luke 24, the scriptures are related either to Jesus' identity (for example, that he is the messiah, Acts 18:28) or to his death and resurrection (for example, "it was necessary for the messiah to suffer and rise from the dead," Acts 17:2–3), not to specific details of his life. One of these nine scenes makes a novel claim about the kind of prophecy Jesus fulfilled: "All the prophets testify about him that everyone who believes in him receives forgiveness of sins through his name" (Acts 10:43). This is both puzzling and revealing. It is puzzling because there seems to be no OT prophecy that people who believe in the messiah will have their sins forgiven through his name. And it is certainly false that *all* the prophets made this specific prediction. So it is most unlikely that Luke here has particular prophecies in mind, or even that he knows of any that are relevant to his claim. Rather, it seems that here Luke, speaking through Peter, is professing his faith that a central element of the Christian message (that commitment to Jesus brings forgiveness of sins) is not some baseless promise or recent innovation of a new religion; on the contrary, it is part of the God of Israel's plan for humanity, proclaimed now for the first time, but foretold long ago by God's inspired oracles. The reference to "*all* the prophets" is more than mere exaggeration; it reveals how confident Luke is that the good news Christians preach is rooted in the ancient, and therefore venerable, tradition of Israel. If the claim in Acts 10:43 were challenged by a skeptical audience, Luke's rhetoric would be shown to be without textual foundation. However, the thought that he might be challenged by skeptics probably never occurred to Luke because he wrote for an audience who already believed in Jesus. Acts 10:43 is thus an especially clear window into how early Christian appeals to the fulfillment of prophecy actually functioned: commitment to Jesus was the foundation for the conviction that he had fulfilled prophecy—not the other way around. People did not come to believe in Jesus because they were told that all the prophets predicted that those who believe in him have forgiveness of sins through his name. Rather it was those who already believed in Jesus who could go on to believe that their experience of being forgiven through his name had been predicted long ago by a long succession of prophets.

Responses to Claims of Fulfillment

In light of the above analysis it is instructive to consider briefly the scenes in Acts that narrate how people respond to the claim that Jesus fulfilled scripture. The lengthiest such scene (Acts 8:26–39) tells of a royal official from Ethiopia pondering a passage from Isaiah. When the apostle Philip, guided to the location by an angel, asks the official if he understands what he is reading, the man replies, "How can I unless someone explains it to me?" (Acts 8:31). Referring to one of Isaiah's passages about the mysterious suffering servant (Isa 53:7–8), the Ethiopian asks Philip, "Of whom does the prophet say this—himself or someone else?" Philip seizes the opportunity: "he launched out with this passage as his starting point, telling him the good news about Jesus" (Acts 8:35). Before long the man asks Philip to baptize him on the spot (Acts 8:36). Luke here narrates an ideal scenario for how prophecy *should* point people to Jesus. Even so, the scene recognizes that the prophets (exemplified by Isaiah) are difficult to understand, and that one must learn how to interpret them from the standpoint of Christian faith before they can inspire belief in Jesus.

Two other summary scenes in Acts are sufficient to show the variety of Jewish responses to the claim that Jesus fulfilled prophecy. In one (Acts 17:10–12) the members of a Jewish synagogue "welcomed the message with great enthusiasm. Each day they studied the scriptures to see whether these claims were true, and many of them came to believe." The other scene comes at the end of Acts. Paul is under house arrest in Rome, and the leaders of the Jewish community in that capital city

> arranged a day to meet with Paul. They visited him at his lodg-
> ings in great numbers. All day long he explained the matter to
> them, testifying to the kingdom of God and trying to convince
> them about Jesus from both the law of Moses and from the
> prophets. Some were convinced by what he had said, while oth-
> ers refused to believe. (Acts 28:23–24)

The results are mixed. Luke is careful not to say that some were convinced by Paul and some were not; Luke instead tells us that some were convinced while others "refused to believe."[5] The lesson Luke imparts here is that once

---

5. The Greek verb here (*ēpistoun*) is in the imperfect tense, which conveys the sense of a continuous action in the past. So it means more than that they *did* not believe.

one has heard a gifted Christian preacher explain how Jesus fulfilled prophecy, the failure to believe can only be a willful act, a refusal to accept the evident truth.

If one wonders why Luke chose to end Acts in a scene of mixed results—why not a scene in which all were persuaded?—it is because Luke has saved a trump card to play as the finale to his narrative. Paul gets the last word as he explains that the very refusal of some to believe that Jesus fulfilled prophecy is itself a fulfillment of prophecy (Acts 28:25–28). Thus, those Jews who resist prophecy unwittingly fulfill it. Luke's understanding of the nature of prophecy is close to what we see in, for example, the Greek tragedy *Oedipus Rex*: humans are powerless to resist prophecy.[6] Even those who consciously and willfully try to defeat prophecy end up fulfilling it against their will and in ways they do not understand at the time.

Another version of this paradox is on display in two other scenes in Acts. In the middle of a long speech in the synagogue in Antioch in Pisidia, Paul says, "Because the residents of Jerusalem and their leaders did not recognize him or understand the words of the prophets that are read every Sabbath, they fulfilled those words by condemning him" (Acts 13:27). Note Paul's logic here: it is *because* the Jerusalemites did not understand the prophets that they fulfilled their words. Similarly, in Jerusalem Peter announces, "Friends, I know that you acted in ignorance, as did also your rulers; *in this way* God fulfilled what he had foretold through all the prophets, that his messiah would suffer" (Acts 3:17–18). The implication here is startling, for it seems that if the people and their leaders *had* understood the prophecies, those prophecies would *not* have been fulfilled (note the "in this way"). According to Luke, God's plan apparently required key players in it to be unaware of it. In these two scenes Jews are described as acting in ignorance, not as consciously defying God's will (as in Acts 28). But even with this variation the theme is the same: God's will, foretold by the prophets, will be accomplished, not only despite human ignorance and resistance, but even *because* of that ignorance and resistance.

The narrative strategy in Acts is brilliantly designed to harness the power of prophecy to validate the Christian message: when people accept that Jesus fulfilled prophecy, they validate the prophetic truth of Christianity; and when people refuse to accept that Jesus fulfilled prophecy, they also validate the prophetic truth of Christianity. Not bad.

It means that they *persisted* in not believing—hence, the translation "refused to believe."

6. Luke's essentially Greek understanding of prophecy as announcing a future event that has the force of fate—i.e., the event is predestined to occur—is also on display in his redaction of Jesus' prediction in Mark 14:21 that "the Human One goes as it is written of him" to "the Human One goes to meet his destiny" (Luke 22:22).

—— 11 ——

The Fulfillment of Prophecy in the Gospel of John

J OHN, LIKE MATTHEW, HAS a significant interest in the fulfillment of scripture,[1] presenting ten scenes in which Jesus fulfills a scriptural prediction. Our study of John's gospel starts with an overview of its fulfillment scenes and discusses this gospel's explicit acknowledgment that only those who believe that Jesus is the resurrected son of God can see that he fulfilled scripture. The chapter then proceeds along the same lines as the chapter on Matthew. It first analyzes how the author we call John helps Jesus fulfill scripture. Then it discusses how John uses the fulfillment theme, situates that theme into its historical context, and assesses its role in the harsh accusations this gospel levels against Jews who do not believe in Jesus.

Overview

The first two things Jesus' disciples say about him in the Gospel of John are "We have found the Messiah" (1:41) and "We have found him about whom Moses in the Law and also the prophets wrote" (1:45). The latter statement expresses the belief that Jesus fulfills scripture in an especially overt way, one that brings out into the open what other NT declarations about Jesus imply: not only that Jesus fulfills the scriptures, but that the scriptures were written *about* him. John reiterates the explicit form of this belief when he has Jesus proclaim that "the scriptures testify on my behalf" (5:39), and that "Moses wrote about me" (5:46). Similarly, John himself adds a comment after he

---

1. Of the ten passages John quotes in his fulfillment scenes, only four come from the prophets; five are from the Psalms and one from the Torah. Therefore, in discussing the Gospel of John it is more appropriate to speak of the fulfillment of *scripture* than of prophecy, unless a specific prophecy is in view.

quotes a passage from Isaiah: "Isaiah said this because he saw his [Jesus'] glory and spoke about him" (12:41).

The Gospel of John has eight scenes that quote OT texts and narrate their fulfillment.[2] Only two of those concern something Jesus does.

- Jesus drives out money changers and animal vendors from the temple (2:14–16).

- Jesus rides a donkey into Jerusalem to the cheers of a crowd (12:12–15).

In the other six scenes scripture is fulfilled when something is done to Jesus.

- God sends Jesus from heaven (6:31–33).

- The Jews do not believe in him (12:37–40).[3]

- Judas betrays Jesus (13:18).

- The "world" hates Jesus for no reason (15:25).

- Jesus' executioners divide up his clothing (19:24).

- Jesus' executioners spear his corpse rather than break his legs (19:33–34, 36–37).

In the pair of scenes in which Jesus himself fulfills scripture, John both times interrupts his narration to tell us that the disciples who witnessed the two events did not understand until after the resurrection that what Jesus had done had fulfilled scripture (2:17[4] and 12:16). It is somewhat curious that the Johannine Jesus, who openly proclaims his divinity to those who seek to kill him,[5] does not point out, even to his followers, which deeds of his fulfill scripture. Jesus tells his enemies that the scriptures were writ-

2. There are two more scenes in which an event fulfills scripture, but no text is quoted. In 17:12 Jesus tells his Father in prayer that Judas "was destined to be lost, so that the scripture might be fulfilled," and in 19:28 Jesus says, "(in order to fulfill the scriptures) 'I'm thirsty.'"

3. John qualifies this blanket statement with the explanation that many Judeans did believe in him (12:42). We can infer—though John would not be pleased—that those who did believe in Jesus were thereby threatening to *frustrate* the fulfillment of scripture.

4. In 2:17 John says simply that the disciples remembered the scripture that Jesus had fulfilled; John does not explicitly mention the resurrection. However, in the other two passages that describe the disciples remembering the scriptural significance of something Jesus said or did (2:22 and 12:16), John indicates that this remembering occurred after the resurrection. Therefore, we should infer that he intends 2:17 in the same sense.

5. John 5:17–18; 8:58–59; 10:30–31.

ten about him but does not enlighten his disciples that anything he has done fulfills a specific scripture—although he points out one scripture that his enemies had fulfilled (15:25) and another one that Judas would fulfill (13:18–19). These are strong clues that John independently agrees with Luke's analysis of why Jesus' followers did not perceive during his lifetime that he had fulfilled prophecy. According to Luke, such insight required supernatural enlightenment that was available only after the resurrection. Luke describes that enlightenment quite concretely in Luke 24:27 and 24:44, scenes in which the risen Jesus interprets for his disciples numerous biblical passages that refer to him. (Unfortunately for us, however, Luke does not reveal which passages Jesus explained.) For John the ability to reflect on the life of Jesus and recognize when it had fulfilled scripture seems to be part of what the holy spirit imparts to the disciples after Jesus' death. Jesus promised that this spirit "will teach you everything and remind you of all I have said" (John 14:26) and "will guide you to the complete truth" (16:13). The risen Jesus transmitted this holy spirit to his disciples on the evening of Easter Sunday (20:22). Earlier that same day, even after they had discovered Jesus' empty tomb, "they did not yet understand the scripture, that he must rise from the dead" (20:9).

John's outlook on this topic is not entirely consistent. As noted above, John describes disciples, long before the resurrection, proclaiming Jesus as the one about whom Moses and the prophets wrote (1:45), and John has Jesus saying right out that "the scriptures testify on my behalf" (5:39), and that "Moses wrote about me" (5:46). Those three statements confirm the basic principle that belief in Jesus is the prerequisite, not the result, of the belief that he fulfills prophecy. John 1:45 is pronounced by a believer and is preceded by the proclamation that Jesus is the messiah (1:41). Jesus' declarations in 5:39 and 5:46 neither lead nor invite his listeners to believe in him. On the contrary, those assertions are polemical ones, accompanied by accusations that "the Jews" have neither God's word nor God's love in them (5:38, 42), and that they do not believe Moses (5:46).

The only place in this gospel where Jesus explains how a scripture is fulfilled in him (rather than in what someone else does) further confirms my thesis. In the scene that sets up Jesus' famous discourse on the bread of life, the crowd tells him,

> "Our ancestors had manna to eat in the desert. As the scripture puts it, 'He gave them bread from heaven to eat.'"
>
> Jesus responded to them: "Let me tell you this: it was not Moses who gave you bread from heaven; rather, it is my Father who gives you real bread from heaven. That is to say, God's

bread comes down from heaven and gives life to the world."
(John 6:31–33)

The scripture the crowd quotes is a paraphrase of Ps 73:24, which in the Septuagint reads,

> He rained down on them manna to eat,
>   and gave them the bread of heaven.

Despite the obvious meaning of that verse, John's Jesus contends that "bread from heaven" does not actually refer to the manna of Exodus, but to the "true" bread from heaven, which is Jesus himself (6:35, 51). Once again it is clear that one needs to believe in Jesus before one can perceive that he fulfills scripture.

Nonscriptural Scripture

One more passage in John merits attention in this overview. It is a curious passage, for it quotes a scripture not found in the OT.

> Jesus cried out, "Let anyone who is thirsty come to me, and let the one who believes in me drink. As the scripture has said, 'Rivers of living water shall flow out of him.'" Now Jesus said this about the Spirit, which believers in him were to receive; for as yet there was no Spirit, because Jesus was not yet glorified. (John 7:37–39)

It is difficult to determine whether to classify this as a fulfillment of scripture or a somewhat vague promise that a scripture will come true. In any case, two features of the passage are important. The first is that there simply is no such quotation in the OT or in any extant ancient text. Even if John is paraphrasing rather than quoting some text, there is no scriptural verse on which "Rivers of living water shall flow out of him" is clearly based; about the best scholars can do is suggest a phrase in Zech 14:8 ("living waters shall flow out of Jerusalem") as a possibility. The second important feature in this passage is the narrator's commentary, which explains that the meaning of this scripture was not understood—and could not be understood—until after the death and glorification of Jesus.

Excursus:

Other Unattributable Quotations

As a fabricated scripture, John 7:38 is similar to Matt 2:23 ("He shall be called a Nazorean"). Those are not the only instances in which a New Testament author showcases an alleged scriptural quotation that cannot be found in any biblical book. For the record, here are three more examples, the first of which might be intended as a fulfilled prophecy.

> Israel failed to obtain what it was seeking. The chosen obtained it, but the rest became obstinate, as it is written,
>
> *God gave them a sluggish spirit,*
>> *eyes that would not see*
>> *and ears that would not hear,*
> *until this very day.* (Rom 11:7–8)

> Whoever wants to be a friend of the world makes himself an enemy of God. Do you think that it's for nothing that the scripture says, *"God jealously longs for the spirit that he has made to dwell in us"*? (James 4:4–5)

Neither of those can be found in the Jewish scriptures or anywhere else. Another mysterious quotation is featured in 1 Corinthians.

> As it is written,
>
> *What eye has not seen, and ear has not heard,*
>> *and what has not entered the human heart,*
> *what God has prepared for those who love him,*
>> *this has been revealed to us through the Spirit.*
> (1 Cor 2:9–10)

Paul regularly uses the quotation formula ("as it is written") to introduce quotations from the scriptures. Although the first line resembles phrases in Isa 64:3, the rest of the quotation is nowhere to be found in the OT. However, the saying is remarkably similar to one in the *Gospel of Thomas*:

> Jesus said, "I will give you what no eye has seen, what no ear has heard, what no hand has touched, what has not arisen in the human heart." (*Thomas* 17)[6]

---

6. See Hedrick, *Unlocking the Secrets*, 47, for a tradition history of this saying.

Whether Paul is freely quoting from this gospel or whether both Paul and *Thomas* are quoting some undiscovered third writing is unknown.

How John Helps Jesus Fulfill Scripture

In this part of the chapter we do for John, though more briefly, what we did earlier for Matthew: analyze the creative ways in which the evangelist matches scriptures to their fulfillments.

Selective Quotation

Half the quotations in John's fulfillment scenes come from OT passages that are not amenable to his christological agenda. In these cases John quotes a single line or statement from a passage for which he otherwise has no use. The way John quotes scripture, therefore, reveals that he does not believe that Jesus fulfills, for example, this or that psalm, but only a single detail within it. Five of John's scriptural quotations allow us to see how judicious he was in selecting which bits of a passage to quote.

John 2:17 (Ps 69:9)

When Jesus disrupts the commerce in the temple, John reports that his disciples remembered a verse from the psalms: "Zeal for your house will consume me." The verses immediately following this one in Psalm 69 are antithetical to John's interpretation of Jesus because they describe the speaker of the psalm doing public penance for sin:

> When I humbled my soul with fasting,
>> they insulted me for doing so.
> When I made sackcloth for my clothing,
>> I became a byword to them. (Ps 69:10–11)

John 13:18 (Ps 41:9b)

After Jesus washes his disciples' feet at the Last Supper, he tells them that the example he has set is not intended for all of them because one of them (Judas) will fulfill the scripture, "The one who ate my bread has lifted his heel against me." John quotes only the second half of Ps 41:9 because the first half does not fit John's description of the relationship between Jesus and Judas. The psalm describes "the one who ate my bread" as "my intimate friend in whom I trusted" (Ps 41:9a, NRSV [modified]). In the psalm that description makes the betrayal in v. 9b all the more treacherous, but John cannot apply v. 9a to Judas because it would contradict John's assertions that Jesus had never trusted Judas. The divine Jesus, who knows everything, always knew that Judas would turn traitor: "Jesus was aware from the start which ones were not believers, and he knew who would turn him in" (John 6:64 [SV]; see also 6:70–71 and 13:10–11).

The verse in the psalm immediately following the line John quotes is equally hostile to his purpose: "But you, O LORD, be gracious to me, and raise me up, that I may repay them" (Ps 41:10). Although the prayer to "raise me up" would be attractive to John, the next phrase ruins it for him because the psalmist asks to be raised up so that he can take revenge on his enemies.

Earlier in Psalm 41 the psalmist prays, "Heal me, for I have sinned against you" (Ps 41:4). John had to choose with care how to quote from this psalm.

John 15:25 (Ps 69:4)

As Jesus reflects on the hatred he has encountered among those to whom he was sent, he reveals that their animosity "was to fulfill the word that is written in their law, 'They hated me for no reason,'" a complaint found in two psalms (Ps 69:4 and Ps 35:19). Perhaps John knew this and studied both of them in search for scriptures that were fulfilled in Jesus. However, since John quotes Ps 69 earlier in his gospel (2:17) and clearly alludes to it later (19:29, see below), that psalm is the likely source for his quotation in John 15:25.

Psalm 69 is a prayer for deliverance and revenge (see Ps 69:22–28) but also an expression of confession and repentance. The very next verse after John's quotation of Ps 69:4 reads, "O God, you know my folly; the wrongs I have done are not hidden from you" (Ps 69:5). John not only had to locate the right piece of the psalm; he also had to remove that piece from its context in order for it to find credible fulfillment in Jesus.

John 19:36 (Exod 12:46 / Num 9:11)

John's passion narrative relates that the soldiers hastened the deaths of the two victims crucified with Jesus by breaking their legs, but that they refrained from breaking Jesus' legs because they could see that he was already dead (19:31–33). John sees in this the fulfillment of the ritual prescription not to break the bones of the slaughtered Passover lamb. John's symbolism of Jesus as the Passover lamb is theologically rich, but the analogy John implies between the treatment of the dead lamb and the dead Jesus is confined to a single point of comparison. The commandments in the Torah relating to Passover contain a number of regulations about the sacrificial lamb;[7] none of them can be imagined to apply to Jesus except the one John quotes. Moreover, the prohibition against breaking the lamb's bones occurs twice, both times in conjunction with directives that cannot apply to Jesus.

> The lamb shall be eaten in one house; you shall not take any of the animal outside the house, and you shall not break any of its bones. (Exod 12:46)

> They shall eat the lamb with unleavened bread and bitter herbs. They shall leave none of it until morning, nor break a bone of it. (Num 9:11–12)

John 19:37 (Zech 12:10)

When, instead of breaking Jesus' legs, a soldier makes sure Jesus is dead by spearing his body as it hangs on the cross, John tells us that thus was fulfilled the scripture that says, "They will look at the one they have pierced." John has plucked this clause from the middle of a passage in which Zechariah prophesies that God "will pour out a spirit of compassion and supplication on the house of David and the inhabitants of Jerusalem," a spirit that moves them to mourn a prophet whom they have killed. All Jerusalem, indeed the whole nation, will regret this killing: "On that day the mourning in Jerusalem will be great" (Zech 12:11); "the land shall mourn, each family by itself" (Zech 12:12). None of this can apply to Jesus, of course, whose death was mourned by only a few in Jerusalem. Moreover, in Zechariah it is those who pierce the prophet who mourn for him, which cannot work in the gospel because it is a Roman who pierces Jesus.

Retrofitted Prophecies(?)

In comparison with the retrofits in the Gospel of Matthew, those in John are quite modest. There are only two of them, and it's hard to say whether they actually meet the definition of retrofitting: the alteration of a prophecy by rewording or removing parts of it that are impossible or inappropriate for

---

7. See Exod 12:3–13, 43–46; and Num 9:11–12.

Jesus to fulfill. In John's two borderline cases, his modifications are slight and subtle. In each case his only touch is to tweak the form of a verb.

(1) *John 2:17* turns "Zeal for your house has consumed me" from Psalm 69:9 into "Zeal for your house will consume me." John has no problem declaring that prophecies with past-tense verbs were fulfilled in his story,[8] so why does he take the small trouble to change this one to the future tense? Most likely it is because he sees this prophecy fulfilled only in Jesus' death.[9] That makes this particular prophecy a unique case in this gospel because it is the only one that Jesus *will* fulfill much later in the story.

(2) *John 19:36* takes an instruction in the Torah about the Passover lamb ("You/They shall not break any of its bones")[10] and changes the verb from active to passive ("None of his bones will be broken"). It is not apparent why John made this adjustment. Perhaps he thought that by changing the verb from active to passive he was converting a commandment ("You shall not break") into a prophetic prediction ("will not be broken").[11]

Conclusion. The barely noticeable alterations in our two examples do not change the meaning of their prophecies. John could have quoted both of them as is and applied them to Jesus with no more awkwardness than in any of his other prophecy-fulfillment scenes. Perhaps John thought the minor modifications in these two scriptures made it more evident that Jesus had fulfilled them. Or perhaps those changes were not deliberate. If John was quoting from memory, changes like those could well be inadvertent. Even if John was working from written texts, it does not stretch the imagination that he could have unconsciously changed the tense or voice of a verb.

8. See the above analyses of John 6:31, 12:38, 12:40, 13:18, 15:25, and 19:24.

9. In its context in Psalm 69, "consume" expresses the "burning intensity of the zeal; John interprets the Psalm to mean that zeal for the Temple will destroy Jesus and bring his death" (Brown, *Gospel of John*, 124).

10. The "you" version is in Exod 12:10 and 12:46 LXX; the "they" version is Num 9:12 LXX.

11. Some scholars propose that the quotation in John 19:36 comes not from the laws of Passover but from Ps 34:20, a guarantee of protection for the righteous: "He guards all their bones; not one of them will be broken." This verse uses the passive voice just as in John. Since, however, it seems clear that John associates the death of Jesus with the Passover sacrifice, it is much more likely that he draws his quotation from a passage about the Passover lamb in either Exodus or Numbers.

Zechariah 9:9 / John 12:15

This is the place to consider the quotation of Zech 9:9 in John 12:15, which differs considerably in length and wording from all known forms of the Zechariah passage.

Zechariah 9:9 LXX

Rejoice greatly, daughter of Zion;
>   proclaim, daughter of Jerusalem.

Look, the king is coming to you,
>   righteous and saving.

He is gentle and riding on a donkey
>   and a young colt.

as quoted by John

Do not be afraid, daughter of Zion.

Look, your king is coming,
>   sitting on a donkey's colt.

John has freely reworded the prophecy and condensed it to about half its original size. Those revisions, however, do not seem to alter any crucial element of the prophecy's meaning. John apparently made the changes to enable the prophecy to function more effectively in its literary and theological context of John 12.[12] John could have applied Zech 9:9 to Jesus without alteration, more or less as Matthew did in Matt 21:5 (though without the double donkey ride—see pp. 135–36). Therefore, John's rewriting of this particular prophecy here does not count as retrofitting.

Stories Created out of Scriptures

In John's unique passion narrative there are several scenes in which he has used the OT as a source for some details in his story. In these cases the interplay between the story and the ancient scriptures goes in both directions: the events in the story fulfill certain scriptures, but those scriptures are also part of the raw material from which John has shaped the story. (We saw this same dynamic in the Gospel of Matthew.) The scriptures John quotes can be fulfilled with unusual precision and literalness because John composed his

---

12. Schuchard, *Scripture within Scripture*, 71–84.

stories with those very passages in mind. There are three such scenes in the passion narrative.

John 19:23–24

The synoptic gospels report that the soldiers who crucified Jesus divided up his clothing by casting lots to see who got what (Matt 27:35 / Mark 15:24 / Luke 23:34). John, however, describes in detail a specific method by which the soldiers made this division. The four soldiers (only John tells their number) divide up Jesus' outer garments; perhaps John means that they cut them into pieces of cloth that could be put to other uses. However, Jesus' tunic, a long undergarment, would apparently be useless if it were to be cut up. So the men gamble for it by casting lots.

> This happened so that the scripture would be fulfilled that says,
>
> "They divided my garments among them,
>   and for my clothing[13] they cast lots." (John 19:24 [SV], quoting Ps 22:18)

John differs here from the synoptic gospels in two ways. First, while the synoptic scene (actually Mark's scene copied by Matthew and Luke) was created on the basis of Ps 22:18,[14] John makes that scriptural basis explicit by quoting the verse.[15] Second, what the synoptics narrate as one action (dividing garments by casting lots), John narrates as two (first dividing the outer garments and then casting lots for the tunic). John goes into this detail because he takes the two lines of Ps 22:18 to be descriptions of two distinct actions rather than synonymous descriptions of the same deed. Since, according to John's interpretation, the psalm foresees a two-step division of Jesus' clothing, then that is what must have happened. John's procedure here is similar to Matthew's when he describes Jesus mounted on two donkeys (Matt 21:1–7). In both cases the gospel writer decided that a poetic verse in

---

13. John evidently identifies Jesus' tunic with the "clothing" in the psalm, even though the psalm's Greek word (*himatismos*) is not the word for "tunic" (*chitōn*) used in John 19:23 (Brown, *Death of the Messiah*, 955).

14. While it might have been standard practice for soldiers to help themselves to the clothing of those they crucified, the detail that the soldiers *gambled* for Jesus' clothing reflects the influence of the psalm. If soldiers routinely gambled for the clothing of the crucified, that detail in the story would not have attracted enough attention for Christians to ponder it in light of the scriptures. If a scripture is fulfilled at every crucifixion, that fulfillment loses its ability to single out Jesus as anyone special.

15. The whole scene in John 19:23–24 might well be fictional, but that would not affect the analysis of how the author used the psalm verse in composing it.

synonymous parallelism described two distinct actions and then fashioned a gospel scene accordingly.

John 19:28–29

As Jesus is about to die,

> he says (in order to fulfill the scripture), "I'm thirsty." A bowl of sour wine was sitting there, so they filled a sponge with wine, stuck it on some hyssop, and held it to his mouth. (SV)

This short scene is unusual because it is the only one in this gospel that claims that a specific event fulfills the scriptures without quoting the scripture it fulfills. It is also the only scene in which Jesus says or does something that causes someone else to fulfill scripture. The scripture to which John alludes is from Psalm 69, a text he knows well, having quoted from it twice before (Ps 69:9 in John 2:17 and Ps 69:4 in John 15:25). This time Ps 69:21 is fulfilled: "for my thirst they gave me sour wine to drink." (The "sour wine" was a vinegary-tasting blend of water and cheap wine.)

The synoptic gospels also describe the crucified Jesus being offered sour wine, but only John (in John 19:23–25) points out that this was done in order to fulfill scripture. John's scene differs from the synoptic one also in that the Johannine Jesus takes the initiative to fulfill scripture by saying "I'm thirsty." In the synoptic scene the soldiers offer Jesus wine on their own initiative (Matt 27:48 / Mark 15:36 / Luke 23:36). In John's gospel Jesus is in full control at all times, especially during his passion[16] and even as he is dying. While the details in this short scene are different in John and the synoptics, both versions have been generated by the OT scripture: both Mark and John (or the Christian storytellers before them) invented the detail about the wine offered to Jesus on the basis of Ps 69:21.

John 19:33–37

In 19:31–32 John narrates the gruesome process in which soldiers broke the legs of the two men crucified with Jesus in order to hasten their deaths. Verses 33 and 34 indicate that since Jesus was already dead, the soldiers did not break his legs, but instead one soldier thrust a spear between his ribs. In 19:36–37 John reports that both what the soldiers did and did not do

---

16. For example, in John's narrative—in contradiction to the synoptic gospels—Jesus does not need anyone's help in carrying the cross; see the emphatic "by himself" in John 19:17 (in contrast to Matt 27:32 / Mark 15:21 / Luke 23:36).

fulfilled scripture: "None of his bones will be broken," and "They will look at the one whom they have pierced."

The entire scene (19:31–37) is unique to John. While the synoptics mention that two men were crucified with Jesus, those gospels show no interest in how the men died, nor do they mention the spear thrust into the corpse of Jesus. John narrates the breaking of the two men's legs only in order to highlight what was *not* done to Jesus. The soldiers do not need to break Jesus' legs because the soldiers "saw that he was already dead" (19:33). So far John's story makes sense. What happens next does not. Why stab a dead man? Readers are tempted to fill in this blank by imagining that the soldier stabbed Jesus to make sure that Jesus was truly dead. But if so, then why did the soldiers refrain from breaking his legs? Perhaps John intended this detail in the story to be illogical, so as to underscore the power of prophecy: the soldier with the spear acted the way he did, not because it made sense to him, but because scripture must be fulfilled and he was the unwitting means to its fulfillment. Despite John's insistence that this particular detail in the story is based on an eyewitness report (19:35), it is difficult to overcome the suspicion that the author's more likely inspirations for this scene are the two scriptures he quotes. Jesus, proclaimed by John the Baptizer as the Lamb of God (1:29), dies on the eve of Passover while the Passover lambs are being slaughtered.[17] So it makes perfect theological sense to John that the dead body of Jesus was treated with the same care as a lamb slaughtered for Passover: "None of his bones shall be broken" (Exod 12:46; Num 9:12). That Roman executioners unknowingly treat Jesus as a Passover lamb is further testimony to the power of the divine plan by which Jesus fulfills scripture.

The Role of Scripture outside the Fulfillment Scenes

It is self-evident that John has the OT in mind in those scenes where he announces that the scriptures were fulfilled. But the role of the scriptures in John's passion narrative is more subtle than explicit quotation, and their influence reaches beyond those obvious examples. When a narrative element is unique to John, and especially when there is something incongruous about it, it is often a helpful hypothesis that John has shaped the story the way he has because he has based it on an OT passage. While some degree of

17. John notes that Jesus was condemned to death on "the day of preparation for Passover, about twelve noon" (19:14), which was the time the Passover lambs began to be slaughtered in the temple. See Brown, *Death of the Messiah*, 847, and the Jewish sources cited there.

guesswork is unavoidable in such theorizing, in a few examples, the connection between the narrative detail and the OT text is fairly clear. In such cases it is easier to imagine that John constructed the story with the scriptural passage in mind than that the narrative detail just happens by coincidence to match up to a certain scripture. We can briefly consider three examples.

John 18:6

All the gospels tell of Jesus' being arrested by armed men, but John's version of this scene is epic in its scale: in addition to the Jewish temple police, an entire Roman military formation, a cohort, which consisted of six hundred troops, is sent to take Jesus into custody. Jesus confronts them and asks, "Who is it you're looking for?" When they say, "Jesus of Nazareth," he identifies himself by saying, in Greek, *Egō eimi* (literally, "I am"). In ordinary speech that means simply "I am he" but is also the name of God (see Exod 3:14), which is how John uses it here. What happens next is probably the most bizarre, yet theologically brilliant, scene in all the gospels: "As soon as he said, 'I am,' they all stepped back and fell to the ground" (John 18:6). Taken literally, the scene is absurd: a massive, combat-ready military unit cowering face down in the dust in front of Jesus. Taken metaphorically, however, the symbolism is perfect: both the armed Jewish officers and the full military might of Rome assume the posture of submission and worship when Jesus reveals his true identity by pronouncing the divine name.

One detail doesn't fit, however. Before the soldiers fall on their knees, they all step back. Why? John depicts them prostrate before Jesus, not falling backwards, so there is no physical reason for them to step back before prostrating themselves. There is also a grammatical oddity in John's Greek here, which literally reads "they went out to the behind" or "they retreated backwards." The prepositional phrase "to the behind/backward" (*eis ta opisō*) is superfluous and clumsy. The incongruities in John's narration and in his grammar correspond exactly to a verse from the psalms: "my enemies shall turn back backwards" (*eis ta opisō*) (Ps 56:9 [55:10 LXX]). A coincidence? Perhaps. But it's much more likely that John inserts this awkward detail into his story because he took a cue from this psalm.[18]

---

18. Hanson, *Prophetic Gospel*, 203.

John 19:5

Another highly dramatic—and justifiably famous—scene in John's passion narrative is the one in which Pilate presents Jesus, wearing a crown of thorns and a purple cloak, to the crowd and says, "Behold the man!" Since this very public spectacle is found only in John its historicity is dubious. Yet its symbolic meaning, unlike the meaning of the soldiers' groveling before Jesus, is not obvious. What is "Behold the man" supposed to signify? If Pilate were to say "Behold your king" the scene would make good sense as realistic fiction because Jesus has been mockingly arrayed with a crown and royal robe. The Johannine irony of that would have been pitch perfect. It is precisely because Pilate's proclamation is enigmatic that we should suspect a scriptural basis for it. The most appealing candidate is Zech 6:12, in which two people are told to go to a high priest named Joshua (which is "Jesus," *Iēsous* in Greek), put a crown on his head and proclaim "Behold the man! His name is Branch . . . for he shall build the temple of the Lord."[19] How much of the context after "Behold the man" John has in mind is impossible to say. Perhaps John saw a connection between "he shall build a temple to the Lord" and Jesus' disruption of the temple, during which he proclaimed, "Destroy this temple and I will raise it up in three days" (John 2:19). "His name is Branch" is obscure. Perhaps—and this is very speculative—John linked the Branch in Zech 6:12 to a messianic oracle in the book of Numbers: "A star shall rise from Jacob, and *the man* shall arise from Israel" (Num 24:17). The connection between the last verse and Branch is easier to see in Greek than in English, for "branch" (*anatolē*) is etymologically related to "rise" (*anatelō*).[20]

John 19:29

When a soldier offers Jesus wine, he does so in a way that is physically impossible: he dips a sponge in wine, sticks the sponge on a stalk of hyssop, and raises it to the lips of the crucified Jesus. Hyssop is a short fernlike plant and is quite incapable of supporting the weight of a soaked sponge. Mark and Matthew give a realistic version of this event in which a soldier uses a stick to lift a sponge (Mark 15:36 / Matt 27:48). Since John's description cannot be meant literally, we naturally suspect that he is interested in hyssop's symbolism, which has to do with its role in the Passover ritual: "Slaughter the Passover lamb. Then take a bunch of hyssop, dip it in the blood . . . and

19. Ibid., 204.
20. Brown, *Gospel of John*, 2:876.

touch the lintel and the two doorposts with the blood" (Exod 12:21–22). The appearance of hyssop at the cross of Jesus has nothing to do with historical memory. John adds this botanically impossible detail in order to reinforce his interpretation of the crucified Jesus as a slaughtered Passover lamb (see above).

One medieval Greek gospel manuscript features an ingenious modification of John 19:29. The copyist substituted *hyssos* (javelin) for *hyssopos* (hyssop), probably in the belief that the text from which he was copying was in error.[21]

Summary

Our analysis of how John pairs prophecies and their fulfillments shows that it was no easy task. In five cases John quotes scripture selectively and precisely, lifting single verses out of contexts that cannot possibly be applied to Jesus. In two cases John's quotations of scripture show very minor alterations from the wording of the originals; these cases might or might not be examples of retrofitting. In the passion narrative all three of the scenes in which John announces the fulfillment of scripture are literary fictions that he created out of the very scriptures that the scenes allegedly fulfilled. John enriched several other scenes in the passion narrative with symbolically significant details taken from scriptures that he believed pointed to Jesus.

As is the case with Matthew's gospel, John's shows that the author used the scriptures carefully and creatively in constructing his argument that Jesus fulfilled them. John's work on the prophecies that Jesus fulfilled is less extensive than Matthew's, and less varied in how he manipulated the texts he quotes, but it betrays the same conviction that belief in Jesus opens up new and unexpected meanings in the scriptures of Israel.

How John Uses the Fulfillment of Scripture

As in the Gospel of Matthew, so too in John's gospel the demonstration that the scriptures were fulfilled in Jesus is a literary and theological achievement that required deliberation and ingenuity. Why did John go to all that effort? Why was it so important to him to try to prove that Jesus fulfilled scripture? In the next few pages I situate the fulfillment of scripture in John's gospel within its anti-Jewish polemic. I argue that the way John presents the fulfillment of scripture is meant to strengthen his accusation that the Jews

21. Ibid., 2:909.

willfully rejected their messiah. I then consider the fairness and plausibility of this accusation, examining the particulars of John's fulfillment scenes so as to assess whether it was reasonable to expect Jews either of Jesus' time or of John's day to be persuaded that Jesus was the one about whom the scriptures testify.

Anti-Jewish Polemic and the Fulfillment of Scripture

The Gospel of John is an acutely anti-Jewish narrative in which the fulfillment of scripture plays a supportive and explanatory role. The Jewish rejection of Jesus is a major theme in this gospel, and John robustly asserts that "the Jews" are culpable for rejecting Jesus (e.g., John 9:41 and 15:22), a sin for which they will be punished (see, e.g., 3:36). John puts forward several theories to explain Jewish disbelief, the most prominent being their unwillingness to be persuaded by the "signs" or "works" that Jesus performs. Those works were designed to testify to Jesus' divine origin (5:36). So persuasive are Jesus' signs supposed to be that simply hearing them narrated long after the fact should be sufficient grounds for belief in him. Indeed, that is the very reason why John wrote his gospel, as he emphatically explains in its closing words (20:30–31).[22] Therefore, the disbelief of those who personally witnessed Jesus' signs must have been willful (12:37; 15:24). The rhetoric of the accusation is hard to miss: "the Jews" do not believe in Jesus, not because the evidence for his divinity is weak or ambiguous or hard to grasp, but because they knowingly reject the truth. "You do not believe me *because* I speak the truth" (8:45). "The Jews" revulsion for the truth is rooted in their satanic nature: they are like their father, the Devil, who has nothing to do with the truth because he is a liar by nature (8:44). That the Jews are "liars" (8:55) is therefore not something they do, but what they are by nature since "the father of lies" is their father.

There is one place in the gospel where a very different—and contradictory—assessment of Jewish intransigence peeks through. In the Last Supper discourse Jesus warns his followers of coming persecution. "The time is coming when those who kill you will think they are offering devotion to God" (John 16:2b). That unique acknowledgment of Jewish sincerity is surprising, coming as it does on the heels of the venomous accusation that those who oppose Jesus "hate God" (15:23–25). Indeed, the sudden (and

---

22. There is a strong scholarly consensus that John's gospel originally ended with 20:30–31. Chapter 21 is a later appendix. See Brown, *Gospel of John*, 2:1077–80, and the extensive scholarly literature cited there.

isolated) recognition of the sincere, though—from John's perspective—misguided motivations of Jews makes the vituperation against them in the rest of the gospel all the more disturbing. John 16:2 proves that the author knows better.

Another reason for the Jews' rejection of Jesus is their disbelief that he fulfills the scriptures, which John characterizes the same way he does their disbelief in Jesus' signs: as a willful refusal of the truth. John analyzes this root cause of disbelief only once and quite briefly (5:39–40, 46–47), but his argument is clear, almost syllogistic. The scriptures "testify on my behalf, yet you refuse to come to me to have life" (5:39b–40). Moses "wrote about me," so "if you really believed Moses, you would believe me" (5:46). But since they do not believe Jesus, it follows that they must not believe Moses (5:47).

John's self-sealing logic equates Jews' not accepting that Jesus fulfills scripture with their rejection of Moses (i.e., of their own Judaism). John does not point to any behavior (e.g., violating Torah) that shows that Jews disbelieve Moses; he infers that solely from their disbelief in Jesus. That inference would be valid only if it were transparently evident that Moses wrote about Jesus. But John openly admits that that was not true. Although he reports that the disciple Philip mysteriously realized that Jesus was the one "about whom Moses wrote" (1:45), John goes out of his way to explain that the disciples failed to understand that Jesus had fulfilled scripture until after the resurrection (2:22; 12:16). Philip's proclamation in 1:45 is but one of numerous examples of things in John's gospel that make sense only in the light of faith in the risen Jesus. Therefore, for John to maintain that the Jews should have recognized that Jesus fulfills scripture is tantamount to holding that they should have known during Jesus' lifetime what his followers failed to realize until after they came to believe in his resurrection.

Two final and closely related explanations for Jewish failure to believe in Jesus make appeal to prophecy. The first says simply that Jewish disbelief is itself a fulfillment of prophecy.

> 37 Although he had performed so many signs before their eyes, they did not believe in him, 38 in order that the word the prophet Isaiah spoke would be fulfilled:
>
> "Lord, who has believed our message?
>> To whom is God's might revealed?"
>> (John 12:37–38, quoting Isa 53:1)

John here hints at more than he says. The opening "although" in John 12:37 seems to imply that since the signs Jesus worked were fully sufficient to elicit belief, there must have been something impeding the Jews' recognition of what was so clearly evident. Verse 38 can thus seem to explain that their disbelief was inevitable, for how can prophecy fail to be fulfilled?

The second explanation, which follows immediately after the first one, makes that implication explicit. John bluntly declares,

> ³⁹ And so they were *unable* to believe, because Isaiah also said,
> ⁴⁰ "He has blinded their eyes,
>
> and closed their minds,
>
> to make sure they don't see with their eyes
>
> and understand with their minds,
>
> or else they would turn their lives around
>
> and I would heal them."
>
> ⁴¹ Isaiah said these things because he saw his glory and spoke about it. (John 12:39–41, freely quoting Isa 6:10)

Given this analysis of the divine will as the cause of Jewish disbelief, John's next sentence is puzzling: "Nevertheless, many did believe in him, even many of the ruling class" (12:42a). The "nevertheless" reveals John's awareness of how strange is the ground on which he now treads: *many* Jews believed in Jesus, (a) despite their God-sent blindness, and (b) in defiance of prophecy. However, the full statement introduced by this report shows that John's purpose is to condemn those believers for not professing their faith publicly.

> ⁴² Nevertheless, many did believe in him, even many of the ruling class, but because of the Pharisees they did not admit it, so they wouldn't be thrown out of their congregations. ⁴³ You see, they loved human glory more than the glory that comes from God. (12:42–43)

John 12:37–38 implies and 12:39–40 directly asserts that the Jews were *prevented* by God from believing. If the reader dwells on this, a theological conundrum about divine justice seems inevitable: how can they be held guilty for not doing what God prevented them from doing? But John does not linger. He takes the reader straightaway to the condemnation in 12:42–43, which indicts, not the unbelievers, but the believers who lack the courage of martyrs. John thus quickly moves his audience from a facile condemnation of outsiders to anxious self-examination. (Do we—or would we—have the courage to profess faith in Jesus in the face of danger?) The rhetoric of v. 43 is especially effective, for it shifts the motivation for silence away from fear to a craven desire for transient glory. To hide one's faith out of fear of persecution is understandable, perhaps even excusable; to do so out of a preference for "human glory" over "the glory that comes from God" is devastatingly reprehensible.

I have drawn attention to how John draws attention *away* from the theological problem that is just below the surface of his two appeals to Isaiah. That John holds Jews morally culpable for not believing in Jesus is abundantly evident. And yet in 12:39–40, and in at least one other place (6:44: "No one can come to me unless the Father calls him"), John asserts that God himself prevented them from believing. John does not attempt to resolve this issue, nor does he even raise it. Perhaps he did not recognize it as a problem.

Who Knew?

How were those who encountered Jesus supposed to realize that the scriptures testify to him (John 5:39)? At the point in the story when Jesus makes that declaration, the only thing that had happened so far that John claims fulfilled scripture was Jesus' disruption of the temple, which John admits that the disciples did not connect to scripture until later (2:17, 22), and which no other gospel presents as a fulfillment of scripture. As for the other fulfillment scenes in John, we can ask about them what we asked about those in the Gospel of Matthew: which of them deal with publicly observable events or circumstances that neutral observers could plausibly have interpreted as fulfillments of prophecy?

- That God had sent Jesus, the bread of life, from heaven (John 6:31–33) in fulfillment of Ps 78:24 ("He gave them bread from heaven to eat") is an obviously Christian interpretation and not something anyone can verify by observation.

- Jesus' entry into Jerusalem on a donkey (12:12–15) was a public event, but John admits that even the disciples did not connect it to prophecy until after they came to believe in Jesus' resurrection.

- That "the Jews" did not believe in Jesus (12:37–40) would be public knowledge; and perhaps it is plausible that the public would perceive the truth behind John's hyperbolic characterization that "the world" hated Jesus (15:25). But there is no good reason to think that people would see those circumstances as fulfilling scripture (Isa 53:1; Isa 6:9–10; Ps 35:19 respectively) unless they already believed that the scriptures were written about Jesus.

- Few people outside those who were present at Jesus' arrest would know that Jesus had been betrayed by one of his followers (John 13:18). Perhaps a few of those few would associate that fact with Ps 41:9 ("The one who ate my bread has lifted his heel against me") and thereby make the connection that Jesus had disclosed privately to his disciples (John 15:25).

- The crucifixion was a public event, to be sure. However, the three details of Jesus' execution that, according to John, fulfill prophecy (the soldiers' gambling for Jesus' clothing [19:23–24], their refraining from breaking his legs [19:32–33, 36], and the spearing of his corpse [19:34, 37]) are almost certainly narrative fictions, created by John out of the very scriptures they fulfill (see above).

In summary, the examination of each of the specific scriptures that John claims were fulfilled in the life and death of Jesus turns up virtually nothing to sustain the case that Jews who saw and heard Jesus should have realized that those scriptures were being fulfilled. And there is no basis at all for them to have concluded that Moses wrote about Jesus.

When John wraps up his narration of Jesus' public ministry, he reflects on Jewish disbelief in Jesus (12:37–40), interpreting it as a double fulfillment of prophecy. First, Jews' disbelief was itself a fulfillment of prophecy (12:38). Second, they were unable to believe because it was prophesied that God would prevent them (12:39–40). Here again John has to distort the quoted prophecy's original meaning in order to apply it to his story. Both quotations are from Isaiah and reflect on the failure of that prophet's own message to elicit a favorable response from Israel. John's recontextualization of both quotations forces them to refer to Jesus' preaching about himself.

John's Audience

All the gospels, and John especially, are stories about the past (the career of Jesus) that have meaning for the author's own present. "The Jews" in John's gospel, although they appear in the story as figures from the time of Jesus, represent for John's audience the Jews of their own day, with whom John's people are in hostile and futile debate. When Jesus tells Nicodemus, "We tell what we know, and we give evidence about what we've seen, but none of you accepts our evidence" (John 3:11), the plural pronouns are transparent indicators that John is using the character of Jesus to speak on behalf of his community to the Jews of his day.

A traumatic situation that seems to have catalyzed the writing of this gospel was a move by Jewish authorities to ban followers of Jesus from the synagogue (see 9:22). John wrote his gospel, not to persuade Jews that Jesus is the messiah—it was too late for that—but to reassure his audience that they were right and the Jews who "persecute" them (15:20) were wrong. Situating John's theme of the fulfillment of scripture in that context helps us understand its function. At a time when Jewish authorities were telling those who believed in Jesus that they had no place in Israel's religion, the argument that the scriptures of Israel were written about Jesus was a powerful means for his followers to reassert their claim to their religious heritage. If the specific arguments that particular details in the story of Jesus fulfilled particular scriptures were ever presented to real-life Jews—as opposed to the fictive Jews in stories told by followers of Jesus—in the hopes of persuading them, by the time John wrote his gospel those arguments were strictly for the benefit of John's Christian audience. In seeking to understand the gospel's impact on its audience, it is beside the point to ask whether those arguments refer to publicly observable events, or whether those events have some evident connection to the scriptures they supposedly fulfill. Those questions are aimed at assessing whether reasonable persons would accept the claim that Jesus fulfilled prophecy. But in the polemical situation in which John writes, opponents are not treated as reasonable people. If John's audience is willing to believe that "the Jews" are children of Satan—and they have to be willing to do so because that is what Jesus himself calls his/their enemies—then we are long past the point where rational arguments can find a forum. From John's perspective, the Jewish rejection of Jesus is both willful and culpable.

> If I hadn't come and spoken to them, they wouldn't be guilty of sin. But as it is, they have no excuse for their sin. Those who hate me also hate my Father. If I hadn't performed feats among them such as no one else has ever performed, they wouldn't be guilty of sin. But as it is, they have witnessed these feats and come to hate both me and my Father. (John 15:22–24)

It should not surprise us that John then asserts that this hatred for Jesus fulfills scripture (15:25).

In light of the historical context of John's gospel, we can adjust our questions about the plausibility of his argument from prophecy. Instead of asking whether the alleged fulfillments of scripture that John points out would have been evident to the Jews in the story at the time of Jesus, we can ask how those fulfillment scenes might be evaluated by Jews of John's time, sixty or so years after the death of Jesus. In that context we don't have to wonder how or if people might realize which specific scriptures were supposedly fulfilled, because John quotes the scriptures he wants readers to consider. Similarly, we don't have to evaluate whether people knew about the events or circumstances that fulfill those scriptures, because John narrates them and coordinates them with the scriptures he quotes. Nor do we have to factor in John's acknowledgement that the disciples connected specific scriptures to certain events only after the resurrection, because John transmits their retrospective insights.

In assessing how Jews of John's day might respond to his message that they should believe that Jesus is the messiah because he fulfilled scripture, we can ask two questions. First, are the scriptures John quotes actually prophecies about the messiah? Second, how persuasive would the claim that Jesus fulfilled the scriptures be to those who were not already his followers?

Messianic Prophecies?

John quotes ten scriptures[23] that he claims were fulfilled in his narrative. It is constructive to canvass the Gospel of John, as we have done for the Gospel of Matthew, to see how many of the quoted texts that it asserts were fulfilled are prophetic predictions, and how many are about the messiah or some messianic figure.

1. *John 2:17 (Ps 69:9)*. "Zeal for your house will consume me." In the psalm, the verb refers to a past event ("has consumed"), which John has moved into the future ("will consume") so that it can point ahead to Jesus' death (see below). The psalm itself makes no prediction and is not about a messianic figure; the "me" in the quote is someone praying for deliverance from persecutors.

2. *John 6:31 (Ps 78:24)*. "He gave them bread from heaven to eat" is a transparent reference to the manna of the exodus. It is not a prophecy.

3. *John 12:15 (Zech 9:9)*. "Your king is coming, sitting on a donkey's colt" is a prediction about the future Davidic ruler, a messianic figure.

4–5. *John 12:38 and 40 (Isa 53:1 and 6:10)*. Both of these pronouncements refer to past actions that affected the prophet's own experience. Neither is a prediction, and neither is about a messianic figure.

23. Two of John's eight fulfillment scenes (12:37–40 and 19:33–37) each quote two passages.

6. *John 13:18 (Ps 41:9).* "The one who ate my bread has lifted his heel against me" is not a prediction. In the psalm it describes a past event. The speaker ("me") is not a messiah.

7. *John 15:25 (Ps 69:4).* "They hated me for no reason" is not a prediction, nor is the speaker a messiah.

8. *John 19:24 (Ps 22:18).* "They divided my garments among them, and for my clothes they cast lots" is not a prediction, nor is the speaker a messiah.

9. *John 19:36 (Exod 12:46 / Num 9:12).* "None of his bones shall be broken" is not a prophecy; it is a ritual commandment about how the slaughtered Passover lamb is to be handled.

10. *John 19:37 (Zech 12:10).* "They will look at the one they have pierced." This cryptic oracle is a prediction, but to whom it refers is unclear. Perhaps the pierced one is a prophet who will be killed by the Israelites to whom he was sent. If so, this verse is very unlikely to be a messianic prophecy, since Jewish messianic conceptions, as diverse as they were in the first century, did not include a messiah who would be killed.[24]

Results

Of the ten quoted scriptures allegedly fulfilled in John's gospel, only one (the prediction from Zechariah in John 12:15) can safely be considered a messianic prophecy.

Plausible Fulfillments?

Our second step in assessing John's use of the fulfillment of scripture is to pose the question, what would Jews of John's day make of his claims that the scriptures he quotes were fulfilled in the life and death of Jesus? Let's consider each of John's fulfillment scenes with that question in mind.

---

24. The traditional Hebrew text (the Masoretic Text) of Zech 12:10 is worded strangely: "They will look at *me* whom they have pierced." In context the "me" can only be Yahweh himself. This extremely odd reading has led most editors of critical editions of the Bible to substitute "the one" for "me," on the reasonable assumption that the Hebrew text is corrupt. A rabbinic interpretation solved the difficulty another way, interpreting the sentence to mean that "they" will pierce the messiah and look to God (Brown, *Gospel of John*, 2:955). However, there is no evidence that this interpretation was known in the first century.

(1) Would many agree that Jesus' "zeal" for the temple had "consumed" him (John 2:14–16)? Some might grant that Jesus' disturbance of the temple was motivated by zeal for God's house. However, in order to see Jesus fulfilling that scripture, one would have to interpret his disruption of the temple to be what motivated his enemies to seek his death. While that is a plausible—though not necessary—way to understand the narrative plot in the synoptic gospels (Mark 11:18),[25] John's gospel does not connect the dots in this way. While the synoptic gospels situate Jesus' demonstration in the temple during the last week of his life, John puts it in chapter 2 and draws no connection between it and the threat to Jesus' life. According to John, the death plot against Jesus was motivated by the authorities' alarm at the large numbers of people who believed in him because of his raising of Lazarus (11:45–53).

(2) None except Jesus' followers would believe that he had been sent from heaven, and so only they would acknowledge that he was the fulfillment of "He gave them bread from heaven to eat" (John 6:31–33).[26]

(3) Jesus rode a donkey into Jerusalem (John 12:15). It's hard to see how that would impress people because it was such a commonplace event. Many people had ridden donkeys into that city, and surely they had not fulfilled prophecy by doing so. So although the prophecy from Zechariah is about a figure who might be considered a messiah, there is nothing particularly messianic about riding a donkey. Besides, unless one already regarded Jesus as a king, one would not agree that he fulfilled the prophecy about a *king* riding a donkey.

(4–5) One would have to already believe that Jesus' expansive claims about himself were true in order to realize that people's disbelief in him was a fulfillment of prophecy (John 12:38 and 40).

(6–7) Only those who already believed that Jesus was the messiah would see much significance in the scriptures that were fulfilled when Jesus was betrayed by a friend (John 13:18) and "hated without cause" (John 15:25), for those scriptures would be fulfilled in countless situations of betrayal and undeserved enmity.

(8) Similarly, some people might be impressed that scriptures were fulfilled when Jesus' executioners gambled for his clothing (John 19:24), but they might also object that such a thing had nothing to do with being the messiah.

---

25. Mark 11:18 does not report that Jesus' enemies sought to kill him because of his act in the temple. It says that they decided to kill him *after* his act there because of the crowd's reaction to his teaching.

26. There is no biblical verse with this wording. John seems to be paraphrasing Ps 78:24 or Ps 105:40 or Neh 9:15.

(9) People would have no reason to agree that the prohibition "You shall not break any of its bones" (Exod 12:46) refers to Jesus' body (see John 19:36) unless they were already willing to see him as a slaughtered Passover lamb, which only his followers might do.

(10) A similar problem attends "They will look on him whom they have pierced" (John 19:37, quoting Zech 12:10). Being pierced by a spear was, unfortunately, not all that rare. Certainly thousands of Jews had died that way in the terrible war with Rome (66–70 CE). Moreover, anyone who knew the Zechariah passage quoted by John would realize that it could not refer to Jesus unless one agreed with John to ignore most of the actual prophecy (see p. 182) and to consider only the one sentence he extracts from it.

Results

The results of this analysis confirm those from Matthew's gospel: unless one already believed in Jesus, the chances are very slim that one would be persuaded by John's fulfillment scenes that Jesus had fulfilled scriptures in any way that made him special.

Conclusion

The Gospel of John is unique in its forthright admission that only those who believe that Jesus is the resurrected Son of God can recognize that he fulfilled scripture (John 2:7; 12:16). John, like Matthew, periodically interrupts the gospel narrative to explain how events in it fulfill specific quoted scriptures. Also like Matthew, John *helps* Jesus fulfill scripture, in three interesting ways. First, John is quite selective in quoting the scriptures that he claims were fulfilled, isolating just the right words to lift from a passage, while avoiding adjacent phrases that cannot apply to Jesus. Second, John reports Jesus' fulfilling a prediction that he quotes as scripture, but that is not actually a biblical text (John 7:37–38). Third, John uses scriptures as raw material in composing certain scenes in which those same scriptures are fulfilled. Scenes composed in this fashion can demonstrate the fulfillment of scripture with unusual clarity.

John's gospel is colored throughout by an undisguised anti-Jewish polemic that heaps moral condemnation on Jews for not believing in Jesus. John, speaking through Jesus, asserts that Jews have no excuse for not embracing Jesus as the Son of God because, among other kinds of "evidence," they should have realized that he fulfilled scripture (John 5:39). This chapter has scrutinized that claim in detail, in regard to Jews both of Jesus' day (the ones portrayed in the narrative) and of John's day (the ones in the imagined audience of his gospel). The analysis in this chapter has argued that for the former group, it is most obscure *how* they were supposed to come to believe in Jesus on the basis of scripture, because the fulfillment scenes that John narrates do not describe events in which neutral observers could reasonably be expected to recognize fulfillments of scripture. In fact, John acknowledges that even Jesus' disciples could not recognize them that way at the time. As for Jews in John's implied audience, I have argued that it is most unrealistic to think that his gospel would persuade them that Jesus was the messiah because he had fulfilled scripture, because only one of the ten quoted passages that John claims had been fulfilled is an actual messianic prediction. Furthermore, the connections John draws between the scenes he narrates and the scriptures he quotes in them are simply not plausible, unless one *already* believes in Jesus.

12

The Fulfillment of Prophecy
in the Letters of Paul

P AUL, WHO CLAIMS TO have been a learned Pharisee before he became an
apostle of Jesus to the gentiles, uses the Jewish scriptures to reinforce and
lend authority to his own teaching. He can quote and allude to them in an
impressive variety of ways, of which it will suffice here to mention a few. Paul
can quote Torah to support his moral teaching (e.g., 1 Cor 9:9). He can adduce
quotations from the prophets that testify to Israel's failure to respond to God's
will (Rom 11:7–10), or to dramatize the sufferings of Christians (Rom 8:36).
Paul can use a prophetic maxim to anchor his teaching about righteousness
(Rom 1:17 and Gal 3:11). He can string together multiple quotations and
paraphrases to pile up scriptural testimonies to the sinfulness of humanity
(Rom 3:10–18) or to God's plan to include gentiles (Rom 15:9–12). He can
explicate an allegorical interpretation of a biblical story (Gal 4:21—5:1), and
utilize pesher techniques (Rom 10:6–8, see pp. 82–83).

These examples are sufficient evidence that Paul had an expert knowledge of scripture and was skilled at using it in a variety of modes. When it
comes to the particular mode of interpretation we are studying (i.e., pointing
out the fulfillment of quoted prophecies, however), Paul uses it sparingly. In
one place he quotes a verse and relates it to Jesus' passion ("For Christ did
not please himself; but, as it is written, 'The insults of those who insult you
have fallen on me'"—Rom 15:3, quoting Ps 69:9), and here the reference to
the passion is implied rather than stated. Other than that fleeting allusion,
Paul does not correlate prophecies to specific events in the life of Jesus. In
fact, Paul tells no stories at all about the life of Jesus, except for a terse recital
of how he established the Lord's Supper (1 Cor 11:23–25). So we will not
find in Paul's letters the explicit fulfillment scenes we see in the gospels.
The closest Paul comes to something similar (other than the quotation in
Rom 15:3 that we just noted) is when he twice quotes from scriptures (in

Rom 9:33 and Gal 3:16) that he understands to be predicting Jesus—but not predicting any specific thing that Jesus did. Considering the range of ways in which Paul handles scripture and not just his overt quotation/fulfillment format, it is apparent that Paul sees prophecy fulfilled not primarily in Jesus himself but in the eschatological establishment of a new people of God (the church) that includes both Jews and gentiles.[1]

Another point of contrast between Paul's letters and the gospels is that while the latter (especially Matthew and John) deliberately create the impression that Jews should have recognized that Jesus fulfilled prophecy, Paul does not even try to pretend that the few fulfillments of scripture he lays out will convince non-Christian Jews. For one, his letters are, obviously, addressed to specific communities who already believe in Christ. What is more important is that Paul articulates a theory—the "veil" theory (2 Cor 3:12–16, see pp. 109–10)—that explains why non-Christian Jews are *unable* to grasp the "true" meaning of their scriptures (i.e., that the scriptures point to and are fulfilled by Christ). It would therefore be irrelevant to ask of Paul's letters the question we asked of the Gospels of Matthew and John: whether the Jews of the author's time could reasonably be expected to accept the claim that the scriptures he quotes were fulfilled in Jesus. In Paul's judgment, non-Christian Jews were prevented by God from seeing the light on this crucial matter.

My task with the letters of Paul is a limited one: to consider a handful of cases in which he claims that a passage he quotes from the Torah, psalms, or prophets has come true in Christ or in the experience of the churches. For each I will consider how the scriptural quotation fits into Paul's argument. Then I will examine those quotations in their original contexts and note the textual and interpretive maneuvers Paul makes in order to show their fulfillment.

Romans 9:25–26 *(Hosea 2:23, 1:10)*

In reflecting on the inclusion of gentiles into the new people of God constituted by the congregations of Christ, Paul quotes the prophet Hosea.

> [25] Those who were not my people I will call "my people,"
>> and her who was not beloved I will call "beloved."
> [26] And in the very place where it was said to them, "You are not my people,"
>> there they shall be called children of the living God. (Rom 9:25–26)

1. Hays, *Echoes of Scripture*, xiii, 86, 110.

Verse 25 is a free quotation, somewhat reworded, of Hos 2:23. Verse 26 is an exact quotation of Hos 1:10b. For Hosea, "not my people" and "not beloved" refers to two children he had fathered with his wife Gomer, a "woman of prostitution" whom Yahweh had commanded Hosea to marry (Hos 1:2). Gomer's designation does not mean she was a literal prostitute; rather, in the metaphorical language of the prophets, the term marks her as one who participated in the fertility rituals of the Canaanite gods.[2] Hosea's marriage thus symbolizes the broken covenant between Yahweh and Israel. Yahweh instructs Hosea to bestow disastrously symbolic names on the children of this marriage, names that signify Yahweh's termination of his covenant with unfaithful Israel. Hosea's daughter is named Lo-ruchamah (literally, "Not Pitied"),[3] and one of his sons is named Lo-ammi, "Not My People" (Hos 1:6–8). Yahweh had epitomized his covenant with Israel with the formula, "You shall be my people and I shall be your God."[4] Hos 1:9 thus announces Yahweh's renunciation of that covenant: "Name him [Hosea's son] Lo-ammi, for you are not my people and I am not your God."

In the context of Hosea's prophecy, the verses used by Paul look forward to Yahweh's gracious restoration of the covenant, a restoration symbolized by the reversal of the rejection signified in the names of the prophet's children: "I will have pity on Not Pitied (Lo-ruchamah), and I will say to Not My People (Lo-ammi), 'You are my people,' and he shall say 'You are my God'" (Hos 2:23). For Hosea, the declarations in 2:23 and 1:10 express the reestablishment of Yahweh's covenant with Israel. Paul, however, reads into these verses a meaning Hosea did not envision: God's incorporation of non-Israelites into a new scheme of salvation.

Romans 10:18 (*Psalm 19:4*)

Paul's exposition of the universal availability of salvation pivots on his famous declaration that "if you confess with your lips that Jesus is lord and believe in your heart that God raised him from the dead, you will be saved" (Rom 10:9). Since salvation depends on confession and belief, Paul voices an obvious worry: "How are they to believe in one of whom they have never heard? And how are they to hear without someone to proclaim him?" (Rom 10:14). Paul responds in 10:18 by asking and answering a question:

2. Wolff, *Hosea*, 13–16.

3. The substitution of "not beloved" in Rom 9:25 for "not pitied" in Hos 2:23 (2:25 in the Hebrew text) follows the wording of the Septuagint.

4. As in, for example, Jer 31:33.

But I ask, have they not heard? Indeed they have: for

"Their voice has gone out to all the earth;

and their words to the ends of the world."

Paul here quotes Ps 19:4 to make the exaggerated assertion that the whole world has heard the good news of salvation. In the context Paul creates, "their voice" and "their words" refer to the preaching of Christian missionaries (chief among them, of course, being Paul himself).

We know even before checking that a biblical psalm will not be about *Christian* missionaries, but Ps 19:4 is not about any words spoken by anyone. In its own context, 19:4 celebrates a stirring paradox: the heavens, especially the night skies, proclaim the glory of the creator's handiwork. The skies are silent, and yet who has not been moved by the magnificence of their testimony?

There is no speech, nor are there words;

their voice is not heard,

Yet their voice goes out through all the earth,

and their words to the end of the world. (Ps 19:3–4)

The psalmist reflects on the mute eloquence of the starry sky. Paul removes those words from their context and puts them into his own, thereby making them refer to the preaching of those who spread the Christian message.

Romans 10:20–21 *(Isaiah 65:1–2)*

20 Isaiah is so bold as to say,

"I have been found by those who did not seek me;

I have shown myself to those who did not ask for me."

21 But of Israel he says, "All day long I have held out my hands to a disobedient and contrary people." (Rom 10:20–21, quoting Isa 65:1–2)

These two quotations from the Book of Isaiah are part of a string of four scriptural quotations in Rom 10:18–21. Verse 18, as we just saw in the last example, quotes Psalm 19 to assert that the whole world has heard the good news about Christ. Verses 19–21 quote three scriptures to assess the contrasting responses to the Christian message. In verse 19 Paul uses a quote from Deuteronomy to predict that Israel will be provoked to jealous anger by the responses of gentiles to the gospel of Christ. Then verses 20 and 21 juxtapose the gentiles' acceptance of God's offer of salvation (v. 20) with

Israel's rejection of it (v. 21). Paul's introduction to verse 21 ("But of Israel he says") makes it plain that he understands verse 20 to refer to gentiles.

What Paul construes as two discrete statements contrasting gentiles and Jews are, in their own context in the Book of Isaiah, part of one continuous divine complaint about intransigent Israel.

> ¹ I was ready to be sought out by those who did not ask,
> > to be found by those who did not seek me.
>
> I said, "Here I am, here I am,"
> > to a nation that did not call my name.
> ² I held out my hand all day long
> > to a rebellious people,
> who walk in a way that is not good. (Isa 65:1–2)

In Isa 65:1 God accuses Israel of refusing to do what it is obliged to do by the covenant ("ask [me]" . . . "seek me" . . . "call my name"), a refusal made all the more blameworthy by God's solicitous desire to remain in covenant relationship with his people. However, Paul, using the Septuagint wording of 65:1, transforms the prophet's *accusation of Israel* into a nonaccusatory *description of gentiles* as those who neither sought God nor asked him to show himself to them. Paul's reliance on the Septuagint version enables him to take advantage of its subtle difference from the Hebrew text. What the latter expresses as Yahweh's willingness ("I was ready") to be sought and found becomes in the Septuagint an expression of an accomplished fact ("I have been found" and "I have shown myself"—see the wording in Rom 10:20). This shade of meaning nicely suits Paul's argument inasmuch as gentiles have already found God through their acceptance of the good news about Christ. Paul's resignification of Isa 65:1 thus enables this prophecy to be fulfilled in his lifetime (and, not incidentally, in part thanks to his own efforts).

1 Corinthians 14:21 (*Isaiah 28:11, 12*)

> In the Law it is written,
> "By people of strange tongues
> > and by the lips of foreigners
> I will speak to this people;
> > yet even then they will not listen to me." (1 Cor 14:21)

This is Paul's free, but faithful, paraphrase of Isa 28:11 and the last clause of 28:12. That Paul attributes this quotation to the Law is probably not a mistake, but rather a customary Jewish way of referring to the whole scripture as the Law. Paul uses this quotation to bolster his nuanced—and confusing—argument about the proper use of glossolalia (speaking in tongues). Paul regards this strange ability as a spiritual gift through which individuals speak to God (1 Cor 14:2) and "build themselves up" (14:4). Paul wishes that all Christians had this ability (14:5), one—he apparently cannot resist pointing out—in which he surpasses everyone else ("I thank God that I speak in tongues more than all of you," 14:18). However, because the utterances of those who speak in tongues are unintelligible, even to the speakers themselves (14:2, 9), no one should speak in tongues in the assembled congregation unless there is someone present who has the spirit-given ability to interpret what is said (14:27–28).

Throughout 1 Corinthians 14 Paul contrasts glossolalia with prophecy, by which he does not mean the recitation of the scriptural prophets' words, but rather the spiritual gift by which one relays messages from God "to other people for their upbuilding and encouragement and consolation" (14:3). Paul argues that prophecy is superior to glossolalia because prophecy is intelligible while glossolalia is not (14:4–19). Paul is worried about the public relations problem posed by glossolalia; "outsiders or unbelievers"[5] who hear a roomful of Christians speaking in tongues will think that they are out of their minds (14:23). And yet—and here it gets confusing—"tongues are a sign not for believers but for unbelievers; prophecy, however, is not for unbelievers but for believers" (14:22).[6] To muddy the waters even more, Paul seems to contradict himself a few lines later by describing how prophecy can lead an *un*believer to salvation (14:24–25).

How Paul's quotation from Isaiah fits into his teaching about the use of glossolalia is unclear. In 1 Cor 14:21, that he means "strange tongues" (cf. Isa 28:11) to refer to glossolalia is obvious, but how he intends the rest of the quotation is puzzling. Who are the "foreigners" (1 Cor 14:21, quoting Isa 28:12)? Does "this people" (1 Cor 14:21; cf. Isa 28:11) refer to Christians or to unbelievers? The last line from Isaiah, "yet even then they will not listen to me" (1 Cor 14:21; cf. Isa 28:12), clearly seems to be an accusation that "they" refuse to heed God's message; but that makes little sense when the message is incomprehensible because it is spoken in tongues. It seems best to conclude that Paul did not intend each clause in the passage to have a specific referent in the worship experiences of his Corinthian audience. Perhaps his purpose for this quotation was simply to make the Corinthians

---

5. The two terms are apparently meant to be synonyms (Conzelmann, *1 Corinthians*, 243).

6. Fee, *First Epistle to the Corinthians*, 676–87, provides a careful and detailed discussion of the problems in this difficult passage.

als *Abweisung*

aware that a scriptural prophecy has been fulfilled in the spiritual gift of glossolalia.

Here are the lines Paul uses, in Isaiah's own words.

> With stammering lip
>> and with alien tongue
> he will speak to his people. (Isa 28:11)

In its original context of Isaiah's time, the "alien tongue" is meant literally; it refers to the language of the Assyrians. The two verses immediately preceding 28:11 describe how Isaiah's opponents mocked his preaching. Since they had scorned Yahweh's message delivered to them in their own language through Isaiah (28:9–10), he threatens in 28:11 that Yahweh will teach them a lesson in the language of an invading foreign army, which in Isaiah's time was Assyrian.

The wording of Paul's quotation matches neither the Septuagint nor the Hebrew text of Isaiah, so we do not know whether Paul chose his own wording or relied on a non-Septuagint Greek translation unknown to us. In either case there is a small but important difference between Paul's version and the original: both the Hebrew text and the Septuagint refer to a single foreign language (Assyrian), while Paul uses the plural "strange tongues." Whether this difference is the result of Paul's conscious retrofitting or whether he found it ready-made in whatever translation he was using, the shift from singular to plural facilitates his new interpretation.

What Isaiah expressed as a threat of divine punishment in the form of a national military disaster, Paul sees "fulfilled" in a spiritual gift intended to enhance the private prayer of Christians.

Galatians 3:16 *(Genesis 15:5 et al.)*

> The promises were made to Abraham and to his offspring. It does not say, "And to offsprings," as of many; but it says, "And to your offspring," that is, to one person, who is Christ. (Gal 3:16)

Here Paul claims that God's covenant promise to Abraham's progeny was not intended for his numerous descendants (i.e., the people of Israel), but for only one of them: Jesus. Paul supports this extraordinarily implausible assertion by making two interpretive moves, one explicit and one covert. The explicit move is to draw attention to a point of grammar: the noun "offspring" (literally, "seed," *sperma* in Greek) is singular in form, not plural. Despite the fact that "seed" is a collective noun in Greek (as well as in

English), Paul here insinuates that God had hidden a secret meaning in plain sight by using the grammatically singular form of the word in his promise to Abraham. Paul's grammatical argument, though disingenuous (see below), is out in the open. His other interpretive tactic, however, is hidden from his audience: he has lifted the phrase "to his seed" out of its context. He had to do that because in its context(s) "to his seed" means the exact opposite of what Paul says it does. Let's have a look.

There are three scenes in Genesis in which Yahweh makes promises about Abraham's seed: Gen 15:5, 17:4–8, and 22:17–18. Each scene uses the singular collective noun "seed" (*zera'* in Hebrew, *sperma* in the Septuagint), and the content of each promise is that Abraham will have *innumerable* descendants.

- *Gen 15:5.* Yahweh instructs Abraham to count the stars if he can. Yahweh then tells him, "So shall your seed be."

- *Gen 17:4–8.* "This is my covenant with you: you shall be the ancestor of a multitude of nations" (17:4). "I will establish my covenant between me and you, and your seed after you throughout their generations" (17:7).

- *Gen 22:17–18.* "I will make your seed as numerous as the stars of heaven and as the sand of the seashore" (22:17).

Out of those three scenes Paul extracts, with surgical precision, only the words "your seed," and on that basis argues that the promises to Abraham's offspring were meant for only one man. We can see why Paul does not quote or describe *what* God promised Abraham, because Paul's interpretation contradicts the plain sense of what God said in each scene. Paul belabors the point that the word "seed" is singular in form, but he is perfectly aware that the word is plural in meaning, for that is how he himself uses it a few paragraphs later: "If you belong to Christ, then *you* (plural) are Abraham's seed (singular), *heirs* according to the promise" (Gal 3:29).

Galatians 4:29

Just as it was at that time, the child who was born according to the flesh persecuted the child who was born according to the spirit, so it is now also. (Gal 4:29)

Paul often uses scripture without quoting it. He can discuss the fulfillment of an unquoted scripture by referring or alluding to a passage or a story, and then applying it to some present reality. In the above example of Gal 3:16 in which Paul quotes a phrase from Genesis, he also alludes to the larger narrative in which that phrase occurs. To round out our cursory examination of Paul's use of the fulfillment of prophecy, we should study one example that does not actually quote a text. Galatians 4:29 shows Paul (mis)using scripture in a highly creative way.

Our verse occurs within Paul's allegorical interpretation of the Genesis narrative about Sarah, wife of Abraham, and Hagar, her slave by whom Abraham fathered Ishmael, his firstborn son (Genesis 16–17). Paul spins this story into an imaginative prediction of the spiritual contrast between Jews (whom Paul symbolizes as Ishmael), who are "enslaved" to Torah, and gentile Christians (whom Paul symbolizes as Isaac), who are "free" from that Law. Galatians 4:29 refers to Ishmael and Isaac, not by their names, but as "the one born according to the flesh" (Ishmael) and "the one born according to the spirit" (Isaac)—even though both were physically fathered by Abraham. Paul alludes to some violence in the brothers' relationship, which he sees fulfilled in the persecution of gentile Christians by Jews: "Just as at that time the one born according to the flesh *persecuted* the one born according to the spirit, so it is now also" (Gal 4:29). Although we do not know what experience is indicated by "it is now also," we have to assume that Paul's Galatian audience did.

However, we should not assume that the Galatians would have understood which scriptural passage Paul alludes to, because there is no part of the Genesis story in which Ishmael persecutes Isaac. In fact, if we see any persecution in the story, it should be in the shameful manner in which Sarah, with Abraham's (and God's) acquiescence, literally "oppresses"[7] the pregnant Hagar (Gen 16:1–6) and later drives her and Ishmael out into the desert (Gen 21:8–14). Genesis 21:9 tells us that Sarah decided to cast out Hagar and Ishmael when she saw the boy "playing (or, literally, "laughing") with her son."[8] In claiming that Ishmael persecuted Isaac, Paul is probably alluding to an imaginative Jewish interpretation of Ishmael's play/laughter as something nefarious.[9] The text of Genesis, however, provides no basis for this biased attempt to excuse Sarah's cruelty. Nowhere does Genesis say, or even imply, that Ishmael persecuted Isaac, or treated him badly in any way.

---

7. The Hebrew verb describing what Sarah did to Hagar in Gen 16:6 (*'anah*) is the same word that describes what the Pharaoh did to the Hebrew slaves in Egypt (Exod 1:11, 12; Deut 26:6).

8. "With her son" is found in the Septuagint but not in the Hebrew text.

9. See the exposition from *Midrash Rabbah* quoted and analyzed in Darr, *Far More Precious*, 142–43.

distort

Paul does not explain how Ishmael allegedly persecuted Isaac, which is probably why he does not quote any passage. That omission makes it all the more troubling that—and how—he proceeds to loosely quote the very next verse after Gen 21:9, the one to which he alludes. We need to note that Gen 21:10 reports *Sarah's* words,[10] because the way Paul "quotes" that verse in Gal 4:30 makes it difficult to overcome the suspicion that he is trying to deceive his gentile audience into thinking that the scripture says that *God*, rather than Sarah, had turned against Ishmael.

> What does the scripture say? "Drive out the slave and her child, for the child of the slave will not share the inheritance with the child of the free woman." (Gal 4:30, Paul's adaptation of Gen 21:10)

Paul's attribution of the quotation simply to "scripture," and his misleading rephrasing of Gen 21:10, clearly give the impression that the quoted verse relays the words of *God* rather than—as the verse itself openly states—the words of Sarah.

Paul needs Ishmael to be the evildoer in order for the story to fit his theological interpretation of the Jewish-gentile dynamic of his own time.[11] If Paul must distort the scripture to make that happen, he seems perfectly willing to do so.

In Paul's Name

Ephesians 4:8 *(Psalm 68:18)*

Critical biblical scholars all but unanimously agree that several NT letters attributed to Paul were not actually written by him:[12] Ephesians, Colossians, 2 Thessalonians, 1 and 2 Timothy, and Titus.[13] These pseudo-Pauline letters have virtually no interest in the fulfillment of scripture. In fact, there seems to be only one place in all these letters where the author quotes scripture and then points to its fulfillment: Eph 4:8, 11. In this lone example, the scripture

10. "She said to Abraham, 'Cast out this slave and her son; for the son of the slave shall not inherit along with my son Isaac.'"

11. Hays, *Echoes of Scripture*, 117–18.

12. See Ehrman, *Forged*, for a thorough and accessible account of the phenomenon of pseudonymity in early Christian literature. Ehrman discusses the evidence for rejecting the authenticity of some NT letters attributed to Paul on pp. 92–114.

13. There is some scholarly dispute about the authenticity of Colossians and 2 Thessalonians. In addition, the Letter to the Hebrews is sometimes mistakenly attributed to Paul, but in the NT the text of this letter is anonymous.

quoted has been retrofitted. The author of Ephesians quotes (or better, para-phrases) scripture in 4:8 in support of what he states in 4:7:

> 7 Each of us was given grace according to the measure of Christ's gift. 8 Therefore it is said,
>
> "When he ascended on high he made captivity itself a captive;
>> he gave gifts to his people." (Eph 4:7–8)

Taking it for granted that the "he" in the quotation refers to Christ, the author of Ephesians explains what "he ascended" both means and implies (4:9–10). The author then indicates that the "gifts" to which the quotation refers are the different authoritative offices of the Christian church. "The gifts he gave were that some would be apostles, some prophets, some evan-gelists, some pastors and teachers" (4:11).

The quotation in Eph 4:8 is a free paraphrase of the first part of Ps 68:18. Here is Ps 68:17–18, with the lines adapted by Ephesians in italics.

> With a mighty chariot force, twice ten thousand,
>> thousands upon thousands,
>> the Lord came from Sinai into his holy place.
> *You ascended the high mountain,*
>> *leading captives in your train*
>> *and receiving gifts from people,*
> even from those who rebel against Yahweh God's abiding there.
> (Ps 68:17–18)

Ps 68:17–18 imagines Yahweh's triumphal procession from Sinai to his temple ("his holy place") in Jerusalem, where he receives tribute from its inhabitants, even from those who oppose his presence in their midst. "The high mountain" was originally a literal expression of the very ancient belief that gods lived on high mountaintops. In the context of Psalm 68, however, "the high mountain" is a grandiose reference to the modest hill in Jerusa-lem, Mount Zion, on which the temple stood.[14]

The author of Ephesians leaves out the word "mountain" in his para-phrase of Ps 68:18. Through that strategic omission, pseudo-Paul trans-forms the psalm's celebration of Yahweh's ascent of Mount Zion ("ascended a high mountain") into Christ's ascension into heaven ("ascended on high"). That interpretation probably came naturally to the author, but it created a problem: how to interpret the next clause in the psalm, "he received gifts from people"? The author solved that problem by rewording that part of the

---

14. Weiser, *Psalms*, 488.

psalm, in two ways. First, he replaced the verb, reversing its meaning so that Christ *gives*, not receives, gifts. Second, the author added a possessive adjective, so that the gifts are given not to people in general, but to *his* people, i.e., to the church. Ephesians' rewriting of Ps 68:18 is thus a textbook example of retrofitting scripture so that it can find its fulfillment in the experience of Christians.

2 Corinthians 6:18 *(2 Samuel 7:14)*

> "I will be your father,
>> and you will be my sons and daughters,"
> says the Lord Almighty. (2 Cor 6:18)

NT scholars are confident not only that whole letters were written in Paul's name but also that some sections in his authentic letters were written after his death and inserted by early editors. One such non-Pauline insertion is 2 Cor 6:14—7:1.[15] Verses 16–18 contain a composite quotation attributed to God and composed of phrases and paraphrases from several OT verses. It concludes with "I will be your father, and you shall be my sons and daughters," which in its present context refers to the relationship between God and Christians. In its original context, however, this declaration—in slightly different words—is made to King David concerning his son Solomon: "I will be a father to him and he shall be a son to me" (2 Sam 7:14). Many OT passages use father-son imagery to characterize the special relationship between Yahweh and the kings. To enable this verse to apply to the relationship between God and Christians, the author of 2 Cor 6:14—7:1 made three surgical modifications in 2 Cor 6:18: "his father" becomes "your (plural) father," "he" becomes "you" (plural), and "son" becomes "sons and daughters." This is an especially clear example of how the NT can take an OT passage and give it new meaning by altering its wording and applying it to a Christian context.

Conclusions

In all the above examples from Paul (and from those who wrote in his name) new meanings are assigned to OT passages, meanings that can be discerned only by rereading the OT in the light of Christian belief. In each case, the new meaning is foreign to the one the quoted scripture has in its

15. See Furnish, *II Corinthians*, 371–83.

own context, which is pretty much par for the course in all ancient efforts to demonstrate the fulfillment of prophecy. In one case (Rom 10:20–21), Paul takes half of his quotation in the same sense it has in its original context, and the other half in a sense antithetical to its original meaning. In another example (Gal 3:16), the meaning Paul gives the quoted scripture overtly contradicts its original meaning, which is why his quotation is so selectively precise, a single phrase extracted from its original context(s) in which his interpretation is impossible. In two cases, Paul's version of a quotation differs from its Hebrew original in ways that make his new interpretation more plausible. In one of those cases (Rom 10:20), the difference Paul exploits is found in the Septuagint. In the other case (1 Cor 14:21), the difference might be the result of retrofitting. Paul's fictionalized plot summary of the story of Ishmael and Isaac in Gal 4:29 is a good example of retrofitting, though an unusual one in that it does not feature a quoted text. Finally, the rewritings of scripture in the pseudo-Pauline Eph 4:8 and 2 Cor 6:18 are paradigm cases of retrofitting.

13

The Fulfillment of Prophecy in the Epistle to the Hebrews

THE EPISTLE TO THE Hebrews has a keen interest in prophecy, as we can see in its very first sentence: "Long ago God spoke to our ancestors in many and various ways by the prophets" (Heb 1:1). Although Hebrews extensively quotes, paraphrases, and alludes to prophetic writings (and other OT texts), it uses prophecy rather differently than do the gospels. The epistle does not focus on the fulfillment of prophecy; it has no formulas ("this happened in order to fulfill *x*") like those in Matthew or John. Hebrews does not quote prophecy in order to *prove* anything about Jesus. The perspective of this epistle is more complex than that. It sees the person of Jesus as God's final revelation to the world. "In these last days God has spoken to us in a son . . . He is the reflection of God's glory and the exact imprint of God's very being" (1:2–3a). In Hebrews we see a sophisticated attempt to correlate the revelation God gave in the past with God's final revelation in Christ.[1] Since the same God has spoken through both Christ and the prophets, the author of Hebrews can look to the prophets for clues to understand Christ and equally to Christ for clues to understand the prophets. As one commentator puts it, "Hebrews interprets Christ in light of the Old Testament and the Old Testament in light of Christ."[2]

The affinity between those two forms of divine revelation is so close in the mind of the author that he can attribute passages from the OT to Jesus himself, as if a verse from a psalm, for example, were a saying of Jesus (see Heb 2:12–13 and 10:5–7). What is perhaps even more unusual, from our perspective at least, is that the author can take the words of psalms that were originally spoken by worshippers to God and represent them as words spoken by God to Jesus, as for example, "In the beginning, Lord, you founded

1. Hughes, *Hebrews*, 57.
2. Koester, *Hebrews*, 117.

the earth, and the heavens are the work of your hands" (Heb 1:10, quoting Ps 102:25).[3]

Because the author of Hebrews proceeds from this interpretive stand-point, he does not set out to persuade outsiders to believe in Jesus and then marshal prophecies as evidence. Whatever the gospels were trying to prove by using prophecy, Hebrews simply assumes. The author's belief about Jesus, as expressed in the eloquent language of 1:2–3, is not something the author seeks to demonstrate; it is rather the starting point for the epistle's theologi-cal reflections. Hebrews thus assumes that faith in Jesus comes first; then, with that faith firmly in place, the believer can recognize Jesus in the OT.

We can see this interpretive process unfold as the author explains the symbolic meaning of a certain arrangement in Israelite worship. The author gives a detailed description of the sanctuary (literally "tent") the Israelites wandering in the desert constructed as their first place to worship Yahweh (Heb 9:1–5). The author explains in particular that this sanctuary tent housed a second, inner sanctuary called the Holy of Holies. The priests used the outer sanctuary on a daily basis,[4] whereas the Holy of Holies was entered only once a year by the high priest (Heb 9:6–7) on the Day of Atonement (see Lev 16:29–34). The author then gives a symbolic interpretation of the distinction between the two sanctuaries, an interpretation he attributes to the Holy Spirit.

> By this the Holy Spirit indicates that the way into the sanctuary has not yet been disclosed as long as the first tent is still stand-ing. This is a symbol [literally, "parable"] of the present time, during which gifts and sacrifices are offered that cannot perfect the conscience of the worshipper, but deal only with food and drink and various baptisms, regulations for the body imposed until the time comes to set things right. (Heb 9:8–10)

The author sees in this symbolic interpretation the key to the meaning of Christ's death: Jesus acted as a high priest entering the Holy of Holies and offering himself as a sacrifice to atone for human sin (Heb 9:11–14).

The Holy Spirit and the (Re)Interpretation of Scripture

What is most interesting in the above passage from Hebrews 9 about the two sanctuaries is the description of the Holy Spirit's role. Prior to chapter 9, the last place that this epistle mentions the Holy Spirit describes its role

---

3. See Hughes, *Hebrews*, 61.

4. See, for example, the daily priestly duties prescribed in Lev 24:1–9.

of relating the OT to "today" (Heb 3:7). What is more, the author there presents a quotation from Psalm 95 as if it were spoken directly by the Holy Spirit: "As the Holy Spirit says, . . ." (Heb 3:7a). In Heb 9:8 it speaks again: "The Holy Spirit indicates that the way into the [second] sanctuary has not yet been disclosed as long as the first sanctuary was still standing," that is, as long as the system of worship represented by the first sanctuary was valid. Within the full context of Heb 9:1–14, the author asserts in 9:8 that even though the high priest entered that sanctuary every year on the Day of Atonement, the "true" way into that sanctuary was not known until the significance of the death of Jesus was understood.

The author is here claiming that those who have received the Holy Spirit (i.e., Christians) have a unique insight into the meaning of the OT that was not possible for earlier readers of the scriptures.[5] That claim is evidence that Hebrews has no interest in the agenda we can see just below the surface in Matthew: accusing Jews of ignoring how Jesus fulfilled prophecy. For the author of Hebrews, the connection between Jesus and the scriptures is revealed by the Holy Spirit.[6] Hebrews 9:8–10 shows both the author's conviction that OT realities are symbols/parables pointing to Christ *and* the author's acknowledgment that such a truth could not be realized until Christ came to earth and the Holy Spirit came to Christians. The OT may point to Christ, but only Christian faith enables one to see *how* it points to him.

The role of the Holy Spirit in making the OT speak directly to the Christian readers of this epistle is in evidence again in chapter 10:

> The Holy Spirit testifies *to us*, saying,
> "This is the covenant that I will make with them
>   after those days," says the Lord:
> "I will put my laws in their hearts,
>   and I will write them on their minds."
>   (Heb 10:15–16, quoting Jer 31:33)

The author attributes the words of Jeremiah to the Holy Spirit, and states that those words were spoken to "us," not to Jeremiah's audience in the past. That is surely why the quotation has been slightly altered. In this prophecy, as it reads in the book of Jeremiah, God promises to make a new covenant "with the house of Israel." But since the audience of the epistle is Christian, not Israelite, the author changed the prophecy to read "with them." This minor change in wording produces a major change in meaning, without which the quotation would not easily apply to "us." The Holy Spirit may speak the

5. Lane, *Hebrews*, 223.
6. Koester, *Hebrews*, 118.

words of prophecy to "us," but the author helped those words apply to us by strategically rewriting them.

In many cases where NT quotations of OT texts are close, but not exact, it is appropriate to wonder whether the changes were made intentionally. Ancient writers often quoted from memory and, at least in some cases, it is entirely likely that small differences are the result of less than perfect memories. (Several times I have consulted a verse I know well and have been surprised that it reads somewhat differently than I remember it. I suspect this kind of experience is fairly common.) However, in the specific case above of Heb 10:16, there can be no doubt that the alteration in wording is intentional because not too far back in this epistle (Heb 8:10) the author quotes the same prophecy from Jeremiah (Jer 31:33), but this time in its original wording.

Heb 8:10	*Heb 10:16*
"This is the covenant that I will make	"This is the covenant that I will make
with the house of Israel	*with them*
after those days," says the Lord:	after those days," says the Lord:
"I will put my laws in their hearts,	"I will put my laws in their hearts,
and I will write them on their minds."	and I will write them on their minds."

Note how Jeremiah's prophecy is introduced the first time the author quotes it:

> God finds fault with them [the Israelites] when he says,
> "The days are surely coming," says the Lord,
>> "when I will establish a new covenant with the house of Israel."
>> (Heb 8:8–9, quoting Jer 31:31).

Comparing Heb 10:15–16 to 8:8–9, we see that when the words of Jeremiah are interpreted as a *criticism* ("God finds fault with them," 8:8), those words are accurately quoted as spoken to "the house of Israel." But when that same prophecy is reinterpreted in 10:15–16 as a *promise*, the author rewords it so that it can be thought of us spoken to "us" (10:15). One begins to see a pattern.

Retrofitting in Hebrews

Since this epistle assumes, rather than argues, that Jesus fulfilled the scriptures, it does not make overt claims like those we see when the gospels quote an OT passage and then describe exactly how Jesus fulfilled it. Nevertheless, Hebrews requires some scrutiny because of the way in which it retrofits OT passages, trimming and rewording them so that they can more easily be interpreted as predictions about Jesus.

For our purposes it is sufficient to examine one example of Hebrews' textual manipulation:[7] the use of Psalm 8 in Heb 2:5–9. Psalm 8 is a masterpiece of poetic reflection, using the immensity and beauty of the night sky to emphasize the paradoxical status of human beings.

> 3 When I look at your heavens, the work of your fingers,
>> the moon and the stars that you have established;
>
> 4 what are human beings that you are mindful of them,
>> mortals that you care for them?
>
> 5 Yet you have made them a little lower than gods,[8]
>> and crowned them with glory and honor.
>
> 6 You have given them dominion over the works of your hands;
>> you have put all things under their feet. (Ps 8:3–6)

Compared to the glories of the heavens human beings are so insignificant that the psalmist wonders why God takes any notice of us. Nevertheless, God has bestowed great dignity on our species, making us "little lower than gods" and entrusting us with "dominion" over all the other creatures of the earth (see Gen 1:26).

The author of Hebrews exploits one particular poetic feature of Psalm 8: its use of singular nouns and pronouns to refer to the human race, just as English speakers use the singular "humanity" (or, in noninclusive language, "man"). Translated literally, with the singular forms italicized, Ps 8:4–6 reads:

7. Other examples include the use of Ps 45:6–7 in Heb 1:8–9 (see Attridge, *Epistle to the Hebrews*, 58–60, and Lane, *Hebrews*, 29–30) and the use of Ps 40:6–8 in Heb 10:5–7 (see Koester, *Hebrews*, 433).

8. The NRSV translates this phrase "a little lower than God" and includes a note indicating that it can also be translated "*than the divine beings* or *angels.*" The Hebrew word in question here is the curious noun *elohim*, which is plural in form, but in the Bible it usually refers to the god of Israel. Whether it means "God" or "gods" must be determined from context. Furthermore, the Hebrew alphabet has no capital letters, and so translators must decide when to capitalize a noun: should it be "Gods" or "gods"? For a discussion of how Israelite belief in polytheism is routinely disguised in English translations, see Penchansky, "No Other Gods."

> ⁴ What is *man* that you are mindful of *him*,
>
>   *the son of man* that you care for *him*?
>
> ⁵ Yet you have made *him* a little lower than gods,
>
>   and crowned *him* with glory and honor.
>
> ⁶ You have given *him* dominion over the works of your hands;
>
>   you have put all things under *his* feet.

(The Hebrew word *'adam* means a human being of either gender. I translate *adam* in verse 4 with the inexact "man" only in order to match the masculine gender of the Hebrew singular pronouns ["him"] and to underline the parallelism with "son of man" [*ben 'adam*]).

The two lines of verse 4 are arranged in a poetic format called synonymous parallelism, a literary device common in biblical poetry, in which two lines express the same thought in different words. The terms "man" and "son of man"[9] thus both refer to human beings in general, or, in this specific context, to insignificant human creatures. The author of Hebrews takes advantage of the ambiguity in the singular form of the words that refer to humanity, and uses that ambiguity to draw an interesting distinction. He starts by making a simple observation about the way things are: it is not yet true that everything in the world is under human control (Heb 2:8). So, the author reasons, the last bit of verse 6 in the psalm ("putting all things under his feet") cannot be true if "his" means "humanity's." Therefore, the author proposes in Heb 2:9 that "his" refers to one extraordinary individual: Jesus (of course). Here is the author's argument in his own words, which come immediately after his quotation of Ps 8:4–6; the ambiguous pronouns are translated here both ways in order to highlight their double meanings:

> ^{8b} Now in subjecting all things to *him/them*, God left nothing outside *his/their* control. As it is, however, we do not yet see everything in subjection to *him/them*, ⁹ but we do see Jesus, who for a little while was made lower than the angels, now crowned with glory and honor. (Heb 2:8b–9a)

The argument is rather ingenious, and it shows how thoughtfully the author engages the OT. Naturally, no one reading Psalm 8 on its own would imagine that it is about a single individual, much less about the messiah. But the author, scrutinizing the psalm from the perspective of belief in the risen

---

9. It is a little surprising that Hebrews does not take "son of man" as a specific prediction about Jesus, since in the gospels that phrase is often his way of referring to himself. This gospel title traditionally translated "the Son of Man" is rendered in SV as "the Human One." For a discussion of the thorny problems in translating this unusual phrase, see Miller, *Complete Gospels*, 208.

and exalted Jesus, can find Jesus in it. However, the synonymous parallelism in the psalm—not the parallelism between "man" and "son of man" in Ps 8:4 (Heb 2:6), but the parallelism between the two halves of Ps 8:5 (Heb 2:7)—works against the author's interpretation. Here is Ps 8:5, translated both from the original Hebrew and from the Greek Septuagint, on which the author of the epistle depends; the differences are in italics.

> *Hebrew*
>
> You have made him/them *a little lower* than the *gods*
>> and have crowned him/them with glory and honor.
>
> *Greek*
>
> You have made him/them *for a little while lower* than the *angels*
>> and have crowned him/them with glory and honor.

In both versions of the psalm, the first and second lines mean the same thing: regardless of whether the first line reads "a little lower than the gods" or "for a little while lower than the angels," it is still clearly equivalent to "crowned with glory and honor." But the author of Hebrews takes these two descriptions to mean opposite things. He was not being arbitrary in reading this verse in this way, however. His interpretation was guided by two small, but significant, changes that the verse underwent when it was translated from Hebrew into Greek: (1) "gods" became "angels," and (2) "a little lower" was translated with a Greek phrase (*brachu ti*) that can also mean "for a little while." "A little lower than gods" in Hebrew thus became in Greek "(for) a little (while) lower than the angels." The author of the epistle found in the Greek version of this verse an opportunity to read Jesus into it. The nuances in the meaning of the verse introduced by its Greek translation allow a Christian interpreter to read it as a description of Jesus: "for a little while lower than the angels, *but* (now)[10] crowned with glory and honor" (Heb 2:9). By contrast, the Hebrew version of Ps 8:5 cannot easily be taken as a description of Jesus, because it would make little sense to say of him, "You have made him a little lower than the gods, *and* have crowned him with glory and honor."

The christological interpretation of Psalm 8 depends entirely on giving the two lines of Ps 8:5 opposite meanings. Thus the author of Hebrews can see Jesus in Psalm 8 only by interpreting it contrary to its natural sense, for the psalm itself presents the two lines in verse 5 in synonymous parallelism,

---

10. The "but" translates the Greek conjunction *kai*, which normally means "and," but can often mean "but" depending on context. The "(now)" is added to the English translation to highlight the temporal contrast connoted by the "but."

whereas our author understands them in sharp contrast to one another. Even so, the epistle's interpretation was not completely arbitrary, for the author seems to have found the clue for it in the subtle transformation in the meaning of the verse that occurred during its translation from Hebrew into Greek.

But our author still faced one problem with the psalm: the first half of verse 6, which, in the Septuagint that our author used, reads, "You have set him [i.e., humanity] over the works of your hands." Here the psalm alludes to the creation story in Genesis 1, in which God grants human beings dominion over the other creatures. The echo of Genesis is reinforced in Ps 8:7–8, which lists the creatures of the land, air, and sea—in an unmistakable allusion to Gen 1:26: "Let us make humanity in our image, according to our likeness; and let them have dominion" over the fish and birds and animals. What problem does "You have set him [i.e., humanity] over the works of your hands" create for the author of Hebrews? That problem is, for the author's interpretation to make sense, he has to argue that "we do not yet see everything in subjection to him [humanity]" (Heb 2:8), despite the fact that the psalm, which the author correctly quotes in 2:8, plainly states that God *had already* set "him" (humanity) over creation, "subjecting all things under his feet."

The author of Hebrews, in effect, is *objecting* to what the psalm asserts. The psalm in its own words directly contradicts the author's interpretation of it. His solution is one we have seen many times before: retrofitting. Here the necessary retrofit was relatively simple; all the author had to do was remove the troublesome sentence from the psalm. Compare these verses of the psalm, translated from the Septuagint, with the edited version of those verses that appears in the epistle:

Psalm 8 (original)	*as quoted in Heb 2:6–8*
⁴ What is man that you are mindful of him,	⁶ What is man that you are mindful of him,
the son of man that you care for him?	the son of man that you care for him?
⁵ Yet you have made him for a little while lower than the gods,	⁷ Yet you have made him for a little while lower than the gods,
and crowned him with glory and honor.	and crowned him with glory and honor.
⁶ You have set him over the work of your hands;	
subjecting all things under his feet,	⁸ subjecting all things under his feet,
⁷ all sheep and oxen,	
and the beasts of the field,	
⁸ the birds of the air,	
and the fish of the sea,	
whatever passes along the paths of the sea.	

The author of Hebrews has handled the psalm with skill. He snipped out the first half of verse 6, and ended his quotation before the psalm gets to verses 7–8, where it alludes to Genesis. Those adjustments make the psalm's references to the creation story disappear. With those elements of the psalm missing, the author can transform the half of verse 6 that he does quote ("subjecting all things under his feet") from a *description* of what God had already done for humanity on the sixth day of creation into a *prediction* of what God will do for Jesus.

The precision with which the author has nipped and tucked the psalm shows how deliberately he worked. The author must have studied the psalm closely, and realized that it did not—indeed, could not—mean what he wanted it to say. However, convinced that the Holy Spirit enabled him to understand the "true" meaning of the scripture, a meaning the psalmist himself could not grasp, the author of Hebrews skillfully edits the psalm so that it can refer to Jesus.

Conclusion

This brief study of the Epistle to the Hebrews discloses some of its complex relationship with OT texts. The author does not present Jesus as the fulfiller of scripture in the direct fashion of the gospels. Rather, the author uses scriptural quotations and allusions to elucidate facets of God's final revelation in Jesus. Conversely, the author also finds in Jesus clues that illuminate the significance of God's past revelation in the scriptures. The connections between the old and the new that sustain this interpretive dynamic are, according to the author, the results of the agency of the Holy Spirit. However, the author does not operate like a passive recipient of inspired interpretations who simply explains the higher meaning of OT passages. Rather, the author of this epistle interacts with the sacred texts by ingeniously and creatively shaping them—editing, selectively quoting, strategically rewording, and retrofitting them—so that they can display their new meanings all the more clearly. The interpretation of Psalm 8 in Heb 2:5–9 is a showcase example of our author's hermeneutical skills. A close-focus analysis of that interpretation reveals a miniature tour-de-force of subtle interpretive moves and textual adjustments that turn the original message of the psalm on its head in order to relate it to Jesus. It seems that for the author of Hebrews, in some cases the "true" significance of a scripture can come to light only by contradicting what it means in its original words.

PART 3

The Argument from Prophecy in Patristic Thought

14

Justin Martyr and the Argument from Prophecy

THE WORK OF JUSTIN is foundational for understanding the traditional Christian perspective on prophecy. The prophets were central to Justin's Christianity. Demonstrating and drawing out the implications of the fulfillment of the scriptures is at the heart of his theological program. He holds up that fulfillment as a compelling proof for the unique truth of Christianity. He devises a rationale for how the Jewish scriptures could be understood as predicting Jesus, and he provides hundreds of concrete examples. At a time when Christians' relationship to those scriptures was up for grabs, and when some were challenging the assumption that Christianity should have anything to do with them, Justin's work amounted to a forceful argument not only that the Jewish scriptures were essential to Christianity but that Christians were the *only* ones with a rightful claim to those sacred writings. Justin links the argument from prophecy directly to Christian supersessionism, that is, the belief that Christians had replaced Jews as the chosen people of God. Justin argues that because Christians had superseded Jews, the Jewish scriptures now belonged to Christians and not to Jews. Justin thus takes Christian tradition a giant step forward in deploying biblical prophecy as a theological weapon against Judaism.

Justin's thinking on prophecy was immensely influential, but not in the sense that many later Christian writers on prophecy depended directly on his exegeses and arguments. What makes Justin's work so significant is that it is the earliest comprehensive articulation of what will become the standard rationalization of Christianity's appropriation of prophecy. Three of Justin's writings (all mid-second century) are extant: the *First Apology*, the *Second Apology*, and the *Dialogue with Trypho*. The dialogue is the longest and will get most of our attention.

I begin by examining a crucial contradiction in Justin's understanding of the relationship between prophecy and Christian faith. I then sketch the overarching anti-Jewish purpose of Justin's argument from prophecy and its context within an intra-Christian theological controversy. I briefly survey the argument from prophecy as Justin presents it in the *First Apology* and then turn to the *Dialogue with Trypho*. I will look at representative samples of his christological exegesis, examine his argument that the prophets foretold the virgin birth, analyze his spurious charge that Jews deleted passages from the scriptures, and look into Justin's curious scriptural "quotations." The chapter concludes with a summary of Justin's contribution to Christian anti-Judaism.

The Place of Prophecy in Justin's Thought

Justin was born in a Roman colony in Samaria between 100 and 110 CE into a wealthy Greco-Roman family. He was well educated and as a young man was devoted to the study of philosophy. After working through the teachings of the various philosophical schools, he identified himself as a Platonist, for it was the philosophy of Plato that he found the most satisfying in his search for the truth about God. Justin became a Christian around 130. He attributes his conversion to his admiration for the courage of Christian martyrs and to a life-changing conversation with a mysterious old man on a secluded beach. In a lengthy conversation the old man maintained that the philosophers were mistaken about the nature of the soul and its ability to know God. Justin then asked, "If these philosophers do not know the truth, what teacher or method shall one follow?" The old man's reply explains the crucial role of the biblical prophets in the search for philosophical truth.

> A long time ago, long before the time of those reputed philosophers, there lived blessed men who were just and loved by God, men who spoke through the inspiration of the Holy Spirit and predicted events that would take place in the future, which events are now taking place. We call these men the prophets. They alone knew the truth and . . . reiterated only what they heard and saw when inspired by the Holy Spirit. Their writings are still extant and whoever reads them with the proper faith will profit greatly in his knowledge of the origin and end of things, and of any other matter that a philosopher should know. In their writings they gave no proof at the time of their statements . . .

but the events that have taken place and are now taking place force you to believe in their words.[1]

The man said much more, but it was his testimony about the prophets that most influenced Justin. After the man departed, never to be seen again, Justin tells us, "my spirit was immediately set on fire, and an affection for the prophets, and for those who are friends of Christ, took hold of me."[2]

The figure of the old man with whom Justin had a sophisticated philosophical exchange looks suspiciously like a convenient autobiographical fiction, a literary device by which Justin can unfold his internal wrestling with his doubts about the sufficiency of Platonism and his attraction to Christianity. In any case, what catches our attention is the central role of the prophets in Justin's conversion. "They *alone* knew the truth and communicated it to humanity." In contrast to the philosophers, who strive for the truth with unaided human reason, the prophets received the truth directly through divine inspiration. Two other assertions in the old man's (i.e., in Justin's) profession of faith are significant for understanding Justin's thought: (1) in order to benefit from the prophetic writings, one must read them "with proper faith," and (2) events that happened long after the prophets spoke "force you to believe their words." Those statements contradict each other. The second one claims that the fulfillment of the prophets' predictions provide objective proof of their truth, whereas the first one recognizes that faith (by which Justin obviously means Christian faith) is necessary to understand what the prophets wrote. The final words of the old man reinforce the necessity of faith to grasp the truth of prophecy. "Above all, beseech God to open to you the gates of light, for no one can perceive or understand these truths unless he has been enlightened by God and his Christ."[3] The recognition that Christ fulfills prophecy is therefore both a *basis* for and a *result* of Christian faith.

Justin seems unaware that his two positions are inconsistent. In all likelihood he saw no tension between them because for him the "grace" to understand the scriptures amounts to the argument from prophecy that Jesus taught to the apostles, through whom it has come to all Christians. "He thus revealed to us all that we have learned from the scriptures *by his grace.*"[4] Justin found the argument from prophecy thoroughly convincing and so, philosopher that he was, inferred that the argument must be

1. Justin, *Dialogue* 7.
2. Justin, *Dialogue* 8.
3. Justin, *Dialogue* 7.
4. Justin, *Dialogue* 100.

thoroughly rational. That is why he thought there was no excuse for those (especially Jews) who were not convinced by it.

> Once the hidden meaning of the scriptures has been brought to light by Christ and the apostles, it shows itself to be rational and convincing, and every denial of its validity and cogency is due either to hatred of the truth . . . or cowardice. There is thus no contradiction between the rationality of the scriptural proof and the necessity of "the grace to understand."[5]

That Justin noticed no contradiction in his twin propositions does not mean that there is none. Think about it. If Justin's argument from prophecy is to be a rational proof of the truth of Christian faith, you need to know what the prophecies predict. Without that knowledge you cannot verify that Jesus fulfilled them. But how can you know what the prophecies predict? According to Justin, you can't know that from the prophecies themselves, for their meanings are obscure (see below). It is only by accepting the interpretation of prophecy that Jesus taught the apostles (and that the apostles faithfully passed on to the church) that you can understand what the prophets were predicting. Justin's argument thus comes full circle. *If* you accept the Christian interpretation of the prophecies, *then* you will see that Jesus fulfilled them.

Furthermore, Justin's premise that the prophecies were opaque until Jesus revealed their meaning depends on a prior belief that Jesus had divine authority to interpret the scriptures. Justin's assertion that the argument from prophecy is rationally compelling is just that: an assertion. Most of his examples of scriptures that predict Jesus are no more persuasive to non-Christians than the interpretations in the Dead Sea peshers were to those outside the Qumran sect. Moreover, any argument that needs to be buttressed by the accusation that those who reject it are haters of the truth automatically invites our skepticism.

We can accept that Justin himself saw no contradiction in asserting, on the one hand, that prophecy can be rightly understood only through Christian faith, and, on the other, that it is objectively evident that Jesus fulfilled prophecy. But the contradiction is there nevertheless. It haunts Justin's longest extant work, the *Dialogue with Trypho*, a messy tour-de-force of the argument from prophecy. Both positions are present in the dialogue but are unevenly matched. Justin's conviction that prophecy proves the truth of Christianity is ubiquitous, whereas his admission that Christian faith is a prerequisite for a true understanding of prophecy comes through in only a few places. The assumption in nearly every chapter of this voluminous

5. Skarsaune, *Proof from Prophecy*, 12–13.

dialogue is that anyone with an open mind should be able to see the over-whelming evidence that the scriptural prophecies are fulfilled in Jesus. Jus-tin clearly intends the argument from prophecy to be a rational argument, one that does not require faith. In fact, in the *First Apology* Justin introduces his argument from prophecy to counter the accusation that Christians have blind faith.[6]

> We do not trust mere statements [without proof], but by ne-cessity believe those who predicted these things before they happened, for we are actual eyewitnesses of events that have happened and are happening in the very manner in which they were foretold. This, we are sure, will appear even to you the greatest and truest proof.[7]

When Justin wraps up the lengthy presentation of "the greatest and truest proof" in the *First Apology* (see below), however, he hedges his confi-dence in ways that betray his awareness that many (most?) are not persuad-ed by the argument from prophecy. Chapter 53, the conclusion to his proof, begins thus: "We could produce many other prophecies, but we refrain from doing so, since we think that those already mentioned are sufficient to con-vince those who have ears to hear and understand." That last phrase builds in the explanation that those who do not agree are either close-minded or not intelligent enough or both. The last sentence of chapter 53, which is Justin's final word on the argument from prophecy, reiterates that explana-tion in harsher terms: "Such self-evident truths should convince and lead to faith those who accept the truth and who are not vainglorious or slaves to their passions."[8] Justin's aggressive rhetoric leaves no doubt about what it implies: since what he proclaims are "self-evident truths," those who claim to be unpersuaded by his arguments must be intellectually dishonest and morally corrupt.

The Dialogue with Trypho and the Argument with Marcion

The *Dialogue with Trypho* is not a genuine dialogue. Justin does 99 percent of the talking. Trypho is cast as a learned Jew, but he functions as Justin's straight man. Once in a while he voices objections to Justin's interpretations, but usually he gets to say only something like "I see; please continue." While

6. Lieu, *Image and Reality*, 79

7. Justin, *First Apology 30*.

8. Justin, *First Apology 53*.

there might have been a historical Trypho with whom Justin had once debated, Trypho, the character in the dialogue, is clearly a literary fiction. No self-respecting Jew would listen in tacit approval to Justin's long-winded and gratuitous "arguments" or tolerate his insulting and disgusting abuse of Jews. The dialogue seems to represent Justin's fantasy of what he would say if he had a docile and helplessly captive Jewish audience.[9]

The dialogue is very long (almost as long as all four gospels combined),[10] repetitive, poorly organized, and padded with numerous extended scriptural quotations. Reading this tome will tax the attention of even the nerdiest scholar. One gets the impression that Justin wanted to include everything he could throw at the issue, so as to bury his fictive opponent in an avalanche of alleged evidence. The scope and depth of the argument shows Justin's huge commitment of intellectual labor to the interpretation of the Jewish scriptures. In several places the details of the argument indicate that Justin is wrestling with actual Jewish objections to some Christian interpretations. Although the Trypho character is Justin's own creation, it seems likely that Justin has argued with real Jews—perhaps among them there was one named Trypho.

The dialogue ends in a failure of sorts: Trypho and his companions are not persuaded. Since Justin (the author, as opposed to the character in the dialogue) knew how the story would end from the start, we can see that the work has two purposes: presenting the argument from prophecy and explaining why Jews reject an argument Justin considers to be transparently true. Hypothetically, Justin could have used the ending of his story to admit that his own scriptural interpretation is not the basis of Christian faith but rather depends on Christian faith. That would have dissolved the contradiction discussed above, for it would have given up the contention that the argument from prophecy is objectively compelling. After all, if an intelligent and fair-minded Jew like Trypho is not persuaded, even after Justin's tidal wave of an argument has washed over him, then it must take more than unaided human reason to see its truth. But Justin does not take this path. Instead he resorts to insult and character assassination, accusing Trypho (and through him, all Jews) of willful blindness, hardness of heart, and the like. In doing so Justin took his cue from the NT and was aided by turning some prophetic denunciations of Israel against the Jews of his own day.

9. Mack, *Who Wrote the New Testament?*, 267.

10. Some of the dialogue is missing. It is structured into two days of "conversation," but the conclusion of the first day and the opening of the second day are missing, as is apparent from the lacuna between chapters 74 and 75. How much text is lost is hard to say, but it is several pages at least. See Skarsaune, *Proof from Prophecy*, 213–15.

(Once again we see a Christian interpretation of Jewish scripture in which its blessings apply to Christians but its condemnations apply to Jews.)

Let's reflect for a moment on what might have been. Trypho remains a Jew as the dialogue ends, but the parting is cordial. Trypho's final quoted words to Justin are, "do not hesitate to remember us as friends when you depart." As they leave, Trypho wishes Justin "a safe voyage and deliverance from every disaster." The last words in the dialogue—Justin's, naturally—express his hope that Trypho and his friends "may some day come to believe entirely as we do that Jesus is the Christ of God."[11]

So, after all the argument, the Jews are still Jewish, but they are not enemies. (Remember, Justin knew before the start how this would all end.) Justin could have used his dialogue to help his readers accept a situation in which Jews and Christians share a body of scriptures that they both venerate but interpret in very different ways. Justin could even insist that Christians understand the scriptures better than Jews do, not because Jews are completely wrong, but because Christians can see deeper (and thus "truer") truths in them than Jews can. Such a scenario would let Christians maintain the superiority of their faith but without denying the legitimacy of the "partial" truth by which Jews live. Such a scenario is not a modern pipe dream anachronistically retrojected to the second century. It is the stance Justin himself takes toward Greek philosophy (see *Second Apology* 13), whose teachings about God had far less in common with Christian beliefs than did Judaism's.

But that was not to be. Justin's argument throughout the dialogue amounts to an uncompromising claim that Jews are utterly in error, and that as a result, the Jewish scriptures belong to Christians and to them alone. That claim takes us to the heart of Justin's project, and to understand it we need to situate it in its own historical and theological context. Justin confronts a problem in the mid-second century that did not exist in the late first century when the gospels were written. What had shifted between then and Justin's time was the Christian relationship to the Jewish scriptures. The evangelists took it for granted that those writings belonged to both Jews and Christians, and that arguing over their meaning was fair game—that was how all Jews of the time worked out their thinking about religion. By the early second century the Christian movement was largely if not overwhelmingly gentile, and its differentiation from Judaism was evident in most regions.[12] A cre-

---

11. I paraphrase that farewell exchange thus:
    Trypho: "I hope you have a safe trip."
    Justin: "I hope you don't end up in hell."

12. See the cautions urged by Knust that in Justin's time one could "not readily identify who was a 'Christian' let alone who was a 'Jew'" (Knust, "Roasting the Lamb," 101,

Marcion

ative Christian thinker, Marcion, son of the bishop of Pontus, studied the writings of Paul and pondered his contrasts between themes such as law and faith, old and new covenant, Adam and Jesus.[13] Marcion thought through those contrasts in his own second-century context and drew a conclusion that would have shocked Paul. Marcion's fundamental insight was that Christianity and Judaism were incompatible. His teaching was elegant, logical, and radical: the god of Israel was a different deity from the God who had sent Jesus. The god of Israel was a god of law and wrathful justice; the Father of Jesus was a God of grace and mercy—does that sound familiar?—a God unknown to humanity until Jesus revealed him. Therefore, Marcion argued, the Jewish scriptures were not sacred to Christians, who should repudiate them along with the god they proclaim.

Mainstream Christian thinkers wanted nothing to do with Marcion's theory, for two main reasons. First, it would make Christianity something brand new, which was not a good thing in a world that was suspicious of innovation and that valued antiquity, tradition, and stability. Second, it would mean that the God who had created the world was inferior and his creation deeply flawed. There was more to all this, of course, but what is important to our agenda is that Christians who rejected Marcion's answer were now compelled to confront the sticky problem of how to relate to the Jewish scriptures. Those writings were obviously about Israel and Israel's God, and they made it clear that the God of Israel's overarching design for its history was "the establishment of a Jewish theocracy in Jerusalem":[14] God would dwell in his temple, and his people would be ruled by his laws and interact with him primarily through the temple cult. The controversy stirred up by Marcion forced a perplexing, and now unavoidable, question: if Christians were not part of Judaism—they did not observe Torah and had nothing to do with the synagogue—then what should they do with the scriptures of Israel?[15] Non-Marcionite Christians needed to find a way to read those scriptures as a story about the God they knew, a story that led up to Jesus (and thus to themselves). In short, Christians had to co-opt a story that did not belong to them, to transform the Jewish scriptures into Christian ones.[16]

Of course Justin did not put it that way. As we can see from his actual interpretations (see the rest of this chapter), he gives no clue that he thought that he was transforming the scriptures at all. He presents his task

---

and the literature cited in note 7).

13. As in, for example, Galatians 3; 2 Cor 3:6–11; and Rom 5:12–21, respectively.

14. Mack, *Who Wrote the New Testament?*, 268.

15. Ibid., 267.

16. Ibid., 268.

Hidden

as discovering their true meaning, which had been there all along but hidden until the coming of Christ allowed it to be seen for what it was.

Justin is clear that the true meanings of the prophecies were hidden. He admits that no one can truly understand prophecy without "a special grace" from God;[17] Jews therefore are "incapable of understanding the truths spoken by God."[18] Justin also asserts that God hid the truth of the scriptures from them in punishment for their sins.[19] The prophecies were so opaque that even demons didn't understand them.[20] Justin explains that the prophets "often expressed themselves in parables and types [prefigurements], thus hiding the truth they held."[21] That the prophecies were actually about Jesus was a complete secret.

> If through the prophets it was obscurely declared that the Christ would suffer and afterwards become Lord of all, it was impossible for anyone to understand this until Christ himself convinced his apostles that such statements were explicitly proclaimed in the scriptures.[22]

Justin's emphasis on the hidden truth of the scriptures pays off for his program because it guarantees that only Christians can possibly understand them. It allows him to deal with Jewish interpretations as debating points to be refuted, but not as anything he needs to take seriously. But this benefit comes at a steep price: Justin's position entails that *the prophecies don't really predict anything*[23] since their meaning can be discovered only in retrospect. Justin seems unaware that this theory of prophecy neutralizes what he elsewhere calls the "work of God": "It is the work of God to announce something before it happens and then to demonstrate that it happened as it was predicted."[24] Justin's understanding of prophecy also effectively undermines the program implicit in the anti-Jewish rhetoric of the gospels, especially Matthew and John. Those two gospels insist that the "Jews" (especially their leaders) should have believed in Jesus after witnessing him fulfill prophecy after prophecy. But that raises the question, if, according to John, the Jews

---

17. Justin, *Dialogue* 92 and 119.
18. Justin, *Dialogue* 38; see also 123.
19. Justin, *Dialogue* 55 and 38.
20. Justin, *First Apology* 54.
21. Justin, *Dialogue* 90; see also 52, 112, 130.
22. Justin, *Dialogue* 76.
23. Mack, *Who Wrote the New Testament?*, 269.
24. Justin, *First Apology* 12.

of Jesus' day could not know what the prophecies were predicting, how were they supposed to realize that Jesus was fulfilling them?

Justin's understanding of prophecy confirms the thesis we deduced earlier in analyzing the fulfillment of prophecy in the gospels: that Jesus' fulfillment of particular prophecies can be perceived only in hindsight, and that, therefore, the conviction that Jesus fulfills prophecy is a result, not the cause, of Christian faith.

Justin's Theory of the Divine *Logos*

Justin's distinctive doctrine of the Word (*logos*) of God was his most productive contribution to the intellectual project of claiming the Jewish scriptures for Christianity. Drawing on the rich and respectable philosophical and theological associations of the term *logos*,[25] Justin developed this pregnant notion into a sophisticated foundation for his Christianizing of the scriptures.[26] Equating the Logos/Word with the Son of God and the "spirit of prophecy," the divine force that inspired all the prophetic utterances in the scriptures, gave Justin a hermeneutical device that enabled him to see the scriptures not only as being *about* Jesus, but as having been *spoken* by him in his pre-earthly existence as the Son of God. Justin goes to great (and wearying) lengths in arguing that it was God the Son, not God the Father, who appeared and spoke to the patriarchs and Moses. One key example will suffice to sample the flavor of his argument. Justin asserts that it was the Word of God (= the Son) who spoke to Moses in the burning bush. (He makes this case in *Dialogue* 59–60 and, somewhat differently, in *First Apology* 63. The latter argument is easier to follow than the one in the dialogue.)

> The Word of God is his Son, and he is called angel and apostle; for as angel he announces all that we must know and [as apostle] is sent out to inform us what has been revealed,[27] as our Lord himself says: "Whoever hears me, hears Him who sent me." This will be further clarified from the following words of Moses: "The angel of God spoke to Moses in a flame of fire out of the midst of the bush and said, 'I am who I am,' the God of Abraham, the God of Isaac, and the God of Jacob, the God of your fathers.'"[28]

25. For a concise summary see Barnard, *Justin Martyr*, 85–87.

26. See Mack, *Who Wrote the New Testament?*, 264–66.

27. The explanation works well in Greek because "angel" (*angelos*) means "messenger" and "apostle" (*apostolos*) is "one who is sent."

28. Justin, *First Apology* 63.

The first premise in Justin's argument is nothing more than a bald asser-tion. Why is the Word/Son also an angel? Because Justin says so. The rest of the argument would not convince a pagan Roman because it rests on the authority of a gospel passage (Luke 10:16). Neither would it convince a Jew because it depends on a key misquoting of the Bible (see below).

There is nothing amiss in Justin's appealing to the authority of the gospels, for he is a Christian. But there is something strange in his assump-tion that non-Christians would accept without question the authority of a Christian text. Justin also plays the gospel card all through his dialogue with Trypho, who lets it pass without objection. That Trypho keeps silence on this matter is one more indication that this dialogue is fictitious and aimed at a Christian audience. But Trypho's silence is more than that: it also helps us see that Justin's central concern is to work out how Christians should re-late to the Jewish scriptures. Justin, the literary character in the dialogue, is trying to convert Jews, but Justin the author is trying to convince Christians to take the Jewish scriptures seriously, to show them how to do that, and to stake a claim to the scriptures as Christian property.

The text of Exodus on which Justin here is focused actually reads, "God said, 'I am who I am'"; it does not read, "the *angel* of God said . . ."[29] Jews attribute the voice from the bush to God himself (which is, after all, what Exod 3:14 plainly states), which is why Justin preempts any Jewish objection by quoting a prophecy against them. Here is how he introduces his argument about the burning bush.

> Even now, all Jews teach that the ineffable God spoke to Moses. That is why the spirit of prophecy, censuring the Jews through Isaiah, said, . . . "Israel has not known me, and my people has not understood me."[30]

Whatever Jews say about God must therefore be wrong.

Justin's logos theory cashes out into the belief that the Jewish scriptures were not only *about* Jesus but *from* him. That belief had three remarkable and far-reaching effects. (1) It lets Justin (and other Christian exegetes) dis-cover clues to Jesus all over the scriptures, in places where they are far from apparent; (2) it transforms the scriptures into words addressed to Chris-tians; and (3) it justifies the Christian claim to own the scriptures—for since Jews do not understand them, they have no moral right to interpret them.

---

29. Exod 3:2 narrates that the angel of the LORD appeared to Moses in the flame. The OT often interchanges God and his angel in scenes where God appears to humans. Justin's quotation is a pastiche of verses 2, 14, and 15 from Exodus 3.

30. Justin, *First Apology* 63, quoting Isa 1:3.

[These prophecies] are contained in your scriptures, or rather *not yours, but ours.* For we believe and obey them, whereas you, although you read them, do not grasp their spirit.[31]

The Argument from Prophecy in the *First Apology*

Before grappling with the argument from prophecy in the *Dialogue with Trypho*, we should survey Justin's other presentation of his argument in the *First Apology*, the opening and closing of which we analyzed above. The basic ideas of the argument in the *First Apology* are the same as in the *Dialogue*, but since the apology is aimed at a Roman audience, Justin lays out his case somewhat differently than he does in the dialogue.

Justin wrote his *First Apology* around 155. He addressed it to the Emperor Antoninus Pius, to his successors Marcus Aurelius and Commodus, and to the Roman Senate. One-third the length of the *Dialogue with Trypho*, the *First Apology* argues that Christians pose no threat to Rome, makes the case for the truth of Christianity and its superiority to Greek and Roman religion, and explains some misunderstood Christian practices. Nearly one-third of the apology (chapters 30–53) is devoted to the argument from prophecy. Justin quotes numerous prophecies (only a few of which are quoted in the gospels) as illustrations of how the details of Jesus' birth, life, and death were predicted in the scriptures. Justin twice tells his audience that they can verify that Jesus did what the prophets predicted from the *Acts of Pilate*,[32] apparently assuming that its attribution to Pilate would give it credibility with Romans.

Although the *First Apology* is addressed to Roman authorities, little of what Justin says about prophecy is tailored for a non-Christian audience. Nearly all the fulfillments of prophecy that Justin lists are presented as self-evident and without supporting arguments. For example, Isa 9:6 ("A child is born to us, / a young man is given to us, / and the government is on his shoulders") "signifies the power of the cross that he [Jesus] placed on his shoulders."[33] Note that Justin casually assumes the paradoxical Christian interpretation of the cross as a sign of power and that Jesus' crucifixion was

---

31. Justin, *Dialogue* 29.

32. The *Acts of Pilate* is an elaborate account of Jesus' trial before Pilate, his crucifixion and burial, events at the empty tomb, and a discussion of Jesus' resurrection by a council of Jewish elders. The prologue to this work claims that it was written in Hebrew by Nicodemus soon after Jesus' death. It was actually written in Greek by an anonymous Christian sometime in the second century.

33. Justin, *First Apology* 35.

a voluntary act. However, a Roman audience would naturally see the cross as a sign of powerlessness, and would not understand a crucifixion as something one does to oneself. Many of Justin's examples would similarly confuse Roman readers, if they would even know what he was talking about. The few cases in which Justin gives arguments to support his christological interpretation of a prophecy do not fare much better because they still assume that the audience accepts the truth of basic Christian claims. For example, Justin quotes a Christian version of Ps 96:10, which reads, "Let them rejoice among the Gentiles, saying, 'The Lord has reigned from the tree.'" ("From the tree" is a Christian gloss; see below.) To connect this verse with Jesus, Justin argues that

> no one before him [Jesus] or after him occasioned joy among the gentiles by being crucified. Yet our Jesus Christ, after his crucifixion and death, arose from the dead, and after ascending into heaven, ruled there; through the good news announced by the apostles in his name to the people of every nation, joy is given to those who look forward to the immortality promised by him.[34]

Justin's argument asserts Jesus' resurrection, ascension, and glorious reign in heaven as simple facts. Justin seems unconcerned that non-Christians would need to be *persuaded* that Jesus rose from death and ascended into heaven. All of this indicates that Justin actually writes for Christians.

An important feature of the argument from prophecy in the *First Apology* is its claim that the Greek philosophers borrowed their wisdom from Moses and the prophets.

> Moses is more ancient than all the Greek authors, and everything the philosophers and poets said in speaking about the immortality of the soul, or retribution after death, or speculation on celestial matters, or similar doctrines, they took from the prophets.[35]

Justin here is retailing an apologetic motif that originated in Hellenistic Judaism. Rooting all of Greek wisdom in the Jewish scriptures makes it all the more important for Justin to claim them for Christians.

Twenty years before Justin wrote the *First Apology*, the Romans had crushed an uprising in the Jewish homeland, the Bar Kochba revolt. The Roman army had sacked and burned Jerusalem, and, aiming to preempt

---

34. Justin, *First Apology 42*.

35. Justin, *First Apology 44*. Justin gives examples of how Plato "plagiarized" from the books of Moses in chapters 59–60.

any future Judean dreams of independence, had banished Jews from the city site. Justin uses the memory of those recent events in his argument.

> You know full well that, as it was foretold to come to pass, Jerusalem has been destroyed. That it would be destroyed and that no one would be allowed to dwell in it was thus foretold by the prophet Isaiah: "Their land is desolate, and their enemies consume it before them, and none of them shall dwell in it." And you are fully aware that it was guarded by you, lest anyone should dwell in it, and that the death penalty was decreed for any Jew caught entering it.[36]

In the verse Justin quotes, Isaiah was speaking to his own people—the biblical text refers to "your" land and "your" enemies—of the Assyrian invasion of Judea in 701 BCE, a disaster through which Isaiah himself lived. Justin's appropriation of this passage here shows the plasticity of early Christian interpretations of prophecy: Isaiah's lament over his devastated land is repurposed to refer to events in Justin's lifetime, events with no discernible connection to the life of Jesus. Justin's interpretation also cleverly implies that Rome was an instrument of the fulfillment of biblical prophecy, though he does not develop that notion. (The same implication is present in the fulfillment of some of the prophecies related to Jesus' death.) Finally, it is crucial to note that Justin's quotation does not match the biblical text, which does not contain the line Justin focuses on most emphatically: "none of them shall dwell in it." Justin either acquired that extra line from his testimony source (see p. 256 below), or else he added it himself. Either way, Isaiah's words have been retrofitted to enable them to "predict" what Christians know has already happened.

The last topic Justin discusses before concluding his presentation on prophecy concerns a hefty body of messianic prophecies that Jesus did *not* fulfill: predictions that the messiah will conquer, reign, establish universal peace, raise the dead, and the like. No doubt Jews had cited those prophecies as evidence that Jesus was not the messiah because he had not fulfilled the messiah's job description. Justin copes with this problem by presenting the theory of the two comings of the messiah.

> The prophets have foretold two comings of Christ: the one, which already took place, was that of a dishonored and suffering man; the other coming will take place, as it is predicted, when he shall gloriously come from heaven with his angelic army, when he shall also raise to life the bodies of all the men that ever were,

---

36. Justin, *First Apology 47*, quoting Isa 1:7.

shall cloak the worthy with immortality, and shall relegate the
wicked . . . into the eternal fire together with the evil demons.[37]

Justin's explanation amounts to "Jesus didn't fulfill those prophecies, but he
will"; it is an unvarnished statement of faith, not a reasoned argument that
would satisfy a non-Christian. But Justin does his best.

> Since we have shown that all those things that have happened
> had been foretold by the prophets before they happened, it must
> necessarily also be believed that those things that were likewise
> foretold, but are yet to happen, shall certainly come to pass.[38]

Justin concludes his presentation in the *First Apology* by emphasizing
that his argument is rationally compelling. In several places he confronts
the inevitable impression of his Roman addressees that much of what Christians say about Jesus had earlier been said about the Greek and Roman gods
and deified heroes. Justin now cashes in the argument from prophecy for
hard evidence that makes Christian claims about Jesus uniquely true. "We
do not make bare statements, such as the fables of the alleged sons of Jupiter,
without being able to prove them."[39] Recalling again the recent defeat of the
Jews in Palestine, Justin holds up the fulfillment of prophecy as conclusive
proof for the divinity of Jesus. He argues that there would be no reason
to believe that a crucified man is the divine savior unless prophecies had
foretold him and "unless we had seen events happen just as foretold, namely
the devastation of the Jewish land, and men of every race believing through
the teaching of his apostles."[40]

As we saw above, Justin's confidence in the persuasiveness of his argument is tempered by his polemic against those not persuaded by it. His finale is a rhetorical flourish: "Truly, such self-evident truths should convince
and lead to faith those who accept the truth, and who are not vainglorious
or slaves to their passions."[41]

---

37. Justin, *First Apology 52*.
38. Justin, *First Apology 53*.
39. Justin, *First Apology 53*.
40. Justin, *First Apology 53*.
41. Justin, *First Apology 53*.

The Argument from Prophecy
in the *Dialogue with Trypho*

The *Dialogue* is not well organized, though it does fall into fairly discernible sections. The first part (1–9) recounts Justin's conversion and sets up the fictitious dialogue. The next part (10–29) deals with Jewish law and explains why Christians do not observe it. The long central section (30–108), well over half of the sprawling work, is devoted to the argument from prophecy. The last part (109–41) makes the supersessionist case that the promises and privileges that God granted to Israel, as well as God's word to them in the scriptures, now belong exclusively to the Christians, since the Jews have forfeited them by not believing in Jesus. Justin's general sequence of topics in the dialogue mirrors the structure of his overall argument in that the argument from prophecy is the basis for his conviction that Christians have replaced Jews as God's chosen people. It is because the scriptures are fulfilled in Jesus that Judaism as a religion has become obsolete, and it is because it is obvious that Jesus fulfilled the scriptures that Jews are without excuse. God has justly abandoned them.

The poor organization of the *Dialogue*, its frequent tangents, and its sheer length make it frustrating to analyze. Rather than try to follow Justin's rambling train of thought, we will focus on a few topics that will help us understand his contributions to the Christian perspective on prophecy.

I start by sampling Justin's exegesis, surveying ten of his interpretations that display the various ways he discerns Christian realities encoded in Jewish texts. Then I examine in closer detail one set of prophecies on which Justin lays great emphasis: those that foretell Jesus' virgin birth, primarily the Emmanuel prophecy of Isaiah 7:14. Justin tries to overcome Jewish objections to the belief that this prophecy predicts a virgin birth, but I argue that he is wrong on every count. Then I investigate Justin's accusation that Jews have deleted scriptural passages that testify to Jesus. The charge is false; in fact, it was Christians who rewrote scriptures and created passages. At that point I will digress for a brief analysis of a work prior to Justin, the *Letter of Barnabas* so that we can appreciate that Justin draws on a Christian tradition of creatively rewriting the scriptures in order to make their fulfillment by Jesus more evident.

Justin's Christological Exegesis

Like all Christian (and Jewish) thinkers, Justin regards all the scriptures as prophecy. Since Moses and David were considered prophets, the writings attributed to them (the Pentateuch and the Psalms) were considered prophetic. Because Justin is convinced that *all* the scriptures testify to Jesus, the slimmest association in the wording, imagery, or symbolism of a passage with something in the Jesus story is enough for Justin to claim that the passage is about Jesus. There are many, many examples in the dialogue. Here are five of them related to Jesus' death and resurrection that tumble out in rapid succession and without supporting arguments in chapter 97.

- Moses' posture during the battle with the Amelekites (Exod 17:8–13) prefigures Jesus' death: "It was no accident that Moses remained until evening in the form of a cross, when his hands were held up by Aaron and Hur, for the Lord also remained on the cross almost until evening."

- A straightforward prayer in thanksgiving for a peaceful night's sleep (Ps 3:5–6) becomes a prophecy of the resurrection: "Then he arose from the dead, as David foretold when he said, 'With my voice I cried to the Lord, and He heard me from his holy hill. I laid down and slept; I awakened, for the Lord sustained me.'"

- "Isaiah foretold the manner of his [Jesus'] death in these words: 'I have spread out my hands / to an unbelieving and contradictory people'" (Isa 65:2). For Justin, "I have spread out my hands" is a prophecy of the crucifixion.

- Isaiah also predicted Jesus' resurrection in these two short and cryptic oracles: "His burial has been taken out of the midst," and "I will give the rich for his death." The first is from Isa 57:2, the second from Isa 53:9. How either of these curious Septuagint renderings—they both differ entirely in meaning from their Hebrew originals—points to anyone's resurrection, much less Jesus', Justin does not say. Trypho neither objects nor inquires.

That a real-life Jewish debate participant would let these interpretations pass in silence is, of course, utterly implausible. That is one of the reasons why we cannot take Justin's writing as representing an actual dialogue. Beyond that, however, it is interesting that Justin gives no supporting arguments for why the scriptures he quotes and alludes to above are about Jesus. At many places in the dialogue Justin gives detailed and occasionally ingenious arguments for his christological interpretations. In many other places, as here, he gives none, confident that his Christian audience will see Jesus prophesied in any passage he mentions.

A few more examples of Justin's exegesis are sufficient to showcase the different kinds of connections he can make between the OT and his Christian interests.

Isaiah 33:16

This verse promises rewards to the righteous. "He will live on the heights; / his refuge will be the fortresses of rock. / His bread will be supplied, his water assured." Justin sees a deeper, Christian meaning here. To him it is "quite evident" that this verse is a prophecy about the sacrament of the Eucharist.[42] All Justin needs is the word "bread." That Justin imagines that Trypho would understand this, much less agree to it, shows that the audience in Justin's mind is Christian.

Isaiah 33:19

Justin wrings another specious interpretation from Isaiah a few verses later. He quotes Isa 33:19 thus: "A shameless people, / and there is no understanding in him who hears." Justin turns this against Jews, as if Isaiah were referring to his own people: "The prophecy also states that . . . they who think they know the very letter of the scriptures, and who listen to the prophecies, have no understanding of them."[43] The wording of the verse Justin quotes here has only a faint resemblance to what we know of Isaiah's actual text, in which the "shameless people" are foreign conquerors, not Israelites, and what the Israelites fail to comprehend is not the prophet's words but the foreign language of the invaders.[44]

Genesis 49:11a

Justin extracts two phrases from Jacob's blessing over his son Judah and reads them as christological prophecies. "Tying his colt to the vine, and the donkey's colt to the tendrils of the vine"

> was a prophecy both of the deeds he would perform at his first coming and of the gentiles' belief in him. For the gentiles, like a

42. Justin, *Dialogue* 70.

43. Justin, *Dialogue* 70.

44. Here is Isa 33:19 in the NRSV (based on the Hebrew): "No longer will you see the insolent people, the people of an obscure speech you cannot comprehend, stammering in a language you cannot understand."

foal, had never been harnessed or felt a yoke upon their necks, until our Christ arrived and sent his disciples to convert them.[45]

If Trypho were allowed to speak, he might point out that the "prophecy" does not mention a yoke, and that Justin's interpretation does not deal with the vine or the tying, the actual images in the text.

Genesis 49:11b

The second phrase in Gen 49:11 on which Justin comments is: "He will wash his robe in wine, and his garment in the blood of the grape." This signifies that

> He would wash in his own blood those who believed in him. For the Holy Spirit called those whose sins were forgiven by Christ his robe; among whom he is always present in power, but among whom he will be manifestly present in person at his second coming. The expression "blood of the grape" indicates allegorically that Christ has blood not from human seed, but from the power of God, for God, not man, has made the blood of the grape.[46]

The associations come so fast that to follow Justin's train of thought can be dizzying. He doesn't say why wine is blood, although those familiar with eucharistic symbolism (i.e., Christians) will get the connection. Justin does try to explain in what sense forgiven Christians could be Jesus' robe. But where does the Holy Spirit (i.e., the scriptures) "call those whose sins were forgiven by Christ his robe"? It almost feels rude to point out that the answer is "nowhere."

Psalm 22:15

In chapters 99–106 Justin undertakes an extensive and meticulous exegesis of Psalm 22, but what he does *not* say about it is as revealing as what he does. This psalm, a poignant cry from the heart by a righteous man tortured by merciless tormentors, must have been used very early on by followers of Jesus to help them come to terms with his horrible death. Its influence on the gospel passion narratives is hard to miss. Justin goes through Psalm 22 nearly verse by verse, relating its various details to the gospel story. Some of

---

45. Justin, *Dialogue 53*.
46. Justin, *Dialogue 54*.

Virgin Birth

his correlations are obvious because he takes them straight from the gospels. Three examples are "My God, my God why have you abandoned me?" (Ps 22:1, see Mark 15:34), "all who see me mocked me" (Ps 22:7, see Mark 15:29), and "they divided my garments among them, / and for my clothing they cast lots" (Ps 22:18, see John 19:23–24). However, most of Justin's interpretations of this psalm should strike us as far-fetched. For example, "my tongue sticks to my jaws" (Ps 22:15), which is a vivid description of the torment of thirst the righteous one endures during his ordeal, is for Justin a prediction that Jesus would stand silent before his accusers.[47] To point out what we have seen already, no one would beforehand reflect on this verse and infer that it foretold that the messiah would be silent at his trial. Justin's interpretation is possible only in retrospect, and only on the basis of the beliefs that Jesus was the messiah and that the most minute details about him were encoded in the scriptures.

Justin shows considerable ingenuity in matching up the various elements of Psalm 22 with details in the story of Jesus. He makes no less than twenty different correlations, interpreting every clause in the psalm except three. Two of those three are professions of lifelong dependence on God ("You are the one who drew me from the womb," and "I was cast upon you from the womb" [Ps 22:9, 10]); they add no new content to the psalm. But the third element in the psalm that Justin ignores is prominently positioned and obviously discordant with his project; if Justin were to acknowledge its existence, it would defeat his announced plan to "show you that the whole psalm referred to Christ."[48] It follows immediately on the first words of the psalm, the words of abandonment that are quoted by Mark and Matthew (Ps 22:1a). Verse 1b LXX reads, "far from my salvation are the words of my sins." Not even the most fanciful interpretation could cope with that clause, and Justin passes over it in discreet silence. This omission could not have been the result of inattention. It had to be deliberate, which proves that Justin knew that some prophecies did not—and could not—apply to Jesus.[49]

Prophecy and the Virgin Birth

Justin treats an impressive array of prophecies in the dialogue, but one topic to which he repeatedly returns is the prediction of Jesus' virgin birth. He

47. Justin, *Dialogue* 102.

48. Justin, *Dialogue* 99.

49. It is ironic, although Justin was unaware of it, that his problem in this line is created by the Septuagint, on which he relies. In Hebrew, Ps 22:1b is harmless: "Why are you so far from helping me, from the words of my groaning?"

emphasizes that the virgin birth is "an irrefutable proof to all men."[50] Justin provides a number of passages in which he sees predictions of the virgin birth (see below), but the one text over which he debates with Trypho is the only one applied by the NT to the prenatal Jesus (quoted here with the crucial noun untranslated):

> Look, a *parthenos* will conceive
> and will give birth to a son,
> and you will name him Immanuel.
> (Isa 7:14, quoted in Matt 1:23).

Justin often brings up the virgin birth, and Trypho several times asks him to prove that it was foretold in prophecy. When Justin eventually gets around to that, he starts by quoting all of Isa 7:10–17,[51] apparently because he considers that context to be crucial to his christological understanding of 7:14. After that long quotation, Justin lets Trypho articulate two objections.[52] The first is that Isaiah's oracle is actually about a young woman, not a virgin. In Trypho's view, Justin's text of 7:14 is mistaken in its wording and meaning. Trypho's position is supported by the Hebrew text and the non-Septuagint Greek translations, which have the Hebrew and Greek words that unambiguously mean "young woman." Justin, on the other hand, quotes this verse from the Septuagint, which has *parthenos*, a Greek word that can, but usually does not by itself, mean "virgin."[53] On the basis of the objective textual evidence, Trypho's "young woman" undoubtedly reflects the original wording of Isaiah's text.

Trypho's second objection is that "the prophecy as a whole refers to Hezekiah[54] and it can be shown that the events described in the prophecy were fulfilled in him."[55] Justin does not let Trypho explain this interpretation—which Justin calls a "lie"—but we can infer that Trypho understands 7:14 within both its immediate narrative context in Isa 7:10–13 (which Justin quotes) and its historical context, which is described in Isa 7:1–9 (which Justin does not quote). If those interlocking contexts are taken into account, the birth of a son announced by Isaiah in 7:14 is intended to be a sign to King Ahaz (Isa 7:10–13) of God's providence in the face of an imminent attack on Jerusalem (Isa 7:1–9). That is why Trypho, representing Jewish

---

50. Justin, *Dialogue 84*.

51. Justin, *Dialogue 66*.

52. Justin, *Dialogue 67*.

53. Miller, "Wonder Baby," 10; and Miller, *Born Divine*, 189–90.

54. Hezekiah was the son of King Ahaz, to whom Isa 7:14 was addressed.

55. Justin, *Dialogue 67*.

interpreters in general, sees Isaiah's sign fulfilled in the birth of Hezekiah, Ahaz's son and heir to his throne. Trypho's interpretation coincides with one common among modern critical scholars.

Justin responds to Trypho's two objections in different places in the dialogue. Pulling them together, we find two counterarguments to the first objection and one to the second. None of Justin's arguments holds up to scrutiny. His first reply is not really an argument but an adamant assertion, laced with insult, of the accuracy of the Septuagint's translation.

> Here too you dare to distort the translation of this passage made by your elders at the court of Ptolemy, the king of Egypt,[56] asserting that the real meaning of the scripture is not as they translated it, but should read, "Behold, a young woman will conceive."[57]

Justin has encountered this kind of Jewish objection before, and he has no patience for it. "Whenever there arises in the scriptures an evident contradiction of their [i.e., Trypho's teachers'] silly and conceited doctrine, they boldly affirm that it was not so written in the original text."[58]

Justin's second argument for why Isa 7:14 predicts the virgin birth is that Isaiah points to the birth as a sign from God, which it could not be if the boy were conceived naturally because there is nothing unusual in that.[59] What Justin overlooks (intentionally?) is that Isaiah specifically intends the sign to be a sign *for Ahaz* (see Isa 7:10–13).[60] The birth of Jesus (virginal or otherwise) eight centuries later could not be a sign for Ahaz.[61] We can surmise that Trypho, like modern critical scholars, understands that the sign is expressed in the timing of the boy's birth, not in the manner of his conception, a point made clear in 7:16, which promises that before the boy is old enough to know right from wrong, the two kings on their way to dethrone

---

56. It was Jewish lore that the Septuagint was produced under the patronage of the Hellenistic rulers of Egypt. The story can be found in the second-century-BCE *Letter of Aristeas to Philocrates*. See Law, *When God Spoke Greek*, 35–39.

57. Justin, *Dialogue 84*.

58. Justin, *Dialogue 68*.

59. Justin, *Dialogue 84*.

60. In "Yahweh himself will give you a sign" (7:14), the "you" is plural in both Hebrew and Greek. But this need mean no more than that 7:14 is addressed to the king and his royal entourage. Isaiah also uses the plural "you" in 7:13, when he addresses Ahaz as "house of David."

61. By definition, a virgin birth could not be a sign for *anyone* (except the mother), because it would not be apparent that the child had no human father. See Miller, *Born Divine*, 166–67 and 263–67.

Ahaz will be as nothing. The birth must therefore be imminent if it is to be a sign to Ahaz in his present crisis.

Justin's attempt to refute Trypho's point that the prophecy in Isaiah 7 was fulfilled in Hezekiah moves the argument to a different, though deceptively similar, oracle from Isaiah 8. When Trypho challenges Justin, "Please show us how that passage [Isa 7:14] refers to your Christ, and not to Hezekiah, as we Jews believe,"[62] Justin's response focuses not on 7:14 but on 8:4, which he argues cannot apply to Hezekiah, but only to Jesus:

> Before the child knows how to call father or mother, he will take
> the power of Damascus and the spoils of Samaria in the pres-
> ence of the king of Assyria. (Isa 8:4 LXX)

Justin here quotes the Septuagint, which can mean something very different than the Hebrew text, depending on how it is taken. The Septuagint verse contains a grammatical ambiguity that Justin construes in a peculiar way. The ambiguity is contained in the third-person singular verb "will take": who is its subject?[63] The common-sense reading of the verse is that an indefinite "one" will take the power of Damascus and the spoils of Samaria, not, as Justin reads it, that the child will do so, though "the child" is the closest antecedent to the verb and thus grammatically the more likely candidate for the subject of the sentence. If we accept the "one will take" option, then the Septuagint has a meaning quite close to the Hebrew text, which says, "Before the child knows how to call 'my father' and 'my mother,' the wealth of Damascus and the spoils of Samaria will be carried away by the king of Assyria." Isaiah's words in Hebrew predict that Assyria will defeat Damascus and Samaria before the promised boy is old enough to say his first words, whereas in Justin's interpretation of the Septuagint the child himself will overpower those two countries under the nose of the Assyrian king. In Hebrew, Isaiah's announcement is the kind of short-term prediction about military affairs that are the stock-in-trade of the prophets. According to Justin, on the other hand, Isaiah foretells a bizarre miracle in which a baby defeats two nations in the jurisdiction of a foreign king.

In arguing that Isa 8:4 (in Justin's version) was not fulfilled by Hezekiah, Justin insists that the prophecy could apply to him only if it did not contain its first clause about the baby's age. Justin presses the point that without that clause the prophecy would indeed be a prediction of the exploits of the adult King Hezekiah. But since the prophecy says "Before the child knows how to call father or mother, he shall take the power of

62. Justin, *Dialogue 77*.

63. Greek, like many inflected languages, does not require a separate pronoun to indicate the subject of a verb. Here the verb *lēpsetai* can mean "he/she/one/it will take."

Damascus and the spoils of Samaria," Justin asserts that "you cannot prove that this ever happened to any of you Jews, but we Christians can show that it did happen to our Christ."[64] How Justin makes the case for that last claim is fascinating and, to modern readers, woefully unconvincing. He maintains that this prophecy was fulfilled when the magi visited the baby Jesus (Matt 2:1–12). Justin's argument requires some freewheeling exegesis, since the gospel story mentions neither Damascus nor Samaria nor the king of Assyria. It does, however, feature King Herod, whom, Justin says, "scripture calls king of Assyria because of his wicked ungodliness." The Bible nowhere does any such thing, which is probably why Justin provides no clue as to his source for this startling and gratuitous assertion. The best he can do is to remind us that "the Holy Spirit often speaks in parables and similitudes,"[65] which might be Justin's cryptic admission that the scriptures do not *actually* call Herod the king of Assyria.

What about the baby conquering Damascus and despoiling Samaria? When did the baby Jesus do that? Justin's explanation needs to be read in his own words.

> "He will take the power of Damascus and the spoils of Samaria" meant that the power of the wicked demon that dwelt in Damascus should be crushed by Christ at his birth. This is shown to have taken place. For the Magi, held in servitude (as spoils) for the commission of every wicked deed through the power of that demon, by coming and worshipping Christ, openly revolted against the power that had held them as spoils, which power the scripture indicated by parable to be located in Damascus. And in the parables that sinful and wicked power is fittingly called Samaria.[66]

It is stating the obvious to say that this interpretation will not convince Jews, or even Christians, except those willing to indulge the most fanciful correlations. Nothing in the Gospel of Matthew hints that the magi are in servitude to a demon. If anything, Matthew portrays them as righteous gentiles. Furthermore, Justin's scenario bends logic: if the magi were enslaved to a demon, why would that demon permit them to seek and worship Jesus? Justin seems to realize how thin his hermeneutical ice is at this point, judging from his lame assertion that "Damascus" and "Samaria" are symbolic names for evil powers. Justin's concluding appeal to Trypho is either naive or cynical (depending on how generous one is inclined to be to Justin): "It would be to

---

64. Justin, *Dialogue* 77.
65. Justin, *Dialogue* 77.
66. Justin, *Dialogue* 78, quoting Isa 8:4 LXX.

your advantage, my friends, to learn what you do not understand from us Christians, who have received the grace of God, and not to exert every effort to defend your peculiar teachings."[67]

After Justin finishes by quoting Isaiah to support his claim that God has removed his grace from the Jews and given it to the Christians, he allows Trypho to register his skepticism by letting him say, "The words of God are indeed holy, but your interpretations are artificial."[68] (Justin could not have imagined that, nineteen centuries later, fair-minded readers would agree with his straw man Trypho.)

There is another irony in this exchange, one that raises troubling questions about Justin's intellectual integrity. Recall how Justin stressed the importance of literary context. Indeed, he admitted that if the prophecy in Isa 8:4 were considered out of its context, Trypho's interpretation of it would be plausible. It is only when the oracle is taken as a whole, and not quoted selectively, that Justin can find a reason for applying it to Jesus. (We leave aside here the problem of Justin's reliance on a dubious reading of the Septuagint.) The irony is that if the oracle in 8:4 is taken in its appropriate literary context, Justin's interpretation of it becomes untenable, for the child spoken of in 8:4 is identified in 8:3 as the son of Isaiah himself, a boy already born and burdened with the weird and unwieldy name Maher-shalal-hash-baz. By severing Isa 8:4 from 8:3, Justin is indulging in the selective quoting at which Matthew and company were adept, so it should not surprise us. But Justin's double standard is glaring; a few pages earlier he had lectured Trypho on the need to pay proper attention to context.

Is this what it seems to be: blatant hypocrisy? The only mitigating factor one might plausibly plead on Justin's behalf is that he genuinely believed that, as a Christian, he was entitled to his double standard. If so, his hypocrisy is sincere. He seemed to think that quoting out of context is wrong when Jews do it, but not when Christians do. Justin apparently saw nothing *intrinsically* improper about ignoring context. When context helps Christians to see the "true" interpretation, context should be considered; when it doesn't, it should be ignored. It seems that the ends justify the means.

Justin's appreciation of the need for context is not a one-time concern. In chapter 65 he criticizes Trypho for distorting a verse (Isa 42:8) by quoting it out of context. Justin counters that he will quote the same verse, but "I will add a few words of the context of the passage quoted by Trypho, and also those that immediately follow them." He then quotes all of Isa 42:5–13, after which he asks—rhetorically of course—whether Trypho can now see that

67. Justin, *Dialogue 78*.
68. Justin, *Dialogue 79*.

the passage is about the messiah. Justin does not bother to interpret what he quotes; he is confident that the context makes his own interpretation obvious. Trypho concedes without objection.

Reading Isa 8:4 in the context of 8:3 not only invalidates Justin's interpretation; it also clarifies the grammatical ambiguity in the verb "will take" in 8:4b LXX, the ambiguity that afforded Justin the tiny opening he needed for his christological interpretation. Since the child in 8:4 is Isaiah's son, it is extremely unlikely that the Septuagint translators imputed to Isaiah a prediction that his own son will conquer countries while still in diapers. Therefore, "*one* [i.e., someone other than the child] will take the power of Damascus" is undoubtedly the proper construal of the sense of the oracle. This brings the Septuagint into agreement with the Hebrew text on the central significance of Isa 8:4: the divine sign is manifested by *when* Damascus and Samaria are conquered (i.e., soon), not by whom. Thus, Justin's interpretation of 8:4 has three strikes against it: it is ruled out (1) by its context in 8:3, (2) by the Hebrew text of 8:4, and (3) by the plain sense of the Septuagint. Justin's christological interpretation of Isa 8:4, wholly aside from its exceeding arbitrariness, could only get off the ground (1) by a strange construal of the grammar (2) of the Septuagint, (3) when 8:4 is extracted from its immediate context.

Conclusions about Isaiah 7:14

Justin's robust attempt to prove that Isaiah predicted the virgin birth must be judged a failure. Justin's arguments, which have to be culled from different places in the dialogue, are structured as refutations of Trypho's two objections to the Christian interpretation of Isaiah 7: first, that Isa 7:14 is about a young woman, not specifically a virgin; and second, that Isaiah's prophecy about the birth of a promised child refers to Hezekiah, son and heir of King Ahaz, to whom the oracle was delivered.

Justin counters the first objection in two ways: by stridently asserting that Trypho is wrong about the wording of 7:14, and by arguing that the birth announced in the prophecy must be a miraculous birth in order to be a sign. Justin's first assertion is nothing more than his insistence that his text of Isaiah (the Septuagint) is right and Trypho's text (either the Hebrew text or a literal Greek translation of it) is wrong. Despite Justin's adamant insistence on the accuracy of the Septuagint,[69] anyone who could read Hebrew

---

69. Justin's insistence on the accuracy of the Septuagint (at least in regard to Isa 7:14) is undoubtedly rooted in the fact that the Gospel of Matthew quotes Isa 7:14 from the Septuagint. However, Matt 2:15 quotes Hos 11:1 in its Hebrew version, rather than

would disagree and would be right to do so. Justin's argument that the birth in 7:14 had to be miraculous in order to qualify as a sign ignores the verse's immediate context (Isa 7:10–13), which shows that the predicted birth will be a sign from God because of *when* the boy will be born, not because of the manner of his conception. That Justin ignores that context *deliberately* is evident from the fact that he quotes 7:10–13 in full, but does not allow it to influence his interpretation of 7:14. Justin tries to refute Trypho's second objection—that the promised sign was fulfilled by the birth of prince Hezekiah—with a complicated interpretation of Isa 8:4, joined with a convoluted and capricious interpretation of the story of the magi in Matthew. Justin's argument here is undermined on several counts, but is decisively ruled out by the plain meaning of Isa 8:3.

Beyond Isaiah 7:14

Even if, for the sake of the argument, we grant Justin's contention that Isa 7:14 predicts the virgin birth, there still is only this one verse that overtly points to that miracle. But Justin does not rest his case on this one verse alone. He discovers allusions to the virgin birth in several passages that do not mention a virgin, and he claims that there are numerous passages that clearly predict it. In chapter 76 he collects and explains four examples (Dan 7:13 and 2:34, Isa 53:8, and Gen 49:11).

> Does not Daniel allude to this very truth [the virgin birth] when he says that he who received the eternal kingdom is "like a son of man?" The words, "like a son of man" indicate that he would become man and appear as such, but that he would not be born of human seed.
>
> Daniel states the same truth figuratively when he calls Christ "a stone cut out without hands;" for to affirm that he was cut out without hands signifies that he was not the product of human activity, but of the will of God, the Father of all, who brought him forth.
>
> The words of Isaiah, "Who shall declare his generation?" show that his origin is indescribable, and no mere man has such an origin.
>
> When Moses affirmed that "He shall wash his robe in the blood of the grape," did he not mystically foretell what I have frequently mentioned to you, namely, that Christ would have

from the Septuagint because the rendering in the Septuagint would make it impossible for Matthew to apply the prophecy to Jesus (see p. 125). It is ironic that Justin's principle of the superiority of the Septuagint would make Matthew's choice in 2:15 invalid.

blood, but not from man, just as it is not man, but God, who gave blood to the grape?

Although Justin maintains that these verses "clearly point to" the virgin birth,[70] it is implausible in the extreme that a Jewish reader would infer from these texts that the messiah would be born to a virgin. Such an interpretation would not occur even to a Christian reader without the expert guidance from Justin's ingenious inferences. Justin can see the virgin birth in these verses only because he knows ahead of time what he is looking for. Once again it is Christian faith that enables one to see a meaning that others do not see, that is, to believe that the scriptures predict Jesus.

Mutilating the Scriptures

Justin several times accuses Jewish leaders of sabotaging the scriptures by removing passages or phrases that he believes clearly refer to Jesus.[71] He gives examples.

- A passage in which Ezra tells the people, "This Passover is our savior," and warns them not to go through with their intention "to humiliate him on a cross."[72] The words Justin attributes to Ezra seem to be modeled on 1 Cor 5:7 ("Our Passover [i.e., Passover lamb], Christ, has been sacrificed"), but there is no evidence that they were ever part of the Jewish scriptures.

- A passage where Jeremiah complains of a plot against his life, in which he says, "I am like a gentle lamb led to slaughter," and his enemies say, "Let us put wood into his bread and cut him off from the land of the living."[73] Justin maintains that the strange reference to wood "proves that the Jews planned to crucify Christ himself," despite the fact that Jeremiah quotes his enemies as they talk about him (Jeremiah), not about a future messiah. Contrary to Justin's accusation, this verse is found in the Bible;[74] it is Jer 11:19, though the phrase about the wood and the bread is from the Septuagint. (The Hebrew version reads, "Let us destroy the tree with its fruit.")

70. Justin, *Dialogue* 75.

71. Justin, *Dialogue* 71, 73, 120.

72. Justin, *Dialogue* 72.

73. Justin, *Dialogue* 72.

74. Justin seems to be in some doubt about this verse. He says that it was removed only recently, which is why it "is still found in some copies of the scriptures in Jewish synagogues" (*Dialogue* 72).

- A verse Justin attributes to Jeremiah: "The Lord God, the Holy One of Israel, remembered his dead that slept in their graves, and he descended to preach to them the good news of his salvation."[75] This passage, found nowhere in the Bible, reflects the early Christian belief that between his death and his resurrection Jesus descended to the underworld to preach to the souls there (see 1 Pet 3:18–20 and *Gospel of Peter* 10).

- A description of the death of Isaiah, "whom you Jews sawed in half with a wooden saw,"[76] which derives from the legendary *Martyrdom of Isaiah* and is alluded to in the NT (Heb 11:37).

Justin also accuses Jews of removing "from the tree" from Ps 95:10: "The Lord has reigned from the tree."[77] Justin assumes that his readers will understand the tree to be an allusion to the cross. But it takes more than that to relate this verse to Jesus. It also requires one to have already interpreted his crucifixion as an enthronement, something only a Christian would do. This is a sign of how deep Justin's conspiracy theory runs. Not only does he imagine that some cabal of Jewish authorities has deleted passages that point to Jesus, but also—amazingly—that those authorities also interpreted the story of Jesus the way Christians do. The evil of these (imaginary) teachers is thus profound: they know the truth and try to hide it from their people. To Justin's mind their sin is worse than the terrible ones committed by the people in the Bible: worshiping the golden calf, sacrificing their children to demons, and slaughtering the prophets. Justin blames the teachers, not the Jewish people as a whole, for he excuses Trypho: "You appear not to have ever heard of the scriptures that I said they had mutilated."[78]

What is the basis for Justin's accusation that Jewish leaders have deleted passages? It must be because he has compared his version of the scriptures with Jewish copies. If his texts have bits that theirs do not, Justin instinctively trusts his own sources over the Jewish ones. And since the passages in question are, in Justin's eyes, obvious prophecies of Jesus, the motives of those Jews responsible must be nefarious. Toward the end of the dialogue referring to the large number of passages he has argued refer to Jesus, he says, "If your teachers had understood them, they would most assuredly have deleted them from the text."[79]

75. Justin, *Dialogue* 72.
76. Justin, *Dialogue* 120.
77. Justin, *Dialogue* 73.
78. Justin, *Dialogue* 73.
79. Justin, *Dialogue* 120.

Excursus:

Justin's Textual Sources

Scholars who have toiled at the task of comparing Justin's biblical quotations with the various second-century versions of the Septuagint have discovered that Justin sometimes quotes from the Septuagint and sometimes from some other non-Septuagint version. In a good number of cases he quotes and comments on two different versions of the same passage, one Septuagint and one not. But there is a problem: Justin thinks that his non-Septuagint quotations represent the true Septuagint, while his quotations that actually match the Septuagint, quotations he calls "Jewish," he regards as non-Septuagintal.[80] Justin refers to those biblical manuscripts as Jewish because in his day pretty much the only available copies of the OT (LXX) were produced by Jewish scribes.[81] Justin's other (non-Septuagint) sources for quotations were not actual copies of the Bible, but rather anthologies of proof texts made by Christians for the express purpose of demonstrating that Jesus had fulfilled the scriptures. Those anthologies are known to scholars by the Latin term *testimonia* ("testimony sources"). No copy of them has survived,[82] but from what scholars can deduce from studying the many variants in how early Christian authors quote the OT, those testimonies were very free quotations, often paraphrased to make the connection to Jesus as clear as possible. The paraphrasing techniques can be described as "targumizing," that is, mixing quotation with creative embellishment. The testimony sources probably also featured quotations that blended material from more than one passage, "composite quotations created with great care."[83] Furthermore, the testimony sources were not simply collections of biblical material; the "quoted" passages were probably accompanied by interpretations and arguments showing how they applied to Jesus.[84]

---

80. "What Justin calls 'LXX' text is the text of his testimony source(s), while the 'Jewish' text is the text of his Biblical MSS" (Skarsaune, *Proof from Prophecy*, 43).

81. Ibid., 44.

82. The Coptic Psalms testimony recently discovered by Hedrick seems to be an exception. See pp. 123–24.

83. Skarsaune, *Proof from Prophecy*, 91.

84. Ibid.

Excursus:

The *Letter of Barnabas*

At this point a short detour through a somewhat earlier work than Justin's will give us an opportunity to see concrete examples of how quotations from testimony sources interweave authentic scriptures with altered phrases and added material. The *Letter of Barnabas*, which was written probably around 130 and anachronistically attributed to Paul's companion, is chock full of OT "quotations" and exegesis aimed at undermining the legitimacy of Judaism and establishing that only Christians truly understand the scriptures. Many of Barnabas' quotations have been cleverly altered to adapt them for Christian use. What follows are two examples. Since both are used by later Christian writers who did not copy them from Barnabas, we can be confident that Barnabas has taken them from testimony sources.

(1) Our first example, *Barnabas* 5:13, uses a clause from Psalm 119 to splice together two clauses from Psalm 22.

> It was necessary that he [Jesus] would suffer on wood. For the
> one who prophesies about him says:
> "Spare my soul from the sword" (Ps 22:20)
>   and "nail my flesh" (Ps 119:120)
> "for a synagogue of evildoers has risen up against me." (Ps 22:16)[85]

In its own context in Psalm 22, the term "soul" in the first line means "life,"[86] and "sword" is a metaphor for human violence. Since this is thus a prayer for God to save the psalmist's life, it cannot function as a prophecy of Jesus' passion if left in its own context—everyone knows that God did not prevent Jesus from being killed. But when "deliver my soul from the sword" is teamed with "nail my flesh" from a different psalm, the soul/flesh contrast changes the meaning of "soul" to one's spiritual essence, and the sword/nail pairing gives "sword" a literal sense. "Spare my soul from the sword" can now be taken as a prophecy about Jesus because it is no longer a plea to be spared from physical death. The price of that adaptation, however, is that it turns the line into nonsense: how can an iron sword harm an immaterial soul?

In the Septuagint the second line reads, "Nail my flesh *with your fear*" (Ps 118:120 LXX), and so has a moral and spiritual meaning, rather than any literal reference to physical suffering. The testimony source deleted

---

85. The translations from the *Letter of Barnabas* are my own.

86. "Deliver my soul from the sword, / my life [literally, "my only one"] from the power of the dog. / Save me from the mouth of the lion" (Ps 22:20–21).

"with your fear," thereby transforming the line in the psalm into an obvious prophecy of the crucifixion.

The "synagogue" (Greek: *synagōgē*) in the third line comes straight from the Septuagint, where it has its natural sense of "assembly." When transplanted into the nakedly anti-Jewish atmosphere of Barnabas' letter, however, the term would be taken to denote a specifically Jewish congregation. This is a textbook example of a passage acquiring a new meaning, not by a shift in its wording, but by its being understood in a new, and in this case, hostile context.

(2) The second example from *Barnabas* deals with the strange episode from the desert wanderings of the Israelites in which God sent poisonous snakes to punish them for complaining about the deprivations of the desert (see Num 21:4–9). Many die from the snakebites, and the people repent. After Moses prays for them, God tells him, "Make a snake and put it on a pole (*sēmeion*)[87] and . . . whenever a snake bites someone, everyone so bitten that looks at it will live" (Num 21:8 LXX).

When Barnabas discusses this scene, he introduces it by explaining its significance.

> Moses makes a prefigurement ["type"] of Jesus, showing that it was necessary for him to suffer and that he whom they thought they had destroyed would bestow life in the sign (*sēmeion*) set up when Israel was falling. (*Barnabas* 12:5)

When Barnabas relates the words of Num 21:8, he changes them from words spoken by God to Moses into words spoken by Moses to the people. The words Barnabas "quotes" are paraphrased and elaborated, making this a showcase example of Christian targumizing.

> Moses said to them, "Whenever one of you is bitten, come to the snake that has been placed on the wood, and hope and believe that the snake, although it is dead, can bestow life, and you will immediately be saved." (*Barnabas* 12:7)

The Christian rewording of this passage loads in transparent references to the cross, resurrection, faith, and salvation, none of which are in the original text. With those unmistakable clues now written directly into the "biblical" text quoted in 12:7, who could question the interpretation spelled out in 12:5?

The textual manipulations we see in these two examples from Barnabas are in no way exceptional. They embody a Jewish-Christian approach to exploring and explaining the Jewish scriptures in the light of Christian

---

87. The Greek word *sēmeion*, literally "sign," here denotes a kind of signal staff.

faith. Believing that Jesus was the promised messiah, and thus the culmination of God's plans for Israel, those Jewish-Christians were convinced they had the key for decoding the real meaning of the scriptures. Their subsequent refashioning of those scriptures, using (by then) traditional Jewish techniques, represents a distinctly Jewish way of expressing Christian theology, "by means of the rearrangement and re-casting of OT texts in such a way that they in fact present new data."[88]

The Influence of Justin's Sources on His Anti-Judaism

What we know about the nature of those early Christian testimony sources can shed light on Justin's experience of and attitude toward the OT. It seems likely that Justin's conversion to Christianity was facilitated not by the OT as we know it, but as he received it from Christians. It came to him "in conveniently doctored form,"[89] complete with interpretive aids that "proved" how the prophetic passages were fulfilled in Jesus. In Justin's subjective experience, then, the christological meaning of the OT seemed natural and self-evident. He might well have been genuinely puzzled when he learned that Jews resisted these Christian interpretations because they considered them to be far-fetched and to violate the clear meaning of the original text in its own context. He would have wondered why Jews, who revered these scriptures, could not (or would not) see their "real" meaning, which was so obvious to Justin. Judging from what we see in the *Dialogue,* Justin's wonderment found two very different resolutions. First, he discovered the explanation for Jewish "disbelief" in the OT itself, in the abundant and fulsome passages that indict Israelites for their hard hearts, wanton sinfulness, and stubborn rebellion against God's will. We have seen this before, a Christian construction of a Catch-22 in which prophecy is fulfilled precisely by Jewish rejection of the claim that Jesus fulfilled prophecy. Second, Justin's wonderment at Jewish disbelief was probably a primary motivation for his writing his huge *Dialogue.* He would gather all the christological interpretations he could find or devise, arrange them into a dialogue with an imaginary Jew, and so demonstrate to his Christian audience how right they were and why the Jews were so wrong.

If, as seems nearly certain, Justin received his Christian indoctrination with the help of testimony sources rather than the OT as we know it, we can understand his reaction to actual biblical manuscripts. We would expect Justin to regard his Christian textual sources with the strong affection and

88. Danielou, *Theology of Jewish Christianity,* 90.

89. Wilson, *Related Strangers,* 271.

gratitude typical of mature converts, for he would revere those texts as a means by which he had found the truth and attained salvation. We should not be surprised that when Justin discovered that Jewish copies of the Bible differed in their contents and wording from his Christian sources that he would easily believe that it was Jews, not Christians, who had tampered with the texts. As noted, that Christian tampering included not only freestyle paraphrasing, targum-like elaborations, and composite quotations, but also the interpolation of nonbiblical passages and interpretive comments. From our perspective we can see that these Christian texts, in effect, rigged the game from the start. But it would be a mistake for us to see those textual manipulations as deliberate forgeries intended to deceive. The targumizing techniques evident in the testimony sources indicate that they were the work of Jewish-Christians, which we would expect a priori anyway, since only (former) Jews would have a deep knowledge of Israel's scriptures. As we have seen in an earlier chapter, the Jewish targumists understood themselves, not as creating new meanings for the scriptures, but as faithfully transmitting their true message. Since the Jewish believers in Jesus who crafted the testimony sources inherited that understanding of how biblical interpretation was practiced, we should see their way of treating the scriptures "as an expression of genuine concern for the deeper meaning of the sacred text."[90] We take it for granted that the meaning of a text must be determined from its wording. But in the Jewish world of interpretation, which was home to both the targumists and the authors of the testimony sources, the meaning of a biblical passage was primary, its wording secondary. Rewording the Bible to help its "true" meaning shine forth was an accepted aspect of the practice of faithful interpretation. Jews, including Jewish-Christians, seemed to understand that.

But Justin did not, and neither did the other Christian authors who relied on testimony sources. Those gentile Christians did not come to the task of interpretation with Jewish presuppositions. Instead, they mistakenly assumed that the doctored texts in the testimony sources were the actual words of scripture. This fed their hostility toward Jews and led to the false accusations that they had mutilated the scriptures.

90. Skarsaune, *Proof from Prophecy*, 91.

Conclusions

Interpretation of Scripture

Our analysis of the argument from prophecy in the *Dialogue with Trypho* has yielded several striking conclusions about Justin's interpretation of scripture.

- His exegeses of prophecies are possible only from the presuppositions of Christian faith. Justin's examples are ample evidence that Christians found Jesus in the OT only because they already knew he had to be there and then went looking for him.

- What Justin takes to be quotations of scripture are often Christian mashups that rewrite and embellish scripture to make it say what Christians want it to say.

- Justin ridicules Jews for deleting passages from scripture that are in fact Christian interpolations.

- Justin's argument for the virgin birth is a textbook example of bad exegesis. It hinges on his insistence on a misleading translation of the original text, a willful ignoring of literary context, a nonsensical construal of grammar, and an interpretation of the magi story that is, frankly, bizarre.

On every important point about prophecy where Justin disagrees with Trypho, Justin is wrong, despite the fact that Trypho is Justin's literary creation. The only reason Justin lets Trypho disagree at all in this shamelessly one-sided "dialogue" is so that its Christian audience can see how baseless Jewish objections really are. Persuasive as Justin's arguments surely were for ancient Christians, today they fall completely flat.

It is tempting to conclude that Justin and Trypho do not truly disagree because they are not interpreting the same thing: Trypho looks for what the author of a passage (say, David or Isaiah) meant, while Justin seeks to understand what the Holy Spirit meant. Making that distinction was a live option for Justin; all he had to do was to invoke the oracular view of prophecy and assert that because the prophets were under divine inspiration, they did not understand the meaning of what they wrote. But Justin does not make that distinction. Though he often refers to the Holy Spirit as the source of scripture, he also believes that he is explaining its natural meaning, which anyone can understand through the use of reason. A perfect example has to do with Psalm 72, "a psalm dictated to David by the Holy Spirit, which you [Trypho] erroneously think refers to your king Solomon, but which in reality refers to our Christ."[91] After quoting the whole psalm, Justin offers a logical argument about Ps 72:8–11. "None of the things foretold in the psalm happened to Solomon: for not all the kings adored him, nor did his power extend to the ends of the earth, nor did his enemies fall down prostrate before him and lick the dust."[92] Justin does not let Trypho voice the obvious rejoinder: neither did any of those things happen to Jesus! Justin doesn't bother to say how those three things apply to Jesus; probably they are among the prophecies that Jesus *will* fulfill at his second coming. In any case Justin intends his argument to show, not that there is a deeper significance to the psalm than Trypho sees, but that Trypho is wrong about its plain meaning.

In this case, as in others, it is clear enough to us that Justin was wrong and Trypho was on the right track. Psalm 72 is a song for a king's coronation, with idealized and exaggerated royal propaganda, complete with prayers for universal sovereignty, which Justin misinterprets by taking literally. Justin's objection that no Jewish king *literally* ruled the whole world cannot be taken seriously, given that Justin elsewhere never lets the literal sense impede his own interpretations. (Herod can be the king of Assyria, and a robe can mean people, for example.)[93] Justin's interest in the literal sense is as opportunistic—and as disingenuous—as his concern for literary context. Moreover, if Justin wants to take Psalm 72 as a literal prophecy about Jesus, he can use it only selectively, for how could he relate "He will be given the gold of Arabia" (Ps 72:15 LXX) and the promise of agricultural fertility (Ps 72:16) to Jesus? Most egregious is Justin's willful ignoring of the psalm's superscription, "to Solomon," which is present in the Septuagint, whose authority Justin elsewhere smugly asserts.

Whatever we might think of the cogency of Justin's interpretation of scripture, we should not doubt that he stood secure in his belief that he was on the side of truth and that the Jews are utterly wrong about the scriptures. His attacks on the Jews are ugly, to be sure, but we need to understand those attacks because they are integral to his theological project. Because it is "self-evident" that the scriptures are about Jesus, the errors of the Jews must be willful and therefore culpable. This polemic is strewn throughout the *Dialogue*; a few examples are more than sufficient to take their measure.

You Jews are a ruthless, stupid, blind, and lame people.[94]

---

91. Justin, *Dialogue* 34.
92. Justin, *Dialogue* 34.
93. See his interpretations of Isa 8:4 (pp. 249–52) and Gen 49:11 (p. 245).
94. Justin, *Dialogue* 27.

You are neither wise nor understanding, but sly and treacherous; wise only for evil actions, but utterly unfit to know the hidden will of God, or the trustworthy covenant of the Lord, or to
find the everlasting paths.[95]

It is only your obstinacy that prevents you from knowing the
mind and will of God.[96]

[*referring to Jesus' entry into Jerusalem on a donkey*]: It had been
explicitly foretold that the Christ would do precisely this; when
he had done it in the sight of all he furnished clear proof that he
was the Christ. And yet, even after those things have happened
and are proved from the scriptures, you persist in refusing to
believe.[97]

For Justin the Jewish interpretation of scripture is a massive sin for
which Jews deserve both the historical punishments God has meted out to
them (the scourge of two wars with Rome, the destruction of the temple in
Jerusalem, and the devastation of their homeland) and the forfeiture of their
status as the chosen people to the Christians. Toward the end of the *Dialogue*, after rattling off a long list of prophecies that supposedly foretell that
God will choose a new people to replace Israel, Justin hammers his point
home by having Trypho incredulously ask, "Do you mean to say that you
are Israel, and that God says all this about you"? Justin eventually responds,

As your whole people was called after Jacob, surnamed Israel,
so we who obey the precepts of Christ, are, through Christ who
begot us to God, both called and in reality are Jacob and Israel
and Judah and Joseph and David and true children of God.[98]

Concerning the destruction wreaked by the Romans, Justin goes so
far as to imply that God had planned those punishments from the time of
Abraham. According to Justin, God's purpose in requiring the circumcision
of Abraham and his descendants was so that the Romans could distinguish
Jews from all others and thus single them out for retribution.

The purpose of this [circumcision] was that you and *only you*
might suffer the afflictions that are now justly yours; that only
your land be desolate, and your cities ruined by fire; that the
fruits of your land be eaten by strangers before your eyes; that

95. Justin, *Dialogue* 123.
96. Justin, *Dialogue* 68.
97. Justin, *Dialogue* 53.
98. Justin, *Dialogue* 123.

not one of you be permitted to enter your city of Jerusalem. Your circumcision of the flesh is the only mark by which you can be distinguished from other men . . . The above-mentioned tribulations were justly imposed on you, for you have murdered the Just One, and his prophets before him; now you spurn those who hope in him [i.e., Christians].[99]

Not only is Justin's theory about the purpose of circumcision hateful,[100] but it also pretends—incredibly—that Judea was the only nation to be crushed by Rome's military might. Moreover, Justin is wrong that Jews were the only people to practice circumcision, and he is well aware that many Christians did so as well.[101]

Anti-Judaism is not some unfortunate by-product of Justin's christological interpretation of scripture. It is the wellspring of his entire theological project. His aim was to claim the Jewish scriptures for Christianity, and not merely to establish that Christians could and must use them, but to show that those writings were genuinely Christian. To do that it was not enough for him to argue that the Jewish understanding of scripture was inadequate, nor even that Jews misunderstand the meaning of the scriptures. The logic of Justin's theological premises drove him to assert that Jews know from the scriptures the truth about Christ and spurn it. How else to explain why God had rejected the people he once chose as his own? From within Justin's theological context, which was strongly influenced by the Marcionite controversy, the only way to vindicate the God of Abraham and the prophets was to delegitimize the Jews.[102]

Justin's *Dialogue with Trypho* is a landmark achievement in that it forges and articulates with eloquence and energy an essential link between the argument from prophecy and supersessionism. That linkage—the belief that the Jews have been abandoned by God because of their refusal to embrace the messiah foretold by the prophets—remained foundational to the long, shameful, and sinful history of Christian anti-Judaism.

---

99. Justin, *Dialogue* 16.

100. In our post-Holocaust context it is horrifying beyond words to imagine a ruthless military superpower using circumcision as a criterion by which to single out Jews for atrocities. If the claim that such a horror is the express purpose of God is not blasphemous, then what is?

101. See Justin, *Dialogue* 47.

102. See Efroymson, "Patristic Connection."

___ 15 ___

Between Justin and Augustine

─────────────

BETWEEN JUSTIN, IN THE mid-second century, and Augustine, in the late fourth/early fifth century, lies most of the patristic era. Justin's and Augustine's studies of the fulfillment of prophecy are bookends to the thought of the theologians between them. There is, naturally, diversity among the patristic authors in their discussions of OT prophecy. But, with one exception, that diversity is fairly narrow in its range because it consists of variations on a set of shared themes, three of which are central to our study: (1) that the prophecies of the OT are fulfilled in Jesus and the church, (2) that the fulfillment of prophecy is a proof of the truth of Christianity, and (3) that Jews are blameworthy for not accepting (1) and (2). Given the general consistency of patristic thought on prophecy and its fulfillment, there is no need in this book for full-length treatments of all the patristic authors, a project that would be a book in itself. This chapter's aim is modest: to offer an impressionistic sample of patristic thought on our topic. It does so in two modes, first with quotations from three representative patristic theologians spanning three centuries (Hippolytus of Rome, Lactantius, and John Chrysostom), then with summary analyses of two writers, Eusebius of Caesarea and Theodore of Mopsuestia. Eusebius deserves a careful look because the narrative in his monumental *History of the Church* became *the* paradigm within which later mainstream Christianity thought about its origins. Theodore, too, is worth examining because his theory of biblical interpretation represents a very small minority, dissenting voice on the topic of OT prophecy. Theodore is the exception that proves the rule.

Hippolytus of Rome

Hippolytus (ca. 170–235) is best known for his *Refutation of All Heresies.* Here is an excerpt.

All parties [of the Jews] alike expect the Messiah, inasmuch as the Law certainly, and the prophets preached beforehand that He was about to be present on earth. Inasmuch, however, as the Jews did not acknowledge the time of His arrival, there remains the supposition that the declarations [of Scripture] concerning His coming have not been fulfilled. And so it is, that up to this day they continue in anticipation of the future coming of the Christ—from the fact of their not discerning Him when He was present in the world. And [yet there can be little doubt but] that, on beholding the signs of the times of His having been already among us, the Jews are troubled; and that *they are ashamed to confess that He has come*, since they have with their own hands put Him to death, because they were stung with indignation in being convicted by Himself of not having obeyed the laws. And they affirm that He who was thus sent forth by God is not this Christ [whom they are looking for]; but they confess that another Messiah will come, who as yet has no existence; and that he will usher in some of the signs which the law and the prophets have shown beforehand, whereas, regarding the rest [of these indications], they suppose that they have fallen into error.[1]

Hippolytus expresses a Christian belief, widely held by the patristic theologians, that Jews actually *know* that Jesus was the messiah, since he so obviously fulfilled the predictions of their own scriptures. Hippolytus (like many other patristic authors) was unwilling to accept that Jews, who understood the prophets, could sincerely not be convinced that Jesus was the fulfillment of prophecy. According to Hippolytus, therefore, Jewish resistance to the Christian claim that Jesus was the messiah is evidence of their refusal to repent for their guilt in rejecting him.[2]

Lactantius

Lactantius (ca. 240–320) wrote *The Divine Institutes*, a lengthy apology addressed to pagans. Here are two brief excerpts. In the first, Lactantius adduces two prophecies, one being from a nonbiblical source. For Lanctantius, these are prophecies of the virgin birth that Jesus "plainly" fulfilled, despite the fact that he was not actually called by the name foretold by one of the prophecies.

---

1. Hippolytus, *Refutation of All Heresies* 9.25 (italics added).
2. Ruether, *Faith and Fratricide*, 149.

Solomon in Psalm 19 says: "The womb of a virgin is impaired and has received a child; and the virgin has become pregnant and she is become a mother in much misery."[3] Likewise the prophet Isaiah, whose words are these: "Therefore the Lord himself will give you this sign. Behold a virgin shall conceive and bear a son, and you shall call his name Emmanuel."

What can be more plainly said than this? The Jews who killed Him read those very words. If anyone thinks that we are making them up, let him ask them. They may take the strongest proof from them. It is firm enough testimony for proving the truth because it is presented by those who are our enemies. He has not been called Emmanuel habitually, however, but Jesus, which in Latin means salvation or Savior,[4] because He came as the bearer of salvation to all peoples.[5]

Lactantius refers to Jews as "our enemies," which seems intended to add force to the common patristic argument that the prophecies about Jesus were not manufactured by Christians after the fact.

In the next excerpt, Lactantius makes the argument for his pagan audience that the fulfillment of prophecy is a more convincing proof of Jesus' divinity than are his miracles.

It is not strange if you, who are far removed from the wisdom of God, understand nothing of the materials which you have read; even Jews, who from the beginning perused the prophets to whom the mystery of God had been entrusted, were ignorant of what they were reading. Get to know, then, and understand, if you have any mind at all, that we believe Him to be God, not because He performed miracles, but because we have seen that He fulfilled all the things that were foretold to us by the preaching of the prophets. He did miraculous things, and we would have considered Him to be a magician, just as you do now and as the Jews did then, had not all the prophets foretold those very deeds. And so we believe that He is God, not only because of His marvelous deeds and works, but also because of that very cross that you touch like dogs, since that, too, was foretold at the same time. Therefore, it is not because of His own testimony—for who

3. The reference here is to the noncanonical *Psalms of Solomon.* This quotation does not exist among those psalms that are extant.

4. It is puzzling that Lactantius, who writes in Latin, mistakenly claims that the name Jesus has a meaning in that language. Perhaps he meant "in Hebrew" instead of "in Latin." In Aramaic (which gentiles routinely mistook for Hebrew), Jesus' name is *Yeshua,* which sounds like the word for "salvation" (*yeshuah*).

5. Lactantius, *Divine Institutes* 4.12.

can be believed when he is speaking of himself?—but because of the testimony of the prophets, who told about all the things that He did and suffered long beforehand, that He is acknowledged by faith to be divine, something that could not happen to Apollonius or Apuleius or any of the magicians, nor can it ever happen to anyone.[6]

Lactantius expresses a common Christian notion: that Jews do not acknowledge Jesus because they do not understand their own scriptures, a view stated by Paul himself in 2 Cor 3:12–16.[7] However, most patristic theologians took the opposite perspective, asserting that Jews know full well that Jesus fulfilled prophecy (see Hippolytus, above, and Chrysostom, below). Lactantius also argues that the fulfillment of prophecy is the *essential* evidence for belief in Christ. If Jesus had not fulfilled prophecy, then his miracles could be written off as magic, not taken as evidence for his divinity. For Lactantius, it is Jesus' fulfillment of prophecy that elevates him above other miracle workers, of whom Lactantius names Apollonius and Apuleius, two of the most famous miracle workers in Antiquity.

John Chrysostom

John Chrysostom (ca. 347–407) was archbishop of Constantinople. Among his many works is the *Demonstration against the Pagans that Christ Is God*, which a later scribe aptly subtitled, *From the Sayings concerning Him in Many Places in the Prophets*. The work is a long and detailed correlation of prophecies to every aspect of Jesus' life. All peoples in the ancient world respected legitimate prophecy, whatever its source. Chrysostom rightly expects pagans to acknowledge the authority of Jewish prophecies, especially owing to their great age and to the fact that they were preserved in writing.

Here are three brief consecutive paragraphs from the *Demonstration*, in which the author's supreme confidence in the persuasiveness of his apology seems shaken. In our first selection, Chrysostom addresses his pagan audience directly.

> Do you see how precisely the prophets took up each point and predicted what was going to happen? How, then, do you still have the audacity to refuse to believe, even though you have been given such proofs of his power, even though you hear the words which foretold it so long beforehand, even though you see

---

6. Lactantius, *Divine Institutes* 5.3 (translation modified).

7. See pp. 109–10, 112–13.

that events did occur to match the predictions and that everything which they foretold has been fulfilled to the last detail?[8]

Chrysostom asserts that the prophecies that Jesus fulfilled are so numerous, so detailed, and so ancient, and Jesus fulfilled them so precisely, that
the proof is overwhelming. Any disbelief, therefore, can only be a willful
refusal to acknowledge what everyone knows is true. Hence Chrysostom's
pointedly rhetorical question, "How, then, do you still have the audacity to
refuse to believe?"

Chrysostom goes on to anticipate an objection: that Christians have
fabricated the prophecies. He counters by pointing out that the prophecies
come from books preserved by hostile witnesses, the Jews.

> These things are not figments of my imagination. As witnesses
> to prove this I give you the very men who were the first to re-
> ceive the sacred books and who still preserve them. It is true
> that these men are our enemies and the descendants of those
> who crucified Christ. But they still preserve these sacred books
> and guard them even to the present day. So I offer them to you
> as my witnesses.[9]

Like Lactantius, Chrysostom characterizes Jews as "our enemies," and imputes to them the inherited guilt for Jesus' death.

Chrysostom now anticipates a further objection: since the prophecies
are found in the holy books of the Jews, does not their unbelief in Jesus
undermine the persuasiveness of the fulfillments that Christians allege?
Chrysostom's response is that Jews know the truth—how could they not,
since it shines so brightly?

> It is a legitimate question to ask how they can have these books
> but have no faith in what they say. It is for the same reason that
> their fathers also refused to believe back in the days when Christ
> worked wonders and marvels for them. So we cannot put the
> blame on Christ, in whom they refused to believe; we must lay
> the blame at the doors of those men who refuse to see the truth
> in the sunlight of high noon.[10]

The rhetoric here is aggressively polemical. For Chrysostom, not only did
Jews of Jesus' time "refuse to believe," but Jews in general do not believe even
their own scriptures: they "have no faith in what they say." Chrysostom's
insinuation is as transparent as it is baseless: Jews reject Jesus not because

8. John Chrysostom, *Demonstration* 11.4.

9. John Chrysostom, *Demonstration* 11.5.

10. John Chrysostom, *Demonstration* 11.6.

they do not understand that the scriptures predict him; they reject him be-cause they do not believe what the prophets plainly say. Chrysostom seems unaware that this malicious accusation is inconsistent with his argument in his previous paragraph (see above), for why would Jews preserve and revere, as sacred, books in which they have no faith?

Eusebius of Caesarea

Eusebius of Caesarea (ca. 265–340) is among the most important shapers of the Christian imagination. His *History of the Church*, completed in the mid-fourth century in the wake of Constantine's bestowal of imperial favor on Christianity, provided the basic narrative framework within which Christianity has told itself the story of its origins ever since. Eusebius' *History* is an impressive and imposing edifice, and the fulfillment of prophecy is the cornerstone with which he anchors its foundations.

When writing a history of anything, where should you start the story? How and at what point in history to begin a historical narrative is a chal-lenge inherent in the historian's task. For Eusebius, getting this decision right was crucial to the success of his project because of the ancient world's universal and innate suspicion of innovation. The world in which Eusebius wrote revered tradition, the more ancient the better. Christianity existed under a cloud of skepticism because it was, even in Eusebius' time in the fourth century, regarded as a *new* religion. The Christian savior was a man who had lived in the same empire that currently ruled the civilized world; Jesus was born during the reign of Augustus Caesar, a "mere" three centu-ries before Eusebius wrote. His primary objective at the very beginning of his history, therefore, is to demonstrate that the Christian religion, although it appeared on the stage of history only recently, is "none other than the first, most ancient, and most primitive of all religions."[11] Eusebius' strategy is to root Christ and Christianity in the religious tradition of the Hebrews, who "are respected by all men for their antiquity,"[12] for their history reaches back to the mists of the past, prior to the Great Flood.

Eusebius executes this strategy primarily by marshaling evidence that the Jewish scriptures foretell Jesus Christ. He presents his case in three parts, arguing that the Old Testament

1. reveals the divinity of Christ and his existence as the Son of God prior to his incarnation on earth;

11. Eusebius, *History* 1.4.10.
12. Eusebius, *History* 1.4.5.

2. prophesies the details of Jesus' life, teaching, death, and resurrection; and

3. anticipates the exact names "Jesus" and "Christ" as names of singular reverence.

(1) Eusebius begins his story of Christ with an explanation that Christ has both a divine and a human nature. "By this means, both the antiquity and the divine character of Christian origins will be demonstrated to those who imagine them to be recent and outlandish, appearing yesterday for the first time."[13] Eusebius quotes a number of biblical passages and interprets them to mean that the divine Son of God existed with God from all eternity. Here are two examples. (i) God the Father was speaking to the Son when he said, "Let us make humankind in our image and likeness."[14] (ii) The passage about Wisdom in Proverbs 8:12–31 refers to God's Son, "a Being, living and subsisting before the world, who assisted the Father and God of the universe in the fashioning of all created things."[15]

(2) In describing Jesus' earthly life, Eusebius emphasizes how it fulfilled prophecy in detail.

> What He did and what He suffered accorded with the prophecies, which foretold that a man who was also God would live in the world as a worker of miracles and would be revealed to all nations as a teacher of the worship due to the Father. They foretold also the miracle of His birth, the new teaching, and the marvels of His works, and furthermore the manner of His death, His resurrection from the dead, and last of all His restoration to heaven by the power of God.[16]

Eusebius does not document these fulfillments by quoting specific prophecies because he has done so elsewhere: "I have collected in special pamphlets the *Selections from the Prophets* that concern our Savior Jesus Christ, and in other works have provided a fuller explanation of the statements about Him."[17]

(3) For Eusebius, not only do the scriptures reveal the divinity of the Son and foretell the details of his life, but they also show that "both 'Jesus' and 'Christ' were names honored even by God's beloved prophets of old."[18]

13. Eusebius, *History* 1.2.1.
14. Eusebius, *History* 1.2.4, quoting Gen 1:26.
15. Eusebius, *History* 1.2.15.
16. Eusebius, *History* 1.2.23.
17. Eusebius, *History* 1.2.27.
18. Eusebius, *History* 1.3.1.

Moses was the first to proclaim the name "Christ," for in his exposition of the laws of the covenant, he bestowed this title on the high priest "as a mark of honor and glory."[19] Eusebius here alludes to the description of the high priest in Leviticus as "the anointed priest." Lev 4:5 LXX, for example, refers to the high priest as *ho iereus ho christos*, literally, "the priest, the anointed one" (see also Lev 4:3, 16; 6:22). Eusebius infers from that title that "it is clear that Moses understood the divine import of the word 'Christ.'"[20] (Actually, Lev 4:3 proves that "Moses," the putative author of Leviticus, did *not* understand the term "anointed" to connote divinity, because that verse describes the sacrificial ritual by which the anointed priest atones for *his own sins*, which bring guilt on the whole people.)

As for the name Jesus, Eusebius exploits the fact that the Christian savior and Joshua, Moses' successor, have the same name—"Jesus" and "Joshua" are both *Iēsous* in Greek.

> Moses was enabled by the Holy Spirit to foresee quite plainly the title Jesus. Never yet heard by human ears until it was made known to Moses, the title Jesus was bestowed by him for the first and only time on the man who—again as a pattern and symbol—he knew would after his own death succeed to the supreme authority.[21]

Just as Joshua inherited Moses' authority, so Jesus "succeeded to the authority over the true and most pure religion."[22] Eusebius points out that it was Moses himself who gave Joshua his name; his parents had named him Hoshea (Num 13:16). "Moses thus bestows on the two men who in his time surpassed all the people in merit and glory—the high priest and the man chosen to follow him as leader—the name of our Savior Jesus Christ as a signal honor."[23]

Eusebius next uses the fact that Israel's kings were anointed. He offers quotations of Lam 4:20 (attributed to Jeremiah) and Ps 2:1–2, 7–8 (attributed to David), both of which refer to kings as "christs" (i.e., as anointed ones).

> Thus, it was not only those honored with the high priesthood, anointed with prepared oil for the symbol's sake, who were distinguished among the Hebrews with the name of Christ, but the kings too; for they, at the bidding of God, were anointed by

19. Eusebius, *History* 1.3.2.

20. Eusebius, *History* 1.3.3.

21. Eusebius, *History* 1.3.3, alluding to Num 26:15–20.

22. Eusebius, *History* 1.3.4.

23. Eusebius, *History* 1.3.5.

prophets and were thus made Christs in image, in that they, too, bore in themselves the patterns of the kingly, sovereign authority of the one true Christ, the divine Word who reigns over all.[24]

The accumulated testimony of the prophetic scriptures provides the evidence with which Eusebius believes he has demonstrated that the roots of Christianity are ancient, thus inoculating it against the charge that it was a recent innovation. For one more prophetic witness, Eusebius calls on Isaiah, who foresaw a people who would appear "all at once" and would be "honored by all with the name of Christ."[25]

> This so amazed one of the prophets, when with the eye of the Holy Spirit he foresaw what was to be, that he burst out:

>> "Whoever heard such things?
>> And who ever spoke thus?
>> Was the earth in labor for only one day?
>> And was a people born at once?"

> The same writer also hinted at the future name of this people:

>> "Those who serve Me shall be called by a new name,
>> which shall be blessed on the earth."[26]

For Eusebius, the "new name" that is "blessed on the earth" is, of course, the name "Christian." This interesting interpretation of Isa 65:15–16 is possible only for the Septuagint version. In the Hebrew text it is God, not the new name, that is blessed: "To his servants he will give a new name; then whoever invokes a blessing in the land shall bless by the God of faithfulness."

At the end of this first section of Eusebius' introduction to his *History of the Church*, he restates his thesis:

> What then is to prevent us from admitting that we, Christ's followers, share one and the same life and form of religion with those who were dear to God so long ago? Thus the practice of religion as communicated to us by Christ's teaching is shown to be not modern and strange but, in all conscience, primitive, unique, and true.[27]

---

24. Eusebius, *History* 1.3.7.
25. Eusebius, *History* 1.4.2.
26. Eusebius, *History* 1.4.3, quoting Isa 66:8 and 65:15c–16a.
27. Eusebius, *History* 1.4.15.

Theodore of Mopsuestia

Theodore of Mopsuestia (ca. 350–428) is the foremost representative of what scholars call the Antioch school of biblical interpretation. Antioch and Alexandria were home to two rather different Christian approaches to the Bible.[28] The Alexandrian school, whose leading representative was the scholar Origen, saw the Bible as a book of symbols expressing spiritual meanings that were available only by going beyond the literal level. The Alexandrian interpreters made extensive use of allegorical interpretations to expound the deeper level of meaning they discovered. The school of Antioch rejected the allegorical method and saw the task of interpretation as understanding the intention of the human author. The school believed that the divine revelation in the Bible was to be found precisely at its literal level, for it was in the actual events of the history of Israel and the events reported in the gospels that God's will and actions were to be discerned. It was this concern for the historical level of meaning that led the scholars of the Antioch school to be wary of interpretations that presuppose that the primary purpose of the OT was to predict Jesus and the church. Theodore of Mopsuestia was especially strict about limiting the christological interpretation of OT passages. He did not rule it out altogether, because he accepted the NT's assertions that Jesus fulfilled certain prophecies, but those specific examples were for Theodore the exceptions to the rule.

Ancient sources report that Theodore wrote commentaries on many OT books, including all the prophets, although none of those works are extant except for his *Commentary on the Twelve Prophets*.[29] Theodore also wrote a commentary on the Psalms, which was lost but has been partially reconstructed.[30]

Theodore certainly acknowledged the predictive dimension of prophecy. To his mind, the most important prophet was David, author of the psalms, which contain short- and long-term predictions "of all that would happen in regard to the [Jewish] people at different times."[31] In Theodore's view, however, the prophets were primarily concerned with their own times. "For the most part, each of the prophets necessarily emerged to mention

28. See Young, "Alexandrian and Antiochean Exegesis."

29. Hill, "Introduction," 3. Since Antiquity it has been customary to distinguish the three "major" prophets (Isaiah, Jeremiah, and Ezekiel) from the twelve "minor" prophets (Hosea, Joel, Amos, Obadiah, Jonah, Micah, Nahum, Habakkuk, Zephaniah, Haggai, Zechariah, and Malachi).

30. Ibid.

31. Theodore, *Commentary on Joel*, preface. ("Preface" here refers to the first section of Theodore's commentary, not to remarks by the translator.)

events whose outcomes were shown to be close at hand."[32] Theodore's position is thus the very opposite of Eusebius's, whose view represents a near consensus among patristic writers: that the prophets did *not* address their own times, because such short-term concerns were too fleeting to be of concern to exalted spokespersons for the eternal God.

Note how Theodore begins the assertion quoted above with "for the most part," a qualification that reflects his belief that the prophets occasionally, and David more than the rest, predicted events beyond the lifetime of their original audiences. However—and this is what marks out Theodore as distinctive—all the predictions (with but one exception) pertained to the time *before* Christ. For example, the sufferings that the prophet Malachi says will purify the people and the priests (Mal 3:1–4) foretell the persecutions inflicted on Jews in the time of the Maccabees. Similarly, Psalm 69, which details the sufferings of a persecuted righteous individual, likewise foretell the tribulations endured by faithful Jews at that time.[33] By contrast, other christological interpretations, and the gospels themselves, relate Psalm 69 to Jesus' passion.

To consider another significant example, the gospel writers also use Psalm 22 in the passion narratives. Indeed, Matthew and Mark portray the crucified Jesus reciting the agonized opening of Ps 22:1: "My God, my God, why have you abandoned me?" (Matt 27:46; Mark 15:34). Theodore, however, relates this psalm to David's anguish when his son, Absalom, led Israel in rebellion against him and drove him from Jerusalem (see 2 Samuel 15). Theodore argues that Psalm 22 cannot be about Jesus because its author "refers to his own sins."[34] That argument exemplifies Theodore's respect for the integrity of scripture. He opposed christological interpretations of verses plucked out of their contexts when other verses in the same passage clearly could not be related to Christ.

As mentioned above, Theodore does not deny altogether that Christ is prophesied in the OT. However, he sees only four passages that refer directly to Christ. Three of those are psalms (2, 8, and 45) in which David adopts the persona of Christ.[35] The sole text from the books of the prophets that Theodore believes directly predicts Jesus is, appropriately, the very last passage in the Christian OT—and thus the last words before the beginning of

32. Theodore, *Commentary on Joel*, preface.

33. Young, "Alexandrian and Antiochean Exegesis." 350.

34. Ibid. Theodore did not know Hebrew and so relied solely on the Septuagint, in which the second half of Ps 22:1 reads, "The account of my sins (*paraptōmatōn*) is far from my salvation." The same sentence, translated from the Hebrew, reads, "Why are you so far from helping me, from the words of my groaning?"

35. Ibid.

the NT: Mal 4:4–6. "Since he [Malachi] was the last prophet of all those who consigned their prophecies to writing, he was right in considering he could then show the end of the Law, on the one hand, and, on the other, show what would come after it."[36] Beyond this small set of passages that are directly about Jesus, Theodore also recognizes a few prophecies that have a secondary application to Christ, that is, passages that the NT claims were fulfilled in Jesus. Theodore regards such interpretations as secondary on two grounds. First, he notes that NT authors alter the wording of some passages to make them match the time of Jesus.[37] Second, he interprets some psalms as David's prophecies that foretell events in the history of Israel, and those events prefigure saving events in the life of Jesus.[38]

Theodore does not endorse the simplified argument that the truth of Christianity is proven by the direct fulfillment of the prophets' predictions.[39] A striking example is Theodore's explication of Hos 11:1 ("I called my son out of Egypt"), in which he makes no mention of Jesus at all, a truly remarkable omission, since Matthew regarded it as a christological prophecy (Matt 2:15). Apparently, Theodore could see no justifiable connection between Hosea's intention and Matthew's use of Hosea's words.

As a Christian, however, Theodore does not deny the NT's repeated proclamation that Jesus and the church fulfilled numerous prophecies. In discussing these claims, Theodore distinguishes between what the prophet himself referred to and a later, and it seems fuller, realization of the prophet's words. Two examples show the subtlety of Theodore's respect for the prophets' own intentions and historical contexts even as he affirms the NT's message. The first example is his explanation of Mic 5:2 ("From you [Bethlehem], will come forth for me one who is to rule in Israel; whose origin is from of old, from ancient days"). According to Theodore,

> It is clear that . . . this refers to Zerubbabel,[40] a successor of David, yet the true fulfillment of the words is achieved in Christ the Lord. While every promise made to David about his descendants reigning seems at first flush to indicate his successors in

36. Theodore, *Commentary on Malachi*, 4.

37. Young, "Alexandrian and Antiochean Exegesis." 350.

38. Trigg, *Biblical Interpretation*, 165.

39. Zaharopoulos, *Theodore of Mopsuestia*, 158.

40. Zerubbabel was a distant descendant of David and the grandson of King Jehoiachin, who was exiled to Babylon. When the Persians took over the Babylonian empire, they appointed Zerubbabel governor of their province of Judah. Some Jews, including the prophets Haggai and Zechariah, hoped that Zerubbabel would become a messianic king who would inaugurate a time of renewed glory for Israel (see Hag 2:20–23 and Zech 4:6–10).

the kingdom of Israel, in reality it foretells Christ the Lord in the flesh, who as a successor to David exercises the true and abiding rule over all.[41]

Here, too, it is noteworthy what Theodore omits from his commentary on this passage. He neither reminds the reader that Jesus was born in Bethlehem nor points out that Matt 2:5–6 quotes this very verse from Micah as a prophecy that Jesus fulfilled.[42]

The second example is Amos 9:11–12 ("I shall raise up the tent of David that is fallen . . . so that the remnant of people may seek me out, along with all the nations on whom my name has been invoked"). In Acts 15:13–17, James quotes this prophecy as authority for the church's inclusion of gentiles. James thereby implies (but does not explicitly assert) that the phrase "I shall raise up the tent of David that is fallen" was fulfilled in Jesus. Theodore explains that Amos was referring to the restoration of the royal line of David after Israel's return from exile in Babylon, that "all who had returned to their own place would have Zerubbabel as a king in the line of David."[43] Theodore integrates the original intent of the prophecy and its later use by the NT as follows:

> Whereas at that time the passage was meant by the prophet to disclose the coming events of the return, the firm and unshakable truth of the words is revealed and established in the person of Christ the Lord and the application of the passage takes its true force from blessed James.[44]

It seems that Theodore endorses the NT's interpretation of this prophecy because Amos' original intention for it was not completely fulfilled: David's line was not actually restored when Israel returned from exile. Theodore's reasoning seems to be that it was only because of this inconclusiveness that James was able to interpret Amos' prophecy as finding its full realization in Christ.[45]

Theodore's refusal to recognize more than a handful of direct predictions of Jesus and the church in the prophetic texts of the OT seems motivated by several factors. One is his primary focus on the historical context of the prophetic writings, which led him to concentrate on the prophets' intended messages to their Israelite contemporaries. Another is Theodore's

41. Theodore, *Commentary on Micah*, 5.

42. Zaharopoulos, *Theodore of Mopsuestia*, 163.

43. Theodore, *Commentary on Amos*, 9.

44. Theodore, *Commentary on Amos*, 9.

45. Zaharopoulos, *Theodore of Mopsuestia*, 162.

respect for the literary integrity of those texts, which led him to reject christological interpretations of single verses removed from their contexts. A
third factor is a "remarkably clear appreciation of the eschatological newness of the NT," and thus his recognition that Jesus had effected a radically
new era in God's saving work.[46] Theodore describes "the time of Christ the
Lord, [as a time] when everything was important and awesome, novel and
really baffling, surpassing what had happened under the Law to the greatest extent imaginable."[47] Theodore thus differs sharply with Eusebius, who
took pains to downplay the newness of Christ, insisting that Christ and the
church are predicted everywhere in the OT.

Theodore's approach to interpreting the OT represents the road not
taken. Through these early centuries, Christians had very little, if any, interest in the prophets' messages to their own audiences. Virtually the only
value the Jewish scriptures had for patristic authors was as sources for understanding Christian revelation and for confirming the truth of Christianity. Except in the nearly negligible minority opinion of Theodore and his
fellow Antiochene exegetes, the OT writings were by then understood as
fully "baptized" members of the thoroughly Christian scriptures. No one
exemplifies that perspective more fully than Augustine, whom we engage
in the next chapter.

46. Young, "Alexandrian and Antiochean Exegesis," 351.

47. Theodore, *Commentary on Joel*, 2.

16

Augustine and the Argument from Prophecy

AUGUSTINE (354–430) IS A towering figure in the history of Christian theology, probably the single most influential thinker in all Christianity. His theology summed up the patristic era in the Latin West and set much of the agenda for the Middle Ages. His writing on the interpretation of the OT is voluminous, much of it devoted to explaining how Christ and the church fulfilled specific prophecies. He also ponders more generally the relationship between Christ and the OT. He explains how demonstrations of the fulfillment of prophecy should help to persuade both Jews and pagans of the truth of Christianity, and why Jews as a whole nonetheless remained unpersuaded. He reflects extensively on Jewish nonbelief that Christ fulfilled prophecy, and theorizes what that nonbelief entailed about the Jews' role in God's ongoing plan and for how Christians should regard and behave toward them. Augustine also wrestles with the problem posed by the fulfillment of prophecies attributed to pagan gods.

Augustine does not devote a distinct treatise to the systematic explication of his thinking on the fulfillment of scripture. He weaves his scriptural interpretations and his methodological, apologetic, and theological reflections on the fulfillment of scripture into many different topics. This chapter, therefore, considers selections of his writing culled from several sources, but primarily from three: the monumental *City of God*, the massive polemic *Reply to Faustus*, and the sermon *In Answer to the Jews*. We will also consult of two his minor works, *Faith in Things Unseen* and *The Divination of Demons*, as well as one selection from his *Tractates on the Gospel of John*. Augustine is a skillful, if prolix, writer and a clear thinker. One seldom has to struggle to understand what he is trying to say. Sometimes the most efficient way to explain his thought is simply to quote him, which this chapter will do often, and a few times at some length.

This chapter has five parts. The first introduces Augustine's general convictions about the fulfillment of scripture and the role it plays in his defense of the truths of Christianity, as well as his principles of interpretation. The second part discusses the thorny topic of what Augustine thought about Jews and Judaism in light of his belief that the OT is fulfilled in Christ. The third part examines Augustine's deployment of the fulfillment of prophecy in his apologetic to pagans. The fourth part showcases examples of Augustine's more far-fetched interpretations of OT passages in which he sees Christ and the Church, and explores what such interpretations reveal about the dynamics that guide them. The fifth part investigates how Augustine copes with the belief (which he shared) that paganism also had prophecies that had been fulfilled.

Introduction

We can begin our study of Augustine's thinking about the fulfillment of prophecy by considering four topics: (1) his belief that *all* Jewish scripture (with a few specific exceptions) foretells Christ; (2) his rationale in support of allegorical and typological interpretation, and the clues in a passage by which he can tell which elements in it are meant to be taken symbolically; (3) his principle that individual verses are not to be interpreted out of context, a principle he understands very differently than we do today; and (4) how and why the fulfillment of prophecy functions as a cornerstone in Augustine's apologetics.

There is no better way to describe Augustine's understanding of the relationship between the OT and Christ than to let him speak for himself.

> To enumerate all the passages in the Hebrew prophets referring to our Lord and Savior Jesus Christ, would exceed the limits of a volume. The whole content of these Scriptures is either directly or indirectly about Christ. Often the reference is allegorical or enigmatical, perhaps in a verbal allusion, or in a historical narrative, requiring diligence in the student, and rewarding him with the pleasure of discovery. Other passages, again, are plain; for, without the help of what is clear, we could not understand what is obscure. And even the figurative passages, when brought together, will be found so harmonious in their testimony to Christ as to put to shame the obtuseness of the skeptic.[1]

---

1. Augustine, *Faustus* 12.7.

Three features of this paragraph merit attention. (1) Although in the context of this manifesto "the whole content of these scriptures" refers to the books of the prophets, Augustine believes that the whole OT is about Christ, something implied by his mention of historical narrative in the next sentence, as well as by his very many statements elsewhere, e.g., "All that Moses wrote is of Christ or relates to Christ, either predicting Him by words and actions, or as illustrating His grace and glory."[2] When Augustine interprets scripture in reference to Christ, his examples come from all over the OT, but mostly from the prophets, psalms, and Genesis.

(2) Augustine acknowledges that the references to Christ in many passages are obscure, difficult to discover, and often hidden in verbal allusions or peripheral narrative details.

(3) Despite those problems, Augustine is confident that the sheer number of passages that testify to Christ will overpower any skepticism.

When it comes to searching for the hidden meanings of scripture, Augustine is aware of the difficulty. "We investigate those hidden meanings of divine scripture as best we can, some finding symbols with more, others with less success."[3] Even if those meanings can be hard to find, Augustine is sure that *all* of scripture is about Christ and the Church: "However, what is certain to all people of faith is, first, that these things were not done and recorded without some prefiguring of what was to come and, second, that they refer *only* to Christ and his Church."[4]

In his treatise *Reply to Faustus*, Augustine qualifies his position that *every* passage predicts Christ: "Every part of the narrative in the prophetic books[5] should be viewed as having a figurative meaning, except what serves as a framework for the literal or figurative predictions."[6] Augustine compares this to a harp: only the strings make music, while the rest of the harp forms the framework for the strings. "So in these prophetic narratives the circumstances selected by the prophetic spirit either predict some future event, or if they have no voice of their own, they serve to connect together other significant utterances."[7]

2. Augustine, *Faustus* 16.9.

3. Augustine, *City of God* 16.16.

4. Augustine, *City of God* 16.16 (italics added).

5. These include the books of Samuel, Kings, and Chronicles.

6. Augustine, *Faustus* 22.94.

7. Augustine, *Faustus* 22.94.

Rationale for Symbolic Interpretation

Augustine is alert to a possible objection from Jews and pagans that typological interpretations are "mere ingenious fancy." Christians, however, "must yield to the authority of the Apostle when he says, 'All these things happened to them for an example,' and again, 'These things are for our examples.'" Those quotations are from 1 Cor 10:11 and 10:6, and they relate to Paul's typological reflections on the Exodus story. Augustine goes on to discuss Paul's allegorical interpretation of the story of Ishmael and Isaac in Galatians 4, using it as precedent for seeking typological meanings in a trove of OT passages where one might not expect to find much meaning.

> If two men, Ishmael and Isaac, are types of the two covenants, can it be supposed that there is no significance in the vast number of particulars which have no historical or natural value? Suppose we were to see some Hebrew letters written on the wall of a noble building, should we be so foolish as to conclude that, because we cannot understand the letters, they are not intended to be read, and are mere painting, without any meaning? So, whoever with a candid mind reads all these things that are contained in the Old Testament, must feel constrained to acknowledge that they have a meaning.[8]

Augustine here refers to elements in biblical stories that seem superfluous ("have no historical or natural meanings") because they do not contribute to the meaning of the story in its own context. His analogy to inscriptions in Hebrew (a language that he tells us he could not read) is revealing: all scripture must be meaningful, and so our inability to understand the meaning of a passage is no reason to doubt that it has one. Augustine argues that the particulars of a passage that have no discernible meanings in their natural or historical sense must therefore have symbolic meanings. Augustine gives a series of examples of what he has in mind. Here are three that have to do with Noah's ark.

> Granting that an ark was required in order to escape from the flood, why should it have precisely these dimensions, and why should they be recorded for the devout study of future generations?
>
> Granting that the animals were brought into the ark to preserve the various species, why should there be seven clean and two unclean?

---

8. Augustine, *Faustus* 12.37.

> Granting that the ark must have a door, why should it be
> in the side [of the ark], and why should this fact be committed
> to writing?[9]

In each case Augustine finds elements of the story that are necessary to
make its point, but then goes on to identify seemingly innocuous details
that surely could have been omitted with no loss to the narrative thread. It
is precisely those details that Augustine urges us to probe for their hidden
meanings.

> A rational mind is led by the consideration of the way in which
> these apparently superfluous things are blended with what is
> necessary, first to acknowledge their significance, and then to
> try to discover it.[10]

In *City of God* 15.26, Augustine shows us what he had discovered concerning two features of the ark. (1) The ark was three hundred cubits long,
fifty wide, and thirty tall—proportions that prefigure the Incarnation. As
the ark was a vessel of salvation, so was the human body of Jesus, the normal
human body having the same ratio of height, length, and width as the ark: a
man lying on the ground is "six times as long from head to foot, as he is wide
from left to right, and he is ten times as long as he is high from the ground
up." (2) The door in the side of the ark symbolizes the wound in the side of
Christ, "the door by which those who come to Him enter in, in the sense
that believers enter the Church by means of the sacraments which issued
from that wound."

Augustine adds another qualification to his stipulation that *all* scripture is about Christ. In *City of God* 17.3 he distinguishes three categories
of prophecies: those that refer to the earthly Jerusalem (which were meant
to be fulfilled within the history of Israel), those that refer to the heavenly
Jerusalem (which were not fulfilled in Israel but that were or will be fulfilled
in Christ and the church), and those that refer both to Israel (literally) and
to the heavenly Jerusalem (figuratively). An example of the first category
is the prophet Nathan's announcement of how God will punish David for
his rape[11] of Bathsheba and murder of her husband (see 2 Kgs 12:9–14).
An example of the second is Jeremiah's oracle about the new covenant (Jer
31:31–33). Examples of the third are the bestowing of the title "city of God"

9. Augustine, *Faustus* 12.38.

10. Augustine, *Faustus* 12.38.

11. Most interpretations of David's interaction with Bathsheba imply that it was
consensual adultery; see, for example, the NRSV's title for 2 Sam 11:1–13: "David Commits Adultery with Bathsheba." But the king's actions against a powerless woman clearly
amount to rape. See Miller, *Born Divine*, 84.

on Jerusalem and the prophecy that God's house would be built there. The third kind of prophecy "has challenged and continues to challenge the interpretative talent of scripture students."

Augustine disagrees with those who maintain that there is no such thing as the first type of prophecy. Such interpreters insist that every prophecy without exception has allegorical meaning. Augustine finds this position "too speculative," but does not refute it; he simply states, "That is my opinion," and then lays out his nuanced position:

> I do not censure those who may have been able to carve out some spiritual interpretation from every historical fact recounted, so long as they take good care first and foremost to adhere to its historical truth.[12]

In *City of God* 13.21 Augustine gives a clear example of how this principle should work. He argues that those "who have allegorized the entire Garden of Eden" err if they then deny the historical truth of the story, as if it "had no purpose but to express meaning for our minds." However, as long as we affirm the literal truth of the narrative, nothing forbids us from seeing

> in the Garden the life of the blessed; in its four rivers, the four virtues (prudence, fortitude, temperance, and justice); in its trees, all useful knowledge; in their fruits, the holy lives of the faithful; in the tree of life, wisdom herself, the mother of all good; and in the tree of the knowledge of good and evil, the experience that results from disobedience to a divine commandment.[13]

In fact, it is even better to read the story as a prophetic allegory of the Church.

> The Garden itself is the Church; the four rivers are the four gospels; the fruit trees are the saints, and the fruit are their works; the tree of life is the Saint of saints, Christ; and the tree of the knowledge of good and evil is the free choice of our will.[14]

Context and Interpretation

We need to consider one more element of Augustine's interpretive method: his insistence that quotations not be interpreted out of context. In discussing

---

12. Augustine, *City of God* 17.3 (translation modified).

13. Augustine, *City of God* 13.21.

14. Augustine, *City of God* 13.21.

the prophetic interpretation of the psalms, Augustine is concerned that because his expositions of them are so brief, "I may appear to be arbitrarily plucking texts out of their contexts to bolster my own views."[15] To counter that impression Augustine lays out the following principle: "The sense of any one verse should be supported by the pattern of the whole psalm or, at least, should not be contradicted by the context . . . To show the valid use of any excerpt, the entire psalm must be expounded."[16] Augustine invites those who are so inclined to read his lengthy commentary on the psalms, in which one will "discover how abundant and magnificent are the prophecies of David, king and prophet, touching Christ the King and the City which he founded, the Church."[17]

This principle seems perfectly congruent with our modern sensitivity about respecting the intent of the author or the integrity of the text, or both. However, two crucial distinctions must be kept in mind, lest we fall into anachronism by imagining that Augustine shared the modern historical-critical understanding of biblical interpretation. First, Augustine is not interested in the meaning intended by the ancient Hebrew author, but in the meaning intended by the divine author who inspired him. Second, the examples of Augustine's interpretation discussed in this chapter show how differently he applies the principle of interpreting in context than we might today. Augustine does not allow context to invalidate his figurative interpretations. Rather, context assures him that details in the text that *seem* not to fit his interpretation actually do fit it, even if he cannot easily figure out how. Context allows the interpreter to understand the obscure details in the text in harmony with verses whose meaning is clearer. The verses that are easy to grasp provide the key to the significance of the elements that are obscure. Augustine articulates his understanding of the function of context.

> Although there exist on any prophetic theme utterances which are literal, plain-spoken and perfectly clear, there has to be some intermingling of figurative language. It is this latter kind of thing which forces upon teachers the laborious task of discussion and explanation—more particularly for the benefit of those who are rather slow to understand. Nevertheless, there are texts which, on a very first hearing, obviously concern Christ and the Church—even if they contain a residue of less readily intelligible points to be clarified at one's leisure.[18]

15. Augustine, *City of God* 17.15.
16. Augustine, *City of God* 17.15.
17. Augustine, *City of God* 17.15.
18. Augustine, *City of God* 17.15.

Augustine offers Psalm 45 as an example of how context should guide interpretation. We will follow closely his interpretation of this psalm because it provides a clear example of how his interpretation proceeds differently than our modern methods allow. Psalm 45 is unusual in that it praises a king, a victorious warrior, on the occasion of his wedding. The psalm is unique in that it calls the king "God" ("Your throne, O God, endures forever," Ps 45:6).[19] For Augustine that title, in conjunction with the description of the king's anointing in verse 7 ("God, your God, has anointed you"), clinches beyond any doubt the christological reference of the psalm.

> Is there any reader—however dull-witted—who does not recognize in this person the Christ whom we preach, in whom we believe? Is there any insider so ill-informed in his faith, any outsider so deaf to its universally known character, as not to be aware that Christ's very name is derived from "chrism," that is, from His anointing?[20]

In considering Augustine's use of context here, the modern interpreter might be put off by the mention of the king's sword and arrows (vv. 3, 5), and object that Jesus did not carry weapons, much less kill his enemies with them ("Your arrows are sharp in the heart of the king's enemies, the peoples fall under you," v. 5). For Augustine, however, the weapons in the psalm do not count against his christological interpretation; they are puzzling details to be cleared up later.

> After that [recognizing Christ the King in the psalm], one may, at his leisure, look into the meaning of the rest that is spoken figuratively—what, for instance . . . his "sword" and "arrows" might be, and much else that is cast in metaphorical language.[21]

The psalm also addresses the king's bride and describes her wedding dress and bridesmaids (Ps 45:10–15). Here too the modern interpreter might protest that the gospels do not describe Jesus as having a wife, much less report details of his wedding. For Augustine, however, this objection would miss the point because the NT describes the Church as the bride of Christ (see Eph 5:32), which is surely the basis for Augustine's elaborate interpretation of the queen in the psalm as the city of God.

---

19. The Hebrew can also be translated "Your throne is the throne of God." However, the Septuagint and Augustine's Latin translation are unambiguous.

20. Augustine, *City of God* 17.16.

21. Augustine, *City of God* 17.17.

The last two verses of the psalm furnish further contextual clues that to us count against its Christianized reading, but to Augustine they reinforce it.

> ¹⁶ In the place of ancestors you shall have sons;
>
> > you will make them princes in all the earth.
>
> ¹⁷ I will cause your name to be celebrated in all generations;
>
> > therefore the peoples will praise you forever and ever. (Ps 45:16–17)

The sense and structure of the psalm demand that we read these verses as addressed to the king—it makes little sense to assume that the psalm concludes by praising the queen. (The "you" and "your" are masculine in the Hebrew text.²² The NRSV helpfully adds "O king" after the first "you," although that word is not in the Hebrew text.) Verse 16, then, steers us away from a christological interpretation, for Jesus had no sons, and nothing in the NT refers to Christians as "sons of Christ." For Augustine, however, who lacked the grammatical guidance of the Hebrew text, that problem does not exist because he reads these verses as addressed to the king's spouse, the Church. "This prediction we see realized before our eyes, because out of her sons come her rulers and fathers all over the earth, as the nations hasten to join in praising her."²³ Augustine proceeds immediately to his interpretive conclusion.

> These truths are perfectly clear and, therefore, any interpreta-
> tion of other parts of the psalm, which are somewhat obscure by
> reason of metaphorical language, must be consistent with what
> we know to be true.²⁴

Apologetics and the Fulfillment of Prophecy

The fulfillment of prophecy is, for Augustine, more than a pillar of Christian faith; it is one of its foundations. He regards the fulfillment of prophecy as sure evidence for the reliability of scripture. "Our scriptures never deceive us, since we can test the truth of what they have told us by the fulfillment of predictions."²⁵ Fulfilled prophecies stand alongside the miracles of Jesus as convincing proof for the truth of Christianity.

---

22. Hebrew, unlike Greek and English, has different masculine and feminine forms of "you" and "your."

23. Augustine, *City of God* 17.16.

24. Augustine, *City of God* 17.16.

25. Augustine, *City of God* 16.9.

There were many grounds for our faith. Not to mention a multitude of miracles that proved that Christ was God, we had the
divinely inspired and utterly authentic prophecy . . . which, after
this fulfillment, are completely cogent.[26]

In fact, when discussing the teaching of the apostles, Augustine argues that
the probative value of prophecy is even greater than that of miracles.

The Apostles quoted the predictions of the prophets to prove the
truth and importance of doctrines. For although their preaching
was accompanied with the power of working miracles, the miracles would have been ascribed to magic . . . unless the apostles
had shown that the authority of the prophets was in their favor.
The testimony of prophets who lived so long before could not be
ascribed to magical arts.[27]

The point Augustine makes here is that the fulfillment of prophecy is not
an article of faith, but rather a basis for it. He does not ask people to *believe*
that Jesus fulfills prophecy. He argues, rather, that people should believe
in Christ and in the truth of Christianity *because* Christ and the Church
fulfill prophecy. Augustine matches prophecies to fulfillments in the confidence that fair-minded, rational people will agree that they have been
fulfilled in just the way he claims. If some are not convinced by such lucid and overwhelming evidence, Augustine's only explanation is that such
people must be defective, either morally corrupt because they are motivated
by some vice to refuse to acknowledge what they know to be true (those
who "prefer their sins to their salvation"),[28] or cognitively impaired because
some impediment makes then unable to recognize the truth. Addressing
an imaginary Jewish audience, Augustine asks, "Those events foretold with
such great authority, fulfilled with such manifestations—do you either with
great blindness fail to consider them, or with remarkable impudence refuse
to acknowledge them?"[29]

Jews and the Fulfillment of Prophecy

Our next task is to track both how Augustine makes the case for the fulfillment of prophecy and how he understands the fulfillment of prophecy to
function within the apologetic project. For obvious reasons he presents the

26. Augustine, *City of God* 22.6.

27. Augustine, *Faustus* 12.45.

28. Augustine, *Faustus* 13.16.

29. Augustine, *Answer* 7.9.

matter differently when the apology is addressed to Jews than when it is addressed to pagans.

Augustine's thinking on Jews and Judaism is complicated. He wrote on this topic often, at length, and over a long arc of time, so there should be no surprise that his writing on these matters contains some inconsistencies. The specific focus of our inquiry here is on how Augustine deploys the fulfillment of prophecy against Jews, how he analyzes their resistance to those arguments, and what that resistance entails for the relationship between Jews and Christians. The sources for our inquiry are Augustine's sermon *In Answer to the Jews*, a few passages in *Reply to Faustus* and the *City of God*, and one of his pieces in his *Tractates on the Gospel of John*.

At the start of *In Answer to the Jews* Augustine acknowledges that it is futile to argue about scripture with Jews. When Christians quote the New Testament to them, "they do not listen to what we say because they do not understand what they read." "What they read" here refers to the Jewish scriptures. Augustine then makes explicit what he just implied.

> They do not understand what they read. Certainly, if they understood what the prophet is foretelling ("I have given you as a light to the Gentiles, that you may be my salvation[30] even to the end of the earth"), they would not be so blind and so sick as not to recognize in Jesus Christ both light and salvation. Likewise, if they understood to whom the prophecy refers ("Their sound has gone out to all the earth, and their words to the end of the world"), which they sing so fruitlessly and without meaning, they would awaken to the voice of the Apostles, and would sense that their [i.e., the Apostles'] words are divine.[31]

Despite the Jews' incomprehension, however, Christians should still confront them with "testimonies selected from sacred scripture, which has great authority among Jews." To what end? "If they do not want to be cured by means of this advantage offered them, they can at least be convicted by its evident truth."[32] Decoding Augustine's rhetoric here is revealing. That Jews need to be "cured" implies that they are afflicted with blindness (see below). That they "do not want" to be cured implies that their blindness is willful (more on this shortly). It seems that the actual purpose of confronting Jews with fulfilled prophecies is so that they can be "convicted," that is, found guilty—by whom?—by Augustine's Christian readers (who else?). Jews are

---

30. Compare Augustine's Latin, "that *you* may be my salvation to the end of the earth," to the Hebrew text: "that my salvation may be to the end of the earth."

31. Augustine, *Answer* 1.2, quoting Isa 49:6 and Ps 19:4.

32. Augustine, *Answer* 1.2.

guilty because the truth of fulfilled prophecy is "evident"—to whom?—to Augustine's readers (who else?). Augustine thus constructs a rhetorical arena in which Jews are on trial, and fulfilled scripture is the evidence against them; Augustine is the prosecutor, and his Christian audience is the jury.

Real-life Jews would, of course, resist such rhetoric. But Augustine is speaking to *Christians* about Jews, even though he imagines himself in dialogue with Jews in a section of this sermon, addressing them in the second person: "It may be well to address the Jews just a little while *as if* they were present."[33] *In Answer to the Jews* is a sermon,[34] and Christian sermons are preached not to Jews but to Christians, for whom the guilt of the Jews was long settled. Toward the end of the sermon, after laying out numerous "obvious testimonies," Augustine calls on Jews (in his imaginary audience) to repent of their unbelief.

> Not I, but the Prophet whom you read—through whom you cannot deny God has spoken, to whom you cannot deny the authority of the sacred Scriptures—at the Lord's command vehemently cries out and lifts up his voice like a trumpet and, rebuking you, says, "O house of Jacob, come and let us walk in the light of the Lord." You, in the person of your parents, have killed Christ. For a long time you have not believed in Him and you have opposed Him, but you are not yet lost, because you are still alive; you have time now for repentance; only come now.[35]

Augustine knows, of course, that Jews will not "repent," and so this rhetorical flourish serves only to underline their guilt. In discussing the Jewish refusal to see the light shining before them, Augustine repeatedly hammers home two interrelated themes: that Jews are blind to the truth of Christ, and that their unbelief fulfills prophecy. Both of those rationalizations serve to preclude any unspoken doubts in his audience (and perhaps in himself) that the avalanche of fulfillments of scripture with which he tries to bury Jews might not be as obvious as he assumes. Such doubts could arise precisely because it was *Jews* who were not persuaded. Who knows the prophets better than they? If even they—who cherish the prophetic books, who can read them in their original language, and who regard them as the words of God—had not by Augustine's time (nearly four centuries since the time of Christ) seen in those hundreds of predictions the light of Christ, then perhaps those predictions might not be as probative as Augustine needs them to be. While he never expresses such a doubt, his apparent need to

---

33. Augustine, *Answer* 7.9.

34. Ligouri, "Introduction," 387–88.

35. Augustine, *Answer* 8.11, quoting Isa 2:5.

repeatedly "explain" Jewish unbelief might well betray a fear that doubts might linger in his Christian readers, or even in himself.

The Blindness/Blinding of Jews

Augustine has two answers to the question of why Jews do not believe in Christ: (1) because they do not want to, and (2) because they do not understand their own scriptures. We have already seen how Augustine works both ends of this paradox in the opening of *In Answer to the Jews,* where he uses the familiar metaphor of blindness for Jewish incomprehension: Jews do not recognize Christ because they are blind; their blindness could be removed if they would listen to (i.e., agree with) the Christian interpretation of Jewish scripture; but they do not want to be cured.[36] This argument moves in a perfect circle: they do not believe because they are blind, and they were blinded because they did not believe. Augustine encapsulates this paradox by borrowing Paul's metaphor of the veil: as long as Jews "are unwilling to turn to God, the veil that covers their minds in reading the Old Testament is not removed; this veil is taken away only by Christ."[37]

A bit later in *Reply to Faustus*, Augustine intensifies the paradox by interpreting Jewish blindness as divine punishment. Jews do not understand (that Jesus is the messiah) because "in the mysterious justice of God they were blinded." Augustine then turns to the Book of Wisdom (also known as the Wisdom of Solomon) for an explanation of why Jews of Jesus' day killed him, and of why Jews of Augustine's day resist Christian interpretations of scripture.

> In the mysterious justice of God they were blinded; and thinking only of the power of the Messiah, they did not understand His weakness, in which He died for us. In the Book of Wisdom it is prophesied of the Jews: "'Let us condemn him to an ignominious death. If he truly is the Son of God, He will help him and deliver him from the hand of his enemies.' Thus they thought, and erred; for their wickedness blinded them." These words apply also to those who, in spite of all this evidence, in spite of such a series of prophecies and their fulfillment, still deny that Christ is foretold in the Scriptures.[38]

---

36. Augustine, *Answer* 1.2.

37. Augustine, *Faustus* 12.11, referring to 2 Cor 3:15–16.

38. Augustine, *Faustus* 12.44, quoting and melding Wis 2:20, 18, 21.

Note how Augustine's quotation from Wisdom links wickedness and blindness: they are blinded because they conspire to this singularly wicked deed, and they do this wicked deed because they are blind. The circularity of that logic is very tight, and it is doubtful that Augustine fully endorses its second half, for it comes close to excusing Jewish guilt for the blood of Jesus. Nor is it likely that Augustine intends the first half of Wisdom's analysis to apply to Jews, inasmuch as he does not hold that their blindness is God's punishment for their killing of Jesus. In Augustine's reasoning, the punishment for that most heinous crime was the destruction of the temple in Jerusalem in 70 CE, the Jews' loss of their homeland, and their continuing dispersal throughout the Roman—and now (in Augustine's time) Christian—empire.

Augustine is alert to the moral problem entailed by the paradox: how can Jews justly be judged guilty for their rejection of Christ if God has blinded them to the truth? Augustine's analysis of this problem takes him into what is for him the impenetrable mystery of God's inscrutability. Augustine's reasoning was boxed in (1) by his inability to recognize the arbitrariness of his Christian interpretations of Jewish scripture, and thus by his inability to imagine that the insight that Christ fulfilled scripture was anything less than overwhelmingly evident, and (2) by his axiomatic trust that God is just. If the Jews had for so long not accepted what for Augustine is utterly obvious—that their scriptures are about Christ—this obduracy could only be the result of blindness. Their blindness could have come only from God; there could be no other source for it, and, besides, it was foretold by the prophets themselves (see below). Since whatever God does is just, because God cannot do otherwise, the Jews' blindness must therefore be a just punishment for sin. But for which sin(s)? Not the murder of Jesus, for that was the *result*, not the cause, of their blindness. The sins that merited the punishment of blindness must have been committed prior to Christ's incarnation. Since those sins are not recorded in scripture, they must be sins known only to God.[39]

Augustine works out this solution in Tractate 53 of his *Tractates on the Gospel of John,* in which he wrestles with John 12:37–40, which links Jewish disbelief with both the fulfillment of prophecy and their incapacitating blindness.[40] John 12:38 declares that God foretold their lack of faith but had not caused it.[41] But then John goes on to state unambiguously that "they *could not* believe" (John 12:39), and follows up in 12:40 with a quotation of Isa 6:10. Augustine recognizes that these words "are more pressing and pose

---

39. Fredriksen, *Augustine and the Jews*, 279–84.

40. See pp. 192–93.

41. See Augustine, *Tr. on John* 53.4.

a deeper question . . . If Jews could not believe, what is the sin of someone not doing what he cannot do?"[42]

But why did God blind them? "I answer that their will earned even this."[43] Their blinding was a "hidden judgment," but it cannot have been an unjust one. Augustine summons Paul as an expert witness. "As the Apostle says when discussing the very same, most difficult question," 'What shall we say then? Is there injustice with God? Not at all.'"[44] Augustine next ponders what the Jews' sin could have been, but retreats to the mystery of the divine will: "Let us shout out with the Apostle, 'Oh the depth of the riches of the wisdom, and the knowledge of God! How inscrutable are his judgments and how unsearchable are his ways!'"[45] Augustine therefore asks his audience not to expect him "to penetrate this depth, to probe this deep abyss, to search out the inscrutable . . . This is higher than my growth, and mightier than my strength."[46] Despite this melodramatic disavowal of his ability to penetrate this mystery, however, a few paragraphs later Augustine is confident that he knows the reason for the Jews' punishment. Taking his cue again from Paul, this time from the tortured caricature in the Letter to the Romans of the Jewish attitude toward the Torah, Augustine explains:

> It is no wonder that they could not believe whose will was so proud that, ignoring God's justice, they wished to establish their own, as the Apostle said of them, "They did not subject them-selves to the justice of God." For they were swollen up not from faith, but, as it were, from works, and, blinded by this very self-inflation, they stumbled on the stone of stumbling.[47]

Augustine is aware that he has now concluded that the Jews' blindness was self-inflicted. That is why he can dissolve "could not" believe into "were unwilling" to believe: "Thus, however, was it said 'they could not,' where it must be understood that they were unwilling."[48] Augustine sums up his analysis thus:

> They are blinded and hardened because in denying divine help they are not helped. God foreknew this about the Jews who were

---

42. Augustine, *Tr. on John* 53.5.

43. Augustine, *Tr. on John* 53.6.

44. Augustine, *Tr. on John* 53.6, quoting Rom 9:14.

45. Augustine, *Tr. on John* 53.6, quoting Rom 11:33.

46. Augustine, *Tr. on John*, 53.7.

47. Augustine, *Tr. on John* 53.9, quoting Rom 10:3.

48. Augustine, *Tr. on John* 53.9.

blinded and hardened, and in this Spirit the prophet foretold
it.[49]

Augustine also discusses the moral problem raised by the intersection
of Jewish blindness and divine justice in *Reply to Faustus,* an earlier work
than his *Tractates on the Gospel of John.* His analysis there is less developed
and relies on different biblical warrants. He puts the problem on the lips of
an impartial pagan.

> If the inquirer objected that it was not the fault of the Jews if
> God blinded them so that they did not know Christ, we should
> try in the simplest manner possible to make him understand
> that this blindness is the just punishment of other secret sins
> known to God.[50]

Augustine then turns to Paul and Jeremiah for support, both of whom made
statements based on the principle that public sins are the penalty for secret
ones. For Paul, Augustine quotes Rom 1:24: "God gave them up in the lusts
of their hearts to impurity, to the degrading of their bodies among themselves." Paul here refers to deviant sexual practices among gentiles, which
he believes are their punishment for the root sin of worshiping images (see
the full exposition in Rom 1:18–32), so it is intensely (and perhaps mali-
ciously) ironic that Augustine would use this quotation against Jews. And it
is an inept example of the principle Augustine wants to illustrate, for there
is nothing secret about image worship among pagans.

Augustine calls next on Jeremiah. The appeal is clever but problematic.

> To revert to the words of Jeremiah, "He is man, and who shall
> know Him?", lest it should be an excuse for the Jews that they
> did not know . . . the prophet goes on to show that their igno-
> rance was the result of secret criminality; for he says, "I the Lord
> search the heart and try the reins, to give everyone according to
> his ways, and according to the fruits of his doings."[51]

Augustine's rhetorical strategy here has two steps. First, he offers a verse
(Jer 17:9) that seems to excuse the Jews for not recognizing Jesus as the
promised messiah. Second, he uses Jeremiah's very next verse (Jer 17:10)
to clarify that the God who sees what is hidden in human hearts always
apportions just rewards and punishments. Augustine's quotation of Jer 17:9
is difficult to understand, though he clearly takes "man" and "him" to refer

---

49. Augustine, *Tr. on John* 53.10.

50. Augustine, *Faustus* 13.11.

51. Augustine, *Faustus* 13.11, quoting Jer 17:9 and 10.

to Christ. That interpretation, however, is possible only because Augustine's Latin version of Jer 17:9 is based on the Septuagint, which differs significantly from the Hebrew text.[52] Because Augustine is using what amounts to a fundamentally different text than the one found in Jeremiah's own language, he can read the prophet's reflection on the darkness of human nature as a christological reference. In Jeremiah's context the next verse follows naturally: the human heart may be inscrutable to us, but not to God (Jer 17:10). Augustine's distorted text of Jer 17:9 enables him to transform Jeremiah's general declaration of divine omniscience and justice in 17:10 into an affirmation of Augustine's a priori verdict on the secret sinfulness of Jews and their consequent culpability for rejecting Christ.

Jewish unbelief fulfills prophecy

Augustine returns to this notion repeatedly, and it will suffice here to quote three succinct examples.

> That the Jews so resolutely refuse to surrender before the clarity of this prophetic witness, which have been so undeniably fulfilled, is itself a fulfillment in them [i.e., in Jews] of prophecy.[53]

> When they refuse to believe in our scriptures and read their own like blind men, they are fulfilling what their own prophets foretold.[54]

> The unbelief of the Jews increases rather than lessens the authority of the books, for this blindness is itself foretold. They testify to the truth by their not understanding it. By not understanding the books which predict that they would not understand, they prove these books to be true.[55]

Which specific prophecies does Augustine have in mind? He doesn't always say, but we can see some of them in the three sections in which the above quotations are found. In the two passages from the *City of God* directly above, Augustine quotes Ps 69:23: "Let their eyes be darkened so that they cannot see." This is a judicious selection for Augustine because it follows Ps

---

52. Augustine's version: "He is man and who shall know him?"
The Hebrew version: "The heart is devious above all else, and inscrutable; who understands it?"

53. Augustine, *City of God* 17.19.

54. Augustine, *City of God* 18.46.

55. Augustine, *Faustus* 16.21.

69:21, a verse to which Matthew and Mark allude in their passion narratives: "They gave me gall for food, and in my thirst they gave me vinegar to drink" (see Matt 27:34, 48, and Mark 15:23, 36). In *Reply to Faustus*, Augustine calls on three passages from Isaiah.

> No one can doubt that Isaiah spoke of the Jews when he said, "The ox knows his owner, and the donkey his master's crib, but Israel has not known, and my people has not understood;" or again, in the words quoted by the Apostle, "I have held out my hands all day long to a wicked and contrary people;" and especially where he says, "God has given them the spirit of remorse, eyes that they should not see, and ears that they should not hear, and should not understand."[56]

After laying out those three quotations Augustine lets it drop that there are "many similar passages."

The Mark of Cain

We need to explore one more aspect of Augustine's thought about how the fulfillment of scripture affects Jews: his reading of the story of Cain and Abel, particularly his highly original interpretation of the mark of Cain. A substantial exposition of the story is found in *Reply to Faustus* 12.9–13, which is part of Augustine's elaborate interpretation of Genesis. He starts by identifying the two brothers. "Abel, the younger brother, is killed by the elder brother; Christ, the head of a younger people, is killed by the elder people of the Jews."[57] That Augustine turns Cain, whose sacrifice God rejected, into Jews is no surprise. That Abel prefigures Christ seems to follow naturally (the asymmetry in which Cain is a people and Abel is an individual does not deter Augustine). Augustine gives each element in the story a detailed and inventive (or fanciful, depending on your taste) interpretation, two of which are relevant to our study. The first is Cain's punishment, which is that he will be "a fugitive and a wanderer on the earth" (Gen 4:12) because "you have driven me away from the soil" (Gen 4:14). Augustine creatively describes this exile as Cain's "losing his earthly kingdom."[58] Augustine replaces the Latin word in this verse, *terra* ("soil/earth"), with *regnum* ("kingdom"), thus alluding to the destruction of the Jewish nation state by the Romans in 70 CE and the Jews' subsequent existence within the Empire as a people with-

---

56. Augustine, *Faustus* 13.11, quoting Isa 1:3, 65:2 [in Rom 10:21], and 6:10.

57. Augustine, *Faustus* 12.9.

58. Augustine, *Faustus* 12.12.

out a homeland.[59] The Christian interpretation of the Roman devastation of Jerusalem as divine retribution for the crucifixion of Jesus is traditional, going back to the New Testament, but the interpretation of the Jewish dispersion as the fulfillment of the punishment of Cain is Augustine's own.[60]

The other interpretation that deserves attention is Augustine's understanding of the mark of Cain. In Genesis, Cain fears that since he has become a homeless fugitive "anyone who meets me may kill me." "Then Yahweh said to him, 'Not so! Whoever kills Cain will suffer a sevenfold vengeance.' And Yahweh put a mark on Cain, so that no one who found him would kill him" (Gen 4:15). Augustine bases his interpretation of this mark on his correct understanding that its purpose was to *protect* Cain. God might have scattered the Jews among the Romans as a punishment, but their continued existence as a distinct people—that is, through the observance of their religious law—is the result of God's providential protection.[61]

> It is a most notable fact that all the nations subjugated by Rome adopted the pagan ceremonies of Roman worship, while the Jewish nation, whether under pagan or Christian monarchs, has never lost the sign of their law, by which they are distinguished from all other nations and peoples. No emperor or monarch who finds under his government the people with this mark kills them (that is, makes them cease to be Jews), but allows them as Jews to be separate in their observances, and unlike the rest of the world.[62]

Augustine combines his paraphrase of God's curse on Cain ("Groaning and trembling shall you be on the earth") with Cain's fear for his life, and interprets both as referring to the manner in which Jews of his own time live: in "terrified subjection to the immensely superior number of Christians."[63] What Jews fear losing is not their lives but their freedom to practice their religion.[64] God protects the observance of Judaism, for that is what constitutes the identity of the Jewish people.

> For whoever destroys them in this way [i.e., forces them to cease Jewish observance] will suffer sevenfold vengeance, that is, shall

59. Fredriksen, *Augustine and the Jews*, 270.

60. Ibid., 322.

61. Ibid., 265.

62. Augustine, *Faustus* 12.13.

63. Augustine, *Faustus* 12.12.

64. Fredriksen, *Augustine and the Jews*, 273.

bring upon himself sevenfold the penalty under which the Jews
lie for the crucifixion of Christ.[65]

For Augustine to find his way to such a conclusion is remarkable, especially in light of his frequent and florid anti-Jewish rhetoric. In numerous
places in his writings Augustine vilifies Jews in high style, utilizing all the
rhetorical resources in the hateful bag of tricks of the well-developed *ad-
versus Judaeos* tradition.[66] He calls Jews blind and he blames them for their
blindness. He also, illogically, hectors them with seemingly sincere calls to
repent, to come to Christ, that is, to cease their practice of Judaism. Yet he
also develops a sophisticated argument that their continued existence as a
distinct, Torah-observant people is the work of God, and he warns rulers
that God protects this people and their religion with fearsome threats.[67]

As remarkable, and unexpected, as that argument is, the affirmation
that God wills and protects the ongoing practice of Judaism is not an end
in itself. Within Augustine's grand vision of the fulfillment of scripture, it
is meant to serve a larger and higher purpose: as a witness to the truth of
Christianity. His explanation is ingenious. Jews live as Jews in communities
scattered throughout the Christian world. The Jewish scriptures they cherish are, consequently, preserved in every part of the world, by a people that
resists Christianity. That is public proof that the numerous prophecies that
have been fulfilled by Christ and the Church are not Christian forgeries.
On the contrary, the fact that these prophetic books are safeguarded by a
people more ancient than Christians, and who continue to be their enemies,
proves the authenticity and antiquity of those sacred books. Jews do not
understand what they read in their books, and therefore derive no benefit
from them. Nevertheless, in God's providence, the Jewish people witness—
without their intention and against their will—to the truth of Christ and the
Church in whom their scriptures are abundantly and manifestly fulfilled.

Augustine elaborates this argument in several places. Three examples
are sufficient to see his argument in his own words.

> One might fear that the inquirer, in the midst of such copious
> evidence, would say that the Christians composed those writ-
> ings when the events described had already begun to take place,
> in order that those occurrences might appear to be not due to a
> merely human purpose, but as if divinely foretold . . . From the

65. Augustine, *Faustus* 12.12.

66. See Fredriksen, *Augustine and the Jews*, 261–62, 304–7, for a helpful distinction between Augustine's anti-Jewish rhetoric and what he "really" thought about actual
Jews.

67. Ibid., 265–72.

Jewish manuscripts we prove that these things were not written by us to suit the event, but were long ago published and preserved as prophecies in the Jewish nation. These prophecies are now explained in their fulfillment.[68]

We have no need of any prophecies other than the ones in our opponents' books, precisely because these enemies, who are scattered over the whole earth wherever the Church is expanding and who possess and preserve these books, are living witnesses, however reluctant, to the truth of our position . . . Although they were conquered and oppressed by the Romans, God did not "slay" them, that is, He did not destroy them as Jews. For, in that case, they would have forgotten and would have been useless as witnesses . . . For, if the Jews had remained bottled up in their own land with the evidence of their scriptures and if they were not to be found everywhere, as the Church is, the Church would not then have them as ubiquitous witnesses of the ancient prophecies concerning Christ.[69]

The Jewish people were scattered over the earth so that, by carrying about with them the prophecies of grace conferred on us, they might everywhere benefit us for a more firm convincing of believers . . . For this reason they have not been exterminated, but dispersed; although they themselves do not possess the faith whereby they might be saved, they still retain in memory that whereby we are aided. They are our supporters in their books, our enemies in their hearts, our witnesses in their scrolls.[70]

Pagans and the Fulfillment of Prophecy

In arguing with Jews Augustine can assume the divine inspiration of the OT because Jews share that belief with Christians. In attempting to convert pagans, however, Augustine must demonstrate the authority of the Bible before it can serve as proof for Christian truths. For Augustine the fulfillment of prophecy is compelling for just this purpose. Two relatively short pieces of Augustine's writing show how he unfolds his argument that the fulfillment of prophecy can serve as a rational basis on which pagans can be persuaded to believe in the Christian scriptures, both the Old and the

---

68. Augustine, *Faustus* 13.10.

69. Augustine, *City of God* 18.46.

70. Augustine, *Faith* 6.9.

New Testament. Our first source is a small section in his formidable *Reply to Faustus*: 13.7–14, a kind of primer on how to use scriptural prophecy to draw in pagan inquirers. Our second source is Augustine's minor treatise *On Faith in Things Unseen*.

Reply to Faustus 13.7–14

> If we say to the pagan, "Believe in Christ, for He is God," and, on his asking for evidence, produce the authority of the prophets, and if he says that he does not believe the prophets, because they are Hebrew and he is a Gentile, we can prove the reliability of the prophets from the fulfillment of their prophecies.[71]

Augustine's first example of such a proof comes from Psalm 2, about which he puts forward a two-step argument. First, he asserts that the opening verses ("Why do the pagans rage, and the people imagine a vain thing? The kings of the earth set themselves, and the princes take counsel together against the Lord, and against his Christ") foretell the persecutions of the early Christians, a historical fact of which everyone is aware. Then Augustine argues that "the rest of the psalm shows that this was not said of David." As evidence, he quotes Ps 2:7–8.

> "The Lord said to me, 'You are my son . . . Ask of me, and I will give you the pagans for your inheritance, and the ends of the earth for your possession." This has never happened to the Jews, whose king was David, but is now plainly fulfilled in the subjection of all nations to the name of Christ.[72]

Augustine's claim that the context of Ps 2:1–2 points to Jesus is plainly refuted by its immediate context. Verse 3 reports what the assembled rulers say in their conspiracy against God and his anointed: "Let us burst their bonds asunder, and cast their cords from us" (Ps 2:3). They do not aim to persecute anyone but to escape their involuntary servitude to the anointed one.

Augustine continues on in *Reply to Faustus* 13.7–9 to interpret at some length a good number of other prophecies that he argues are fulfilled in the decline of idolatry, which is another well-known historical fact, especially since the time when Christianity became the dominant religion of the Roman Empire. Augustine structures the next five sections (13.10–14) around

---

71. Augustine, *Faustus* 13.7.

72. Augustine, *Faustus* 13.7, quoting Ps 2:7–8.

a series of objections he anticipates from open-minded unbelievers. Each objection is answered by the evidence of fulfilled prophecy.

The first objection raises doubts about the authenticity of the prophecies themselves. The sheer amount of fulfilled prophecies might lead an inquirer to suspect that the books containing them were Christian forgeries, written after the events the prophecies allegedly foretell. Augustine replies that those books are preserved by Jews who can verify their antiquity.[73]

The inquirer might well then wonder, if the prophecies are so plainly fulfilled, why are the Jews not persuaded? (I treated this problem in full a few pages earlier; here I summarize Augustine's answer to it in 13.11.) Augustine replies that their very unbelief was predicted with undeniable clarity. "The prophecies of the unbelief of the Jews no one can avoid seeing, no one can pretend to be blind to them."[74] He quotes three prophecies to make his point, and asserts that there are "many similar passages." The last one quoted says that God gave the Jews "eyes that they should not see, and ears that they should not hear, and should not understand" (adapted from Isa 6:10), a troubling prophecy that Augustine anticipates will create a further difficulty.

> If the inquirer objected that it was not the fault of the Jews if God blinded them so that they did not know Christ, we should try in the simplest manner possible to make him understand that this blindness is the just punishment of other secret sins known to God.[75]

In support of this theory, Augustine quotes Jeremiah, who teaches

> that their ignorance was the result of secret criminality; for he says, "I the Lord search the heart and try the reins, to give to every one according to his ways, and according to the fruits of his doings."[76]

If the pagan inquirer hesitates to assent to the truth of Christianity because of the "divisions and heresies among those called Christians," Augustine assures him that this too was foretold. He offers only one prophecy (which is actually a proverb), and it is an odd one: "The partridge is clamorous, gathering what he has not brought forth, making riches without judgment" (Jer 17:11).[77] Augustine explains that just as partridges are quar-

---

73. Augustine, *Faustus* 13.10.
74. Augustine, *Faustus* 13.11.
75. Augustine, *Faustus* 13.11.
76. Augustine, *Faustus* 13.11, quoting Jer 17:10.
77. Augustine's version, based on the Septuagint, differs from the Hebrew: "Like a

relsome, heretics argue, not to find the truth, but to win arguments any way they can. They "gather what they have not brought forth" inasmuch as they mislead those who are already Christian. "Thus they make riches not with judgment, but with considerable haste."[78]

Augustine sees another objection as the final obstacle troubling the mind of his hypothetical inquirer, for at this point "the clear fulfillment of so many predictions compelled him to believe in Christ."[79] However, having seen the light of Christ, the inquirer now faces one more quandary: bewildered by the many divisions among Christians, how to discern which of them teaches the truth.

> The inquirer would next ask by what plain mark a young disciple, not yet able to distinguish the truth among so many errors, might find the true Church of Christ.[80]

Augustine's solution to this problem is found in scripture, in the verse "a glorious high throne is our sanctuary" (Jer 17:12). Augustine interprets this to mean that the true church is "conspicuously visible," an interpretation he supports with four quotations from Paul, Jesus, and Daniel. Augustine's logic here is not easy to discern. The visibility of the Church is reinforced by Jesus' proverb, "A city set on a hill cannot be hid" (Matt 5:14). Augustine starts with Matthew's hill, adds his own assertion that "the true city is on a mountain," with which he sets up a verse in Daniel: "the mountain is that which, as we read in Daniel, grew from a little stone until it filled the whole earth" (see Dan 2:35). Apparently, what all this means is that the true Church is the one that is the most public and widespread. We are entitled to some doubt about how convincing this dizzying argument would be to a novice inquirer, especially one who is repeatedly told how *clearly* prophecies are fulfilled.

Nevertheless, Augustine believes that the apology has now accomplished its goal, which is to offer the fulfillment of prophecy as rational evidence that the prophets were divinely inspired. At this point, and only then, should one expect a pagan to "reasonably receive the testimony of these prophets about the divinity of Christ." At this point it is worthwhile letting Augustine speak for himself at some length.

> After considering these instances of the fulfillment of prophecy about kings and people acting as persecutors, and then becoming

partridge hatching what it did not lay, so are all who amass wealth unjustly."

78. Augustine, *Faustus* 13.12.

79. Augustine, *Faustus* 13.13.

80. Augustine, *Faustus* 13.13.

believers, about the destruction of idols, about the blindness
of the Jews, about their testimony to the writings which they
have preserved, about the folly of heretics, about the dignity of
the Church of true and genuine Christians, the inquirer would
most reasonably receive the testimony of these prophets about
the divinity of Christ. No doubt, if we were to begin by urging
him to believe prophecies yet unfulfilled, he might justly answer,
"What have I to do with these prophets, of whose truth I have
no evidence?" But, in view of the obvious fulfillment of so many
remarkable predictions, no candid person would despise either
the things which were thought worthy of being predicted in
those early times with so much solemnity, or those who made
the predictions. To none can we trust more safely, as regards
either events long past or those still future, than to men whose
words are supported by the evidence of so many notable predictions that were fulfilled.[81]

On Faith in Things Unseen

This sermon argues that it is reasonable to believe in things we cannot see.
While its audience is Christian, it takes the form of an address to pagans,
thereby functioning as a model of how to persuade pagans of Christian
truth. Prophecy is a key component in Augustine's argument. Since pagans
do not believe in the divine authority of the Bible, Augustine admits that it is
futile to expect them to believe in the gospel stories or that Jesus fulfilled the
prophecies mentioned in the New Testament. He works through a familiar
list of events in the gospels—the virgin birth, Jesus' miracles, his passion,
resurrection, and ascension—presenting for each some of the prophecies
those events fulfilled. These are among the things pagans "refuse to believe"
because those events occurred in the past and so are unable to be seen firsthand. Augustine therefore bases his argument from prophecy on *present*
facts about Christ that anyone can see, "things that you behold, which are
not narrated to you as of the past, nor foretold to you as of the future, but
are clearly demonstrated to you as present."[82] The "things" Augustine holds
up for consideration is actually one thing, the worldwide predominance of
Christianity: "All humankind runs its course in the name of the One Crucified." Augustine presents several ways in which prophecies are fulfilled by
the ubiquity of Christianity.

81. Augustine, *Faustus* 13.14.
82. Augustine, *Faith* 4.7.

- God's word to Abraham: "In your seed shall all the nations of the earth be blessed." (Gen 22:18)

- God's declaration: "You are my son / . . . / Ask of me, and I will make the nations your heritage, / and the ends of the earth your possession." (Ps 2:7–8)

- "All the ends of the earth shall remember / and be converted to the LORD." (Ps 22:27–28)

- "To you, O Lord, shall all the nations come / from the ends of the earth." (Jer 16:19)

- "To him shall bow down, / each in its place, / all the coasts and islands of the nations." (Zeph 2:11)

In discussing Christ's ascension to heaven, Augustine divides a single verse into what pagans do and do not see.

> You have not seen what was foretold and fulfilled concerning the ascension of Christ ("You are exalted, O God, above the heavens"), but you do see what results from it: "And your glory over all the earth."[83]

Augustine sums up his argument thus far.

> All these things [in the gospels] already accomplished and transacted concerning Christ you have not witnessed, but you may not deny that you do see things that are taking place here and now in the Church.[84]

The only reason Augustine imagines why pagans would not be persuaded by this presentation of fulfilled prophecies is that they would suspect that Christians had forged the prophetic books after the facts that they "predict" were already evident in order to deceive others into assuming that the prophecies were earlier than what they foretell.[85]

This is the point in the argument where Augustine plays his Jewish card, capitalizing on his interpretation of the mark of Cain (see above). "If they suspect this, let them search through the books of our opponents, the Jews."[86] Pagans should not be surprised that Jews do not understand the Christian truth so evident in their own scriptures, for their unbelief itself fulfills prophecy, and "by a hidden and just decree of God" is "due pun-

83. Augustine, *Faith* 4.7, quoting Ps 108:5.

84. Augustine, *Faith* 4.7.

85. Augustine, *Faith* 5.8.

86. Augustine, *Faith* 6.9.

ishment to be paid according to their merits."[87] Augustine winds up this section of his sermon with a rhetorical flourish: because Jews preserve the books containing the prophecies that validate Christian faith, "they are our supporters in their books, our enemies in their hearts, our witnesses in their scrolls."[88]

Augustine is now ready to draw a line under this argument and make one final inference: because the worldwide growth of the Church proves that biblical prophecies have been fulfilled, it is reasonable to put faith in the teachings of the apostles (i.e., in the books of the New Testament).

> Since it [the triumph of the Church] came to pass exactly as it was foretold, who is so foolish as to say that the Apostles lied about Christ whom they preached as having come, just as the prophets long before predicted?[89]

As icing on the cake, Augustine points out that there is even a prophecy about the apostles themselves: "There are no speeches nor languages where their voices are not heard; their sound has gone out to all the earth, and their words to the ends of the world."[90] This is another one of Augustine's interpretations that is possible only because he uses a Latin translation that veers away from the Hebrew text. Augustine's version of Ps 19:3 echoes the thought of 19:4 that their voices are heard everywhere. In the Hebrew original, to the contrary, verses 3 and 4 express a paradox: "There is no speech, no words; / their voice is *not* heard" (Ps 19:3, italics added). In the Hebrew "their voice" can refer only to the silent eloquence of the heavens (see Ps 19:1–2). Augustine, presumably taking his cue from Paul's use of Ps 19:4 in Rom 10:18,[91] makes "their voice" refer to the apostles' preaching.

Augustine concludes triumphantly with a rhetorical question:

> Who, therefore, except a man blinded by extreme foolishness, or hard and unyielding with a strange stubbornness, will not place faith in the sacred writings that have foretold the faith of the whole world?[92]

---

87. Augustine, *Faith* 6.9.

88. Augustine, *Faith* 6.9.

89. Augustine, *Faith* 6.9.

90. Augustine, *Faith* 6.9, quoting Ps 19:3–4.

91. See pp. 204–205.

92. Augustine, *Faith* 7.10.

Examples of Augustine's Unusual Interpretations

Augustine offers many dozens of prophetic scriptures that he interprets as prefiguring Christ and the church. "To enumerate all the passages in the Hebrew prophets referring to our Lord and Savior Jesus Christ would exceed the limits of a volume."[93] For our study there is no need to survey them extensively. Nor is there need to distinguish those interpretations that are original to Augustine from those that he repeats from interpreters before him: here I am interested in Augustine not as an original interpreter but as a representative one. It is sufficient for my purpose to consider eight examples (a small sample of the total) of highly imaginative interpretations. As I proceed, I will note the textual circumstances and interpretive choices that led Augustine to his conclusions. Appreciating the intellectual effort Augustine invested in these unusual interpretations affords us a crucial insight into the relationship between prophecy and fulfillment in his thought.

(1) At the end of his discussion of Psalm 50, Augustine offers an interpretation of its final verse.

> The closing of the psalm makes God's purpose quite evident: "The sacrifice of praise shall glorify me; and there is the way by which I will show him the salvation of God." What in truth is the salvation of God if not the Son of God, the Savior of the world . . . whose arrival the New Testament has revealed?[94]

(2) Interpreting the eschatological prophecy about Mount Zion in Isa 2:1–4, Augustine comments on the mountain itself.

> "The mountain of the house of the Lord shall be prepared on the top of mountains, and it shall be exalted above the hills, and all the nations shall come to it." Christ is represented by the mountain lifted high above the tops of the mountains because by His height he transcends all heights.[95]

(3) In discussing the Book of Proverbs Augustine admits that sometimes it is not easy to see the prophetic significance of its contents, and that

> to show their significance to Christ and the Church would require too elaborate a discussion to be undertaken here, as it would carry me beyond all proper bounds. However, there is one text in Proverbs, so far from being obscure that its relationship to Christ and His possession, the Church, can be grasped

93. Augustine, *Faustus* 12.7.

94. Augustine, *Answer* 6.8, quoting Ps 50:23.

95. Augustine, *Answer* 7.9, quoting Isa 2:2.

without any such trouble. Wicked men are speaking: "Let us unjustly hide away in the earth the just man, let us swallow him up alive like hell. Let us abolish his memory from the earth, let us lay hands upon his precious possession." This is very similar to what the Lord Jesus Himself, in one of the gospel parables, puts into the mouths of the wicked vinedressers: "This is the heir; come let us kill him, and we shall have his inheritance."[96]

(4) "There is nothing better for a man than to eat and drink" (Eccl 8:15). Augustine explains that the only reasonable interpretation of this saying is that it alludes to the Eucharist.[97] Augustine prudently excludes from his quotation the final element in the verse that follows directly after "to eat and drink": "and enjoy himself."

(5) In *Reply to Faustus*, Augustine reports that his Manichean opponent argued that the OT was not inspired by the God of goodness by pointing out the many immoral actions of OT figures whom Augustine calls "men of God." In responding to this argument, Augustine considers the passages that Faustus mentioned, "to see the meaning of the actions recorded what they typify, and what they foretell."[98] Augustine argues that

> in the prophetic scriptures, where both good and evil actions are recorded, the narrative, being itself prophetic, foretells something good even by the record of what is evil, the credit being due not to the evildoer, but to the writer.[99]

Here are two examples that illustrate this principle.

(i) *David rapes Bathsheba and murders her husband Uriah* (2 Samuel 11). What the literal David did was "a heinous crime," but it prefigures a profound truth if we see Uriah as the devil and David's lust for Bathsheba as Christ's love for the church. Here is how Augustine interprets David's spying on Bathsheba while she bathed, his killing of her husband, and his subsequent marriage to her:

> Christ loved the Church when washing herself on the roof, that is, when cleansing herself from the pollution of the world, and in spiritual contemplation mounting above her house of clay, and trampling upon it . . . He puts to death the devil, whom He first entirely removes from her, and joins her to Himself in

---

96. Augustine, *City of God* 17.20, quoting Prov 1:11–13 and Matt 21:38.

97. Augustine, *City of God* 17.20.

98. Augustine, *Faustus* 22.82.

99. Augustine, *Faustus* 22.83.

perpetual union. While we hate the sin, we must not overlook its prophetic significance.[100]

(ii) *Moses kills an Egyptian and hides his body in the sand* (Exod 2:11–12).

> Moses' killing the Egyptian in defending one of his brothers re-minds us naturally of the destruction of the devil, our assailant in this land of strangers, by our defender the Lord Christ. And as Moses hid the dead body in the sand, even so the devil, though slain, remains concealed in those who are not firmly settled . . . Those who hear the Lord's word and do it, He compares to a wise man who builds his house on rock . . . and those who hear and do not, He compares to a fool who builds on the sand.[101]

(6) In one section of *City of God* Augustine surveys all twelve books of the minor prophets in order to demonstrate that *every* prophet foretold Christ. In some cases, Augustine's interpretation is based on readings that are peculiar to the Septuagint. Here are three examples.

(i) *Amos 4:12–13*

> Be prepared to meet your God, O Israel; for behold I am the one who forms the thunder and creates the wind, *and declares to people his Christ.*

In the Hebrew text, the final clause reads "and reveals his thoughts to peo-ple." The italicized reading is based on the Septuagint, which reads "and declares to people his anointed one (*christos*)." In the Septuagint version, "his *christos*" probably means the king, the anointed ruler appointed by God. Augustine's Latin text reads "*Christus,*" a transliteration—rather than a translation—of the Greek *christos*. Naturally, Augustine takes *Christus* as Jesus' name.[102]

(ii) *Nahum 2:1*

Augustine's quotation is based on the Septuagint: "He who breathes into your face and rescues you from tribulation has come up." The Hebrew text reads: "A shatterer has come up against you [Nineveh]. Guard your ram-parts." In the context of Nahum's prophecy against Assyria's capital Nineveh, the "you" is obviously that city, which is soon to be attacked. Augustine takes "he who comes up" in his version as a reference to the risen Jesus.

---

100. Augustine, *Faustus* 22.87.

101. Augustine, *Faustus* 22.90, referring to Exod 2:11–12 and Matt 7:24–27.

102. See Augustine, *City of God* 18.28.

> Anyone who knows the gospels will recognize who it was that
> came up from hell and breathed the Holy Spirit into the face of
> Judah, that is, into the face of His Jewish disciples.[103]

The mention of Jesus' coming up from hell refers to the belief that between
his death and resurrection he "descended into hell," that is, the realm of the
dead, to preach to the souls imprisoned there (see 1 Pet 3:18–20 and the
Gospel of Peter 10:3–5). Jesus' breathing the Holy Spirit onto the disciples
alludes to an appearance of the risen Jesus in John 20:19–22. Why Augustine understands Nahum to be addressing Judah is puzzling, especially since
Nah 1:1 (in both the Hebrew text and the Septuagint) identifies the prophecy as "an oracle against Nineveh."

(iii) *Habakkuk 3:2*

> O Lord, I have heard your renown, and was afraid;
>
> Lord, I have considered you work and was astonished.
>
> *You will be recognized between two living beings.*

The italicized line appears in the Septuagint but not in the Hebrew text. (I
confess that I have no idea what it means.) Augustine proposes three interpretations: "Here is Christ set between two Testaments, or hanging between
the two thieves, or standing between Moses and Elijah when they conversed
with Him on the mountaintop."[104]

(7) The next example is interesting because Augustine considers and
then rejects an interpretation different from his own. The topic is the identity of Isaac's sons, Esau and Jacob. Although they were twins, Esau was le-
gally the elder because he was the firstborn. The prophecy Augustine quotes
identifies the sons as ancestors and embodiments of two peoples. "The Lord
said to Rebekah, 'Two nations are in your womb, and two peoples born to
you shall be divided; the one shall be stronger than the other, the elder shall
serve the younger'" (Gen 25:23). Augustine's comment speaks for itself.

> Practically every Christian has taken this to mean that the
> "elder" people, the Jews, will serve the "younger" people, the
> Christians. Now certainly it is true that there seems to be a pos-
> sible fulfillment of this in the Idumeans who are descendants
> of the elder (who was called both Esau and Edom, whence the
> name "Idumeans") and who were destined to be overcome by
> the people that sprang from the younger, namely, the people of
> Israel, and to be subject to them. Nevertheless, it surely is better
> to believe that there is something of greater significance in the

103. Augustine, *City of God* 18.31.

104. Augustine, *City of God* 18.32.

> prophecy: "One people shall overcome the other, and the elder
> shall serve the younger." And can this be anything else than
> what is obviously fulfilled in the Jews and Christians?[105]

Why the Christian interpretation is of "greater significance" Augustine does
not say. He even points out that the Idumeans (called Edomites in the OT)
are expressly identified by the Bible as "Esau," an identification made by the
very story on which Augustine comments (Gen 25:30).[106] Augustine thus
overrules Genesis' own interpretation of the prophecy about Esau and Jacob
in Gen 25:23, in favor of an interpretation that subordinates Jews to Christians. Augustine does not elaborate on what he means when he says that
Jews will serve Christians. His discussion of the mark of Cain (see above)
indicates that he does not envision literal servitude, but rather the Jews' carrying out their role as the keeper of their scriptures, a servile task[107] they
perform for the benefit of Christians.

(8) My last example is more complex than the ones previously discussed, in two ways. First, it shows Augustine offering a brief argument for
his interpretation, something he seldom does. (He usually simply presents
his interpretations, apparently confident that his audience will agree without needing to be persuaded.) Second, this is a good example of how he
links different prophecies so that one helps to interpret the other, which he
does frequently. The text is from Malachi.

> I have no pleasure in you. I will not receive a gift from your
> hand. For from the rising of the sun to its setting, my name is
> great among the Gentiles, and in every place sacrifice is offered
> to my name, a pure offering. (Mal 1:10–11, as quoted in *In An-
> swer to the Jews* 9.12)

Before taking up Augustine's interpretation, we should note two things
about the original text and context of Mal 1:10–11. First, the Hebrew text
says, "in every place *incense* is offered to my name, and a pure offering."
Augustine's Latin version features "sacrifice" rather than "incense," a word
that would spoil his interpretation. Second, It is clear from the context in
Malachi both before and after the bit Augustine quotes that the reason God
rejects their sacrifice is that corrupt priests are offering defective animals
(ones that are blind, lame, sick, and blemished, or even stolen); see Mal

105. Augustine, *City of God* 16.35, quoting Gen 25:23.

106. See also Obad 6, 8. Malachi 1:2–5 also equates Esau with Edom, interpreting God's preference for Jacob over Esau as prefiguring Edom's devastation and Israel's
continued existence.

107. Augustine uses different terms for this task, terms that describe the work of
slaves (Fredriksen, *Augustine and the Jews*, 320–21).

1:7–8, 13–14. Augustine reads the prophecy as if it were addressed to the Jews as a people in his own day, ignoring the fact that Malachi describes his prophecy as God's word to the corrupt priests ("you, O priests, who despise my name," Mal 1:6).

> "I have no pleasure in you; I will not receive a gift from your hand." Certainly you cannot deny that here the Lord not only refuses to receive a gift from your hands, but you do not offer Him a gift with your hands.[108]

Augustine explains that last statement by arguing that Jews no longer offer sacrifices because the temple in Jerusalem, which "you have lost through your own fault," was the only place God's law allowed sacrifices to be offered. No temple means no sacrifices. Augustine argues that Jews are not permitted even to offer praise to God. (Augustine imagines them quoting, "Offer to God the sacrifice of praise," from Ps 50:14.) "Even here He opposes you who say, 'I have no pleasure in you.'"[109]

Augustine turns to the rest of Malachi's prophecy, pointing to its fulfillment in the worship offered by Christians.

> Open your eyes at last, at any time, and see, from the rising of the sun even to its setting—not in one place as established with you, but everywhere—the sacrifice of the Christians is being offered to Him, the one who foretold these events, the God of Israel.[110]

To cope with the fact that Christian worship does not involve animal sacrifice, Augustine turns for help to another scripture, which he believes portends the Christian liturgy, which is offered "everywhere, even in Jerusalem itself, according to the order of Melchizedek, not according to the order of Aaron."[111] Melchizedek was a mysterious figure who suddenly turns up in the story of Abraham and is never seen again. He was a king of Salem (later equated with Jerusalem—see Ps 76:2) and a priest of God Most High, who "brought out bread and wine" and blessed Abraham (Gen 14:18–20). Augustine quotes Ps 110:4, which he asserts "was said to Christ about Christ": "The Lord has sworn, and he will not change his mind, 'You are a priest forever according to the order of Melchizedek.'" Augustine takes God's oath not to change his mind to imply that God had changed his mind about the previous priesthood (the order of Aaron), but that he will never do so about

108. Augustine, *Answer* 9.12, quoting Mal 1:10.
109. Augustine, *Answer* 9.12.
110. Augustine, *Answer* 9.13.
111. Augustine, *Answer* 9.13

the order of Melchizedek. "We see the fulfillment of both: of Aaron, there is no longer any priesthood in any temple; of Christ, the priesthood continues everlastingly in heaven."[112] Augustine assumes that his audience will make the connection between Christ's priesthood in heaven and the Christian priesthood that offers sacrifice (i.e., the Eucharist) everywhere on earth. When Augustine picked up this same subject in *City of God*, he spelled out what he assumed in *In Answer to the Jews*.

> The priesthood and sacrifice according to the order of Aaron are nowhere to be found, whereas priests everywhere today are offering, under Christ the Priest, the sacrifice that Melchizedek symbolically offered when he blessed Abraham.[113]

What These Examples Show

The interpretations sampled above are among Augustine's most fanciful. It is safe to say that it is far from obvious, for example, that Ecclesiastes' exhortation "to eat and drink" portends the Eucharist (example 4 above), or that Christ is like a mountain because of his "height" (example 2), or that lust leading to rape prefigures Christ's love for the Church (example 5). How did Augustine arrive at such unusual interpretations? In some cases he could do so only because he relied on a Latin translation (itself translated from the Septuagint) that in places departs significantly from the Hebrew original (see his readings above of Amos, Nahum, and Habakkuk). In some cases he ignores obvious clues from context that would spoil his interpretation (e.g., in Malachi). In other cases he quotes only selected words from a verse, carefully avoiding those that would preclude his interpretation (e.g., in Ecclesiastes). In another case Augustine contradicts Genesis' interpretation of its own story (the Esau-Jacob story).

It was not Augustine's fault that his translation of the Bible was defective. He could not read Hebrew. We should assume that he trusted that his Latin translation conveyed the true meaning of the scriptures. However, Augustine's procedures sketched above—ignoring context, quoting selectively, and rejecting a book's own interpretation of its story (as well as the other tricks of the trade that facilitate interpretations featured earlier in this chapter)—are evidence of the intellectual labor needed to extract the christological interpretations Augustine desired. Those interpretations were not, as it were, lying on the surface waiting for him to find. He had to exert

112. Augustine, *Answer* 9.13.

113. Augustine, *City of God* 17.17.

considerable effort to dig down into the passages to unearth the prizes he thought they concealed.

I have focused on examples of Augustine's interpretations that strike us as outlandish because they show how far he was willing to go to find *some* prefigurement of Christ or the church, even in unpromising passages. Only an interpreter who was convinced that such passages must point to Christ would invest the effort and imagination it must have taken to "discover" those interpretations. This confirms what we have seen elsewhere concerning the basis for christological interpretations of the OT. It is not the case that Augustine sees christological meaning everywhere in the Bible, and on the basis of that evidence concludes that *all* scripture prefigures Christ. Rather, it is because he believes that all scripture prefigures Christ that he can go hunting for hidden christological interpretations. That is the same dynamic we tracked, for example, in the Gospel of Matthew. The belief that Jesus fulfills prophecy is the cause, not the result, of the ingenious interpretations of prophetic passages that find him prefigured there.

Demons and Pagan Prophecy

As we have seen, the fulfillment of prophecy plays a central role in Augustine's apologetic project. Fulfilled prophecies validate both the prophets who pronounced them and the Christian religion to which they point. However, in Augustine's world, the Bible did not have a monopoly on accurate prophecy. It was widely recognized that there were numerous fulfilled predictions in various formats from pagan sources. If the fulfillment of biblical prophecy was evidence for the truth of Christianity, did not the fulfillment of pagan prophecies similarly lend credibility to pagan beliefs? Augustine was aware of this problem, and his solution to it affords us further insight into his understanding of the nature of prophecy and its role in confirming faith. I will argue that in his desire to neutralize the theological validity of the fulfillment of pagan prophecy, Augustine ends up undermining the foundational principle for his own apologetic use of the fulfillment of biblical prophecy.

Earlier in this chapter I analyzed a section of *Reply to Faustus* (13.7–14) that argues that the fulfillment of biblical prophecy provides ample evidence through which open-minded pagans can be persuaded to believe in the Christian scriptures. Immediately after concluding that argument in 13.14, Augustine appends a comment on pagan prophecies. His interest is not in those prophecies in general but in a highly specific category of them: predictions about Christ.[114] Even in the case of this extraordinary class of

---

114. This is a topic to which Augustine gives much attention in books 8 and 9 of *City*

predictions (pagans predicting Christ!), Augustine is quick to deny that their fulfillment legitimizes those who produce them.

> If any truth about God or the Son of God is taught or predicted in the Sibyl or Sibyls, or in Orpheus, or in Hermes (if there ever was such a person), or in any other of the pagan poets, or theologians, or sages, or philosophers, it may be useful for the refutation of pagan error, but cannot lead us to believe in these writers. For while they spoke, because they could not help it, of the God whom we worship, they either taught their fellow-countrymen to worship idols and demons, or allowed them to do so without daring to protest against it.[115]

Augustine's standard for the evidential value of prophecy is thus an un-abashedly double standard. It seems that the fulfillment of prophecy, by itself, proves nothing; what matters is whether the prophet whose predictions are fulfilled promotes the worship of the one true God. The fulfillment of biblical (i.e., "our") prophecies thus establishes the truth of what those prophets teach, but the fulfillment of pagan (i.e., "their") prophecies does not. Augustine's final sentence in *Reply to Faustus* 13.15 sums it up: "In a word, the predictions of pagan ingenuity regarding Christ's coming are as different from sacred prophecy as the confession of devils from the proclamation of angels."

It is a signal reminder of how different Augustine's world was from ours that he does not deny that pagan prophets could accurately foretell the future. If the biblical prophets receive their predictive ability from divine inspiration, what is the source of pagan prophecy? For Augustine the answer is simple and can be stated in one word: demons. Augustine here draws on a long-standing belief going back to Hellenistic Judaism that the gods of the gentiles were not divine in the way that the God of Israel was divine. But neither were they imaginary nothings. They were real spiritual beings, vastly inferior to God and in rebellion against him. Augustine was quite interested in these beings and drew extensively on the work of other ancient writers, both Christian and pagan, in discussing the nature of demons and their cognitive abilities, which he does at great length in books 8 and 9 of *City of God*. It is convenient for us that Augustine devoted a separate treatise, *The Divination of Demons*, specifically to explaining how pagan prophets are able to foretell the future.

---

of God, in which he combs through pagan oracles and the writings of pagan thinkers for evidence that they occasionally and unknowingly glimpsed partial truths that would find their full realization in Christ and Christian monotheism.

115. Augustine, *Faustus* 13.15.

How Demons Foretell the Future

In his introduction to *The Divination of Demons* Augustine reports that he wrote the treatise to respond to questions from his congregation about how Christians might discuss with pagans the topic of divination, which in the context of Augustine's treatise means the seeking of knowledge about the future by supernatural or ritual means. Augustine tells us that those questions were occasioned by a report that the destruction of the famous temple of Isis and Serapis in Alexandria had been foretold by Serapis's priests. (That temple was demolished in 391 by the patriarch of Alexandria, following an edict by the Christian emperor Theodosius.)

> I replied that one should not marvel that demons could know and predict the impending downfall of their own temples and images, and other events, also, insofar as it is allowed them to know and foretell.[116]

In Augustine's view, God permits demons to know and predict the future—otherwise they could not—but Augustine draws a careful distinction: God allows them to make predictions, but those predictions are not to be attributed to the power of God.[117] Augustine's theory is that demons' knowledge of the future derives from their nature as beings with rational souls and "aerial bodies." (Humans have "earthly" bodies.)

Augustine discusses at length the nature and abilities of demons. Aerial bodies have keener sense perception and far greater mobility than earthly bodies, and those abilities enable demons to see and foretell many things in the future. Augustine emphasizes that those abilities are not supernatural; they are natural powers of aerial bodies. Such abilities seem supernatural to us only because the sense perceptions natural to our earthly bodies are so much less acute. The superior abilities of demons are no reason to revere them, no more so than we revere dogs for their superior sense of smell, or vultures and eagles for their superior eyesight.[118]

Demons live much longer than humans and so they have far more experience in understanding how the natural world works. This long experience has taught them how to predict certain natural events, an ability that differs only in degree, not in kind, from the skills by which farmers time the planting of crops or by which sailors predict storms.[119] The demons' accuracy in predictions of this sort is aided by their ability to perceive natu-

---

116. Augustine, *DivDem* 1.1.
117. Augustine, *DivDem* 2.6.
118. Augustine, *DivDem* 3.7.
119. Augustine, *DivDem* 4.7.

ral signs imperceptible to humans.[120] Demons can also predict events that they themselves intend to effect. Moreover, they can predict many things that people intend to do because they can discern human intentions from minute clues in their tone of voice or body language, signs too subtle for humans to read.[121]

Because the demons' ability to see into the future is natural to them, and not the result of divine revelation, which is the source of authentic (that is, biblical) prophecy, demonic predictions are fallible. Some of their predictions turn out false because angels intervene to make sudden, unforeseeable changes in natural phenomena.[122] Sometimes demons lie about the future out of malicious delight in deceiving people. Then when their predictions fail, "they take pains that their failures be attributed to their seers and to the interpreters of their signs."[123]

Rounding off his explanation for how demons predict the future, Augustine returns to the event with which he opened his treatise, the destruction of the temple of Serapis. Augustine proposes a final source for the foreknowledge of demons.

> When downfall was already impending for temples and idols—
> a downfall that the prophets of the most high God foretold so
> long in advance—Serapis, a demon, revealed the event, close at
> hand, to some of his own worshippers, so that he, though yield-
> ing and fleeing, might in a sense commend his own divinity.[124]

Up to this point in the discussion, Augustine has attributed demonic foreknowledge to the superhuman—but not supernatural—abilities inherent in demons' nature as beings with aerial bodies. Now he adds that demons also have access to divine revelation insofar as they are aware of the utterances of biblical prophets. With artful irony, the prophecy that Augustine here highlights is a prediction of the defeat of the pagan gods.

> The Lord will shrivel all the gods of the earth,
>   and to him shall bow down,
>   each in its place,
>   all the coasts and islands of the nations. (Zeph 2:11)

---

120. Augustine, *DivDem* 5.9.

121. Augustine, *DivDem* 5.9.

122. Augustine, *DivDem* 6.10.

123. Augustine, *DivDem* 6.10.

124. Augustine, *DivDem* 6.11.

The gods/demons knew that the God of Israel had proclaimed their even-tual downfall. They had hidden this fate from their worshippers either because they doubted the word of God or because they feared losing devo-tees. However, when Serapis sensed that the time for the fulfillment of this prophecy was approaching in his case, he foretold the coming destruction of his temple so that he would not be considered "ignorant and vanquished."[125]

The Price of Augustine's Refutation of Pagan Prophecy

Augustine does not deny that pagan gods, whom he regards as demons, can predict the future. However, he argues that this ability does not mean that they are divine. He attributes their predictions either to natural abilities inherent in their aerial bodies or to their knowledge of biblical prophecy. Augustine thus accepts the authenticity of some pagan prophecies (they accurately predict the future) but denies their theological legitimacy (they do not originate from true divinity). The double standard here is transpar-ent. The fulfillment of biblical prophecy proves the theological reliability of the Bible (and therefore the true divinity of the God of the Bible), but the fulfillment of pagan prophecy does not prove the true divinity of the pagan gods. In his apologetic to pagans, Augustine uses the fulfillment of biblical prophecies as evidence for the truth of Christianity, on the assumption that the ability to predict the future comes only from the one true God. However, Augustine's attempt to discredit the legitimacy of pagan prophecy enables us to see that his case for the evidential value of prophecy also relies on a second, unstated, premise: the fulfillment of prophecy proves the theo-logical legitimacy of the source of that prophecy, but *only if* that prophecy promotes true religion, i.e., the worship of the God of the Bible. Only with that premise in place could Augustine argue that the fulfillment of "our" prophecies proves the truth of our religion, while the fulfillment of "their" prophecies does not. The unstated premise shows that Augustine's argument from prophecy is perfectly circular: the fulfillment of biblical prophecies proves the legitimacy of the Bible, and the Bible guarantees the legitimacy of its prophecies.

Augustine's argument that pagan prophecy originates from demons shows that for him the fulfillment of prophecy, by itself, proves nothing. This seriously undermines the foundation of his apologetic to pagans. Keep in mind that Augustine does not argue that the fulfillment of prophecy sim-ply *confirms* Christian faith (though that is certainly its primary function

---

125. Augustine, *DivDem* 7.11.

in his writing). Rather, he argues that prophecy fulfillment is a *basis* for faith in Christ. However, by using Christian faith as the standard by which to distinguish which prophecies have divine origin, Augustine, probably unwittingly, subverts his own argument.

CONCLUSION

Augustine professes the conviction that *all* of the OT (with some specific exceptions) foretells Christ and the church. Because Christ is ubiquitous, though hidden, in the scriptures, symbolic prefigurements can be found even—and especially—in seemingly innocuous textual details. Augustine believes that individual verses must be interpreted within their contexts. For him, however, "context" means the larger pattern of symbolic meaning intended by divine inspiration, not the literary context within which we today discern the intention of the human author.

Augustine regards the fulfillment of prophecy to be irrefutable proof for the divine origin of the Old and New Testaments, and thus for the truth of Christianity. He therefore makes it a cornerstone of his apologetics, both to Jews and to pagans. In wrestling with the problem of why Jews reject the (to him) obvious truth that Christ fulfills their scripture, Augustine resorts to a self-serving paradox: Jews do not see that Christ fulfills prophecy because they are blind, and their blindness is a punishment from God. As to the question of what sin merited that dire (but just) punishment, Augustine both pleads ignorance and asserts that their sin was pride. He also emphasizes that the Jews' unbelief is itself a fulfillment of prophecy.

What Augustine labels as the Jews' "unbelief" is actually their persistence in the practice of Judaism, and it is interesting that Augustine sees providence at work in that persistence. In a fascinating interpretation of the mark of Cain, Augustine argues that the existence of Jewish communities within the Christian world serves as witness to the truth of Christianity: by preserving their scriptures, Jews thereby underwrite the credibility of the prophecies fulfilled by Christ, by proving that those prophecies are not Christian forgeries.

Augustine maintains that pagans can be persuaded that Christ fulfills OT prophecies; that even pagans can see this truth should, according to Augustine, be enough to validate the Bible's divine origin to those who do not take its authority on faith. Augustine takes up several problems involved in the effort to convert pagans: how to explain why Jews do not believe in the fulfillment of prophecies from their own scripture, why there are divisions among Christians, and how to discern which version of Christianity is the true one. He solves each of these with appeals to scripture. In *Faith in Things Unseen*, Augustine outlines another strategy for the apologetic use of prophecy with pagans: presenting prophecies that are fulfilled, not in the past life of Jesus, but in the present realities of Christianity. This approach does not require skeptical pagans to trust the gospel stories about Jesus, but only to correlate ancient prophecies with contemporary and undeniable public facts about the church.

In sampling a few of Augustine's more imaginative interpretations of prophecies that are fulfilled in Christ, we see the lengths to which Augustine can go in finding Christ in the OT. By tracking the interpretive steps by which Augustine asserts that Christ is prefigured in those texts, we glimpse the traces of the intellectual effort he exerted in the process. Such investment of effort is best explained by the supposition that Augustine knew what he was looking for in the OT and was confident that he would find it. His interpretive labors therefore confirm the dynamic we see enabling the NT presentation of prophecies that are fulfilled in Jesus: the belief that the scriptures prophesy Jesus is the basis for the interpretations asserting that individual prophecies were fulfilled by him.

Finally, Augustine confronts the problem posed by the fulfillment of prophecies attributed to pagan gods. He acknowledges that those prophecies were accurate but argues that their accuracy is not evidence for the divinity of the spiritual beings who inspired them. Those whom pagans worship as gods are actually demons. Their ability to see the future stems from their superhuman, but not supernatural, sensory and cognitive powers and from their knowledge of the oracles of biblical prophets. Augustine argues, in effect, that the fulfillment of prophecy, by itself, proves nothing. He thus undermines the basis for his own apologetic use of prophecy.

PART 4

Modern Reckoning with the Argument from Prophecy

17

Modern Christian Thought and the Fulfillment of Prophecy

AT THIS POINT THE outline of this book leaps from Augustine to the modern period. A brief explanation is in order. If my purpose were to write a comprehensive history of our subject, this very large gap would be indefensible. But the purpose of this book is limited: to study in depth the fulfillment of prophecy in the NT, to sketch the religious and literary foundations in Israel and Greece for the NT's use of prophecy, to track the apologetic development of the fulfillment of prophecy in the patristic era, and to survey its use in modern Christianity. The many centuries between Augustine and the modern period no doubt contain much Christian interpretation of the fulfillment of prophecy that is interesting and important in its own right. However, to responsibly investigate all that would be beyond my competence, and probably my life span. This book is long enough as it is. What calms my intellectual conscience about ignoring what most of Christian history might contribute to our topic is that what we can learn about the fulfillment of prophecy in the literatures of ancient Israel and Greece, from the NT, and from the patristic writings seems fully adequate for the purpose of understanding the uses of and reflection on the fulfillment of prophecy in modern Christianity.

The argument from prophecy is deeply rooted in the Christian intellectual tradition. The belief that Jesus fulfilled scripture is as early as any Christian belief that historians can track. When Paul, whose writings are the earliest surviving texts from the Jesus movement, asserted that Christ died and rose "according to the scriptures," Paul emphasized that this belief "was handed on" to him by those who were believers before him (1 Cor 15:3–4). Common to every recognizable group in the early Jesus movement is the belief that the scriptures of Israel predict Jesus.[1] That belief wells up

1. This seems true even for the implied audiences of Christian texts that do not

in multiple literary expressions in the NT that vary both in the number of prophecies invoked and in the ingenuity brought to bear by their interpretation. The NT testimonies that Jesus fulfilled specific prophecies continued to develop in the patristic era (roughly the second through sixth centuries). They became full-fledged apologies (arguments to justify Christianity) that invoke a multitude of OT passages and rationalize their fulfillments with increasing sophistication and intensity. The work of Augustine is the high-water mark of this flood of rhetorical creativity. He articulated the argument from prophecy with extraordinary intellectual energy.

In later centuries Christian thinkers accepted the validity of the argument from prophecy without question. It was assumed to be an irrefutable *proof*, and it became a staple in the demonstration of Christianity's truth and its superiority to Judaism and, occasionally, to paganism. The persuasiveness of this apologetic seemed irrefutable to the Christian mind. That perception prevailed until the late eighteenth century, when the historical-critical study of the Bible emerged in the wake of the Enlightenment. Only then, when scholars began to privilege the effort to understand each individual biblical writing on its own terms and within its own context, did the reinterpretation of OT prophecies by NT authors begin to seem problematic.

Previous chapters in this book have laid out the considerable problems that the historical-critical study of the Bible creates for the traditional argument from prophecy. This chapter analyzes a handful of short academic treatments of the fulfillment of prophecy in modern Christianity. I trust that the works selected for analysis, despite their brevity, constitute a fair representation of the spectrum of available academic perspectives. We will also take a look at a webpage that brokers an extravagant version of the argument from prophecy to a contemporary popular audience.

Within those sectors of contemporary Christianity that reject or ignore historical criticism, various apologetic efforts restate the traditional argument that Jesus' fulfillments of prophecies prove the truth of Christianity. Such apologies offer numerous OT texts as evidence, unhampered by the slightest concern for their original meanings. Nothing about that is new; the only creativity is in how the arguments are presented and which prophecies are invoked. The Internet provides an environment in which such apologies can easily proliferate, but there is a steady sameness to most of the websites

---

relate Jesus to specific OT passages. For example, the *Gospel of Thomas* tells that Jesus' disciples said to him, "Twenty-four prophets have spoken in Israel, and they all spoke of you" (*Thom* 52:1). That is all the more interesting, not only because *Thomas* nowhere quotes the OT (although *Thom* 16:3, like Matt 10:35 and Luke 12:52–53, attributes to Jesus a saying that parallels Mic 7:6), but also because there is no evidence that *Thomas* even knows the OT (Hedrick, *Unlocking the Secrets*, 6).

that display them, as anyone can see from a casual search. These uncritical similarities are more or less what one expects in apologies that are untroubled by—and probably unaware of—the numerous problems generated by the historical-critical study of the fulfillment of prophecy.

Historical criticism, as an academic discipline, abstains from the apologetic use of the fulfillment of prophecy. Historical-critical study aims to discover and describe what the biblical books *meant* to their original authors and audiences; it does not prescribe what they *should mean* to contemporary believers. As to assertions in the NT itself about the fulfillment of prophecy, historical criticism strives to understand how the different NT authors interpreted OT passages and related those reinterpreted prophecies to Jesus or the church. Historical criticism cannot argue that Jesus really did fulfill prophecy and then treat that fulfillment as evidence that he was the messiah. Historical criticism simply has no method by which to construct such an argument.

Of course, Christian scholars can—and many do—make such arguments. But when they do, they step beyond the domain of historical criticism. One's exegetical method need not delimit one's theological beliefs. A scholar of good faith and intellectual honesty might conclude, on the basis of historical criticism, that the prophets had no intention of predicting Jesus but nevertheless believe that Jesus was the messiah who fulfilled prophecy. The same goes for a scholar who rejects a literal interpretation of the first chapter of Genesis, and who yet believes that God is the creator. In both examples, the *exegetical conclusions* flow from the application of an academic method, whereas the *religious beliefs* are anchored in theological commitments. However, there are also scholars who attempt to harmonize the belief that Jesus fulfilled prophecy with the findings of historical-critical exegesis by creating a place for that belief *within* that academic method. They run into great difficulty, as we will see.

Many Christian biblical scholars, while recognizing that apologetics lies beyond the methodological jurisdiction of historical criticism, nevertheless endorse the argument from prophecy. They do so not because they think it can be supported by historical criticism, but because they believe that the teachings of the NT constitute divine revelation. The underlying reasoning, though implicit, is bold and clear: Jesus fulfilled prophecy because the NT says he did, and he fulfilled all the specific prophecies quoted in the NT, for the same reason. I maintain that there need be nothing amiss intellectually in openly admitting that one holds a belief taught by the Bible that cannot be supported by one's critical interpretation of the Bible. Most people, including highly rational people, believe many things they cannot justify on intellectual grounds.

However, many people, especially scholars, feel constrained not to hold beliefs that lack solid rational bases. They spontaneously seek justifications for their beliefs within intellectual disciplines that use rational methods for acquiring and verifying knowledge. Scholars who attempt to justify, on historical-critical grounds, the belief that Jesus fulfilled prophecy face a daunting problem: how to explain the validity of the novel meanings that NT authors attributed to OT prophecies. Not only are there numerous cases in which those new meanings were not intended by the OT authors, there are also many cases in which the new meaning is clearly incompatible with the original one (cases, for example, in which the new meaning is possible only if the context of the OT passage is ignored). There is no special challenge in describing *how* that happened—that is a straightforward task within historical criticism. Rather, the challenge is to *justify* the new interpretations, by explaining how they express the *true* meanings of those old prophecies.

As we have seen, that was not difficult for the ancients, since they understood prophecies as oracular utterances, and thus assumed that the prophets sometimes did not understand the meaning of what they prophesied. But an oracular interpretation of prophecy is not viable in historical criticism, which is founded on the methodological principle that all authors, including biblical authors, attempt to communicate intelligible meanings to their intended audiences. For historical-critical scholars defending the NT argument from prophecy, the challenge is to explain *both* how NT authors interpret OT passages in ways that violate the principles of historical criticism *and* how those new meanings are true and valid (which they must be because they are the result of divine inspiration). Put more bluntly, the challenge is to demonstrate how texts that mean what their authors intended them to mean can *really* mean something their authors did not intend.

That problem, I maintain, is insoluble *within historical criticism*. However, if that problem is reframed as a question *within Christian theology*, it seems easy to answer. One simple solution proceeds like this: What the Bible teaches is true, and therefore what the NT teaches about the OT is likewise true. If there are some examples of the fulfillment of prophecy that raise the confusing problem of how the same prophecy can have a meaning in its NT context that is incompatible with its meaning in its OT context, then those examples merely show the limitations of human understanding. Since the Bible is God's book, it can mean whatever God wills it to mean, and God is not limited by human standards of consistency.

That explanation resolves the problem theologically by removing it from human jurisdiction—a move based on the belief that our inability to understand how two seemingly incompatible meanings can both be true need not undermine our confidence in the truth of God's word. The problem is not really solved; it is just taken off the table. Even those who accept this nonsolution might wonder why God would so confound our ability to understand a book intended for our instruction.

However, the problem does not go away so readily for those persuaded by the basic logic of historical criticism, which requires the presupposition that the human authors of the Bible were genuine authors, and so their writings meant what they intended them to mean. Therefore, whatever divine revelation the Bible might convey would be communicated through the meanings intended by the human authors. From that standpoint, the problem of incompatible meanings is an acute one.

What follows are six case studies. Five are close analyses of brief treatments of the fulfillment of prophecy, modern academic works selected from across the methodological and theological spectra. The sixth analyzes a nonacademic example from the Internet, a medium that cannot be overlooked in any survey of modern apologetics. In chronological order, my six cases are

1. a work of thoroughgoing historical criticism unconstrained by Christian doctrine, written by Samuel Reimarus (1778), a pioneer of modern critical scholarship

2. a mid-twentieth-century apology untouched by historical criticism, in a Catholic textbook on apologetics

3, 4, 5. attempts to meet the challenge described above, by three academic works, two Catholic and one evangelical, in different genres: an article on prophecy in *The New Catholic Encyclopedia* (1967), an essay on biblical inspiration in the *Jerome Biblical Commentary* (1968), and an introductory textbook, *How to Read the Bible for All Its Worth* (2014)

6. an Internet site unaffected by any historical criticism, Present-Truth.org/, that claims to prove that Jesus was the messiah because of the hundreds of prophecies he fulfilled

Samuel Reimarus' Critique of the Fulfillment of Prophecy (1778)

Samuel Reimarus' groundbreaking work, *On the Intentions of Jesus and His Disciples*, was published posthumously in 1778. It is the first historical-critical study of the New Testament to attempt to distinguish the historical Jesus from the Christ portrayed in the gospels. Reimarus devotes only a few pages to the argument from prophecy, in a section of his book aimed at refuting some of the standard apologetic arguments for the truth of Christianity.

Reimarus begins by stipulating commonsense criteria for recognizing a true prophecy: it "should state beforehand legibly, clearly, and distinctly that which no man could previously have known, and that the same should thereafter take place at the time appointed."[2] A prophecy is to be judged false or doubtful if, among other things,

- "it can only be verified through allegorical interpretation";

- "it be only composed of dark and dubious words, and the expressions it contains are commonplace, vague, and uncertain";

- "the words used refer to some other matter and are applied to the prophecy by a quibble."[3]

He then states his thesis: "If, then, we judge by these rules and commence an investigation of those Old Testament prophecies which have been applied to the New Testament, we shall find them to be worthless and false."[4]

Reimarus lays out three arguments in support of his thesis. First, those messianic prophecies that "are most clearly expressed never come to pass; for example, that the Messiah should sit upon the seat of David on Mount Zion and reign from one sea to another, even unto the end of the world, and all besides that was prophesied of the deliverer of Israel."[5] Second, "other prophecies are merely adapted through quibbles, and in reality refer to quite other things."[6] Third, "other passages again contain matters which are applied by the apostles allegorically to Christ,"[7] for which Reimarus gives two examples: Jonah's being inside a whale for three days and three nights, and God's declaration about Solomon, "I will be his father and he shall be my son" (2 Sam 7:14). Reimarus characterizes apologetic arguments that rely on such passages as circular arguments that try "to prove the truth of the New Testament and its doctrines through the prophecies of the Old, and the things said or meant in the Old Testament through the New."[8] Reimarus summarizes with a sweeping assertion.

2. Reimarus, *Intentions of Jesus*, 235.
3. Ibid., 235–36.
4. Ibid., 236.
5. Ibid.
6. Ibid.
7. Ibid.
8. Ibid.

> In short, I may affirm that one cannot refer to a single quoted prophecy that is not false; or if you would have me speak more mildly, I will only say that they are all ambiguous and doubtful.[9]

Reimarus goes on to tease out a crucial element in the logic underlying the argument from prophecy: the inference that Jesus is proven to be the messiah because he fulfilled so many messianic prophecies. Reimarus argues that even if we grant—for the sake of the argument—that the prophecies are rightly interpreted by the NT, "it does not at all follow that Jesus of Nazareth was meant by them."[10] For example, if we grant that it was prophesied that the messiah would be born in Bethlehem, this prophecy would be fulfilled by everyone born there, so why single out Jesus as its unique fulfillment? Reimarus anticipates the apologist's reply: "when all the signs are fulfilled in one person, that person must be meant, and no other."[11] Reimarus responds, "But here we relapse again into the same old circle." He explains what he means by "the same old circle" by analyzing the process through which NT authors identified the many prophecies they believe were fulfilled by Jesus. First, they noted the particulars of his life. Second, in their attempt to make him into the messiah, "they pretend that these particulars had been prophesied and fulfilled in him."[12] However, there was a problem: "prophecies that really corresponded could not be found." So, third, "they, through quibbles and allegories, twisted and turned this or that passage in the Old Testament to suit their purpose."[13]

Reimarus here in one paragraph encapsulates most of the basic elements of the process that I reconstruct in detail in parts 2 and 3 of this book. I argued there that Christian writers started with the belief that Jesus was the messiah and then, convinced that the scriptures must contain prophecies about Jesus, harvested passages that they could correlate to details from the story of his life by attributing new meanings to the prophecies they collected, meanings foreign to their original sense. The Christian authors sometimes rewrote the prophecies to clarify their new meanings, and sometimes shaped their stories about Jesus to fit the prophecies with which they were paired. Reimarus summarizes the basic steps by which the earliest Christians identified and reinterpreted the prophecies that applied to Jesus. However, his short summary does not discern the full range of the literary creativity that I have attributed to the NT authors in their presentation of

9. Ibid., 237.
10. Ibid., 237–38.
11. Ibid., 238.
12. Ibid.
13. Ibid.

Jesus as the fulfiller of prophecy. Reimarus stops short of arguing that the gospel writers shaped or invented stories about Jesus to match prophecies, and he does not explicitly assert that those authors rewrote prophecies, although that seems implied by his claim that they "twisted and turned" the OT passages. Even so, his skeptical stance is clear.

Reimarus' treatment of our topic is quite brief, though adequate to his purpose of refuting the argument from prophecy in the context of a comprehensive critique of traditional Christian apologetics. Although his discussion lacks detailed analyses of specific examples of how the NT uses prophecy, Reimarus does expose the incompatibility of the historical-critical interpretation of the prophets and their prophecies with the apologetic uses of the prophecies in the Christian tradition. That Reimarus could get so much right, in so few pages, shows how easily historical criticism can illuminate the circularity in the argument from prophecy, which must assume the truth of Christianity in order to demonstrate the truth of Christianity. The argument from prophecy presumes that the OT means what the NT says it means, in every case.

Evidence for Our Faith (1948–1959)

Evidence for Our Faith by Joseph H. Cavanaugh was first published in 1948 by University of Notre Dame Press in its University Religion Series, subtitled Theology for the Layman. Its third edition, in 1959, was completed after the death of its author by a committee from Notre Dame's Religion Department. The original preface begins, "This textbook is the product of my classes in Apolgetics at the University of Notre Dame." (The apolgetics course was required of all undergraduates at Notre Dame until 1959.)[14] This textbook thus provides a window into what students at an American Catholic university were expected to understand about the rational basis for Christianity in the decades before Vatican II and the blossoming of historical-critical study of the Bible by Catholic scholars.

The preface to the book exudes the effortless confidence of an apologetic environment in which a Catholic theologian teaches (mostly) Catholic students at a premier Catholic university about the truth of Catholicism. The author explains that the book

> is an attempt to present the case for Catholicism. The difficulty
> has been, not to find sufficient evidence for the case, but to se-
> lect the best evidence and to present it convincingly in such a

14. According to Fr. Robert Pelton, who became chairman of Notre Dame's Religion Department in 1959. Private e-mail correspondence, May 2, 2014.

little book. If a student thinks that the evidence for any point is insufficient or the explanation unsatisfactory, he can consult the books mentioned in the bibliography, for the more he searches through the evidence, the more reasons he will discover for accepting the Catholic faith.[15]

Imagine also the subliminal but unsubtle message communicated to students by the physical context of their study: the professor wears a Roman collar and is addressed as "Father," a crucifix adorns the classroom, and classes begin with prayer. The textbook is "written in honor of our Blessed Mother at the University she has blessed so abundantly."[16]

The argument from prophecy occupies less than three pages, most of which are taken up by a list of prophecies that are distilled into and organized by propositions supported by citations, such as "The Messiah will be begotten of God (Ps 2:7)." The brevity of the treatment is itself revealing and is an important aspect of its rhetorical force: this matter is presented as if it were so self-evident that it requires little explanation and only the briefest of argument. Some of the prophecies on the list are those quoted in the NT, but many are not. Strangely, in many cases the cited passage does not actually relate to the alleged prediction. Here are some examples.

- Psalm 5:10 (5:9)[17] is cited to substantiate that the messiah will rise from the dead. But that verse does not refer to a messiah, nor does it mention death or resurrection. It simply reads, "There is no truth in their mouths; their hearts are vain."

- "He will die for sinners" is supported by citing Isa 53:7; 50:6; Zech 11:12; 12:10; 13:1; Ps 21:7 (a typo for 21:8); 68:22. *None* of those passages speaks of a messiah, or anyone else, dying for sinners (though Isa 53:7 can be read that way if we enlarge the citation to 53:4–7).

- Zech 11:12, Isa 50:6, Ps 21:8, and Ps 68:22 are cited as evidence of prophecy that "through his passion and death he will enter into his glory." None say anything even close to that, as the two psalm citations can illustrate. Psalm 21:8 (22:7) reads, "All who saw me mocked me; / they spoke with their lips / and shook their heads." Ps 68:22 (69:21) reads, "They gave me gall for my food, and in my thirst they gave me

---

15. Cavanaugh, *Evidence*, ix.

16. Ibid. That female students were excluded from the University of "Our Lady" is an irony that I presume (and hope) was invisible to the author. Notre Dame first admitted women in 1972.

17. Biblical citations are from the Vulgate, which numbers the Psalms and their verses differently than contemporary translations do. Since Cavanaugh relied on the Vulgate, the quotations that follow are my own translations from the Vulgate.

vinegar to drink." Although these two psalm texts clearly influenced the passion narratives, in neither case does the psalmist (the implied speaker) die, much less die as a prelude to glorification.

- Psalm 109:4; Isa 66:21; and Mal 1:11 are cited as examples of the prophecy that "the messiah will be a priest and [sacrificial] victim." Ps 109:4 (110:4) is addressed to the king of Israel: "You are a priest forever according to the order of Melchizedek." This can, with some imagination, be taken as a messianic prophecy. However, it is difficult to see how the other two prophecies predict that the messiah will be a priest. Isaiah 66:21 reads, "I will take from among them priests and Levites." "Them" refers to exiles returned to Jerusalem (see Isa 66:20). Malachi 1:11 says that "in every place there are sacrifices, and a clean oblation is offered to me."

Despite the many specious citations, students are assured, "These texts were not chosen at random but constitute an integral part of the Messianic tradition."[18]

It is worth noting that "the Messianic tradition" is a Christian fiction. To be sure, many Jews at the time of Jesus—though not all—hoped for a messiah, and some of those hopes were inspired by specific prophecies. But the kind of figure the messiah would be was variously construed, the expectations about him were diverse, and the lists of prophecies taken to foretell him were far from uniform and not codified. The notion that there was such a thing as "the Messianic tradition"—a kind of authoritative and well-known checklist of transparent predictions waiting to be fulfilled by God's anointed—is a rhetorical fiction of Christian apologetics. This fiction has both positive and polemical functions. The positive function is rather obvious: the one who fulfills the prophecies in the messianic tradition (Jesus, of course) is thereby certified as the messiah.

> Jesus so perfectly fulfilled all the prophecies that an honest student is forced to admit a providential coincidence between the Messianic prophecies and the life of Christ. Surely the fulfillment of all the prophecies in one individual could not have been due to chance or human contrivance, but must have been God's work. Jesus was, therefore, the promised Messiah.[19]

The polemical function of this imaginary prophetic checklist is equally important to the apologetic task, for it incorporates a premise that allows a satisfying answer to the implicit question stalking all apologies: if the truth

18. Cavanaugh, *Evidence*, 73.

19. Ibid.

is so obvious, why doesn't everyone embrace it? When apologetics is tied
to the fulfillment of prophecy, the question is the age-old one: if Jesus unquestionably fulfilled the prophecies about the messiah, why did his Jewish
contemporaries not recognize that? From as early as the Gospel of Matthew,
we know that this question readily invites an anti-Jewish response. "This
objection is easy to answer," and Cavanaugh offers four answers: (1) a few
Jews did recognize Jesus as messiah; (2) the majority of Jews, however, were
evil; (3) their leaders viciously so; and (4) the Jews' moral bankruptcy led
them to misunderstand the prophecies. Lest you think my summary of the
last three answers is exaggerated, here is the textbook in its own words:

> Secondly, the Jewish people at that time were, for the most part,
> morally corrupt . . . Their evil minds were closed to the message
> of Christ. Thirdly, their leaders, the Scribes and Pharisees, hated
> Christ vehemently. After he condemned their pride, arrogance,
> and hypocrisy, they bitterly opposed him. Finally, the Jews had
> misinterpreted some of the prophecies. Blinded by nationalism
> and materialism they looked in vain for a temporal king rather
> than a spiritual king.[20]

This glib indictment of Jewish culpability should by now sound familiar. Although it was written in the twentieth century, it could have been
written by Justin Martyr in the second century, for it simply reproduces the
boilerplate slander endemic to patristic anti-Judaism. Yet, there is an interesting difference. Unlike with Justin and company, the analysis here is confined to Jews of Jesus' time. It offers no reasons why *twentieth-century* Jews
have not acknowledged that Jesus fulfilled prophecy. We can only speculate
as to why this is missing. Perhaps the author realized how ludicrous it would
be to apply his analysis to contemporary Jews. Perhaps uncomfortable experiences with the rare Jewish student in the classroom—if any there were—
had taught professors not to raise the issue. It seems more likely, however,
that the question simply did not occur to the author, since the only Jews of
any significance to Christian theological interests were Jews of the past, that
is, the people of the OT and the caricatures in the gospels.

Two other features of Cavanaugh's apologetic presentation invite
comment. First, his textbook reads the gospels uncritically, which is why
it can simply footnote the Gospel of Matthew as sufficient proof that Jesus "fulfilled the prophecies about the Messiah." Students who relied on
the textbook for their understanding of OT prophecy would, therefore, be
unaware (as Cavanaugh also probably was) of the various ingenious textual manipulations by which the NT writers match obscure prophecies to

20. Ibid., 73–74.

their alleged fulfillments in Christ. Second, the rhetoric of "the messianic tradition," analyzed briefly above, conveniently disguises (presumably out of ignorance) that the implied list of prophecies about the messiah did not exist until Christian thinkers pieced it together in hindsight. As my chapters on Matthew and John demonstrate in detail, the belief that Jesus fulfilled prophecy preceded the identification of the specific prophecies that he supposedly fulfilled. It was only after Christians knew what to look for in the Jewish scriptures that they were able to find the specific passages useful to their purpose. Christians found passages that could be taken to refer to Christ or the church only after they set out specifically to find such passages. The simplistic and uncritical apologetic in *Evidence for Our Faith* seems unaware of the circular reasoning on which it is based.

Amid the list of fulfilled prophecies collated in the textbook, one item merits further attention, because it is showcase evidence that the messianic prophecies were gathered retrospectively: the alleged prediction that "the Messiah will be a spiritual king and legislator,"[21] for which a dozen prophecies are cited.[22] *Four* of those dozen mention a king, but none of those four indicates that the king is anything other than a literal king. Besides, what does the term "spiritual king" even mean? (What if someone today were called a "spiritual president" or "spiritual prime minister"?) This baffling term makes sense only in light of the scene in the Gospel of John in which Pilate asks Jesus, "Are you the king of the Jews?" (18:33) and he replies, "My kingdom is not of this world" (18:36). Only with the prior belief in place that Jesus was a king who lacked an earthly kingdom could the strange notion arise that the messiah would be a spiritual king. Only then could Christian scholars comb through the scriptures looking for prophecies that could be (mis)taken to predict such a figure. Their logic can be easily reconstructed: (1) Jesus, the messiah, was a spiritual king; (2) therefore, the scriptures must have prophesied that the messiah would be a spiritual king; and (3) therefore, prophecies about an ideal king must actually refer to a spiritual king, the kind of king Jesus was.

The New Catholic Encyclopedia (1967)

Our third case study is an article on the "Theology of Prophecy" in *The New Catholic Encyclopedia* (1967) by F. X. Redmond. It includes two paragraphs on "Apologetic Proof from OT Prophecy," which mainly explicate

21. Ibid., 72.

22. Zech 9:9–10; 13:21; Ps 2:6; Jer 23:5; 1:31–34 (presumably a typo for 31:31–34, since Jeremiah 1 ends at verse 19); Isa 1:7; 9:7; 11:10–16; 33:20; 59:21; 62:11; Joel 2:28.

"presuppositions regarding the purpose and significance of OT prophecies."[23] Three presuppositions are discussed. (1) "Only the general and consistent tenor of these prophecies was meant to be literally fulfilled in the great majority of cases." Presumably, this is an inference from how OT prophecies are handled in the NT. If that is the case (and there seems no other explanation), this first presupposition implies that NT applications of OT prophecies to their fulfillments is actually the means by which we discover what the prophets intended their prophecies to mean. (2) "NT fulfillment was not just equal to OT expectations, but surpassed them. Although the Prophets had no blueprint of the messianic era, they would have recognized in it the overfulfillment of their prophecies." On this view, it seems that the prophets would *not* have been concerned that many of their prophecies were "underfulfilled" or not fulfilled at all (e.g., most of their eschatological oracles about the messianic age). (3) "Ordinarily, details in the OT prophecies cannot be used in a prophetic proof for a number of reasons:" the prophets did not intend the details of their messages to be essential to their meaning; prophecies can blend events separated in time; some prophecies are implicitly conditional; the prophets described the messiah and the messianic age "in terms of their own generation."

> The Prophets knew that their prophecies were only approximations, that the new covenant would be different from the old, even though their knowledge and their mentality forced them to describe the new covenant in terms of the old, which they knew.

Redmond concedes, in other words, that the prophets did their best. Their knowledge of the future was vague and imprecise. Although the prophets would have recognized the fulfillment of their predictions, in Redmond's view, they would have been surprised at *how* their predictions were fulfilled, that is, fulfilled beyond their expectations by Jesus and the church. This concession is interesting for its double-mindedness. On the one hand, we can discern presuppositions of historical criticism, for the concession respects the integrity of the prophets as genuine authors. Their knowledge of the future might be vague, but they knew what their prophecies meant, and they did not intend them to mean what later NT authors said they meant. On the other hand, the imagined surprise of the prophets at *how* their prophecies were fulfilled necessarily implies that their words had some level of meaning of which the prophets were not aware. Redmond seems to imagine the prophets, maybe in heaven, saying something like, "I never meant to predict the event or situation that the NT identifies as the

---

23. All quotations in this section are from Redmond, "Prophecy, Theology of," 864.

fulfillment of my prophecy, but I can see how my words came true in a way I didn't expect." Redmond would not imagine a prophet saying, "No, that's not what I predicted; the NT misunderstands and even twists my words."

The belief that the prophets predicted the advent of Jesus requires one of two theories as a premise: either (1) the prophets knew that their prophecies were about Jesus, or (2) the prophets were unaware of the "real" (i.e., christological) meaning of their prophecies. Since, as we have just seen, Redmond denies the first theory, he must therefore hold some version of the second. He does just that, by proposing the theory of "overfulfillment." "The starting point for the proof [from prophecy] should lie in the NT fulfillment and not in OT prophecy." Redmond here acknowledges that the meanings the prophets intended to convey do not lead to the meanings proclaimed in the NT. He recognizes that OT prophecies can be applied to their NT fulfillments only if their original meanings are modified. What comes next in Redmond's argument is crucial: he shifts his rhetoric so that the new meanings attributed by the NT to the prophecies are described, not as violating the prophets' intentions, but rather as *surpassing* them.

> The NT fulfillment greatly surpasses the OT prophecies. If one tries to find in OT prophecy what would come to pass in the NT, he is trying to find the greater in the less. The conclusion would contain more than the premises warrant. Hence, this method compels adjustments and modifications in the meaning of the OT prophecies to equate them to their NT fulfillment. On the other hand, beginning with the NT fulfillment, [which is] the greater, one can show that the OT prophecies relate to their NT overfulfillment.

Unfortunately, no sooner does Redmond propose a solution to the paradox of how to honor the intentions of both the prophets and the NT writers, than he drops the subject. Redmond fails to explain what it means for a fulfillment to "surpass" or "overfulfill" its prophecy. Without some concrete content for this concept and some analyses of specific examples of it (i.e., demonstrating how a particular NT passage shows that Jesus "overfulfills" a specific OT prophecy), the viability of this proposal cannot be assessed. We are left with the suspicion that while it gives the impression of being a solution, it is actually no solution at all. It is a rhetorical adjustment that merely camouflages the problem.

Raymond Brown and the *Sensus Plenior* (1968)

We next take up an article, "Hermeneutics," by Raymond Brown, the greatest Catholic biblical scholar of the twentieth century. The article appears in *The Jerome Biblical Commentary* (1968), which was for decades—and for many still is—the Catholic bible (so to speak) on historical-critical biblical studies. Brown devotes a section of his article to "The *Sensus Plenior*," which he defines as

> the deeper meaning, intended by God but not clearly intended by the human author, that is seen to exist in the words of Scripture when they are studied in the light of further revelation or of development in the understanding of revelation.[24]

Although Brown's essay was published only nine years after the final edition of *Evidence for Our Faith*, and although both works were authored by Catholic theologians and duly approved by ecclesiastical authority, their perspectives on the Bible seem centuries apart.

Brown prefaces his analysis of the sensus plenior with the candid admission that "the NT has much exegesis of the OT that cannot be accepted today as valid exegesis."[25] He also acknowledges that some Catholic scholars "adamantly reject the sensus plenior because they fear such exegesis will endanger the hard-fought-for primacy of the literal sense."[26] The "literal sense" is a term of art that Brown defines as "the sense which the human author directly intended and which his words convey."[27] It is crucial to note that the technical meaning of this term has nothing to do with what is commonly referred to as "taking the Bible literally" or "literalist" interpretation. Brown introduces the topic with great caution. He states that even though

> we show ourselves sympathetic to the validity of a carefully delineated more-than-literal exegesis, we insist that one must be familiar with the many abuses evident in the past history of this exegesis and that the objections of those who oppose it reflect real dangers against which one must take precautions.[28]

Brown clearly leads us to expect a carefully nuanced discussion.

How do we know that the sensus plenior exists? Why not limit the meaning of a text to its literal sense? Brown's answer is a theological one:

24. Brown, "Hermeneutics," 616.
25. Ibid.
26. Ibid.
27. Ibid., 607.
28. Ibid., 615.

because authoritative sources have interpreted OT passages "in a way that goes beyond their literal sense."[29] For Brown, that inference is inescapable. Since the OT itself is divine revelation, the only sources with divine authority to interpret it are the NT (further revelation) and, consistent with fundamental Catholic doctrine, the church fathers, and church pronouncements, which articulate authoritative developments in the understanding of revelation. Through those ecclesiastically sanctioned sources, God "can make clear the full purpose, not hitherto recognized, that he had in inspiring a particular section of scripture."[30]

Nevertheless, Brown is justifiably wary of the highly imaginative meanings that Christian writers have attributed to biblical passages. He poses the question, "How can one distinguish the SPlen [sensus plenior] of a text from an accommodation that attributes to a text a meaning that goes beyond even God's intention?"[31] Brown proposes two criteria. The first is implied in what he had already said about authority: "The surest guide to a SPlen is an authoritative interpretation" from the sources mentioned above.[32] This criterion aims to ensure against "oversubjectivity" by individuals. The second criterion is called the criterion of "homogeneity."

> The second criterion is even more effective in avoiding misunderstanding about the role of the SPlen. This criterion is that the sensus plenior of a text must be homogeneous with the literal sense, i.e., it must be a development of what the human author wanted to say.[33]

As an example, Brown tentatively offers the use of the Immanuel prophecy (Isa 7:14) by Matt 1:23, which "*may* fit this criterion of homogeneity."[34] Brown argues that Matthew's application of Isa 7:14 was certainly not intended by Isaiah, but (perhaps) it is not foreign to Isaiah's intention, inasmuch as Jesus was later believed to be "a sign of the continuance of the Davidic line and represented God's presence with his people."[35] Brown seems to mean that Matthew sees in the birth of Jesus a sign from God that is *similar* to the sign Isaiah promised with the birth of Immanuel.

---

29. Ibid., 616.
30. Ibid.
31. Ibid., 617.
32. That is, Catholic doctrine, the church fathers, and church pronouncements.
33. Brown, "Hermeneutics," 617.
34. Ibid. (italics added).
35. Ibid.

Brown is unambiguously clear that some scriptural interpretations in the NT and elsewhere do not qualify as instances of the sensus plenior.

> Now, and this is extremely important, scholars do *not* suggest that every more-than-literal use of the words of Scripture advocated by the NT, the Fathers, the liturgy, or Church documents is a SPlen.[36]

He later restates that

> certainly the *majority* of the NT citations of the OT in a more-than-literal sense and the *overwhelming majority* of the liturgical and patristic citations of Scripture do not meet the criteria for a valid SPlen.[37]

As an example, Brown cites the use of Jer 31:15 (the prophecy about Rachel weeping for her children) in Matthew's story about the massacre of the baby boys (Matt 2:18). Here Matthew "is not developing the SPlen of Jer but simply accommodating."[38] (See below for the significance of this term.)

Brown's analysis entails an important but restricted role for historical criticism in the assessment of the sensus plenior. On the one hand, historical criticism per se cannot detect whether a given passage has a sensus plenior. That is because historical criticism aims to determine the literal sense (i.e., the sense intended by the human author), whereas the sensus plenior is the extraliteral sense intended by God. Hence, the *only possible* evidence that a text has a sensus plenior would be the fact that the text has been interpreted in a more-than-literal way either by further revelation (NT) or by an authoritative interpretation of revelation in church tradition—and, according to Brown (see the last quotation above), such evidence is rarely present. On the other hand, Brown allots a crucial role to historical criticism: determining whether an authoritative more-than-literal interpretation is a valid sensus plenior, by assessing whether it meets the criterion of homogeneity. As it turns out, rather few texts pass that test.

In the schema Brown expounds, there are three kinds of valid meanings in the Bible: (1) the *literal sense* intended by the human author, and two kinds of "meaning intended by God that go beyond what the human author intended," which are (2) the *sensus plenior*, "flowing from the words of scripture," and (3) the *typical sense*, "flowing from 'things' described in Scripture."[39] The latter is the meaning derived from typological interpre-

36. Ibid., 616 (italics original).
37. Ibid., 617 (italics added).
38. Ibid.
39. Ibid., 619.

tation, which Brown defines as "the deeper meaning that things (persons, places, and events) of Scripture possess because, according to the intention of the divine author, they foreshadow future things."[40] I will not pursue the typical sense further, since it does not directly relate to the fulfillment of prophecy, inasmuch as prophecies are words, not things. I bring up the typical sense only to isolate another catch-all category of nonliteral meaning that Brown posits alongside the intentions of both the human and divine authors: "accommodation."

> This is not a sense of Scripture but a sense given to Scripture; it is not a product of exegesis but of eisegesis. The range of accommodation is immense, running from catechetical application to literary embellishment. Much of the more-than-literal exegesis in the Fathers and in the liturgy is accommodation.[41]

Here is where things get sticky. There are NT passages that accommodate OT texts. Brown gives one example (Matthew's use of the prophecy about Rachel weeping; see above), but there are many more, to be sure. According to Brown's definition, an author who accommodates a text imputes to it a meaning intended neither by its human author nor by God. It seems impossible to avoid the inference that there are many places in which the NT interprets an OT text in a way *not* intended by God.

Brown raises the question, "Is accommodation justified?" He answers that "a certain tolerance can be extended to accommodation when it is done with intelligence, sobriety, and taste."[42] But his answer relates only to how accommodation should be used today. Brown has nothing to say about the theological problem inherent in NT accommodation of OT passages.

As for the topic of the fulfillment of prophecy, Brown leaves unresolved the problem at its core: that in the NT's presentation of Jesus as the fulfiller of prophecies, those prophecies (with a few possible exceptions) are given meanings that are not only beyond but *foreign to* the meanings intended by their OT authors. In Brown's terminology, what the NT shows Jesus fulfilling are not only the "fuller" meanings of prophecies, but also accommodated meanings of prophecies—and in Brown's estimation, the latter far outnumber the former. Brown's analysis implies, therefore, that, in most cases, NT authors read meanings into prophecies that not even God intended.

40. Ibid., 618.
41. Ibid., 619.
42. Ibid.

This becomes clear in the example that Brown offers. When Matthew claims that Herod's mass murder of baby boys fulfills Jeremiah's "prophecy" about the ancestral mother of the northern tribes of Israel figuratively lamenting their exile by Assyria (Matt 2:16–18), the prophetic prediction fulfilled in Matthew's narrative is one that Matthew himself invents and reads *into* Jeremiah's words. Here "Matthew is not developing the SPlen of Jer but simply accommodating the OT passage."[43] What the story fulfills, therefore, is a prediction intended neither by Jeremiah nor by God, one that exists only in Matthew's imagination. Similarly, when Matthew claims that Hosea's remembrance of God's summoning the Israelites out of Egypt to escape slavery was fulfilled when the infant Jesus was taken to Egypt as his parents fled there seeking safety, the only "prophecy" Jesus fulfilled is one that Matthew creates and reads into Hosea's words, giving them a meaning contrary to what both Hosea and (according to Brown) God intended.

When it comes to the fulfillment of prophecy, the NT accommodation of the OT is the elephant in the room. Within Brown's Catholic theological framework, the NT authors are inspired vehicles of revelation. Therefore, the NT accommodations must be authoritative *mis*interpretations of other authoritative texts. Those accommodations generate a paradox similar to the one in the classic question of whether God can create a stone too heavy for him to lift. Here, the question is how God can inspire a misinterpretation of an inspired passage—or, to put it more sharply, how can God inspire an interpretation that he did not inspire? One person's paradox is someone else's contradiction. And calling that last question a paradox seems to me too charitable.

Brown was both a stalwart champion of historical-critical exegesis and a faithful son of his church. His dual loyalties put him in the position of insisting on the primacy and integrity of the literal sense *and* of needing to find a theological rationale for the nonliteral senses authorized by Catholicism's understanding of the nature of revelation. Judging Brown's theory on its own theological terms, we see how it can explain only a few of the NT's claims that Jesus fulfilled prophecy. For all its subtlety and nuance, Brown's theory cannot untangle the contradiction inherent in believing that God inspired a misinterpretation of an earlier inspired text. At the end of the day, it seems that the oil of theologically authorized nonliteral interpretations cannot mix with the water of historical-critical exegesis, no matter how skillfully they are stirred together.

43. Ibid., 617.

How to Read the Bible for
All Its Worth (1981–2014)

How to Read the Bible for All Its Worth by Gordon D. Fee and Douglas Stuart (1981; 4th ed., 2014) is an introductory textbook written by two seminary professors for students at evangelical colleges. It aims to help beginners acquire some sophistication about the art of biblical interpretation and to encourage them to think critically about the topic, but always within the safe framework of evangelical beliefs about the Bible. The book has been extremely popular; its front cover boasts, "over 900,000 copies sold." One may assume that it has been very influential.

Fee and Stuart devote six pages in their chapter on the prophets to "Some Hermeneutical Suggestions," starting with a treatment of the fulfillment of prophecy under the heading, "A Caution: The Prophet as Foreteller of the Future." The authors begin by underscoring that "it was not the prophets' primary task to predict the distant future. They did indeed predict future events, but for the most part *that* future is now past."[44] Fee and Stuart caution, "Too great a zeal for identifying New Testament events in Old Testament prophetic oracles can yield strange results."[45] As an example, the prediction in Isa 49:23 that kings "will bow down before you with their faces to the ground" is taken by many as a prophecy fulfilled in the magi's visit in Matt 2:1–11. Fee and Stuart argue that such an interpretation is invalid because it ignores the context, intent, style, and wording of Isaiah's text, where the "you" before whom the kings bow down unmistakably refers to the nation of Israel. "We must be careful that we do not make prophetic oracles, or any part of Scripture, say what we would like it to say. Rather, we must try to hear what *God* intends it to say."[46]

That appropriate warning comes from a straightforward application of historical criticism in the service of a theological reading of the Bible. For those who practice historical criticism and believe that the prophets were inspired by God, the interpretive task is to discover what God intends to say by discovering what the prophets intended. All of this is clearly laid out in Fee and Stuart's first chapter, which takes up the topic of hermeneutics in its last pages, describing it as the quest for the "Bible's meaning in the 'here and now.'"[47] The authors insist that hermeneutics must be based on and controlled by historical-critical exegesis. "The only proper control for herme-

---

44. Fee and Stuart, *How to Read the Bible*, 206 (italics original). *Note*: all references are to the 4th (2014) edition, unless otherwise indicated.

45. Ibid., 207.

46. Ibid. (italics original).

47. Ibid., 33.

Conflict

neutics is to be found *in the original intent of the biblical text.*[48] Without
that framework, hermeneutics can devolve into "pure subjectivity."[49] Fee
and Stuart caution that hermeneutics is difficult and that there is no strong
consensus on how it should proceed.

> On this one statement, however, there must surely be agree-
> ment. *A text cannot mean what it could never have meant for
> its original readers/hearers.* Or to put it in a positive way, the
> true meaning of the biblical text for us is what God originally
> intended it to mean when it was first spoken or written.[50]

One thing, however, spoils the purity of this methodological elegance for
those who believe that all scripture is inspired by God: NT authors clearly
make some OT passages mean what they never meant.

> Someone will surely ask, "But is it not possible for a text to have
> an additional [or fuller, or deeper] meaning, beyond its original
> intent? After all, this happens in the New Testament itself in the
> way it sometimes uses the Old Testament." In the case of proph-
> ecy, we would not close the door to such a possibility, and would
> argue that, with careful controls, a second, or fuller, meaning is
> possible.[51]

Opening the door to the possibility of a "second, or fuller" meaning creates a
theological conundrum: how is it that God, speaking through Matthew, for
example, can intend a passage from Hosea, for example, to mean something
it did not mean when God, speaking through Hosea, originally spoke it?

The Difference a New Edition Makes

I have copied the last quotation from a previous edition of Fee and Stuart's
book because that quotation reads rather differently in the earlier edition
than in the current fourth edition, and the difference invites consideration.
The difference between the third (2003) and fourth editions involves just
two words, but both shift the statement's meaning significantly: "a second,
fuller meaning" at the end of the quotation in the earlier edition becomes "a
second, or ultimate, intended meaning" in the fourth edition. One change
is that "fuller" has become "ultimate"; the second meaning is no longer just

---

48. Ibid. 33–34 (italics original).

49. Ibid., 34.

50. Ibid., 34–35 (italics original).

51. Ibid., 31 (3rd ed., 2003).

a deeper meaning, but rather its ultimate, i.e., its most meaningful, most *real* meaning. The superiority of the second meaning over the first is more emphatic in the current edition. The other revision is the addition of "intended." This one word dissolves the conundrum identified above: there is no longer the question of how God can intend a prophecy to mean in the NT what it did not mean originally, for now both meanings were *intended* from the start.

Fee and Stuart develop their solution to the problem of fuller/ultimate meanings in their chapter on interpreting the prophets, in a three-page discussion, "A Concern: Prophecy and Second Meanings," which is introduced by the observation, "At a number of places in the New Testament, reference is made to Old Testament passages that do not appear to refer to what the New Testament writers seem to suggest they do."[52] Fee and Stuart use the example of Matthew's interpretation of Hos 11:1 ("I called my son out of Egypt"), pointing out that Hosea obviously intended "my son" to refer to Israel and "out of Egypt" to refer to the exodus. I will again quote from an earlier edition, because Fee and Stuart described Matthew's use of Hosea's words quite differently in their second edition than they do in later ones. In the second edition, they did not pull their punches:

> Matthew does *not* apply those words to Jesus on the basis of a typical exegetical-hermeneutical principle or process. Rather, he takes those words out of their original context and gives them a whole new meaning.[53]

In that second edition, Fee and Stuart continue by warning the student not to do to any passage what Matthew did to his text from Hosea. Matthew "has the authority to do this. We can only read and appreciate what he has done. We cannot, however, do this same sort of thing on our own with any given passage." Earlier in the paragraph, Fee and Stuart claim that "Matthew had something we do not have. He had authoritative inspiration from the same Spirit who inspired Hosea to compose Hosea 11:1."[54]

That stark contrast between Hosea's and Matthew's meanings, and the strict warning from Fee and Stuart, both disappear after the second edition. Instead, the authors take care to emphasize the *continuity* of Matthew's interpretation with Hosea's meaning.

> Matthew is not suggesting that Hosea was "prophesying" that the Messiah would someday come "out of Egypt." Rather, he is

52. Ibid., 208.

53. Ibid., 185 (2nd ed., 1993; italics original).

54. Ibid. (2nd ed., 1993).

seeing an *analogical "fulfillment"* in which the Messiah as God's true "Son" now *reenacts* Israel's own history as God's "firstborn son." This kind of "second meaning," therefore, should not be thought of as playing games with the Old Testament; rather, as God's inspired servant, Matthew is retelling the story of Israel, God's son, as that which has been reenacted by God's true and greater Son.[55]

The difference between this explanation and the earlier one that it replaced is remarkable, given the contrast between the second edition's candid assessment that Matthew takes Hosea's words "out of their context and gives them a whole new meaning," and the assurance in the later editions that Matthew was not "playing games" with the OT. In a similar vein, Fee and Stuart replace their earlier prohibition against imitating Matthew's manner of interpretation with a mild caution.

> We also may be able to see such analogies as we read the story of Jesus; but it is unlikely as a valid hermeneutics that we can legitimately use the language of "fulfillment" in this way without Matthew's own inspiration by the Spirit.[56]

The approach of Fee and Stuart to the problem of second meanings is the same in every edition of their book: they justify the NT's novel interpretations by appealing to divine authority. NT writers were authorized to find new, "fuller" or "ultimate" meanings in the OT, but today's student is not (in the second edition), or is advised not to try (in later editions).

Can an Inspired Interpretation Be a Misinterpretation?

For Fee and Stuart, the *only* OT passages that we know have fuller meanings are those indicated as such in the NT. "Unless something is identified as a *sensus plenior*[57] in the New Testament, it cannot confidently be identified as such from the Old Testament by us on our own authority."[58] The example of Hosea 11:1 is well chosen to illustrate the authors' point. "When Israel was a child I loved him, and I called my son out of Egypt" explicitly refers to the nation of Israel and to an event in Hosea's past. It makes no prediction and cannot refer to an individual. It can bear the new meaning Matthew gives it only if its first half is deleted and its historical reference ignored.

---

55. Ibid., 211 (4th ed., 2014; italics original).

56. Ibid.

57. See p. 337 for an explanation of this term.

58. Fee and Stuart, *How to Read the Bible*, 210.

The evangelical beliefs about the truth of the Bible that ground Fee's and Stuart's work preclude characterizing Matthew's interpretation of Hosea as what it plainly is from the perspective of historical-critical exegesis: a *distortion* of Hosea's meaning—although they unmistakably imply that Matthew's interpretation of it would be a distortion if someone other than a divinely inspired author had made it. Since both Hosea's original meaning and Matthew's new meaning are inspired by God, the new one cannot distort the original one. From that premise, it logically follows that the new meaning must have been divinely planned when the original was written. Fee and Stuart imply as much when, in their fourth edition, they assert that the new meaning is both "ultimate" and "intended." In the second edition, this explanation is more directly stated: "The Holy Spirit had, as it were, 'planted' those choice words in the book of Hosea to be ready for reuse in connection with the events of Jesus' life."[59] The key word here is "reuse." Fee and Stuart certainly seem uncomfortable with how Matthew treated Hosea's nonprediction, but their theology of inspiration can apparently expand to accommodate reusing old "choice words" for a new purpose.

As Fee and Stuart point out, Matthew makes Hos 11:1 refer to Jesus by quoting only half of it and thereby quoting it out of context. Matthew thus distorts (my word, not theirs) Hosea's meaning, but does not alter Hosea's words. One wonders how Fee and Stuart would explain other methods by which NT authors conjure new meanings from the OT. For example, NT authors occasionally combine pieces of different passages to create novel composite ones (as in, for example, Mark 1:2–3 and Matt 21:5).[60] Perhaps Fee and Stuart's concept of divinely authorized "reuse" could be stretched to include assembling new customized passages out of parts of preexisting ones. That stretching gets precarious, however, in cases of NT retrofitting, where prophecies are actually *altered* so that they can apply to Jesus.[61] It is difficult to justify characterizing that kind of textual manipulation as mere "reuse." The version of theological inspiration endorsed by Fee and Stuart loses coherence if it theorizes that the Holy Spirit authorized a NT author to find a new meaning in a passage by altering that passage. A theory of inspiration can hardly assert that the Holy Spirit authorized a biblical writer to alter the words of another biblical writer and then to falsely attribute the altered text to the original author. Finally, Fee and Stuart decline to describe

---

59. Ibid., 185.

60. See the analyses on pp. 157 and 136.

61. See, for example, Matt 1:23; 2:6; 3:3; and 11:10—see pp. 140–41.

the role of the Holy Spirit in New Testament authors' *creating* oracles and attributing them to the prophets (see Matt 2:23 and 27:9–10).[62]

Fee and Stuart forgo analyzing any of the above examples of an old passage being given a new meaning. Had they confronted the hard cases, their facile theoretical assurances would have to be abandoned. In their evangelical ecclesiastical context, Fee and Stuart are probably doing the best that can be done. Christian scholars who practice historical criticism and adhere to traditional beliefs in inspiration are stuck between a rock and a hard place when dealing with the fulfillment of prophecy. That the authors have continued to wrestle with the problem in new editions of their book testifies to their intellectual integrity, for they could easily have let the problem alone and rested on the laurels earned by their hugely successful textbook. Still, the specific difficulties identified above indicate that Fee and Stuart do not yet have a coherent and comprehensive proposal for how to harmonize the NT's creative interpretations of prophecy with historical criticism. The several revisions of Fee and Stuart in their discussion of this problem are evidence of how thorny it is. On the one hand, their exegetical method aims to discover what the prophets originally meant in their own contexts. A theology of inspiration informed by historical criticism locates God's inspired meaning within the intentions of the original prophets, a point Fee and Stuart rightly and repeatedly emphasize. On the other hand, the NT finds meanings in OT passages that their human authors[63] did not intend (and, at least in cases of retrofitted passages, *could not* have intended). NT authors thus, to speak anachronistically, break the rules of historical-critical exegesis. That is why Fee and Stuart warn readers not to imitate how NT authors interpret the Old Testament. Attempting to reconcile a theory of deeper or ultimate meanings with historical-critical exegesis is like trying to fit a square peg into a round hole.

Fulfillment of Prophecy on the Internet

The Internet abounds with websites purporting to document Jesus' fulfillment of prophecy. Most of them are framed by the rhetoric of "proof." Having often encountered the claim that Jesus fulfilled over three hundred prophecies,[64] I was curious about that number. So I googled "300 prophe-

62. See my analyses on pp. 126–31.

63. Fee's and Stuart's assertion that the NT meanings were "intended" (see above) refers to *God's* intentions, not those of the prophets.

64. See, for example, Warren, "Biblical Prophesies [*sic*]: What Are the Odds?", the devotional blog post discussed in the opening pages of this book.

cies" and within ten seconds found a web page that indeed listed more than three hundred specific OT passages correlated with NT citations.[65] (This page is a component of the website Present-Truth.org, which also features anti-Catholic polemics. Ironically, its approach to prophecy is the same as the mid-twentieth-century textbook for Catholic colleges, *Evidence for Our Faith*, discussed above.) On Present-Truth.org, the prophecy page displays the headline, "THERE WERE OVER 300 PROPHECIES FULFILLED IN THE LIFE OF JESUS CHRIST! HERE ARE JUST A FEW." The page actually lists 324, with this introduction:

> ALL of these prophesies [*sic*] were made hundreds, sometimes thousands, of years before Jesus Christ was born. Looking in the face of how He literally fulfilled them all (plus hundreds more), it is an impossibility that He is not Messiah, Saviour of the world.

There is no need for a thorough examination of this very long list. A cursory analysis will suffice, with a few examples to illustrate.

The webpage features three kinds of references. First, as one would expect, there are OT passages that are quoted in the New Testament and explicitly identified there as fulfillments of prophecy. Second, there are OT passages quoted by the New Testament without being identified as fulfilled prophecies (e.g., "Psalm 8:2, The mouths of babes perfect his praise, Matt 21:16" and "Deut 21:23, Cursed is he that hangs on a tree, Gal 3:10–13"). Third, there are OT passages arguably alluded to but not quoted in the NT, and likewise not presented as fulfilled prophecies (e.g., "Isa 53:9, Buried in a rich man's grave, Matt 27:57" and "Psalm 22:16–18, They parted his garments, John 19:23–24").

As the web page indicates, the NT suggests an imaginative connection between a prophecy and Jesus that is fairly apparent. For example, there are dozens of citations of Psalm 22, which has many echoes in the passion narratives, and from Isaiah 53, the poem about the suffering servant. But for many other items, any connection between the OT and Jesus is due entirely to the ingenuity of the anonymous compiler. One example is, "Ps 68:18, Ascended to the right hand of God, Luke 24:51." The psalm reads, "You ascended the high mountain, leading captives in your train and receiving gifts from people." The sole connection to the ascension scene in Luke 24:51 is the word "ascend." Another example is, "Num 24:17, Time: 'I shall see him, but not now,' Gal 4:4." The full verse from Numbers reads,

> I see him, but not now;
>   I behold him, but not near—

65. http://www.present-truth.org/1-Jesus/300-PROPHECIES-FULFILLED.pdf/.

devine

> a star shall come out of Jacob,
>> and a scepter shall rise out of Israel;
> it shall crush the borderlands of Moab,
>> and the territory of all the Shethites.

Gal 4:4 says only, "When the fullness of time had come, God sent his son." The description of the conqueror in Num 24:17 cannot possibly apply to Jesus because he did not "crush" the territories specified in the verse. But even if we ignore the full verse and attend only to its first clause, its connection to Gal 4:4 is pure fancy.

Moreover, a number of entries refer to predictions that are so vague or so generic that they point to nothing particular about Jesus, for they have been fulfilled by thousands ("Deut 21:23, Hung on a tree" [i.e., crucified]), or millions ("Gen 12:3, Of the seed of Abraham" [i.e., Jewish or Muslim]), or even by everyone ("Gen 3:15, Born of the seed of a woman" [i.e., human]).

As is repeatedly the case with patristic claims about the fulfillment of prophecy, numerous OT passages listed on this web page cannot be verified as fulfilled by Jesus unless one presupposes his supernatural status. Needless to say, examples like these do not prove that Jesus was divine on the evidence that he fulfilled prophecy; rather, they can only "prove" that he fulfilled prophecy because he was divine. If you don't already believe in Jesus, you have no basis for recognizing that he fulfilled this type of prophecy. These examples presume the very conclusion they are supposed to prove.

Some of the entries misrepresent the cited passages, which simply do not say what the web page claims. Here are three examples. (1) "Ps 22:20, 21, Satanic power bruising the Redeemer's heel, Heb 2:14." The psalm does not mention Satan, and neither it nor the NT verse mentions bruising or a heel. (2) "Ps 22:22, His Resurrection declared, John 20:17." The psalm here says only, "I will tell of your name to my relatives," which does not even slightly allude to resurrection. (3) "Deut 18:15, Would be a prophet to the children of Israel, Matt 2:15." The verse from Matthew says only that Joseph remained in Egypt until Herod died, which "was to fulfill what had been spoken by the Lord through the prophet, 'Out of Egypt I have called my son.'"

A large portion of the entries are transparent examples of retrospective identification of alleged messianic prophecies. The results of this process are entries in which the allusion to Jesus in the OT passage is extremely dubious, if not obviously absent. Such entries make it onto the list only because the compiler—like nearly all before him who have sought prophetic proof that Jesus was the messiah—has worked backwards, starting with something in the NT and then hunting in the OT for a passage to pair with it, no matter how strained or fanciful the connection. Here a few examples.

Ex 12:21–27, Christ is our Passover, 1 Cor 5:7.

Isa 12:2, Called Jesus-Yeshua, Matt 1:21.[66]

Ps 22:7, They shake the head, Matt 27:39.

Ps 38:11, His friends stood afar off, Luke 23:49.

Ps 41:9, Betrayed by a friend, John 13:21.

Ps 72:10, Presented with gifts, Matt 2:1, 11.

Ps 72:16, The corn of wheat to fall into the ground, John 12:24.

Lev 23:37, The Drink Offering: "If any man thirst," John 19:31–36.[67]

No one reading those OT texts without Jesus already in mind would have any clue that they might be predictions about the messiah. The last two examples make this embarrassingly clear. "May there be an abundance of grain in the land" (Ps 72:16), can be transformed into a messianic prophecy only in the minds of Christians who try to find some OT precedent, however far-fetched, for Jesus' teaching in John 12:24 ("Unless a grain of wheat falls into the earth and dies, it remains just a single grain; but if it dies, it bears much fruit"). A similar retrospective process, with an even more implausible result, produces the claim that the prescription in Lev 23:37 that "all offerings, including drink offerings, should be performed on the appointed day" is a messianic prophecy that Jesus fulfilled when he declared, "Let anyone who is thirsty come to me, and let the one who believes in me drink" (John 7:37). These associations, although delivered by twenty-first-century Internet technology, are just as fanciful and far-fetched as prophecy-fulfillment fantasies expressed in the early centuries of Christianity.

Conclusion

This chapter has analyzed a few small-scale modern Christian engagements with the traditional belief that Jesus fulfilled prophecy. These analyses reveal a spectrum of approaches. At one end of the spectrum, Reimarus forthrightly rejects the traditional belief, on the basis of a historical-critical interpretation of the Bible that is unconcerned with defending Christian doctrine. At the other end, Cavanaugh's textbook and the anonymous Internet page,

---

66. The Isaiah verse reads, "God is my salvation." The Hebrew word for "salvation" is *yeshuah*, and Jesus' name in Aramaic is Yeshua.

67. The reference should be to John 7:37–38.

despite their contrasting ecclesiological locations, both uncritically accept Christian doctrine in a self-confident apologetic that is unconcerned with the historical-critical interpretation of the Bible.

In between those two end points are three attempts (by Redmond, Brown, and Fee and Stuart) to reconcile the traditional belief with historical criticism. They each seek a way to uphold the authority of the Bible or the church, or both, even while affirming the historical-critical conclusion that the NT's proclamation that Jesus fulfilled prophecy was achieved by reading meanings into OT passages that violate their historical, philological, and literary integrity.

I have argued that none of those three attempts yields viable results. Redmond's proposal about "overfulfillment" is a label without an explanation, so it turns out to be a content-free nonsolution. Brown's acknowledgment that most of the NT's fulfillment passages are cases of "accommodation" rather than of sensus plenior leads to either a befuddling paradox or an outright contradiction (depending on how gracious one wants to be about it). The conclusion of Fee and Stuart that OT passages cannot mean what they never meant, except in specific cases for which God authorized new meanings incompatible with their original ones, is an appeal to religious authority that might silence the question but cannot provide a rational solution to it.

Although I have argued that those three attempts do not succeed, I in no way dismiss them as undeserving of consideration. The authors are all sincere, their proposals are intellectually honest, and their arguments are learned ones. I regard all three as worthy attempts to solve a problem that is inherently intractable.

18

Reckoning with the Argument from Prophecy

MODERN HISTORICAL CRITICISM NEITHER affirms nor denies any version of the belief that the Bible is inspired. However, as the preceding chapter has illustrated, Christian scholars who are committed to the principles of historical criticism and who also believe in inspiration construe the inspired meaning of a passage to be the meaning intended by the human author and received by his original audience. Historical criticism, therefore, is incommensurable with an oracular theory of inspiration, which construes the inspired meaning of a prophecy to be the meaning given it by later interpreters. The belief that the prophets were really (if unwittingly) referring to Jesus thus exists outside historical criticism, and is a historical phenomenon to be studied in its own context within the historical development of beliefs within and about the Bible. That is precisely how historical-critical exegesis approaches the fulfillment of prophecy in the NT; the goal is to understand the meaning that Matthew, for example, intended to communicate when he asserts that a particular event fulfilled a specific prophecy. Exegetically, that is a straightforward task that focuses on tracking how Matthew appropriates an OT text; how he interprets it within his historical, religious, and literary contexts; and how that reinterpreted text contributes to the meaning communicated by the Gospel of Matthew.

When Matthew's use of the OT is studied in this particular way, it becomes clear that he attributes meanings to OT passages that they do not (and cannot) have in their original historical and literary contexts. It also becomes apparent that Matthew was well aware of this, as evidenced by the different ways he manipulated the prophetic texts to get them to mean what he wants them to mean: carefully quoting them out of context, selecting among various versions of a passage when one is better suited to his purpose, and even rewriting prophetic scriptures as needed (the process I call retrofitting).

Historical investigation of how Jewish intellectuals in the Hellenistic period interpreted the scriptures helps us to realize that when Matthew manipulated prophecies in the ways he did, he was using hermeneutical techniques that were traditional in his day.[1] Other Jewish scholars of Matthew's time would have been surprised by his interpretations, but probably not by his interpretive methods. That is important to recognize because it confirms that Matthew was playing by the rules, as it were, of his own time. We should, therefore, assume that Matthew, although he knew he was attributing meanings to prophecies that were not intended by the prophets, nonetheless believed that his interpretations of those passages represented their *true* meanings, of which the prophets themselves were unaware.

By situating the fulfillment of prophecy in its own first-century Jewish context, we can thereby achieve some methodologically valid and historically useful understanding of what Matthew (to stick with him as our example) tried to accomplish with the fulfillment of prophecy and the means he used in that effort. Historical-critical exegetes for whom such historical understanding is the sole goal of the study of the Bible will be satisfied that they have (at least partially) achieved it.

But Christian scholars who both practice historical-critical exegesis *and* believe that Matthew's message about the fulfillment of prophecy remains theologically true confront a conundrum: how can one believe that Jesus fulfilled specific prophecies when they do not (and never did) mean what Matthew makes them mean?[2] Matthew could believe that Jesus fulfilled prophecy because that belief cohered with Matthew's interpretive methods, which were sanctioned by the intellectual culture of his day. But Matthew's methods are not those of modern biblical criticism, for they violate the basic principle of historical-critical exegesis: that texts—in this case, prophecies—should be interpreted on their own terms and in their own contexts. This problem is especially acute in those instances where Matthew rewrites, and occasionally even creates, prophecies, for in such cases the prophecies that Jesus is alleged to have fulfilled did not actually exist, at least not in the form in which Matthew quotes them. Furthermore, how can Jesus' fulfillment of prophecy demonstrate that he was the messiah when, in some cases, the stories in which Jesus fulfills a prophecy have been shaped by Matthew so that they fit the very prophecies Jesus was supposed to fulfill?

---

1. See chapters 5 and 6.

2. The previous chapter analyzed three scholarly, but unsuccessful, attempts to answer that question. See pp. 334–47.

Presup 1-5

Five Presuppositions and Their Flaws

The findings of historical-critical exegesis raise grave problems for the traditional argument from prophecy, which claims that Jesus' fulfillments of prophecy, as reported in the NT, prove that he was the promised messiah. That argument rests on numerous presuppositions, five of which relate to biblical interpretation.[3]

Presupposition 1. *The prophecies quoted by the NT exist in the OT.*

Presupposition 2. *The specific prophecies that Jesus is reported to have fulfilled are prophecies that make predictions about a coming messiah.*

Presupposition 3. *The quoted prophecies mean what the NT authors interpret them to mean.*

Presupposition 4. *The specific events or circumstances that the NT authors claim fulfill specific prophecies are convincing, or at least plausible, fulfillments of the prophecies to which they are matched.*

Presupposition 5. *The gospel stories that narrate events in which Jesus fulfilled prophecy report actual historical events.*

None of those five presuppositions holds true across the board for the fulfillment passages in the NT. The following five points expose the gaps and flaws in the above five presuppositions by drawing on the findings of the chapters of this book dealing with the NT.

(1) Some prophecies quoted in the NT are tailor-made by combining pieces of more than one OT passage, some are rewritten or retrofitted, and a few are nowhere to be found in the OT.

(2) Few prophecies quoted in the NT are in any apparent way predictions about the messiah. Many of the quoted passages are not predictions at all, for they refer to persons or events that were already in the past history of the prophets who pronounced them. Moreover, most of the passages that make actual predictions are not about a messiah.

(3) Most of the prophecies quoted in the NT's fulfillment passages are given new meanings that make little or no sense in their OT contexts, but relate instead to the NT's religious, historical, or literary contexts. For example, Matt 2:15 makes "I called my son out of Egypt" (Hos 11:1) refer to an individual son, a meaning impossible in the context of Hos 11:1. New meanings like these are often facilitated by ingeniously selective quotations,

---

3. There are additional presuppositions that have to do with the internal logic of the argument from prophecy. See below.

which reveal that the NT authors worked carefully to remove the quoted texts from their original contexts in just the right way to enable them to carry the new meanings assigned to them.

Furthermore, in some cases the meanings assigned to OT passages by the NT do not make sense in their original OT wordings, but only in the wordings that appear in NT quotations of them. Sometimes, those differences are deliberately introduced through rewriting or retrofitting. In other cases, the differences result from the NT's use of the Septuagint. It is likely that all the NT authors quoted (nearly all) their prophecies from the Septuagint,[4] and in some cases the wording of prophecies in the Septuagint significantly alters what they mean in Hebrew.

To summarize, to agree that the prophecies quoted in the NT truly mean what the NT authors interpret them to mean, one must assent to two dubious principles: (a) in order to understand the true meaning of some OT passages, we must interpret them in isolation from their original literary or historical contexts, and (b) in order to understand the true meaning of some OT passages, we must interpret them as reworded in the NT, not in their original wordings in the Hebrew Bible. Neither of these is admissible in historical criticism.

(4) In some cases the connection between the prophecy and the fulfillment seems highly implausible. For example, it seems far from obvious at best, and nonsensical at worst, that Jesus' healings and exorcisms fulfill the prophecy that "he took our infirmities and bore our diseases" (Matt 8:17, quoting Isa 53:4—which is not even a prediction, much less one about a messiah). Likewise, it seems most odd to claim that when Jesus bound those he had healed to secrecy, he fulfilled the prophecy about God's servant who "will not wrangle or cry aloud, nor will anyone hear his voice in the streets" (Matt 12:15–21, quoting Isa 42:1–4).

(5) Some of the events that the gospels report as fulfillments of prophecy are fictional. It's a safe bet that some of those fictions were created on the basis of the very prophecies they are said to fulfill.[5] This takes us into the murky waters of historical Jesus studies, where competent and critical scholars disagree about the historicity of many gospel stories. However, some stories are surely fictitious. To cite an easy case, there is no evidence, and no serious historical argument, that the infant Jesus—contrary to Luke's story[6]—lived for a time in Egypt (Matt 2:13–15) and was therefore eligible to fulfill Hos 11:1 by being "called out of Egypt."

---

4. Law, *When God Spoke Greek*, 99–116.

5. See, for example, the cases analyzed on pp. 185–87.

6. In Luke's gospel, the parents of the infant Jesus take him from Bethlehem to the

I need to emphasize that I am not arguing that *none* of the fulfillments of prophecy are convincing, or, put another way, I am not arguing that Jesus fulfilled no prophecies at all. Of the prophecies quoted in the NT, (1) all but a few are actual OT prophecies, (2) a few do make predictions about a messianic figure, (3) some mean in the gospels more or less what they mean in their own contexts, (4) some seem easily relatable to the events that supposedly fulfill them, and (5) some of the events and circumstances that are said to fulfill prophecy are very likely or probably historical.

However, for the apologetic argument from prophecy to even get off the ground, *all five* presuppositions must be true for at least some of the fulfillment scenes. How many of those scenes can pass this rigorous test? Very, very few. The detailed analyses in my chapter on Matthew—the gospel that is most emphatic about the fulfillment of prophecy—turned up very meager results: only two of the fourteen quoted passages are actually prophecies about a messianic figure, and they predict a messianic king who will be born in Bethlehem and ride donkeys into Jerusalem.[7] That is an extremely thin basis for a convincing apologetic argument. To make matters worse, one must overcome some steep hurdles to apply even those two prophecies to Jesus:

- Many people besides Jesus were also born in Bethlehem and rode into Jerusalem.

- It is doubtful that the historical Jesus was born in Bethlehem;[8] and while it is likely that he rode into Jerusalem, it is beyond credulity that he did so in the ludicrous manner narrated by Matthew: on two donkeys of different sizes.

- In order to agree that Jesus fulfilled these two prophecies, one must first believe that Jesus was a *king*, which he indisputably was not in any literal sense.

Even the two Matthean passages that feature genuine messianic prophecies are fraught with difficulties for the argument from prophecy. These two cases supply yet more evidence that only those who already believed in Jesus would be persuaded that he fulfilled prophecy.

Results from the other three gospels are no better than the results from Matthew.

---

temple in Jerusalem and then directly home to Nazareth (Luke 2). Luke's storyline has no gaps in which to fit the sojourn in Egypt that only Matthew narrates. See Miller, *Born Divine*, 12–13.

7. See pp. 150–54.

8. See Miller, *Born Divine*, 181–83.

Mark's gospel quotes only one scripture that it applies to Jesus: "The stone that the builders rejected has become the cornerstone" (Mark 12:10, quoting Ps 118:22). Mark implies that Jesus fulfilled this scripture in his death and resurrection, and so only those who believe in his resurrection can see him fulfilling this prophecy.

Luke reports that Jesus claimed three times (twice after his resurrection) that he had fulfilled numerous prophecies, but without giving any particular examples.[9] Luke has only two scenes that present Jesus fulfilling a specific quoted prophecy (Luke 4:11–21 and 22:37). Both are found only in Luke's gospel. Neither makes a prediction. The first quotation is carefully edited and retrofitted to match the story of Jesus' public career.[10] The second ("He was classed with criminals" [Isa 53:12]) can apply to anyone who has been arrested.

John. Of the ten quoted scriptures Jesus allegedly fulfilled in this gospel, only one is a prediction about a messiah: the quote from Zechariah about a king riding a donkey into Jerusalem (see John 12:15). For five of the ten scriptures quoted by John, one can agree that they were fulfilled by Jesus only if one already believes that he was a king, or was sent from heaven, or died as a Passover lamb.[11] Three more of the ten quoted scriptures refer to events or circumstances that apply to Jesus but also to so many unfortunate people (prophecies that one will be betrayed by a friend, gratuitously hated, or pierced by a spear) that Jesus' fulfilling them does not make him special or distinctive.[12]

Three More (Problematic) Presuppositions

The five presuppositions analyzed so far are presuppositions for the argument from prophecy, presuppositions that have to do with the interpretation of either OT passages that allegedly refer to Jesus or the NT passages that quote them. However, even if we grant, for the sake of the argument, that those five presuppositions are accurate, there are three additional presuppositions (numbers 6–8 below) that have to do with how the argument from prophecy makes inferences from Jesus' fulfillment of prophecy to establish his status as the messiah. These three presuppositions, in other words, are presuppositions about the *logic* of the argument.

---

9. See pp. 164–65.
10. See pp. 166–67.
11. John 6:31–33; 12:15, 38, 40; 19:36 (see pp. 198–200).
12. John 13:18; 15:25; 19:37 (see pp. 198–200).

Presupp

Presupposition 6. *Jesus' fulfillment of the reported prophecies constitutes convincing evidence that he—and he alone—was the messiah.*

This presupposition entails that other people besides Jesus were born in Bethlehem, or healed people, or were pierced by spears, and yet were not considered messiahs, even though they had fulfilled prophecies that the NT offers as evidence that Jesus was the messiah. Since fulfilling prophecies like these was not sufficient to make someone a messiah, what makes Jesus' alleged fulfillment of them a special case? Does the argument from prophecy presuppose that one needs to fulfill a certain number of prophecies to be a messiah? If so, how many, and why?

Presupposition 7. *The messianic prophecies that Jesus did not fulfill do not disconfirm his messianic status.*

Relevant here are the numerous eschatological prophecies that anticipate the glories of the messianic age, for the messiah was expected to bring about an era of, among other things, universal peace and justice, agricultural abundance, and political dominance for the people of God.[13] Those few Jews, then and now, who think about the question of whether Jesus was the messiah, reasonably conclude that he was not because he did not inaugurate the messianic age foretold by the prophets. Jesus did not, for example, bring about international peace or universal justice. Christian apologists have a ready response: Jesus *will* fulfill those prophecies when he returns to earth at the end of history—a tactical reply at least as old as Justin Martyr.[14] This way of explaining away the messianic prophecies that Jesus failed to fulfill is nothing more than a profession of Christian faith and so will persuade only those who do not need to be persuaded.

Presupposition 8. *In a number of cases, one must believe that Jesus had some exalted status or that he was raised from the dead before one can recognize that he fulfilled a relevant prophecy.*[15]

Of course, if one believes Jesus to have been God's son, God's servant, and "your king" whom God raised from the dead, one does not need

13. For a few examples of these extravagant prophecies, see Isa 2:1–4; 11:6–9; 35:1–10; 49:19–23; 60:1–22.

14. See pp. 240–41. Some contemporary apologetic presentations of the argument from prophecy feature two lists of prophecies: one that Jesus fulfilled at his first coming, and another that he will fulfill at his second.

15. For example, it is necessary to believe that Jesus was God's son before one can see that he fulfilled Hos 11:1 (Matt 2:15), or that he was God's servant before one can see that he fulfilled Isa 53:4 (Matt 8:17), or that he was "your king" before one can see that he fulfilled Zech 9:9 (Matt 21:5).

fulfillments of prophecy as evidence to believe that he was the messiah. Examples like these demonstrate perfectly a central thesis of this book: the belief that Jesus was the messiah preceded—and is the presupposition for— the belief that he fulfilled prophecy.

A Fundamental Fallacy

Next I briefly spotlight a fallacy that is inherent in, and fatal to, any argument that uses the NT to prove that Jesus fulfilled prophecy. (Presupposition 5, above, is a partial statement of this more general fallacy.) I use the term *fallacy* in the technical sense it has in philosophy: to name a particular kind of error in logic, that is, an error in how one reasons from premises to a conclusion. The fallacy I refer to here is circular reasoning, and it dooms *any* argument that contains it. Circular reasoning, in its most general definition, is presupposing in a premise the truth of the very conclusion that needs to be proven. A simple example involving a scriptural argument from outside Christianity is the Islamic argument that the Quran is true because certain passages in the Quran say that it is true. Here is the argument, expressed formally:

> *Premise*: The Quran says that the Quran is true.

> *Conclusion*: Therefore, the Quran is true.

It is easy to spot the fallacy: the conclusion must be true in order for the premise to be true. In other words, the conclusion has been smuggled into the premise.

Circular reasoning is built into the basic structure of any argument that uses the NT to validate the fulfillment of OT predictions. The argument that you can know that Jesus fulfilled this or that prophecy because the NT says that he did requires that you presuppose the historical accuracy and theological veracity of the NT in order to verify that, yes, Jesus did indeed fulfill a particular prophecy. However, if you presuppose that whatever the NT says is true, you will be persuaded that Jesus fulfilled prophecy without the need to consider the "evidence" of particular examples. You will believe that Jesus fulfilled prophecy simply because the NT says he did. Conversely, if you do *not* presuppose that whatever the NT says is true, then the argument from prophecy gives you no independent or objective evidence that Jesus fulfilled the listed prophecies. The paradox is complete: the argument can persuade only those who are already persuaded, and it cannot persuade those who don't already believe what it tries to prove. In other words, the argument works only for those who don't need it.

Assessment of the Logical Form of the Argument

In academic philosophy, the study of logic since the time of Aristotle has distinguished two basic ways arguments can fail: by being *invalid* or *unsound*. An argument is a series of statements, one of which (the conclusion) is supposed to follow from the others (the premises). In order for an argument to succeed rationally, that is, to prove its conclusion, it must have true premises and a logically valid structure (the conclusion must logically follow from the premises). For example:

> *First premise:* All cats are mammals.
>
> *Second premise:* Daisy is a cat.
>
> *Conclusion:* Therefore, Daisy is a mammal.

The first premise is true by biological definition. The second premise is true as a matter of fact: "Daisy" is the name of my cat. The conclusion follows logically from true premises, and is, therefore, demonstrated to be true. An argument is *unsound* if some of its premises are not true. If "Daisy" were actually the name of my pet gecko, the second premise would be false, and therefore the conclusion would not be demonstrated to be true, even though it followed logically from the premises. An argument is *invalid* if its conclusion does not logically follow from its premises. Consider the following argument:

> *First premise:* All cats are mammals.
>
> *Second premise:* Daisy is a mammal.
>
> *Conclusion:* Therefore, Daisy is a cat.

This argument is invalid—despite the fact that all of its statements are true—because its structure is illogical: the conclusion does not follow from the premises. "Daisy" happens to be the name of a cat, but what if it were the name of a dog? In that case, the two premises would be true, but the conclusion false. When true premises do not yield a true conclusion, the structure of the argument is illogical, which means that the argument itself is invalid.

You can probably see where this is going: toward a failing grade for the argument from prophecy. The exegetical and logical analyses of the argument from prophecy a few pages back add up to the verdict that it fails in both ways: it is *both unsound and invalid.* Either defect by itself dooms the rationality of the argument. For the sake of convenience, the argument from prophecy can be stated in its most basic form as follows:

Premise: Jesus fulfilled prophecies.

Conclusion: Therefore, Jesus was the messiah.

The analyses of the first five presuppositions above show the argument from prophecy to be *unsound* because its premise depends on various presuppositions that historical criticism shows to be untrue. The analyses of presuppositions 6–8 show the argument from prophecy to be *invalid* because its conclusion does not logically follow from its premise. Note that the argument would still be invalid *even if* the premise were true.

The overall verdict is clear enough: *inasmuch as the argument from prophecy is presented as a rational argument*—that is, as a structured attempt to use evidence and logic to persuade the intellect—*it is a failure.* It is a bad argument. It should not be used if the goal is to persuade rationally.

Bad arguments are rationally unpersuasive, but many people are persuaded by them nonetheless. People can be persuaded by invalid or unsound arguments for any number of reasons. Some people might not have enough knowledge to properly assess the truths of an argument's premises. Other people might believe to be true things that are false. Or they might not fully understand the argument. Some might not be familiar with the rules of logic. Some might not know how to, or just do not want to, think critically about an argument. Politicians and advertisers, for example, routinely depend on people being persuaded by rationally flawed arguments. Invalid or unsound arguments can be persuasive in different ways. They might be psychologically compelling because they successfully appeal to non-rational emotions or irrational prejudices. Bad arguments might exploit people's lack of knowledge by introducing inaccurate information or lies that seem convincing. A few minutes' of analyzing the content of politically slanted "news" media will supply plenty of examples of bad, but persuasive, arguments.

So, the verdict that the argument from prophecy is invalid and unsound does not mean that it lacks persuasive power. It has persuaded, and it still persuades, many people—on nonrational grounds. But, because the argument from prophecy is invalid and unsound, it is *not rationally* persuasive, for it provides neither the true premises nor the logical reasoning required to demonstrate what it tries to prove.

The Argument from Prophecy and
Anti-Judaism: Ethical Implications

The extensive effort in the NT to show that Jesus and the church were the fulfillment of scripture reflects a belief of the followers of Jesus that the history of God's dealings with Israel had culminated in their movement, and that they were the rightful heirs of God's promises to Israel. The flip side of that conviction was their belief that Jews who did not embrace Jesus (i.e., all but a tiny minority) must have misunderstood their own scriptures, rejected the fulfillment of God's plan for Israel, or both. Thus the NT proclamation of the fulfillment of prophecy carries, in its ideological DNA as it were, an anti-Jewish polemic. Mark's gospel illustrates this perfectly. The only specific scripture that Mark claims was fulfilled in Jesus is a verse that reflects on the rejection—and murder—of God's chosen one (Ps 118:22, quoted in Mark 12:10).[16] And Mark situates the parable that announces the fulfillment of that scripture (Mark 12:1–11) in a narrative context that emphasizes how wrong—and evil—Jews were for rejecting and (in Mark's judgment) for killing Jesus (see Mark 12:8, 12).

Anti-Jewish polemic is expressed overtly in the gospels, and occasionally in wildly implausible accusations. Consider the charge, for example, that the Jewish people *as a whole* knowingly accepted guilt for the death of Jesus and called that guilt down on their descendants (Matt 27:20–25);[17] or that the Jewish authorities knew that Jesus had been raised from the dead but conspired to cover up that truth (Matt 28:11–15); or that Jews of Jesus' generation were morally responsible for *every* murder in all of history (Matt 23:35–36//Luke 11:49–50); or that Jews who oppose Jesus *hate* God (John 15:23) and are children of Satan (John 8:43). To be sure, none of those hyperbolic slanders are directly entailed by the argument from prophecy, but they all are watered by the same spring: the conviction of a tiny sect of Jews, joined by some gentiles, that the rest of the Jews had rejected God's promised messiah. *That* conviction *does* depend directly on the argument from prophecy, for that argument provided the "evidence" to support the claim that Jesus was the Promised One, that is, the one promised and predicted by the prophetic scriptures.

The extravagant and disgusting anti-Jewish polemics of some patristic theologians, amply exemplified in the writings of Justin Martyr, John Chrysostom, and Augustine,[18] flow from the argument from prophecy more

---

16. See p. 158.

17. Note Matthew's emphatic assertion that "all the people" (Matt 27:25) called for Jesus' death.

18. See pp. 262–64, 268–70, and 290–94, respectively.

directly than do those in the NT. Patristic writers submit their accusations of hard-heartedness, willful blindness, and moral culpability as explanations for why Jews, in the words of Chrysostom, "refuse to see the truth in the sunlight of high noon"[19]—which is impressive rhetoric, but actually refers to nothing more than that Jews remain unpersuaded by the argument from prophecy. Moreover, Justin ties the argument from prophecy explicitly to supersessionism,[20] and his logic in so doing seems unimpeachable: if the Jewish scriptures truly do reveal that Jesus was the Promised One, then it seems to be an unavoidable conclusion that following Jesus is the *only* way to participate in God's ongoing will for Israel. In the minds of Justin and company, Jews who "reject" the revelation of their scriptures (i.e., Jesus) thereby forfeit their status as the people of God.

The bitter and overblown anti-Jewish barbs in the gospels can seem farcical, even pathetic, in the historical context of the first century when they were written, a time when the followers of Jesus composed a miniscule group within Judaism. Centuries later, however, when Christians dominated the politics of the Roman Empire, and Jewish communities survived at the pleasure of Christian rulers, the NT polemics, especially when amplified by aggressive patristic voices, became menacing. The brutal history of Christian anti-Judaism is a toxic legacy of the patristic logic of supersessionism[21] and is, therefore, an indirect result of the argument from prophecy.

The Argument, Not the Belief, Is the Problem

In my 2003 *Born Divine*, I argued that Christians should relinquish the belief that Jesus was the fulfillment of prophecy. I no longer hold that position. In writing this book, I have become convinced that the intellectual and ethical pitfalls I have analyzed inhere in the *argument* from prophecy, not the *belief* in the fulfillment of prophecy. The distinction is crucial. To *believe* that Jesus fulfilled prophecy is one thing; it is something else entirely to *argue* that Jesus' fulfillment of prophecy proves that he was the messiah. I will conclude this book by summing up my case against the argument from prophecy. But before that, I offer two brief explanations of why and how sincere expressions of belief that Jesus was the fulfillment of prophecy

19. John Chrysostom, *Demonstration against the Pagans that Christ is God* 11.6. See p. 269.

20. See p. 264.

21. See "The Negation of the Jews in the Church Fathers" (Ruether, *Faith and Fratricide*, 117–82).

can avoid the debilitating intellectual and ethical problems inherent in the argument from prophecy.

First, if the belief is put forward expressly *as a belief* rather than as an argument, it cannot, by definition, be a bad argument. Therefore, there are no intellectual problems involved in the mere belief that Jesus fulfilled prophecy. Those problems arise only with the claim that there is objective evidence, rational arguments, or both, for that belief, or that the belief proves something.

Second, a robust statement of belief in the fulfillment of prophecy need not carry anti-Jewish implications. For a Christian to discover a new depth of meaning in a certain prophecy does not require that Christian to insist that the new meaning invalidates its original OT meaning. Nor does that Christian's discovery entail that those who do not accept that new meaning misunderstand the scriptures. An affirmation made with that kind of humility implicitly admits, and can even celebrate, the fact that it is only through faith in Jesus that the new meaning becomes apparent, even while graciously conceding that non-Christians, and other Christians with different theological orientations, need not agree that the new meaning is objectively present in the original passage. This kind of belief in the fulfillment of prophecy is fully compatible with the understanding of the nature of scripture presupposed by the historical-critical approach to the Bible. Moreover, this kind of belief shows no disrespect for Judaism, which interprets the Jewish scriptures without reference to Jesus. And it accomplishes those two very important things without compromising the meaningfulness of one's experience of how faith in Jesus can open up new, and distinctively Christian, insights into scriptures from the Jewish Bible.

In short, stating this belief in the fashion outlined above is a way of professing what one believes, without asserting, or even implying, what others should believe. Therefore, there are no ethical problems involved if belief in the fulfillment of prophecy is expressed as a belief rather than as an argument.

Retiring the Argument from Prophecy

I trust that I have made it clear that the *belief* that Jesus fulfilled prophecy is one that Christians can hold with theological and ethical integrity. But the *argument* from prophecy (the argument that Jesus' fulfillment of prophecy proves that he is the messiah) is a different matter entirely, inasmuch as it illegitimately treats a belief as if it were evidence that proves something to be objectively true. I maintain that Christians should retire the argument from prophecy, for three reasons: (1) it's the right thing to do intellectually, (2) it's the right thing to do ethically, and (3) the argument from prophecy is anachronistic and entirely unnecessary.

Retiring the Argument from Prophecy
Is the Right Thing to Do Intellectually

The argument from prophecy stands on two distinct, but linked, propositions: (a) that it is historically (that is, verifiably) true that Jesus fulfilled prophecy, and (b) that Jesus' fulfillment of prophecy compels rational people to accept the conclusion that he was the messiah. Neither of those legs of the argument holds up under rational scrutiny.

a. To assert that Jesus' fulfillment of prophecy is a matter of historical truth rather than of religious belief, one needs to accept the first five unacceptable presuppositions analyzed above, and to be unaware that the argument from prophecy defeats itself by its circularity (also analyzed above).

b. *Even if* (a) were verifiably true from the historical evidence that Jesus fulfilled prophecy, it would not necessarily follow that Jesus was the messiah, for three reasons. First, almost none of the OT passages that Jesus allegedly fulfilled are actually predictions about a messiah (see presupposition 2 above). Second, other people besides Jesus fulfilled prophecies but were not therefore considered messiahs (see presupposition 6 above). Third, there are numerous important messianic prophecies that Jesus manifestly did *not* fulfill (see presupposition 7 above).

In short, Christians should retire the argument from prophecy because—as an argument—it is invalid and unsound (see my reasoning above). Rational people have the intellectual duty to reject invalid and unsound arguments.

Retiring the Argument from Prophecy
Is the Right Thing to Do Ethically

The argument from prophecy is ethically compromised because it denigrates Jews, inasmuch as it implies that Jews who do not believe in Jesus either misunderstand their own scriptures or knowingly reject the truth about

Jesus that those scriptures clearly and repeatedly[22] predict. I am not implying that everyone who endorses the argument from prophecy is anti-Jewish
any more than I would imply that every fan of the Washington Redskins
harbors overt racial animus toward Native Americans. However, ethically
reflective people usually want to be aware of the ethical implications of positions they endorse or of loyalties they express, especially when those are
associated with histories of violence. We can grant that endorsing the argument from prophecy need not mean that one consciously endorses anti-
Judaism. Still, reasonable people should recognize that the anti-Jewish edge
built into the argument from prophecy fosters a demeaning and distorted
view of Judaism, inasmuch as it denies that someone could truly understand
the Hebrew Bible and also remain a Jew in good faith.[23] There is an ethical
duty to abstain from arguments that demean others and distort their beliefs,
all the more so when the argument in question is rationally unsound.

The Argument from Prophecy
Is Anachronistic and Unnecessary

I have argued in this book that although the argument from prophecy might
seem to have been aimed at converting outsiders, it actually functioned to
reassure insiders. To use Matthew and John again as examples, they—obviously—wrote to and for their own small Jewish-Christian communities, to
support their loyalty to Jesus in a time when that loyalty was viewed with
suspicion within Judaism.[24] Both Matthew and John send the message that
since the scriptures confirm that Jesus is the messiah, his followers have
every right to consider themselves true Israelites, despite what the vast
majority of other Jews might think about that. Such a message would have
offered encouragement to fragile sectarian groups like Matthew's and John's
communities, in circumstances when believing that Jesus was the messiah
might make one an outcast in Jewish society.[25] Believing that Jesus was the
fulfillment of prophecy helped to reassure his first-century Jewish followers

22. See the emphasis on "over 300 prophecies" in some Christian apologetics (pp.
2 and 347–48).

23. There are splinter groups of "messianic Jews," sometimes known as "Jews for
Jesus," who accept the doctrines of Christianity *and* claim to observe Judaism, an extremely contested claim among Jews.

24. In this paragraph and the next I reprise and expand on my argument in Miller,
Born Divine, 172–73.

25. If, as seems likely, the hostile social situations reflected in John and Matthew are
not entirely fictive (see, for example, John 9:22; 15:18–21; 16:2–3; and Matt 10:16–23;
23:34).

of the rightness of their cause, at a time when the prestige of Jewish authority could make that cause seem religiously illegitimate.

But that time no longer exists. It has not existed for nineteen centuries. The viability of Christian beliefs is not even remotely threatened by Judaism. Today there is not the slightest possibility that Christians will renounce their religion because Jews do not regard Jesus as the messiah. In the first century, it was certainly useful, and perhaps even necessary, for Christians to believe that other Jews did not understand the true meaning of their scriptures. Today, however, Christianity can survive—and thrive—without that belief. Matthew and John had to *convince* their communities that the legitimacy of their faith in Jesus did not require the validation of Jewish religious authorities. Not only do modern Christians not need to be persuaded about this, but even to imagine telling them that their faith does not need the approval of Jews seems silly.

The argument from prophecy outlived its usefulness long ago. It is implicated in ugly anti-Jewish attitudes that are, at best, ethically dubious and, at worst, grotesquely immoral. And if that weren't enough, the argument is illogical and rationally indefensible. It is long past time for thoughtful Christians to retire the argument from prophecy.

I use the word "retire" advisedly. To retire something does not mean to denounce or condemn it. It means to take it out of service, to put it on the shelf, to give it an honorable discharge. If one is reluctant to part with it—perhaps because it played some meaningful role in the development of one's faith—one can envision an imaginary retirement ceremony, in which the argument from prophecy can be thanked for its contribution and then told, respectfully but firmly, that its services are no longer required. Then it can be conserved in the Museum of Obsolete Ideas.

Appendix 1

Muhammad in the Bible?

IT WAS ALL BUT inevitable that Muslims would go looking for, and therefore find, biblical prophecies about Muhammad. According to Islam, the revelation given to Muhammad and recorded verbatim in the Quran completes and perfects the revelations given to Moses and Jesus.[1] Muslims believe that the Jewish and Christian scriptures, called "Torah" and "Gospel" by the Quran,[2] contain authentic revelations delivered by Moses and Jesus, as well as by the other prophets whom Allah sent to Israel, even though those revelations have been corrupted and blended with material of human origin in the long processes by which the biblical books were written. Islam teaches that although these scriptures mixed divine truth with human opinion, biblical passages that are compatible with the teaching in the Quran can safely be regarded as true. Muslims who study the NT can see how it interprets obscure verses from the OT as prophecies about Jesus. Muslims would not be surprised that earlier prophets would make predictions about Jesus, a later prophet. It is natural, therefore, that some Muslims would learn from the example of the NT and set out to discover biblical prophecies about Muhammad, the "seal" of the prophets. The Quran itself reveals that Jesus had prophesied the coming of Muhammad: "I [Jesus] am sent to you from God to confirm the Torah already revealed, and to give good news of a prophet who will come after me whose name is Ahmad" (Quran 61:6)—"Ahmad" being an alternative form of "Muhammad." Muslims who live among Christians and who are inclined to apologetics would sense the

---

1. The explanations of the beliefs and history of Islam in this chapter reflect basic information available in any introductory textbook or chapter on Islam in a textbook on world religions. Two sources I can recommend are Esposito's *Islam* and Hussain's "Muslim Traditions."

2. Quran 3:3 and 5:46, for example.

persuasive power of demonstrating that the Bible contains prophecies about Muhammad.

The brief exploration of this topic in this chapter draws on two articles, both with the title "Muhammad in the Bible," one by Khalil Ahmad Nasir and available on the Internet,[3] the other by Jamal Badawi, published in a journal for Muslim university students.[4] Both articles are aimed at general readers and both show evidence of a close and respectful study of biblical texts. I could find no biographical information on Nasir beyond the fact that he uses the title "Doctor." Badawi was, at the time of the publication of his article, associate professor of Business Management at St. Mary's University in Halifax. I have no idea how representative the positions and interests of these articles are in the Muslim world, though I suspect that their arguments appeal mainly to educated Muslims in countries with significant Christian populations.

I will analyze and assess Nasir's and Badawi's interpretations of five biblical passages (two from the Gospel of John, one from Deuteronomy, and two from Isaiah), in which, they argue, Jesus, Moses, and Isaiah predicted the prophetic ministry of Muhammad and a crucial military event in his life.

Did Jesus Predict Muhammad?

From the Islamic perspective, the revelation conveyed by the prophet Jesus was authentic, although incomplete—the complete revelation would be delivered by Muhammad six centuries after Jesus. Muslims have various explanations for why the revelations prior to Muhammad were incomplete, the most common being that humanity was not yet ready to receive the fullness of revelation. Reflecting that theory, Nasir asserts, "Again and again Jesus said that he was sent to the world only to give as much guidance as the people of his own time could bear."[5] Nasir does not cite any gospel evidence for this claim, but he probably has John 16:12 in mind: "I have much to tell you, but you cannot bear it just now." Contrary to Nasir's interpretation, Jesus said this kind of thing once, not repeatedly, and in its context John 16:12 cannot mean what Nasir claims. The reason the disciples cannot bear to hear more is because of their grief and fear, for Jesus has been speaking of his imminent death, and not humankind's spiritual immaturity. From the

3. Nasir, "Muhammed in the Bible."

4. The journal is *Al-Ittihad* (Arabic for "The Union"), a defunct quarterly publication of the Muslim Students Association of the United States and Canada.

5. Nasir, "Muhammad in the Bible," para. 7.

start of Nasir's essay, therefore, it is clear that he interprets the Christian Bible, not on its own terms or in its own context, but with Islamic assumptions about what it *should* say.

Nasir finds two passages in which Jesus prophesies the coming of Muhammad: John 14:26 and 16:7–14. Both refer to the "Comforter"[6] who will come to the disciples after Jesus departs.

John 14:26

> The Comforter, the Holy Spirit, whom the Father will send in
> my name, will teach you everything, and remind you of all that
> I have said to you.

Nasir claims, "Only the Prophet of Islam could have fulfilled this prophecy of Jesus."[7] It is hard to understand what Nasir means here, for three reasons. (1) Muhammad did not claim to be sent in the name of Jesus. Nevertheless, Nasir argues that Muhammad was sent in the name of Jesus "because he [Muhammad] bore testimony to his [Jesus'] truth"[8]—which seems to mean that Muhammad declared Jesus to be a messenger of God. (2) The prophecy anticipates the sending of the Comforter within the lifetime of the disciples; the "you" can refer to no one else. Nasir does not address this problem. (3) Nasir does not explain in what sense Muhammad can be the Holy Spirit. A few verses earlier in John's gospel, Jesus tells how his disciples will recognize the Comforter: "he will dwell in you and will remain in you" (John 14:17). Nasir ignores or is unaware of that description.

John 16:7–14

Nasir gives an elaborate interpretation of this passage, breaking it down into six distinct descriptions of the Comforter, which, Nasir asserts, together demonstrate that the prophecy applies only to Muhammad.

- "The Comforter will come after the departure of Jesus,"[9] which Muhammad did.

---

6. "Comforter" is the King James translation of the Greek *paraklētos*, which other translations (such as the NRSV and SV) render as "Advocate."

7. Nasir, "Muhammad in the Bible," para. 8.

8. Ibid.

9. Ibid., para. 11.

- "He will reprove the world of sin, justice, and truth" (from John 16:8). Nasir takes this to mean that he will reprove the followers of Jesus. (However, in John's gospel, "the world" always refers to those who are *not* Jesus' followers.) "Obviously, he [the Comforter] could not be a Christian or a Jew."[10] (Nasir does not say why.) Nasir takes "reprove" to mean "respect Jesus and promote reverence for him," which Muhammad did when he defended Jesus' honor by denying that he had been crucified (Quran 4:158), that is, that he "was saved from that accursed death designed by his enemies."[11]

- The Comforter "will guide the world into all truth" (based on John 16:13). "Muhammad was the only prophet who claimed to have brought a universal and perfect law."[12]

- "The book revealed to him [the Comforter] will contain no human word."[13] This is Nasir's interpretation of John 16:13 ("The Spirit of truth . . . will not speak on his own, but will speak whatever he hears"), although that verse neither mentions nor implies a book. Nasir argues that the Quran is the only such book, and quotes the Quran to prove it: "He [Muhammad] does not speak out of his own desire; it is naught but revelation that is revealed" (Quran 53:4–5).

- "Of the promise, 'He will show you things to come' [from John 16:13b], we need only say that "no prophet has told the world of things to come as much as has the prophet of Islam."[14]

- "He will glorify Jesus and clear him of all charges."[15] (The first half of this statement is based on John 16:14; the second half has no basis in John 16:7–14, which does not mention charges against Jesus). Nasir does not say what these "charges" are. In fact, he gives no explanation at all of his last point.

Nasir has no doubt about the conclusion to be drawn: "Now when we take this prophecy point by point, it is unmistakably proven that it applies to none else but the Holy Prophet Muhammad."[16] (Nasir does not explain

---

10. Ibid., para. 12.
11. Ibid., para. 13.
12. Ibid., para. 18, citing Quran 5:4.
13. Ibid., para. 11.
14. Ibid., para. 14.
15. Ibid., para. 11.
16. Ibid., para. 12.

how the details in John 16:9–11,[17] which he omits from his analysis, apply to Muhammad.) But the author is aware of an objection: "Sometimes an unsuccessful attempt is made to dim the glory of this marvelous prophecy by claiming that this Comforter was the Holy Ghost."[18] Nasir gives several reasons why this cannot be so. The only one I can make sense of[19] is a grammatical argument: the prophecy refers to the one to come as male ("he"), "which could not possibly refer to a spirit"—which seems an odd assertion for a Muslim, inasmuch as the Quran refers to Allah with masculine pronouns, as any page of the Quran will confirm. In John, the choice of pronouns is governed by the masculine gender of the Greek word for "Comforter," *paraklētos*.[20] Apart from the issue of grammar, Nasir's argument is futile on its face because in John's gospel it is Jesus himself who equates the Comforter with the Holy Spirit in 14:26 (see above). Nasir quotes this verse in full earlier in his essay, presenting it as Jesus' prophecy of how God would complete Jesus' partial revelation with "complete teaching which could stay forever with mankind."[21] Immediately after quoting John 14:26—which states that the Comforter is the Holy Spirit—Nasir adds, "Only the prophet of Islam could have fulfilled this prophecy of Jesus."[22]

17. Those verses predict that the Comforter will prove the world wrong "about sin, because they do not believe in me" (v. 9); "about righteousness, because I am going to the Father and you will see me no longer"; and "about judgment, because the ruler of this world has been condemned" (v. 11).

18. Nasir, "Muhammad in the Bible," para. 19.

19. Here are Nasir's other reasons: "Was not the Spirit of Truth supposed to come only after the departure of Jesus? Should it be then assumed that the Holy Ghost was not with Jesus? Obviously no devoted Christian will accept this assumption. One can also inquire where that truth is which is not found in the New Testament but was later brought by the Holy Ghost" (ibid.).

20. A very popular English-language study edition of the Quran has the following footnote for Quran 61:6, in which Jesus prophesies the coming of a prophet named Ahmad (quoted above). "'Ahmad,' or 'Muhammad,' the Praised One, is almost a translation of the Greek word *Periclytos*." (*Periklytos* means "famous" or "renowned.") "In the present Gospel of John . . . the word 'Comforter' in the English version is for the Greek word 'Paracletos' . . . Our doctors contend that Paracletos is a corrupt reading for Periclytos, and that in their [*sic*] original saying of Jesus there was a prophecy of our Holy Prophet *Ahmad* by name" (Ali, *Meaning of the Holy Quran*, 1461). The Islamic "doctors" thus maintain that Christian scribes either deliberately sabotaged or inadvertently botched the original text of John's gospel, which mentioned Muhammad "by name." This pseudo-scholarly conjecture, though clever, is unsupported by any textual evidence.

21. Nasir, "Muhammad in the Bible," para. 7.

22. Ibid., para. 8.

Did Moses predict Muhammad?

> I [God] will raise up for them a prophet like you [Moses] from
> among their brothers. I will put my words into his mouth, and
> he will speak to them everything that I command. (Deut 18:18)

The consensus among biblical scholars is that this prophecy promises a line of prophets after Moses, for the context (Deut 18:19–22) clearly presupposes multiple prophets. The prophecy is thus an assurance that every generation in Israel will have the benefit of prophetic guidance. In the Hellenistic period, when many Jews perceived that God had stopped sending prophets to Israel,[23] the prophecy in Deut 18:18 was reinterpreted eschatologically, as a promise that one ideal prophet would arise in the Last Days.[24] Christians, naturally, applied this prophecy to Jesus (e.g., in Acts 3:22).

A biblical prophecy about a coming prophet-like-Moses would attract the interest of Muslims, for the Quran often describes Muhammad as completing the prophetic revelations given to Moses and Jesus. Both Nasir and Badawi argue that Deut 18:18 predicts the coming of Muhammad, not Jesus. Both authors argue that the prophet foretold by Deut 18:18 cannot be Jewish because he will come from among "their brothers," a term that Nasir and Badawi claim refers to a people related to Israel, not to the Israelites themselves.[25] Muhammad fulfilled this prophecy because he was a descendant of Ishmael, brother of Isaac. However, this reading of "brothers" defies the sense of the passage and the use of that term elsewhere in Deuteronomy. The prophecy says that God will raise up a prophet "for them," that is, for the people of Israel. How could a foreign prophet, even one from a related people (such as the Arabs), be construed as having a mission for Israel? Furthermore, Deut 17:15 ordains that when the Israelites choose their king, he must be "from among your brothers," (i.e., from among the Israelites), which is explicitly reinforced by "not a foreigner."

Deut 18:18 predicts that the prophet(s) to come will be "like Moses." In the context of Deuteronomy, a prophet "like Moses" means simply a prophet that is appointed by God rather than self-appointed; see Deut 18:20–22, which explains how to tell if a prophet is truly sent by God. Nasir

---

23. See Aune, *Prophecy*, 103–5, and the texts cited there; for example, 1 Macc 9:27: "There was great distress in Israel, such as had not been since the time the prophets ceased to appear among them." Aune demonstrates that this perception, although attested in a number of sources, was not universally shared, and is contradicted by other evidence.

24. Ibid., 125–26.

25. Nasir, "Muhammad in the Bible," para. 26; Badawi, "Muhammad in the Bible," 40.

and Badawi both impute very specific meanings to "like Moses," meanings that enable them to interpret this detail so that it points to Muhammad but excludes Jesus. Nasir asserts that "like Moses" means that the prophet will govern a new nation and promulgate "a new Law . . . to replace an old one."[26] Since Jesus denied replacing the Law of Moses (Matt 5:17–18), and since the Quran claims to be a guide for the righteous (Quran 2:3), the prophecy in Deuteronomy points to Muhammad, not Jesus. Badawi goes much further than Nasir, and arranges a series of comparisons that demonstrate, not only that Muhammad and Moses were "very much alike in many respects," but also that the "Prophet Jesus does not fit this particular prophecy."[27] Badawi points out, for example, that Muhammad and Moses were born naturally, were married and had children, died of natural causes, were "heads of states," were forced to flee as adults to escape plots to kill them, defeated enemy armies sent to destroy them, and gave "comprehensive codes of law."[28] Jesus shared none of those similarities with Moses.

In assessing this argument, we start with the observation that any two individuals are like each other in some respects and unlike each other in other respects. In his comparisons of Moses to Muhammad and then to Jesus, Badawi selects criteria that allow him to draw the preordained conclusion, ignoring the ways in which Muhammad is *unlike* Moses. A different set of comparisons could be devised that leads to an opposite result. For example, Moses and Jesus were rescued as infants from a mass murder of baby boys ordered by a king; Moses and Jesus worked miracles; Moses and Jesus chose those who would inherit their authority. Muhammad shares none of those similarities with Moses. Whether Jesus or Muhammad (or Jeremiah, for that matter) is more like Moses is not an objective judgment based on neutral criteria.

The remaining element in Deut 18:18 is, "I will put my words into his mouth, and he will speak to them everything that I command." Badawi acknowledges that his description fits any messenger of God.[29] He therefore does not argue that Jesus did *not* fulfill this aspect of the prophecy. Instead he argues that Muhammad fulfilled it par excellence. Nasir takes a different tack, arguing that the description does not apply to Jesus. "Strange as it may seem, there is not a single example of words which Jesus may be said to have received from God with the command to pass them on."[30] When put in

26. Nasir, "Muhammad in the Bible," para. 23.

27. Badawi, "Muhammad in the Bible," 40.

28. Ibid., 41–42.

29. Ibid., 42.

30. Nasir, "Muhammad in the Bible," para. 29.

this strict form, Nasir's comment is true: the gospels nowhere depict Jesus prefacing his teaching with "Thus says the Lord," as is the custom for the OT prophets. But then Nasir overplays his hand, pointing out that "Jesus did not claim to be a prophet,"[31] citing Matt 16:13–16, in which Nasir believes that "Jesus denied being either John the Baptist or Elias or one of the prophets." This misinterprets the Matthean passage, which reports only that Jesus did not acknowledge being a prophet from the past come back to life. Furthermore, Nasir's implication that Jesus was not a prophet is bizarre for a Muslim to make because Islam reveres Jesus as a great prophet.

Did Isaiah Predict Muhammad?

Nasir and Badawi present other OT prophecies as predictions about Muhammad, of which I briefly sample two from the Book of Isaiah.

Isaiah 42

Badawi finds in the so-called Servant Song of Isaiah 42 "a comprehensive profile [of a future prophet] which not only fits Prophet Muhammad but fits no one else."[32] Badawi makes this case in detail, but listing just a few of his points will help to show the kind of argument he makes. (a) The one of whom Isaiah spoke is called servant (42:1), chosen (42:1), and messenger (42:19). While those descriptions apply to all prophets, "no prophet in history is as universally called by these titles as is Muhammad."[33] (Badawi ignores the fact that Isa 42:19 describes the messenger-servant as blind and deaf.) (b) The servant will not cry out or be heard in the street (42:2). Muhammad spoke quietly; we know this because the Quran enjoins people to speak quietly (Quran 31:19) and warns that Allah does not love harsh speech (Quran 4:148). (c) Isa 42:4 declares that "the isles shall wait for his law"; the only prophet with a "complete and comprehensive code of law," a code that spread across the earth, was Muhammad.[34] (d) Badawi reads Isa 42:13 to mean that the future prophet will "prevail against his enemies"; Jesus did not "live long enough to prevail over his enemies,"[35] whereas Mu-

31. Ibid., para. 30.

32. Badawi, "Muhammad in the Bible," 47.

33. Ibid., 44.

34. Badawi's argument here hinges on the word "law" in the King James translation of Isa 42:4. The Hebrew word is *torah*, which is more appropriately translated as "teaching" (as in the NRSV) or "instruction."

35. Badawi, "Muhammad in the Bible," 45.

hammad did. (Badawi ignores the fact that Isa 42:13 explicitly declares that it is *God* who defeats his enemies.)

Isaiah 21:13–17

> Within a year, according to the years of a hireling, all the glory of Kedar shall fail. And the residue of the number of archers, the mighty men of the children of Kedar, shall be diminished. (Isa 21:16–17, KJV)

Nasir comments on this obscure passage in Isaiah, which no doubt drew his attention because it is labeled "the burden [i.e., oracle] of Arabia" (Isa 21:13).

> This prophetic passage is a picture of the Battle of Badr which took place about a year after the Holy Prophet's migration from Mecca to Medina. In this battle the sons of Kedar, the people of Mecca and the territories around it, unable to withstand the fierceness of Muslim swordsmen and archers, sustained disastrous defeat.[36]

Nasir thinks that the phrase "within a year" was fulfilled in the date of the Battle of Badr (622 CE), the date of Muhammad's migration to Medina.[37] Nasir takes "Kedar," a biblical name for an Arabian tribe,[38] as a reference to the people of Mecca, whose army was defeated by the followers of Muhammad. In Isaiah's historical context, "within a year" means exactly that: soon after Isaiah pronounced the oracle. His prediction of the defeat of Kedar foresaw the results of Assyrian military attacks in Arabia in connection with King Sennacherib's campaign in the eighth century BCE to conquer Babylon.[39]

Conclusion

Nasir and Badawi provide articulate examples of how Muslims can find prophecies about Muhammad in the Bible. These authors quote biblical passages without regard for their literary or historical contexts. They also

36. Nasir, "Muhammad in the Bible," para. 38.

37. The Battle of Badr occurred in April 624, nearly two years after Muhammad's *hijra* (flight or migration) to Medina.

38. See Coogan, "Kedar," 523. Kedar is also mentioned in Isa 42:11 and Ezek 27:21.

39. Kaiser, *Isaiah 13–39*, 134.

quote those passages selectively, ignoring relevant elements in or nearby those passages that do not fit or that undermine the desired interpretations. Anyone who studies the passages critically can easily spot the problems in Nasir's and Badawi's arguments. Many of their interpretations of specific terms or phrases are arbitrary, asserted without argument or without acknowledging the possibility of differing interpretations. The few times when these authors argue against a Christian interpretation, their arguments cannot persuade Christians because those arguments are framed by Islamic assumptions. Neither Nasir nor Badawi was writing for Christians readers. Like all apologetic literature, these essays function to reassure insiders, not to convert outsiders. Both authors use the belief that the Quran is true and that Muhammad was a prophet—assumptions that only Muslim readers will share—as foundations for their arguments.

So, has Nasir or Badawi shown that the Bible foretells Muhammad? Only Muslims might think so. Anyone who respects the meanings that biblical passages had for their original authors and audiences can see that Muslims can find Muhammad prophesied in the Bible only because they expect to find him there, and then they read him into the biblical texts. And yet—and here is the most important point—*what these Muslim interpreters do to the Christian scriptures is no different from what Christian interpreters (including NT authors) did to the Jewish scriptures.* Both sets of interpreters quote selectively and out of context; both ignore relevant biblical material that would wreck their interpretations; both show no interest in what the passages meant in their ancient settings; both impute dubious and arbitrary meanings to the texts; both read their biblical passages within the framework of religious assumptions that emerged centuries after those passages were written. However, early Christian authors manipulate scripture in at least two ways that our Muslim interpreters do not. Christian interpreters (including NT authors) sometimes create customized passages by combining pieces from different scriptures, and they sometimes rewrite prophecies. Nasir and Badawi do neither. Muslim interpreters thus show more respect for the textual integrity of scripture than do authors of the NT.

The Christian project of finding Jesus predicted in the OT and the Muslim project of finding Muhammad in the Bible share the same fundamental apologetic objective: using sacred texts originating in an older, and rival, religion to legitimize a newer one that claims to fulfill and supersede its predecessor. Christian readers of these Islamic apologetics can therefore get a small taste of what it might feel like to modern Jews who encounter Christian claims that Jesus fulfilled the scriptures of Israel.

Appendix 2

Adam and Edom[1]

CHAPTER 15 OF THE Acts of the Apostles is a fictionalized account of how early leaders of the Jesus movement amicably resolved the divisive issue of how to treat non-Jews who wanted to join. One party believed that the Jesus movement should be fully Jewish and that non-Jews must convert to Judaism upon joining the Jesus community. Others, most notably Paul, opposed this requirement and envisioned a movement that encompassed both Jews and gentiles. According to Acts 15, Paul and other representatives of this inclusive position came to Jerusalem to convene with the "Jewish-only" leaders and seek a resolution of their differences. The author of Acts—let's call him Luke since he also wrote the third gospel—portrays an assembly in Jerusalem listening raptly as Paul and his preaching partner Barnabas tell "of all the signs and wonders that had been done through them among the gentiles" (Acts 15:12). Then James, the brother of Jesus and leader of his followers in Jerusalem, declares that the gentiles' reception of the Christian message fulfills prophecy:

> This agrees with the prophets, as it is written,
> "After this I will return
>> and rebuild the dwelling of David, which has fallen;
>>> from its ruins I will rebuild it,
>>> and I will set it up,
> so that all other peoples may seek the Lord—
>> even all the gentiles over whom my name has been called."
>> (Acts 15:16–17)

---

1. This chapter is a slightly revised version of Miller, "Adam and Edom: The Costs and Benefits of Monotheism."

379

The quoted prophecy promises that God will rebuild Jerusalem to be an international beacon of religious truth, one that will draw gentiles to seek the God of Israel. The hope this prophecy expresses is that Jerusalem's recovery from its devastation—by the Babylonians in 587 BCE—will seem so miraculous that other peoples will be awed by the power and mercy of Yahweh and therefore seek to serve him. In its renunciation of a narrowly nationalist view of Yahweh's intentions, this passage is remarkably inclusive for its time: God will rebuild Jerusalem not for the aggrandizement of his covenant partner Israel, but for the benefit of "other peoples." Indeed, this prophecy blurs the boundaries of the covenant altogether by stating that God has "called his name over" all the gentiles. This expression is an idiom that declares ownership, as we see in 2 Sam 12:26–28, where Joab, one of David's generals, sends word to David urging him to bring his army and conquer a certain city or else "I myself will take the city and I will call my name over it."

The structure of the prophecy lets us glimpse its author's reasoning about the universal sovereignty of Israel's God: because all the peoples belong to Yahweh, his merciful generosity to Israel is not intended for that nation alone; rather, the recovery of Jerusalem is a means by which Yahweh will reach out to the gentiles through the blessing of Israel. This passage resonates with the same universalism that concludes Yahweh's very first words to Abraham: "I will make of you a great nation" so that "in you all the families of the earth shall be blessed" (Gen 12:2–3). It seems Luke chose exactly the right prophecy to have James quote at the Jerusalem conference in order to dramatize the proclamation by the Jewish followers of Jesus that their revered teacher was God's blessing on Israel sent for the salvation of the whole world.

Tradurre è tradire
(To translate is to deceive)

In its original context the passage quoted in Acts 15 has a very different meaning—in fact, quite the *opposite* of what it has on the lips of James. The Hebrew translates thus:

> On that day I will raise up
>> the booth of David, which has fallen,
> and repair its breaches,
>> and raise up its ruins,
>> and rebuild it as in the days of old;

so that they may possess the remnant of Edom
    and all the gentiles over whom my name has been called.
    (Amos 9:11–12)

For ease of comparison, here are the three versions of Amos 9:12, translated literally in order to highlight their differences.

from the Hebrew text:

so that they may possess the remnant of Edom
    and all the gentiles over whom my name has been called

from the Septuagint:

so that the remnant of humanity may seek,
    and all the gentiles over whom my name has been called

as quoted in Acts 15:17:

so that the remnant of humanity may seek the Lord,
    and all the gentiles over whom my name has been called

The difference in meaning between the Hebrew text of Amos and the version in Acts comes from three significant differences in wording.

1. Amos mentions "the remnant of Edom"; Acts, following the Septuagint, reads "all other peoples"—in Greek, *hoi katalopoi tōn anthrōpōn* (literally, "the remnant of humanity").

2. Amos says that the people will "possess"; Acts, again following the Septuagint, has "seek."

3. The Acts version has all the nations seeking not Edom, but "the Lord," an appellative found in neither the Hebrew text nor the Septuagint.

Clearly, something is wrong here. Why is the version of the oracle in Acts so different from Amos' original? The answer is simple: Luke quotes from (and embellishes) the Septuagint, not the Hebrew text. It's not that Luke has altered a prophecy. As far as we can tell, Luke did not know Hebrew; he was quoting the only version of Amos he could read. Luke was misled by his source. The only substantive problem this poses is for those who insist that the Bible is inerrant: shouldn't we expect an inerrant author to correct an errant source? Critical scholarship notes that this instance of (mis)quotation results from an incongruous scenario: Luke has the Aramaic-speaking James quoting a scripture found only in the Greek Bible. This

inadvertent but striking flaw in Luke's carefully crafted verisimilitude adds
to the impressive evidence that the Acts of the Apostles is historical fiction.[2]

But why is the Greek passage of Amos so different from the Hebrew
text? The reason is that although the Septuagint usually offers an accurate
translation of the Hebrew, it sometimes does not—and some of those differences are intentional. Indeed, the Septuagint is often more an interpretation
than a strict translation. (As any translator knows, the distinction between
translation and interpretation is fuzzy at best.) In the present passage,
however, the first difference is most likely the result of a simple mistake.
The Hebrew word for the nation of Edom, *'edom* (אדום), is very close to the
word for "humanity," *'adam* (אדם). Perhaps the Septuagint translator was
confused by what he read in his Hebrew scroll, or perhaps his scroll had a
copying error or misspelling of this word. Either way, the mistake would be
easy to make. As for the second difference—the Hebrew "possess" versus
the Greek "seek"—it is difficult to see how this could be a translation error.
More likely it represents a deliberate adjustment by the Greek translator
to make better sense of the sentence in which "the rest of humanity" has
become the grammatical subject. The third variation is the result of Luke's
editing. With "all other peoples" as the subject in the third line of the Greek
version (instead of the people of "the booth of David [Jerusalem]," which
is the "they" in the third line of the Hebrew text), the Greek sentence has
no direct object for the new verb, "seek." Therefore, the Septuagint simply
leaves the sentence incomplete, though it seems likely that "me" (that is,
God, the speaker) is the implied object. Luke reasonably enough adds "the
Lord" to the quotation to clarify the sense of the Septuagint version.

Dueling Meanings

The Hebrew and Greek versions of Amos 9:11–12 differ somewhat in their
wordings but immensely in their meanings. In fact, the two point in opposite directions: in Acts the restoration of Jerusalem is intended to benefit
other nations, while in Amos it is the prelude to Israel's conquest of other
nations.

To understand Amos 9:11–12 properly we need to appreciate its literary context. It occurs in a part of the Book of Amos that critical scholars
consider a later appendix (9:8b–15).[3] Amos 9:11–12 is thus not from the

---

2. For an accessible section-by-section collaborative analysis of Acts that argues
that most of it is fictive, see Smith and Tyson, *Acts and Christian Beginnings*.

3. "The ending of the book [9:8b and 11–15] is almost universally regarded by
critical scholars as redactional [i.e., added by editors]" (Leclerc, *Introduction*, 212).

historical Amos, who prophesied around 750 BCE and whose predictions of impending doom were fulfilled in the Assyrian conquest of the northern kingdom of Israel in 721. Virtually all critical scholars of the biblical prophets agree that the Book of Amos originally ended with these devastating words:

> The eyes of Lord Yahweh are on this sinful kingdom
> and I will destroy it from the face of the earth. (Amos 9:8a)

The scroll of Amos was revised (along with the scrolls of other prophets) during the period of the Babylonian Exile, sometime after the destruction of Jerusalem in 587 BCE. Amos' exilic editors added new oracles promising restoration and good fortune for Israel in order to offset somewhat the extravagantly violent oracles of doom in the rest of the Book of Amos. By the time the text was revised, the destruction it threatened had long since occurred. Because the scroll of Amos originally ended with no hope for Israel's survival (Amos 9:8a), Amos' exilic editors provided a happy ending for this scroll when they revised it.[4] The literary seam where the original scroll ended and the revised appendix begins is both obvious and striking, since the last clause blatantly contradicts the first two.

> The eyes of Lord Yahweh are on this sinful kingdom
> and I will destroy it from the face of the earth
> —except that I will not utterly destroy the house of Jacob.
> (Amos 9:8)

Amos' own prophecy came—and remained—true. The hopeful promise added in 9:8b by his editor has not: the "house of Jacob," one of Amos' synonyms for the northern kingdom of Israel, vanished from history after its destruction by Assyria in 721 BCE.

The short collection of editorial additions in Amos 9:11–15 expresses postexilic hopes for the restoration of David's kingdom.[5] The specific shape of that hope in 9:11–12 is both interesting and ugly. What is interesting is the notion of Yahweh as a deity with jurisdiction over all the nations, not just over Israel. The appearance of this monotheistic assertion in the appendix to Amos is both fitting and ironic. It is fitting because it comes so soon (literarily, not historically) after the stunning affirmation of Yahweh's universal patronage in Amos 9:7:

---

4. Blenkinsopp, *History*, 92; and Wolff, *Joel and Amos*, 113, 346–47.
5. Blenkinsopp, *History*, 92; and Wolff, *Joel and Amos*, 113, 352–53.

god desire [handwritten annotation in margin]

> "Are you not like the Ethiopians to me,
>   O people of Israel?" says Yahweh.
> "Did I not bring Israel up from the land of Egypt,
>   and the Philistines from Caphtor, and the Arameans from Kir?"

Yahweh here proclaims that his solicitude for Israel is not unique; he watches over the Ethiopians, Philistines, and Arameans as much as over the Israelites. Amos 9:7 might be the most radical statement in the Hebrew Bible, inasmuch as it denies that Yahweh has favorites among the nations, a denial that undercuts the very basis of the concept of the covenant.

The irony is that while in 9:7 Yahweh's universal sovereignty is adduced to humble Israel, to tell them that they have no exclusive claim on God's protection, 9:12 cites Yahweh's international jurisdiction as the basis for a revenge fantasy. Note the train of thought in 9:11–12: Yahweh will rebuild Jerusalem "as in the days of old" (that is, as in David's reign when the nation was at the height of its military power) *in order that* Israel may possess what is left of Edom and the other nations, all of which belong to Yahweh.

Why Edom?

Edom comes in for special mention because it was Israel's most hated enemy. Edom bordered Israel, its language was close to Hebrew, and its people were ethnically related to the Israelites; Genesis traces their ancestry to Esau, son of Isaac and brother of Jacob-Israel (Gen 36:1, 8). According to the Torah, the Edomites had refused permission to Moses and the Israelites to pass through their country on the journey from the Sinai into Canaan (Num 20:14–21). In intermittent warfare over several centuries Edom was twice conquered by Israel and twice regained its independence.[6] What most inflamed Israel's enmity toward Edom was the story that the Edomites had rejoiced in the destruction of Jerusalem (Ps 137:7) and had joined in the looting after it fell to the Babylonians (Ezek 35:12) and, most notoriously, that Edomites had hunted down Israelite war refugees and sold them into slavery (see Obad 10–14). We do not know how much of that is historically true or, if any of it is, whether it involved more than rogue bands of Edomite marauders. Nevertheless, the florid oracles against Edom (Isa 34:5–17, Jer 49:7–22, and the entire brief Book of Obadiah) exude a vicious hatred. Indeed, the hostility toward Edom was so intense that the fifth-century-BCE prophet Malachi continued to vituperate against Edom even though it had been conquered a century earlier by the Babylonians (Mal 1:2–5).

6. See MacDonald, "Edomites."

In light of Israel's antipathy toward Edom, it is all the more interesting that prophets of Israel acknowledged Edom's reputation as a seat of wisdom (Jer 49:7, Obad 8). In fact, Job, that paragon of wisdom, was probably an Edomite; his home region, Uz (Job 1:1), is most plausibly located in Edom (see Lam 4:21).

The Ironies of Monotheism

Our analysis of the two versions of this prophecy—in its original context in Amos and in its altered form in the Acts of the Apostles—shows that belief in the universal sovereignty of God can serve contrasting and indeed contradictory purposes:

a. to ground a hope for military domination in the theological legitimation of an ethnic group's desire for violent revenge (in Amos)

b. to ground a hope for universal salvation in the invocation of divine approval for the inclusion in a religious movement of those outside the ethnic group in which it originated (in Acts)

There is abundant irony here. The first usage, which panders to one of our most deplorable impulses, is based on the wording of the prophecy in its original language; the second usage, which serves one of the noblest human aspirations, is based on an error in translation. In a further irony, the prophecy that grounds the first hope, an actual passage in the scroll of a Hebrew prophet, turned out to be false: Israel never again invaded or possessed the land of Edom. But the Acts version of this prophecy, which exists only in a Greek (mis)translation, has come true on a scale far beyond Luke's expectations: the God of Israel is today worshipped by Jews, Christians, and Muslims in nearly every region of the globe. Thus, a final irony can be noted. Much of the NT's claim that Jesus and his movement fulfill the Jewish scriptures turns out, on close examination, to be a shell game of dubious interpretations and textual manipulation. In the case of Acts 15:16–17, however, an exalted prophecy that was never actually uttered by the prophet to whom it is ascribed has been genuinely and abundantly fulfilled.

Translations of Ancient Sources

Aristotle

Rhetoric. Translated by W. Rhys Roberts. Compiled and edited by Lee Honeycutt. http://rhetoric.eserver.org/aristotle/.

Augustine

City of God. Books 1–7. Translated by Demetrius Zema and Gerald Walsh. Writings of Saint Augustine 6. FC 8/1. New York: Fathers of the Church, 1950.
———. Books 8–16. Translated by Gerald Walsh and Grace Monahan. Writings of Saint Augustine 7. FC 14. New York: Fathers of the Church, 1952
———. Books 17–22. Translated by Gerald Walsh and Daniel Honan. Writings of Saint Augustine 8. FC 24. New York: Fathers of the Church, 1954.
Reply to Faustus the Manichaean (Contra Faustum). The Gnostic Society Library. http://www.gnosis.org/library/contf.htm/.
The Divination of Demons. In *Treatises on Marriage and Other Subjects*, 417–40. Translated by Ruth Wentworth Brown. Writings of Saint Augustine 15. FC 27. New York: Fathers of the Church, 1955.
In Answer to the Jews. In *Treatises on Marriage and Other Subjects*, 391–414. Translated by Sister Marie Liguori. Writings of Saint Augustine 15. FC 27. New York: Fathers of the Church, 1955.
On Faith in Things Unseen. In *Writings of Saint Augustine* 2:451–69. Translated by Roy Deferrari and Mary Francis McDonald. 19 vols. FC 4. New York: Cima, 1947.
Tractates on the Gospel of John, 28–54. Translated by John W. Rettig. FC 88. Washington, DC: Catholic University of America Press, 1993.

Barnabas

Translations from the Letter of Barnabas are my own.

Bible

Translations of texts from the Hebrew Bible and New Testament are from the New Revised Standard Version (occasionally modified to highlight comparisons of parallel texts and in rendering the divine name—see Preface). Copyright © 1989, Division of Christian Education of the National Council of Churches of Christ in the U.S.A. Used by permission; all rights reserved. Translations of some gospel texts are from the Scholars Version as found in Miller, Robert J., ed. *The Complete Gospels*. 4th ed. Salem, OR: Polebridge Press, copyright © 2010. Used by permission; all rights reserved.

Dead Sea Scrolls

Note: Most excerpts are from Vermes; a few are from Garcia Martinez. In some cases I have blended these two translations and/or modified them slightly for clarity and style.

Vermes, Geza, trans. *The Dead Sea Scrolls in English*. 3rd ed. Pelican Books. London: Penguin, 1987.

García Martínez, Florentino, ed. *The Dead Sea Scrolls Translated: The Qumran Texts in English*. Translated by Wilfred G. E. Watson. 2nd ed. Leiden: Brill, 1996.

Eusebius of Caesarea

The History of the Church from Christ to Constantine. Translated by G. A. Williamson. London: Dorset, 1984.

Hippolytus

Refutation of All Heresies. http://www.newadvent.org/fathers/050109.htm/.

John Chrysostom

Demonstration against the Pagans that Christ Is God. Translated by Paul W. Harkins. In *Saint John Chrysostom: Apologist*, 163–262. Translated by Margaret A. Schatkin and Paul W. Harkins. FC 73. Washington DC: Catholic University of America Press, 1985.

Josephus

Whiston, William, trans. *The Works of Josephus: Complete and Unabridged*. Peabody, MA: Hendrickson, 1987 (originally published 1736).

Justin Martyr

Falls, Thomas B., trans. *Writings of Saint Justin Martyr*. FC 6. New York: Christian Heritage, 1948 (occasionally modified for style).

Lactantius

McDonald, Mary Francis, trans. *The Divine Institutes, Books I–VII,* by Lactantius. FC 49. Washington DC: Catholic University of America Press, 1964.

Plato

Unless otherwise noted, all translations are from Hamilton, Edith, and Huntington Cairns, eds., *The Collected Dialogues of Plato*. Bollingen Series 71. Princeton: Princeton University Press, 1961.

Phaedrus. Translated by R. Hackforth (pp. 475–525)
Meno. Translated by W. K. C. Guthrie (pp. 353–84)
(Socrates' Defense) Apology. Translated by Hugh Tredennick (pp. 3–26)
Timaeus. Translated by Benjamin Jowett (pp. 1151–1211)

Septuagint

The Septuagint Version of the Old Testament and Apocrypha: With an English translation and with various readings and critical notes. Charles Lee Brenton. 1851. Reprinted, Grand Rapids: Zondervan, 1978.

Targum Jonathan

Smolar, Levy, and Moses Aberbach. *Studies in Targum Jonathan to the Prophets; and Targum Jonathan to the Prophets*, by Pinkhos Churgin. New York: Ktav, 1983.

Theodore of Mopsuestia

Hill, Robert C., trans. *Commentary on the Twelve Prophets*, by Theodore, Bishop of Mopsuestia. FC 108. Washington, DC: Catholic University of America, 2004.

Bibliography

Ackroyd, Peter R. *Exile and Restoration: A Study of Hebrew Thought of the Sixth Century BC.* OTL. Philadelphia: Westminster, 1968.

Allen, Leslie C. *Ezekiel 20–48.* WBC 29. Dallas: Word, 1990.

Ali, Abdullah Yusuf. *The Meaning of the Holy Quran.* New ed. with rev. translation and commentary. Brentwood, MD: Amana, 1992.

Attridge, Harold W. *The Epistle to the Hebrews.* Hermeneia. Philadelphia: Fortress, 1989.

———, gen. ed. *The HarperCollins Study Bible: New Revised Standard Version, including the Apocryphal/Deuterocanonical Books.* Fully revised and updated. Student ed. San Francisco: HarperSanFrancisco, 2006.

Augustine, Saint. *Treatises on Marriage and Other Subjects.* Edited by Roy J. Defferrari. Translated by Charles Wilcox et al. FC 27. New York: Fathers of the Church, 1955.

Aune, David E. *Prophecy in Early Christianity and the Ancient Mediterranean World.* 1983. Reprinted, Eugene, OR: Wipf & Stock, 2003.

Badawi, Jamal. "Muhammad in the Bible." *Al-Ittihad* 19/1 (1982) 25–47.

Barnard, L. W. *Justin Martyr: His Life and Thought.* Cambridge: Cambridge University Press, 1967.

Barton, John. *Oracles of God: Perceptions of Ancient Prophecy in Israel after the Exile.* New ed. New York: Oxford University Press, 2007.

Bernstein, Moshe J. "Pesher Habakkuk." In *Encyclopedia of the Dead Sea Scrolls*, edited by Lawrence H. Schiffmann and James C. VanderKam, 2:647–50. New York: Oxford University Press, 2000.

Berrin, Shani L. "Pesharim." In *Encyclopedia of the Dead Sea Scrolls*, edited by Lawrence H. Schiffmann and James C. VanderKam, 2:644–47. New York: Oxford University Press, 2000.

———. "Pesher Nahum." In *Encyclopedia of the Dead Sea Scrolls*, edited by Lawrence H. Schiffmann and James C. VanderKam, 2:653–55. New York: Oxford University Press, 2000.

Blenkinsopp, Joseph. *A History of Prophecy in Israel.* Philadelphia: Westminster, 1983.

———. *Isaiah 1–39.* AB 19. New York: Doubleday, 2000.

Brenneman, James. *Canons in Conflict: Negotiating Texts in True and False Prophecy.* New York: Oxford University Press, 1997.

Brown, Raymond E. *The Birth of the Messiah: A Commentary on the Infancy Narratives in Matthew and Luke.* Garden City, NY: Doubleday, 1977.

————. *The Death of the Messiah: A Commentary on the Passion Narratives in the Four Gospels*. New York: Doubleday, 1994.

————. *The Gospel according to John*. AB 29–29A. 2 vols. Garden City, NY: Doubleday, 1966–1970.

————. "Hermeneutics." In *The Jerome Biblical Commentary*, edited by Raymond E. Brown et al., 2:605–23. Englewood Cliffs, NJ: Prentice Hall, 1968.

Burkert, Walter. *Greek Religion*. Translated by John Raffan. Cambridge: Harvard University Press, 1985.

Carroll, Robert P. *Jeremiah: A Commentary*. OTL. Philadelphia: Westminster, 1986.

————. *When Prophecy Failed: Reactions and Responses to Failure in the Old Testament Prophetic Traditions*. London: SCM, 1979.

Cavanaugh, Joseph H. *Evidence for Our Faith*. University Religion Series: Theology for the Layman. 3rd ed. Notre Dame: University of Notre Dame Press, 1959.

Collins, Adela Yarbro. *Mark: A Commentary*. Hermeneia. Minneapolis: Fortress, 2007.

Conzelmann, Hans. *1 Corinthians: A Commentary on the First Epistle to the Corinthians*. Translated by James W. Leitch. Hermeneia. Philadelphia: Fortress, 1975.

Coogan, Michael. D. "Kedar." In *Harper's Bible Dictionary*, edited by Paul J. Achtemeier et al., 523. San Francisco: Harper & Row, 1985.

Danielou, Jean. *The Theology of Jewish Chistianity*. The Development of Christian Doctrine before the Council of Nicaea 1. London: Darton, Longman & Todd, 1964.

Darr, Katheryn Pfisterer. *Far More Precious than Jewels: Perspectives on Biblical Women*. Gender and the Biblical Tradition. Louisville: Westminster John Knox, 1991.

Davies, Philip R. et al. *The Complete World of the Dead Sea Scrolls*. New York: Thames & Hudson, 2002.

Davies, W. D., and Dale C. Allison. *A Critical and Exegetical Commentary on the Gospel according to Saint Matthew*. Vol. 3, *Matthew 19–28*. 3 vols. Edinburgh: T. & T. Clark, 1997.

Dodds, E. R. *The Greeks and the Irrational*. Berkeley: University of California Press, 1951.

Edersheim, Alfred. *The Life and Times of Jesus the Messiah*. 8th ed. 2 vols. New York: Longmans, Green, 1897.

Efroymson, David P. "The Patristic Connection." In *Antisemitism and the Foundations of Christianity*, edited by Alan Davies, 98–117. New York: Paulist, 1979.

Ehrman, Bart D. *Forged: Writing in the Name of God*. New York: HarperOne, 2012.

Elliott, John H. *1 Peter: A New Translation and Commentary*. AB 37B. New York: Doubleday, 2000.

Ellis, E. Earle. *Prophecy and Hermeneutic in Early Christianity: New Testament Essays*. 1978. Reprinted, Eugene, OR: Wipf & Stock, 2003.

Esposito, John. *Islam: The Straight Path*. 3rd ed. New York: Oxford University Press, 1998.

Evans, Craig A. *Noncanonical Writings and New Testament Interpretation*. Peabody, MA: Hendrickson, 1992.

Fee, Gordon D. *The First Epistle to the Corinthians*. New International Commentary on the New Testament. Grand Rapids: Eerdmans, 1987.

Fee, Gordon D., and Douglas Stuart. *How to Read the Bible for All Its Worth*. 2nd ed. Grand Rapids: Zondervan, 1993.

————. *How to Read the Bible for All Its Worth*. 3rd ed. Grand Rapids: Zondervan, 2003.

————. *How to Read the Bible for All Its Worth*. 4th ed. Grand Rapids: Zondervan, 2014.

Ferguson, Everett. *Backgrounds of Early Christianity*. Grand Rapids: Eerdmans, 1987.

Fishbane, Michael. *Biblical Interpretation in Ancient Israel*. Oxford: Clarendon, 1985.

Fredriksen, Paula. *Augustine and the Jews: A Christian Defense of Jews and Judaism*. New York: Doubleday, 2008.

Furnish, Victor Paul. *II Corinthians: Translated with Introduction, Notes, and Commentary*. AB 32A. Garden City, NY: Doubleday, 1984.

Gray, Rebecca. *Prophetic Figures in Late Second Temple Jewish Palestine: The Evidence from Josephus*. New York: Oxford University Press, 1993.

Greenberg, Moshe. *Ezekiel 21–37: A New Translation with Introduction and Commentary*. AB 22A. New York: Doubleday, 1997.

Hanson, Anthony T. *The Prophetic Gospel: A Study of John and the Old Testament*. Edinburgh: T. & T. Clark, 1991.

Hays, Richard B. *Echoes of Scripture in the Letters of Paul*. New Haven: Yale University Press, 1989.

————. *Reading Backwards: Figural Christology and the Fourfold Gospel Witness*. Waco, TX: Baylor University Press, 2014.

Hedrick, Charles W. *Unlocking the Secrets of the Gospel according to Thomas: A Radical Faith for a New Age*. Eugene, OR: Cascade Books, 2010.

————. "Vestiges of an Ancient Coptic Codex Containing a Psalms *Testimonia* and a Gospel Homily." *Journal of Coptic Studies* 8 (2006) 1–41.

Hill, Craig C. *In God's Time: The Bible and the Future*. Grand Rapids: Eerdmans, 2002.

Hill, Robert C. "Introduction." In *Commentary on the Twelve Prophets* by Theodore, Bishop of Mopsuestia, 1–34. FC 108. Washington, DC: Catholic University of America Press, 2004.

Hughes, Graham. *Hebrews and Hermeneutics: The Epistle to the Hebrews as a New Testament Example of Biblical Interpretation*. SNTSMS 36. Cambridge: Cambridge University Press, 2004.

Hussain, Amir. "Muslim Traditions." In *A Concise Introduction to World Religions*, edited by Willard G. Oxtoby and Alan F. Segal, 208–71. 2nd ed. Don Mills, ON: Oxford University Press, 2012.

Juel, Donald. *Messianic Exegesis: Christological Interpretation of the Old Testament in Early Christianity*. Philadelphia: Fortress, 1988.

Kaiser, Otto. *Isaiah 13–39: A Commentary*. Translated by R. A. Wilson. OTL. Philadelphia: Westminster, 1974.

Klauck, Hans-Josef. *The Religious Context of Early Christianity: A Guide to Graeco-Roman Religions*. Translated by Brian McNeil. Minneapolis: Fortress, 2003.

Knust, Jennifer Wright. "Roasting the Lamb: Sacrifice and Sacred Text in Justin's *Dialogue with Trypho*." In *Religion and Violence: The Biblical Heritage*, edited by David A. Bernat and Jonathan Klawans, 100–113. Recent Research in Biblical Studies 2. Sheffield: Sheffield Phoenix, 2007.

Koenig, Don. "The Rebuilding of Babylon." *The Prophetic Years*. http://www.the propheticyears.com/reasons/babylon.htm/.

Koester, Craig. *Hebrews: A New Translation with Introduction and Commentary*. AB 36. Garden City, NY: Doubleday, 2001.

Kooij, Arie van der. "Isaiah in the Septuagint." In *Writing and Reading the Scroll of Isaiah: Studies of an Interpretive Tradition*, edited by Craig C. Broyles and Craig A. Evans, 2:513–29. VTSup 70/2. Leiden: Brill, 1997.

Kugel, James L., and Rowan A. Greer. *Early Biblical Interpretation*. Philadelphia: Westminster, 1986.

Lane, William L. *Hebrews 1–8*. WBC 47A. Dallas: Word, 1991.

Law, Timothy Michael. *When God Spoke Greek: The Septuagint and the Making of the Christian Bible*. Oxford: Oxford University Press, 2013.

Leclerc, Thomas L. *Introduction to the Prophets: Their Stories, Sayings, and Scrolls*. New York: Paulist, 2007.

Lieu, Judith M. *Image and Reality: The Jews in the World of the Christians of the Second Century*. Edinburgh: T. & T. Clark, 1996.

Ligouri, Marie. "Introduction to *In Answer to the Jews*." In *Treatises on Marriage and Other Subjects* by Saint Augustine, 387–89. Edited by Roy J. Defferrari. Translated by Charles Wilcox et al. FC 27. New York: Fathers of the Church, 1955.

Lindars, Barnabas. *New Testament Apologetic: The Doctrinal Significance of Old Testament Quotations*. London: SCM, 1961.

Lundbom, Jack R. *The Hebrew Prophets: An Introduction*. Minneapolis: Fortress, 2010.

MacDonald, Burton. "Edomites." In *Harper's Bible Dictionary*, edited by Paul J. Achtemeier, 246–47. San Francisco: Harper & Row, 1985.

Mack, Burton L. *Who Wrote the New Testament? The Making of the Christian Myth*. San Francisco: HarperSanFrancisco, 1995.

Mason, Steve. *Josephus and the New Testament*. Peabody, MA: Hendrickson, 1992.

Mattingly, Gerald L. "Shepherd." In *Harper's Bible Dictionary*, edited by Paul J. Achtemeier, 941–42. San Francisco: Harper & Row, 1985.

McKnight, Scot. *A New Vision for Israel: The Teachings of Jesus in National Context*. Studying the Historical Jesus. Grand Rapids: Eerdmans, 1999.

Menn, Esther. "Inner-Biblical Exegesis in the Tanak." In *The Ancient Period*, edited by Alan J. Hauser and Duane F. Watson, 55–79. A History of Biblical Interpretation 1. Grand Rapids: Eerdmans, 2003.

Meyers, Carol L., and Eric M. Meyers. *Zechariah 9–14: A New Translation with Introduction and Commentary*. AB 25C. Garden City, NY: Doubleday, 1993.

Miller, Robert J. "Adam and Edom: The Costs and Benefits of Monotheism." *The Fourth R* 20/3 (2007) 8–10, 20.

———. *Born Divine: The Births of Jesus & Other Sons of God*. Salem, OR: Polebridge, 2003.

———. "*The Messianic Secret* by Wilhelm Wrede." *The Fourth R* (forthcoming).

———. "The Wonder Baby: The Immanuel Prophecy in Isaiah and Matthew." *The Fourth R* 28/2 (2015) 5–10, 16–18.

———, ed. *The Complete Gospels*. 4th ed. Salem, OR: Polebridge, 2010.

Nasir, Khalil Ahmad. "Muhammad in the Bible." www.alislam.org/books/in-bible.

O'Daly, Gerard J. P. *Augustine's "City of God": A Reader's Guide*. Oxford: Clarendon, 1999.

Overman, J. Andrew. *Matthew's Gospel and Formative Judaism: The Social World of the Matthean Community*. Minneapolis: Fortress, 1990.

Patte, Daniel. *Early Jewish Hermeneutic in Palestine*. SBLDS 22. Missoula, MT: Scholars, 1975.

Penchansky, David. "No Other Gods: The Bible as a Polytheistic Book." *The Fourth R* 21/2 (2008) 3–10.

Pervo, Richard. *Acts: A Commentary*. Hermeneia. Minneapolis: Fortress, 2009.

Rajak, Tessa. "Talking at Trypho: Christian Apologetics as Anti-Judaism in Justin's *Dialogue with Trypho the Jew*." In *The Jewish Dialogue with Greece and Rome: Studies in Cultural and Social Interaction*, 511–34. AGJU 48. Leiden: Brill, 2001.

Redmond, R. X. "Prophecy, Theology of." In *The New Catholic Encyclopedia*, edited by William McDonald et al., 11:861–66. New York: McGraw-Hill, 1967.

Reimarus, Samuel. *On the Intentions of Jesus and His Teachings*. In *Reimarus: Fragments*, 59–269. Edited by Charles H. Talbert. Translated by Ralph S. Fraser. Lives of Jesus Series. 1970. Reprinted, Eugene, OR: Wipf & Stock, 2009.

Remus, Harold. "Justin Martyr's Argument with Judaism." In *Anti-Judaism in Early Christianity*, edited by Stephen G. Wilson, 2:59–80. 2 vols. Studies in Christianity and Judaism 2–3. Waterloo, ON: Wilfrid Laurier University Press, 1986.

Ruether, Rosemary Radford. *Faith and Fratricide: The Theological Roots of Anti-Semitism*. 1974. Reprinted, Eugene, OR: Wipf & Stock, 1996.

Schäfer, Peter. "The Hellenistic and Maccabean Periods." In *Israelite and Judaean History*, edited by John H. Hayes and J. Maxwell Miller, 539–604. OTL. Philadelphia: Westminster, 1977.

Schuchard, Bruce G. *Scripture within Scripture: The Interrelationship of Form and Function in the Explicit Old Testament Citations in the Gospel of John*. SBLDS 133. Atlanta: Scholars, 1992.

Scott, Kenneth. *The Imperial Cult under the Flavians*. Stuttgart: Kohlhammer, 1936.

Skarsaune, Oskar. *The Proof from Prophecy: A Study in Justin Martyr's Proof-Text Tradition*. Novum Testamentum Supplements 56. Leiden: Brill, 1987.

Smith, Dennis E., and Joseph B. Tyson, eds. *Acts and Christian Beginnings: The Acts Seminar Report*. Salem, OR: Polebridge, 2013.

Smolar, Leivy, and Moses Aberbach. *Studies in Targum Jonathan to the Prophets*. Library of Biblical Studies. New York: Ktav, 1983.

Stendahl, Krister. *The School of St. Matthew and Its Use of the Old Testament*. Lund: Gleerup, 1954.

Sweeney, Marvin A. *Isaiah 1–39: With an Introduction to Prophetic Literature*. Forms of the Old Testament Literature 16. Grand Rapids: Eerdmans, 1996.

Tate, Marvin E. *Psalms 51–100*. WBC 20. Dallas: Word, 1991.

"There Were over 300 Prophecies Fulfilled in the Life of Jesus Christ!" http://www.present-truth.org/1-Jesus/300-PROPHECIES-FULFILLED.pdf/.

Trigg, Joseph W. *Biblical Interpretation*. Message of the Fathers of the Church 9. Wilmington, DE: Glazier, 1988.

VanderKam, James C. *The Dead Sea Scrolls Today*. 2nd ed. Grand Rapids: Eerdmans, 2010.

Vermes, Geza. *An Introduction to the Complete Dead Sea Scrolls*. Minneapolis: Fortress, 1999.

Warren, Rick. "Biblical Prophesies [*sic*]: What Are the Odds?" *Daily Hope with Rick Warren*, May 21, 2013, http://rickwarren.org/devotional/english/biblical-prophesies-what-are-the-odds-_221#.U4pMYGzD_cc/.

Weiser, Artur. *The Psalms: A Commentary*. Translated by Herbert Hartwell. OTL. Philadelphia: Westminster, 1962.

Williams, Michael J. *The Prophet and His Message: Reading Old Testament Prophecy Today*. Philipsburg, NJ: P & R, 2003.

Wilson, Stephen G. *Related Strangers: Jews and Christians 70–170 CE*. Minneapolis: Fortress, 1995.

Wolff, Hans Walter. *Hosea: A Commentary on the Book of the Prophet Hosea*. Translated by Gary Stansell. Hermeneia. Philadelphia: Fortress, 1974.

———. *Joel and Amos: A Commentary on the Books of the Prophets Joel and Amos*. Translated by Waldemar Janzen et al. Hermeneia. Philadelphia: Fortress, 1977.

Young, Frances. "Alexandrian and Antiochene Exegesis." In *A History of Biblical Interpretation*. Vol. 1, *The Ancient Period*, edited by Alan J. Hauser and Duane F. Watson, 334–54. Grand Rapids: Eerdmans, 2003.

Zaharopoulos, Dimitri Z. *Theodore of Mopsuestia on the Bible: A Study of His Old Testament Exegesis*. Theological Inquiries. New York: Paulist, 1989.

Ancient Texts Quoted

Texts that are noted but not quoted are not listed.

Texts marked with an asterisk (*) receive significant attention, but are not quoted.

Old Testament (*Catholic canon*)

Genesis

1:26	222, 271
4:12	296
4:14	296
4:15	297
8:21	29
12:2–3	380
17:4	209
17:7	209
20:7	17
21:10	211n10
22:17	209
22:18	304
25:23	309, 310
49:11	244, 245, 253

Exodus

2:11–12*	308
4:15–16	18
7:1–2	18
12:21–22	189–90
12:46	182, 187, 198, 200
23:20	157
34:29–33*	112

Leviticus

4:5*	272
23:37	350

New Testament

Matthew

Mark

Luke

John

Nahum Pesher (4QpNah)

frag 1+2	72	I 6–8	73
I 1–3	72	III 5–7	73

Josephus

Antiquities of the Jews		*Wars of the Jews*	
8.408	100	3.351	99
8.417	101 (2x)	3.352	98
8.419	101	3.401–2	99
10.79	97	3.406	99
10.107	102	3.407	99
10.141	102	6.312–13	99
10.276	98		
13.64	98		
13.68	98		

Targum Jonathan

Isa 22:3	94	Isa 51:20	93
Isa 22:22–25	95	Hab 3:17	93
Isa 26:16	94		

Greek Philosophical Texts

Aristotle		*Meno*	
Rhetoric		99c	60
1407b	62		
		Phaedrus	
Plato		244a	58
Apology		244b	58
22c	61		
		Timaeus	
		72ab	61
Ion			
534d	58		

Early Christian Religious Texts

Patristic Texts

Augustine

Reply to Faustus

In Answer to the Jews

City of God

The Divination of Demons

On Faith in Things Unseen